THE CONTEMPORARY READER OF GENDER AND FAT STUDIES

The Contemporary Reader of Gender and Fat Studies is a key reference work in contemporary scholarship situated at the intersection between Gender and Fat Studies, charting the connections and tensions between these two fields.

Comprising over 20 chapters from a range of diverse and international contributors, the *Reader* is structured around the following key themes: theorizing gender and fat; narrating gender and fat; historicizing gender and fat; institutions and public policy; health and medicine; popular culture and media; and resistance. It is an intersectional collection, highlighting the ways that "gender" and "fat" always exist in connection with multiple other structures, forms of oppression, and identities, including race, ethnicity, sexualities, age, nationalities, disabilities, religion, and class.

The Contemporary Reader of Gender and Fat Studies is essential reading for scholars and advanced students in Gender Studies, Sexuality Studies, Sociology, Body Studies, Cultural Studies, Psychology, and Health.

Amy Erdman Farrell is the James Hope Caldwell Memorial Chair and Professor of American Studies and Women's, Gender, and Sexuality Studies at Dickinson College. The author of *Yours in Sisterhood: Ms. Magazine and the Promise of Popular Feminism* and *Fat Shame: Stigma and the Fat Body in American Culture*, she has shared her research on national popular media, including *Bitch*, *The New Yorker*, *Psychology Today*, NPR, CNN, and *The Colbert Report*. From 2019 to 2020 she served as an American Council of Learned Societies fellow and in 2021–2022 she was in residence at the Harvard Radcliffe Institute, where she worked on a project focusing on key moments in the history of the Girl Scouts of the United States of America.

THE CONTEMPORARY READER OF GENDER AND FAT STUDIES

Edited by Amy Erdman Farrell

Routledge
Taylor & Francis Group

LONDON AND NEW YORK

Designed cover image: 'Take Up Space', copyright Chiaralascura

First published 2023
by Routledge
4 Park Square, Milton Park, Abingdon, Oxon OX14 4RN

and by Routledge
605 Third Avenue, New York, NY 10158

Routledge is an imprint of the Taylor & Francis Group, an informa business

British Library Cataloguing-in-Publication Data
A catalogue record for this book is available from the British Library

Library of Congress Cataloging-in-Publication Data
Names: Farrell, Amy Erdman, editor.
Title: The contemporary reader of gender and fat studies /
edited by Amy Erdman Farrell.
Description: Abingdon, Oxon ; New York, NY : Routledge, 2023. |
Includes bibliographical references and index.
Identifiers: LCCN 2023011176 (print) | LCCN 2023011177 (ebook) |
ISBN 9780367691660 (hardback) | ISBN 9780367691684 (paperback) |
ISBN 9781003140665 (ebook)
Subjects: LCSH: Women's studies. | Body image in women. |
Overweight women. | Sex role. | Sexism. | Discrimination.
Classification: LCC HQ1180 .C658 2023 (print) |
LCC HQ1180 (ebook) | DDC 305.4–dc23/eng/20230411
LC record available at https://lccn.loc.gov/2023011176
LC ebook record available at https://lccn.loc.gov/2023011177

ISBN: 978-0-367-69166-0 (hbk)
ISBN: 978-0-367-69168-4 (pbk)
ISBN: 978-1-003-14066-5 (ebk)

DOI: 10.4324/9781003140665

Typeset in Bembo
by Newgen Publishing UK

An electronic version of this book is freely available, thanks to the support of libraries working with Knowledge Unlatched (KU). KU is a collaborative initiative designed to make high quality books Open Access for the public good. The Open Access ISBN for this book is 9781003140665. More information about the initiative and links to the Open Access version can be found at www.knowledgeunlatched.org.

In memory of Cat Pausé

CONTENTS

FIGURES

CONTRIBUTORS

Roshaunda L. Breeden, PhD (she/her), is an assistant professor in Educational Leadership at East Carolina University. Her practice and research interests revolve around equity and justice for Black students, families, and communities; fat students on campus; and first-generation and low-income students.

Rabbi Minna Bromberg is the founder and president of Fat Torah, and is passionate about bringing her three decades of experience with fat activism to working at the nexus of Judaism and body liberation. She received her doctorate in Sociology from Northwestern University in 2005, with a dissertation on identity formation in interfaith couples, and was ordained at Hebrew College in 2010. In addition to growing Fat Torah, Minna is a singer, songwriter, and voice teacher who specializes in helping people who use their voices in leading prayer. She lives in Jerusalem with her husband and their two children.

Heather A. Brown holds a bachelor of arts degree from Lake Forest College, a master of theological studies from Harvard Divinity School, and a doctorate in education in adult and higher education from Northern Illinois University. Her research is focused on the connections between weight and learning and how to promote academic achievement in fat women in postsecondary education. She is the Assistant Director of the University Writing Center at A.T. Still University. She currently serves as a co-editor of *Adult Literacy Education: The International Journal of Literacy, Language, and Numeracy*. Her work has appeared in many academic journals as well as in *The Fat Pedagogy Reader: Challenging Weight-Based Oppression in Education* and *Thickening Fat: Fat Bodies, Intersectionality, and Social Justice*. She is the co-editor of *Weight Bias in Health Education: Critical Perspectives for Pedagogy and Practice*.

Joy Cox is a body justice advocate using her skill set in research and leadership to foster social change through the promotion of body diversity, equity, and inclusion. Cox received her PhD in Communication from Rutgers University in 2018, writing her dissertation on the facilitation and hindrance of the Fat Liberation Movement. Much of Cox's work over the past ten years has focused on racism and weight stigma in health care, bringing attention to matters of intersectionality, accessibility, and "health." She is also the author of *Fat Girls in Black Bodies: Creating Communities of Our Own* released in 2020, and has been featured on several podcasts and media productions, not limited to CNN's Chasing Life with Sanjay Gupta, Christy Harrison's Food Psych podcast, the Tavis Smiley Show, and the *New York Times*.

Amanda M. Czerniawski is a Professor in Sociology at Temple University. She is the author of *Fashioning Fat: Inside Plus-Size Modeling* and actively writes for both academic and nonacademic audiences and appears on television, film, and radio.

E. Cassandra Dame-Griff is Assistant Professor of Critical Race and Ethnic Studies at Gonzaga University in Spokane, WA (USA). Her work examines the interplay between anti-fat and anti-Latina/o/x discourse and policy in the United States.

Kimberly Dark is a writer, professor, and storyteller, working to reveal the hidden architecture of everyday life so that we can reclaim our power as social creators. She's the author of *Damaged Like Me, Fat, Pretty, and Soon to be Old, The Daddies* and *Love and Errors*, and her essays, stories, and poetry are widely published in academic and popular online publications alike. Her ability to make the personal political is grounded in her training as a sociologist, and you can find her course offerings in Sociology at Cal State San Marcos and Writing/Arts at Cal State Summer Arts. www.kimberlydark.com

Amy Erdman Farrell is the James Hope Caldwell Memorial Chair and Professor of American Studies and Women's, Gender, and Sexuality Studies at Dickinson College. The author of *Yours in Sisterhood: Ms. Magazine and the Promise of Popular Feminism* and *Fat Shame: Stigma and the Fat Body in American Culture*, she has shared her research on national popular media, including *Bitch, the New Yorker, Psychology Today*, NPR, CNN, and *The Colbert Report*. From 2019 to 2020 she served as an American Council of Learned Societies fellow and in 2021–2022 she was in residence at the Harvard Radcliffe Institute, where she worked on a project focusing on key moments in the history of the Girl Scouts of the United States of America.

Jeannine A. Gailey is a professor of sociology in the Department of Sociology and Anthropology at Texas Christian University. Her research focuses on gender, sociology of the body, fat studies, sexualities, and deviance. She is the author of *The Hyper(in)visible Fat Woman* and co-editor of *Fat Oppression Around the World*.

Hannele Harjunen is an associate professor in sociology of sport in the department of Social Sciences in Sport at University of Jyväskylä, Finland. Harjunen's research focuses on gendered body norms, fat stigma and discrimination. Her publications include a monograph *Neoliberal Bodies and the Gendered Fat Body* (2017, Routledge) and articles in journals such as *Feminism and Psychology, Feminist Theory and Fat Studies: Interdisciplinary Journal of Body Weight and Society*. She publishes her research in Finnish and in English.

Da'Shaun L. Harrison is a Black trans theorist, cultural worker, and abolitionist in Atlanta, GA. Harrison is the author of *Belly of the Beast: The Politics of Anti-Fatness as Anti-Blackness*—which won the 2022 Lambda Literary Award for Transgender Nonfiction—and lectures on Blackness, gender, fatness, disabilities, and their intersections. Between the years 2019 and 2021, Harrison served as Associate Editor—and later as Managing Editor—of *Wear Your Voice* Magazine. Harrison currently serves as Editor-at-Large at *Scalawag Magazine* and is the co-host of the podcast "Unsolicited: Fatties Talk Back."

Erin N. Harrop is an assistant professor at University of Denver and a licensed medical social worker. Erin's research focuses on eating disorders, weight stigma, and patient–provider communication. Erin's clinical work also involves trainings at the provider level, introducing interprofessional clinicians to weight-inclusive practices that honor patients' unique intersecting identities.

April Michelle Herndon is the author of *Fat Blame: How the War on Obesity Vicitmizes Women and Children*, and is Full Professor in the English Department at Winona State University. She is an interdisciplinary scholar whose scholarship often works at the intersections of Fat Studies and Disability Studies. She is particularly interested in how public health "wars" affect people already marginalized in U.S. society.

Susan E. Hill is Professor and Head of the Department of Philosophy and World Religions at the University of Northern Iowa. Previously, she was the founding director of UNI's Center for Excellence in Teaching and Learning. She is the author of *Eating To Excess: The Meaning of Gluttony and the Fat Body in the Ancient World* (Praeger, 2011).

Substantia Jones is the founder of and photographer for the photo-activism campaign, The Adipositivity Project. She has spoken about body politics on NPR, Sirius/XM, and the Pacifica Radio Network, as well as a number of podcasts and on radio stations in Canada, Australia, and New Zealand. She's also the producer and host of the four-part radio series *PolitiSIZE* on WBAI-FM in New York City. She's contributed to books by Random House, Seal Press, Ten Speed Press, and Vignette, and lectures annually on her photography at Parsons School of Design, The New School in New York City.

Meridith Lawrence: *Meridith Lawrence* wrote about herself: Despite having grown up learning to hate myself, I am having one hell of a great life! I love going to the beach, eating out, traveling, swimming, and driving around with the radio blaring (among other things). My heartfelt thanks to Mary Nodairy (aka Wisniewski) for turning me on to fat liberation. It saved my life. Note: In 2015 Meridith and Judith Stein, whose interview with Susan Stinson is in this volume, moved to the Bay Area where they enjoyed connecting with fat liberationists. Sadly, Meridith died suddenly in January 2020. She and Judith had been loving partners for 37 years.

Nikkolette Lee is currently a fourth-year PhD student at UC Berkeley. Prior to coming to Berkeley, she received a BA in Ethnic Studies and Sociology at Brown University. Her undergraduate thesis investigated the intersections of racialization and fatness of students at Brown University. Now, her graduate work focuses on weight loss surgery, public health discourses on fatness, and social stigma. Broadly, she is a medical sociologist, interested in questions of fatness, the body, and how modern medicine and social identity intersect.

Emily R.M. Lind is a College Professor of Gender, Sexuality and Women's Studies at Okanagan College.

Lindsey Mazur is a Registered Dietician, Vanier Scholar, and PhD student in Community Health Sciences at the University of Manitoba. Her research focusses on weight stigma and prenatal health policy.

Deborah McPhail is Associate Professor in Community Health Sciences at the University of Manitoba, Canada. Her work focusses on the production of "spoiled" embodied marginalities through medicalization and health care exclusion for fat people and 2SLGBTQIA+ communities.

Chiara Meloni is an author, illustrator, activist, and co-founder of Belle di Faccia.

Mara Mibelli is an author, activist, and co-founder of Belle di Faccia. Belle di Faccia was born in 2018 as an Instagram page and became an organization in 2019. The idea originates from the need to bring fat bodies back to the center of the Italian body positive movement, with a particular focus on fat acceptance and fat liberation. In 2021 they published *Belle di faccia, tecniche per ribellarsi a un mondo grassofobico* (Pretty faces: strategies to rebel against a fatphobic world).

Cat Pausé was a Fat Studies scholar at Massey University in New Zealand. She was the lead editor of *Queering Fat Embodiment* (Ashgate) and the *International Handbook of Fat Studies* (Routledge), and coordinated three international conferences, most recently *Fat Studies: Past, Present, Futures*. Tragically, she died in 2022, leaving a gaping hole in the worlds of fat activism and Fat Studies scholarship.

Ava Purkiss is a historian and Assistant Professor of American Culture and Women's and Gender Studies at the University of Michigan. She studies the intersection of race, gender, health, and the body and is the author of *Fit Citizens: A History of Black Women's Exercise from Post-Reconstruction to Postwar America* (UNC Press, 2023).

Rachele Salvatelli is a Research Fellow at Northumbria University. She is the lead for the People, Health and Society theme at Insights North East. Her research interests include sociology of the body, sociology of health and illness, social determinants of health, sociology of stigma, narrative methodologies and fat studies.

Judith Stein stopped dieting at age 15 in an act of teenage rebellion; it was one of the smartest things she ever did. That was the same year she participated in her first sit-in; she's been a political activist in some fashion ever since. Her fat liberation essays and short stories were published in a variety of alternative and feminist press. She wrote and published a series of secular Jewish lesbian holiday materials published under Bobbeh Meisehs Press. She recently moved to senior housing in Oakland where she is trying to foment what John Lewis called "good trouble."

Terah J. Stewart, PhD (he/him), is Assistant Professor in the School of Education at Iowa State University. His research and writing focus on people and populations that are hypermarginalized and/or have stigmatized identities including: college students engaged in sex work, fat students on campus, identity-based student activism, and antiblackness in non-Black Communities of Color.

Susan Stinson is the author of the novels *Martha Moody, Fat Girl Dances with Rocks, Venus of Chalk*, and *Spider in a Tree*, as well as *Belly Songs: In Celebration of Fat Women*, a collection of poetry and essays. She has taught fiction writing at Smith College and Amherst College.

Jason Whitesel is Associate Professor of Sociology, and Women's, Gender and Sexuality Studies at Illinois State University. He teaches Queer Studies, Sociology of the Body, and Racial, Class, and Gender Inequality. Renowned for his book, *Fat Gay Men*, his attention has turned to global communities of fat-gay/queer BIPOC creatives.

ACKNOWLEDGMENTS

This has been a project of long duration, originating many years ago when Alexandra McGregor approached me at a conference to inquire about my work in Fat Studies and to see if I would be interested in editing a volume on gender and fat. I would like to thank Alexandra for initiating this collection and shepherding it through its earliest stages. When Alexandra's responsibilities at Routledge shifted, the project became the responsibility of Charlotte Taylor, who carefully worked with me to shape the project into its current form. And throughout, Eleanor Catchpole Simmons served as a very capable, friendly editorial assistant, responsive to countless emails throughout the long process. I thank them all.

Extraordinary thanks go to all the contributors—scholars, artists, and activists who carefully shared their research and writing and then responded to requests for revisions and what probably seemed like endless queries. I am grateful for your patience, your friendship, and your passionate writing. I wish especially to thank Joy Cox, with whom I partnered on the Anti-Bigotry Project at Boston University's Center for Anti-Racist Research at the same time I was editing this project, and who came through at the last minute with some optimistic concluding words for our readers.

I had the great fortune to be part of two amazing intellectual communities while I was editing this book. During the 2021–2022 academic year I was in residence at the Harvard Radcliffe Institute, where the fellowship and cutting edge research of my colleagues pushed my thinking in so many ways. And throughout the entirety of this project, my community at Dickinson College has enveloped me in a world of deep creativity and friendship. I wish especially to thank my colleagues and friends in American Studies, Women's, Gender, and Sexuality Studies, Food Studies, and Health Studies and all my students in the Fat Studies courses I have taught who deeply enriched my life and my scholarship.

I wish also to thank the American Council of Learned Society, who supported my research during the 2019–2020 academic year.

I wish especially to thank Dickinson for sabbatical support to work on this project and for the funding of a series of Dana student research interns. It was wonderful to work with many undergraduates on this project, including, in the beginning stages, Emily Benson and Elizabeth Roy, and, at the end, Alyssa Monsanto. Particular thanks go to Adena Cohen, who read every chapter along with me, suggested thoughtful revisions, and then turned to the detailed work of citations and formatting. Such a pleasure it was to work with you, Adena!

Much gratitude as well to our now-grown children, Nick and Catherine, who have become writers and artists in their own right and who inspire me with their creativity and community. And to John, my life partner of almost 35 years—thank you, well, for everything.

My final thanks go to the extraordinary scholar, writer, and community builder, Cat Pausé, whom we lost much too early in 2022. This volume is dedicated to her, with deep gratitude for her friendship and for the vision she created of a truly fat-inspired world.

PART I

Introduction

Though connected, Gender Studies and Fat Studies have different points of origin and often seem to speak to each other only tangentially. This book seeks to remedy this omission. Most particularly, it uses an intersectional lens to explore how gender and fat connect to each other and even often constitute each other. In this chapter, readers will delve into histories of feminism, intersectionality, and stigma in order to see the multiple ways that gender and fat interact and will explore how the concepts of personhood and race are fundamental to understanding why these categories of gender and fat are so salient today. This chapter also suggests alternative ways of pairing the essays in this volume.

DOI: 10.4324/9781003140665-1

1

CONNECTING GENDER AND FAT

Feminism, Intersectionality, and Stigma

Amy Erdman Farrell

In the early days of the coronavirus quarantine, my Facebook feed was inundated with postings about the effects of both—Covid and the quarantine—on jobs, on health, on social connection. The fear was palpable. Amidst all the headlines and dire information, another thread appeared—about the bodies that would be produced during months of inactivity and nervous snacking. One was a chubby dog, clad in green bikini bottoms: "Due to coronavirus my summer body will be postponed until 2021. Thank you for understanding." Another showed Batman grown large, a hairy belly hanging over a too tight yellow waistband. In yet another, captioned in both Italian and English, we see a buff, swaggering man dancing erotically; after the quarantine we see him fattened, his proud stance looking goofy. There was a separate thread of Barbie dolls, blonde hair, and pink dresses, the "before" slender with a tiny waist and perky breasts—the "after" a doll with a double chin and droopy chest. And one showed a woman pulling up a pair of jeans: "When none of your jeans fit after being quarantined so now you have thigh high boots." I imagine people posted these memes to encourage a moment of laughter, imagining that a bit of fat shaming would ease the burden of a tremendously frightening period. But they also illuminate a pulsating cultural anxiety about fatness. Indeed, in these memes, the dread of a fattened body scurries alongside other fears—of lost jobs and evictions, of groceries hard to get, of air that carries dangerous particles, of unknown futures, of mortality. Even in this moment of danger, fat looms big. Indeed, in these memes fat marks death— both physical "morbidity" associated with "obesity," and also social death, the becoming of an abhorrent body, a monster body, embarrassing and too much. And so much of that social death is connected to the way fatness messes up gender. Batman is no longer buff and masculine, but soft and hairy. The dancing man is no longer erotically seductive; he is goofy and embarrassing. The Barbie doll's double

DOI: 10.4324/9781003140665-2

chin has cancelled her femininity; she looks "silly" in that precious pink dress. And the idea of awkwardly donned non-fitting jeans as sexually charged thigh boots is absurd. These newly fat bodies all "do" gender wrong.

These memes—and the way they worry over fat and gender—illuminate the general question that this volume addresses: What are the connections between fatness and gender? On a visceral level—the feelings that fat and gender evoke; on a structural level, the ways that fatness and gender not only relate but actually constitute each other; on an academic level—the association between these two fields of Gender Studies and Fat Studies? To begin on the academic level, these two fields, Gender Studies and Fat Studies, have a lot to say to each other, the former even having explicitly supported the founding of the latter. Gender Studies is rooted in more than 50 years of scholarship, activism, and institution building, if we note the establishment of the first women's studies program at San Diego State University in 1972 and the creation of the National Women's Studies Association in 1977 (Shuster and Van Dyne 1985). Of course, the study of gender has a much longer history, if we choose to look at the history of women's resistance to patriarchy—just in a North American and European context we could go back to Simone de Beauvoir's (1949) *The Second Sex*, the 19th and 20th century struggles for women's suffrage and its attendant multitude of writings that accompanied the activism, the voices of Black feminist activists like Ida B. Wells Barnett in the early 20th century and Sojourner Truth almost a century before in the 1850s (Guy-Sheftall 1995). But even if we address solely its *academic* founding, Gender Studies has a much longer history than Fat Studies, with a legacy of just over 20 years, if we take as its institutional "founding" the publication of Esther Rothblum's and Sondra Solovay's *The Fat Studies Reader* in 2009 and the first issue of the interdisciplinary journal *Fat Studies* in 2012. Both these academic fields share a number of crucial attributes: an indebtedness to the activists who pushed for the founding of the academic disciplines, a commitment to liberation and anti-oppressive practices, a centering of the voices and experiences of those most affected. Within Gender Studies, the term "queer" has long been adopted, following the lead of the street activists who reclaimed this term from cultures that had used it as a disparaging weapon. And, likewise, Fat Studies has reclaimed the term fat—eschewing the term "obesity" as a medicalization and pathologizing of a normal bodily attribute and terms like "plump" or "round" as euphemistic terms that presume the horror of fatness.

Gender Studies and Fat Studies also share a core focus on intersectionality, to draw from the term that Kimberlé Crenshaw coined in 1991 to speak to the ways that the U.S. legal system limited the understanding of the complex and complicated ways that discrimination worked out in real people's lives, whose identities were never just limited to "one" arena. How could an African American woman parse out the precise ways that either sexism or racism served as the source of discrimination in her workplace, when she knew it was an intertwined, inseparable mix of the two, Crenshaw asked. Both Gender Studies and Fat Studies have been—from their respective origins—resoundingly criticized for centering the experiences and voices of white people for whom the discrimination on the basis of gender or of body size seem easier to "see." Within a decade of their institutional foundings, both fields saw powerful voices resisting this white-centering in collections like, for Gender Studies, Cherrie Moraga and Gloria Anzaldua's (1983) *This Bridge Called My Back: Writings by Radical Women of Color* and Lisa Albrecht and Rose Brewer's (1990) *Bridges of Power: Women's Multicultural Alliances* and, for Fat Studies, May Friedman, Carla Rice, and Jen Rinaldi's (2020) *Thickening Fat: Fat Bodies, Intersectionality and Social Justice.*

Significantly, Fat Studies, and fat activism before it, found one of its most generative and welcoming homes within feminist activisms and Gender Studies academic conferences and interdisciplinary departments. Elsewhere I have documented some of these histories in great detail, particularly the importance of feminist independent publishing to one of the most pathbreaking early texts that bridged fat activism and early Fat Studies, the 1983 anthology *Shadow on a Tightrope* (Farrell 2018). In the United States, the key Gender Studies academic organization, the National Women's Studies Association, has had a Fat Studies "stream" since the first decade of the new millennium, with focused sessions on Fat Studies at the annual conference and a vibrant group of scholars and activists who share meals, ideas, and plans for both future scholarship and action. Introductory textbooks to the field of Women's, Gender, and Sexuality Studies generally include at least one essay devoted to Fat Studies work. Verta Taylor, Nancy Whittier, and Leila Rupp's (2019) *Feminist Frontiers*, for instance, published Johnston and Taylor's essay on the Dove "Real Beauty" campaign and fat activism. L. Ayu Sarasati, Barbara Shaw, and Heather Rellihan's (2020) *Introduction to Women's, Gender and Sexuality Studies: Interdisciplinary and Intersectional Approaches* includes Kimberly Dark's "Big Yoga Student." And Susan Shaw and Janet Lee's (2019) *Gendered Voices, Feminist Visions* anthologizes both Susie Orbach's early "Fat Is Still a Feminist Issue" and Francis Ray White's "The Future of Fat Sex."

Of course, just as there are fundamental disagreements within these two fields, significant points of divergence exist between the two areas. The presumptions of one particularly well-known gender theorist, the late Lauren Berlant, are so at odds with Fat Studies scholarship that it's difficult to imagine the synchronicities between the two fields. Berlant describes "obesity" as a form of "slow death," a result of the inexorable pressure of capitalism that exhorts people to try to find some release in "sex, spacing out, [and] food that is not for thought." These kinds of characterizations of the fat person as inherently on the road to death, as lacking in control or good choices, are the precise types of assertions that Fat Studies scholars not only abhor but see as their object of inquiry and interrogation (Berlant 2007). For the most part, though, scholars in Women's, Gender, and Sexuality Studies sees Fat Studies as an allied field because it is recognized as another layer fundamental to the diversity of gendered experience. As Verta Taylor and her co-editors write in the introduction to *Feminist Frontiers*, the field emphasizes the "diversity of women's experiences and the intersection of gender with race, ethnicity, class, sexuality, nationality, and ability." Even if not everyone who is fat identifies as fat (or, as Marilyn Wann put it in her 1998 pathbreaking *Fat!So?*, has "come out" as fat—a topic taken up by one of the contributors for this volume, Rachele Salvatelli), for Gender Studies scholars fat is definitely another nexus of potential and real discrimination and another site that bares the lie that anyone experiences life "solely" as a gendered being outside the range of intersecting histories and experiences.

In *Unbearable Weight*, written before Fat Studies had coalesced as a field, Susan Bordo (2003) wrote that fat is "a women's issue: Fat is a gendered issue. Often immediately thought of as fat is a women's issue. It certainly is. But if it's a women's issue, it means it is a gendered issue." In these pithy sentences, Bordo was getting at the cruel facts of discrimination and experience that were clear even then: women suffer more than men from weight-based discrimination, women take part in weight loss clinics more than men, women have more trouble than men finding sexual and life partners if they are fat. Today we can point to even higher stakes, as Nikkolette Lee discusses in her essay in this volume, with many more women than men undergoing debilitating weight loss surgeries, from liposuction to extraordinary gastric bypass and stomach banding. This collection of essays certainly confronts some of these difficult facts, including the reality that mothers are particularly blamed for not only their own weight "issues" but those of their children and partners as well. But it also lingers on the second half of Bordo's comment, that fat is a "gendered" issue. Indeed, scholars such as Jason Whitesel, whose essay on fat gay men's fat-affirming cultures is included here, point out that weight-based discrimination and pressure to conform to sizing is not so much solely a generalizable division between men and women but has to do with gendering itself—that people whose sexual partners are men tend to have more negative experiences regarding weight, that people who identify as "femme," no matter their gender, will experience more pressure to conform to smaller sizes, for instance.

Indeed, significant recent scholarship emphasizes the extent to which fat and gender not only relate but actually *constitute* each other. In their important essay "Embodying the Fat/Trans Intersection" in the anthology *Thickening Fat: Fat Bodies, Intersectionality, and Social Justice*, Francis White (2020) argues that we need to see fat as "an active producer, enabler, or even destroyer of gender." White's careful analysis illuminates the way that fat in the "right" places (breasts and hips for transwomen, for instance) actually creates a sense of gender, both an internal sense of gender and a gender recognizable and legible to people around them. And, in opposition, fat in the "wrong" places can wreak havoc with one's internal sense of gender and the ways others "read" them—so much so that among the interviewees it was a consistent area of concern, prompting surgery and dieting. In their much earlier essay S. Bear Bergman's writing (2009) shed light on the opposite phenomenon—the way that gender constituted fat. As they put it in their pithy title, they were only a "part-time fatso," observed as a "big guy" when read as male or masculine, but as a "fat so," an object of pity and scorn, when read as female and feminine. In other words, what both White and Bergman reveal is that it's not just that fatness and gender are related, it's that they actually work as the building blocks of each other, the formative characteristics that constitute both a deep sense of self and the ways that one is perceived and read in the world.

Fat Studies and Gender Studies share a deep-seated concern with the question of humanity, or, to be more exact, with the question of who gets to be defined as *fully* human. As historians, philosophers, Critical Race scholars, and feminist scholars have explored, the *body* connotes meaning. The representation and reading of the body confers status, identity, and power. The problem of the *female body* has been the way it marks its bearer as a partial person, a "second" sex, to paraphrase Simone de Beauvoir, or, dependent upon its additional markings of age, nationality, and color, as a nonperson entirely. The problem of the *fat body* is this: within a Western context, fat is *irreconcilable* with personhood. Instead, fat works as a sign of a degenerate, primitive body, a state incommensurate with selfhood. The category of "body size" and of "gender," then, are key signifiers of whether or not one is considered a full human or citizen, or only a "partial human being," to draw from the term Erving Goffman used in his pathbreaking 1963 work *Stigma*.

All these classifications, of course, are deeply imbricated in the Enlightenment project of racialization, of the categorization of people and cultures in a hierarchical ordering from the most "civilized" to the most primitive, from the most human to the most animal-like, from the most perfected to those containing degenerate traits displaying a failure of evolution. Taking a look at almost any form of white-dominated literature, religious text, or philosophical treatise from the Enlightenment through the 20th century, one can see these ideas both explicitly and implicitly assumed, studied, and expressed. As I (2011) charted in my book *Fat Shame*, scientists like the French Georges Cuvier (particularly in his work "on" Sara Baartman) and the Italian Cesare Lombraso (in his work "on" prostitutes and women criminals) worked from a baseline presumption regarding the superiority of Europeans, the inferiority of women, and the meaningfulness of the body—particularly bodily fat—in providing "evidence based science" to prove their assertions about the inferiority of Africans, the biological degeneracy of sex workers, and the irrationality of women. The project of physiognomy—the study of human bodies for evidence of character traits and evolutionary status—was key to this process of racialization and gender-based hierarchicalization that provided the scientific rationale for entire systems of racialized empire, slavery, and the segregation and legal oppression of women and queer people within those racialized categories. As Sabrina Strings (2019) elaborates on in her carefully researched *Fearing the Black Body: The Racial Origins of Fat Phobia*, drawing from popular and scientific writings from the Renaissance through today, fatness has been continually marked as a sign of "savagery" and thinness as "beauty," key markers that masquerade as pure aesthetic judgments or as health values when they actually function fundamentally as tools in the oppressive discourse of race and gender science. And we can see these ideas at work, as Strings demonstrates, in everything from scientific journal articles to religious tracts to the popular articles found in magazines like *Harper's Bazaar*. Indeed, once one begins to note these connections, they can be seen everywhere. Just a few years ago, for instance, I was rereading Charlotte Brontë's 1847 classic novel *Jane Eyre* to accompany a younger family member on a summer reading requirement. And there it was again: the protagonist and heroine of the novel, Jane, is slim and white, dainty and fair skinned. The out of control, maniacal wife Bertha—the "madwoman in the attic" in the words of the literary scholars Sandra Gilbert and Susan Gubar (1979)—is Caribbean, dark, and described as "oversized." Both women are constrained by the legal and cultural force of the man of the house, Mr. Rochester, but only one—the light-skinned, the European, the slender, is allowed a place—legally and affectively—within the bounds of man in whose house they both reside. The trifecta of race, body size, and gender work closely together.

What is also noteworthy when following the example of Bertha within *Jane Eyre* is the extent to which Brontë seems to want to evoke in reader powerful emotions when considering her person and her situation. The most positive of these might be pity—who wants to see a person imprisoned or so unhappy—but more likely disgust at her behavior, outrage at her violence, fear at what she might do. Throughout this volume we will see these feelings discussed and interrogated— the visceral sensations of grossness and disgust at what Julia Kristeva (1982) called the abject, that which must be expelled or rejected in order to maintain a sense of self devoid of the reality of mortality and morbidity. And, indeed, one can even see clearly how this manifests into the very question of who deserves to be alive and whose lives deserve punishment and derision—whether we think of that as the constant belittlement and torment of TV shows like *The Biggest Loser*, to the torture and killing of Black people like Eric Garner at the hands of U.S. police, to the ways that a neo-Nazi writer described Heather Heyer, the woman killed at the Charlottesville, Virginia protest by another neo-Nazi, as a "fat, childless, 32-year old slut" and a "gross creature" (Khazan 2014; Weber 2017). In other words, the derogatory presumptions about fatness in circulation within Western cultures are linked to historic ideas about race and gender and generate (and legitimate) extraordinarily oppressive behaviors (Mollow 2017).

Even as we discuss the ways these categories—fatness, race, gender—intersect and construct each other, and even as we pay careful attention to the fundamental way that the origins of fat stigma are linked to the historical construction of racialization and gendering—we must also attend to the fact that over time these connections have changed shape. Even in the United States, where the "war on obesity" has gained steam since the late 20th century, there has also been an equally powerful alternative movement, one that advocates against discrimination and for new ways of understanding fatness. And these new ways of seeing fat often uproot conventional ideas about gender as well; in her novel *Martha Moody*, for instance, Susan Stinson (1995) creates a world that welcomes queer identities, sexuality outside of monogamous heterosexuality, and the beauty and power of fat bodies. Moreover, as we ponder the significance and connections between fat and gender in this volume, we need to remember that the categories themselves are mutable, fluid, and historically situated; Susan E. Hill's essay in this collection on fat and gender in the ancient world gives us the starkest reminder of how we need to specify our historical location before drawing conclusions. And so many of our contributors, and Cat Pausé most explicitly, alert us to the powerful ways that transgender identities and body modification challenge any understanding of gender as static and unchanging. Fatness itself is a category that shape shifts, ranging from the fact that a person can be fat at one moment and, without changing size, thin in another (the "plus size" models that Amanda M. Czerniawski discusses, for instance, would be considered thin in any other context). But it's not just a question of relativity—people often choose to change size, from the men who work to hasten their fatness in Jason Whitesel's study of fat gay men's cultural arenas to the weight loss worlds that Ava Purkiss and Nikkolette Lee ask us so thoughtfully to consider. This volume, then, pushes forward a conversation about the connections between gender and fat even while attending to complexities— the complexities of intersectionality, particularly the ways that race and historic context shape the encounter—and the complexities of mutable categories, ones that can shape shift even as we pay close attention.

Both the fields of Gender Studies and Fat Studies share another characteristic along with a commitment to anti-oppressive practices—a rejection of false "objectivity." That is, both fields emphasize the importance in situating the writer and researcher as "knowers" whose lives, whose bodies, whose background influences how we see and understand the world, how we create the scholarship, from the questions we ask to the methods we use. This does not mean that one has to "be" a certain identity in order to do the work, but it does mean that one should be clear about the perspective from which one is writing. For me, as a cisgendered, heterosexual, middle aged white U.S. woman, I recognize the ways my position can blind me to oppressive presumptions and biased questions. And though I was bullied tremendously as a child for being fat, so I tangibly feel that pain when I write or think about fat children, my weight as an adult affords me both access to most everything I need (furniture, clothing, seating in public places) and the important attribute of being "unremarkable" in public settings, the important courtesy that Jeannine A. Gailey describes in her essay on hyper(in)visibility. Throughout the volume readers will notice how frequently the contributors note their own body size, experiences, or activism—sometimes in their contributor's notes, sometimes in the body of their essay—a practice observed within both Fat Studies and Gender Studies as a way to create what scholar Donna Haraway called in her pathbreaking 1988 essay "situated knowledge." Sometimes this acknowledgment of the way the author is situated will be explicit, as in my description above; sometimes it will be brief but important, as when E. Cassandra Dame-Griff uses the term "our presence," placing herself directly within the category of "Latina women"; sometimes it will constitute the bulk of the essay, as with Kimberly Dark's autoethnography or Mara Mibelli and Chiara Meloni's analysis of the fat activist group that they began in Italy. What connects each of these pieces, however, is an understanding that no scholar works from an omniscient place, outside of a context that will shape how one sees and understands the world. This is a perspective keenly important to both the Fat Studies and Gender Studies, fields which deny the separation of knowledge from embodiment and which emphasize the importance of listening to and learning from the most effected and marginalized within any historic moment.

The contributors to this volume come to their work not only with a diversity of lived experiences—as I note above—but also with a range of disciplinary perspectives, from history and literature to psychology and sociology. Some of the contributors identify explicitly as fat activists as well as scholars, though even if they deflect the identification as activist they are all keenly aware of fat stigma and its extraordinarily painful and widespread effects. Some of the essays come from people who primarily identify as artists, writers, and activists, an important point to note as much of the most powerful knowledge about fat and gender has originated far outside of academia. All of the contributors are English-speaking, though some make clear that English is not their first language or language of choice. This volume skews to the United States, but the volume also includes contributions from Canada, Finland, Italy, Israel, and New Zealand. The contributors identify as African American, Latinx, white, straight, and queer.

The first section of the volume focuses on some broad discourses of gender and fat, perspectives that can help readers to think about the conceptual ways that our understandings of gender and fat manifest themselves. Discourse refers to a way of constituting knowledge and understanding and is key to how power is produced and maintained. Language is the most obvious discursive formation, but there are also other discursive formations—from medical systems to social practices to religious theology and the list goes on. Significantly, as Stuart Hall explains, one might even consider the fact that "nothing exists outside of discourse"—which is not to mean that there is no physical reality, but rather that nothing has any *meaning* outside of discourse. So, a person's body may have particular genitalia that we call either a vulva or a penis, but the meanings we attach to those parts, the assumptions we make about how the person identifies and comports themselves are discursive—the discourse of gender. Likewise, adipose tissue exists, but the meaning of that bodily tissue—as fat, as not-thin, as excess—are completely discursive. These discursive foundations frequently rely on binary distinctions— male v. female, thin v. fat, white v. Black, with one half of that binary carrying significantly more positive connotation. Significantly, various institutions both draw from already existing discourses about fat and about gender and *also*, in their laws, customs, and practices, work themselves discursively to shape the parameters and lived experiences of both fat and gender (Foucault 1972; Hall 1997; Butler 1990).

The Essays

In this first section of the volume, four scholars—Jeannine A. Gailey, Hannele Harjunen, Cat Pausé, and Da'Shaun L. Harrison—each speak to four broad discursive understanding of gender and fat, all of which help us to understand distinct ways to make sense of foundational, ideological shapings of these categories. Jeannine Gailey, in her essay "Hyper(in)visibility and the Gendered Fat Body," illuminates the ways that contemporary U.S. and European cultures both highlight and demonize the gendered fat body and render it invisible, limiting the possibilities of what Erving Goffman called good "life chances." Hannele Harjunen in her essay "Gendered Fat Bodies as Neoliberal Bodies" interrogates the ways that a neoliberal discourse, one focusing on individualism and self-promotion—have exacerbated and insidiously influenced anti-fat gendered experiences. Cat Pausé turns her attention to the queering of fatness, the ways that fat itself dismantles and reconstructs the discursive formation of gender itself as well as how people experience their own gendering. Da'Shaun L. Harrison confronts the fundamental antiblackness of gendered anti-fat discourses, illuminating the ways that this racial formation shapes every aspect of contemporary life, with particularly deleterious effects on Black people.

Following this section on "Discourses" the volume turns to a unit entitled "Narrative," in which two extremely accomplished writers take us on a journey regarding the stories we and others tell about fat, about gender, and about their tangled connections. The ability to understand and reflect upon narrative is key to almost any kind of analysis of how fat and gender intertwine and to imagining new ways of experiencing and thinking about these categories. Kimberly Dark, in her piece which is both sociology and autoethnography, illuminates the ways that her own and others' embodiments influence everything regarding the ways we understand body size and liberation. Susan Stinson offers a nuanced analysis of so many narratives—from those embedded in the work and experiences of scientists who have studied fatness to those of fat activists and novelists—underscoring the ways they both foreclose possibilities regarding gender and fat and offer emancipatory potential.

The following section, "Historicizing Fatness," emphasizes how crucial it is for readers to understand how discourses and experiences of gender and fat manifest themselves in distinct ways dependent upon historic context. The two contributors for this section focus their attention on two very different historic periods. Susan E. Hill introduces readers to the perspectives on fat and gender in the ancient world, paying particular attention to the ways that historians themselves have written about the past (what we call historiography) have been shaped by their own contemporary thinking—much of it limited by their own fat-phobic and sometimes even misogynistic perspectives. Ava Purkiss takes us to the last 150 years, as she traces the ways that Black women in the United States have strategically used body modification as a way to buffer the antiblack, racist context in which they were living.

The following sections each focuses on different discrete areas of concern and the ways that gender and fat manifest within them. The first focuses on gender and fat within institutions and public policy. April Michelle Herndon explores how anti-fat discourse disproportionately effects women and children in the United States. E. Cassandra Dame-Griff zeroes in on the ways that anti-fatness and misogyny work in tandem to both harm Latinx communities and to legitimate xenophobic and anti-immigration policies in the United States. Heather A. Brown moves us to the realm of education, where she details the research on how anti-fatness and gender discrimination work inextricably to limit the opportunities and achievement of fat girls and women in higher education.

The following section attends to the area of health and medicine. Erin N. Harrop explores how anti-fat and misogynist paradigms have influenced the work of practitioners who treat eating disorders; they explore in particular the work of feminist eating disorder specialists who are at the fore of challenging these limiting perspectives. Nikkolette Lee analyzes the many detailed interviews she has collected with people who have decided to undergo bariatric (aka weight loss) surgery, pointing out the complex rationale and experiences of patients, most of whom are women. Emily R.M. Lind, Deborah McPhail, and Lindsey Mazur examine the intricate and problematic ways that presumptions about fat and gender negatively influence infertility treatments and the care of pregnant people.

The next section attends to a variety of perspectives on gender and fat within popular culture and the media. Amanda M. Czerniawski surveys the world of plus size modeling, detailing the ways that it reproduces misogyny even as it was supposed to liberate fat women. Jason Whitesel provides a very detailed discussion of the multiple ways that fat men within gay communities have created art and media and formed activist and social groups to affirm their own identities. In the final essay in this section, Roshaunda L. Breeden and Terah J. Stewart analyze the problematic representations of Black, fat women in popular media, concluding with the provocative question of why many of these have actually been constructed by Black women themselves.

The final section of this volume turns our attention to possibilities— possibilities for new ways of seeing gender and fat, new ways of understanding gender and fat, new ways of experiencing gender and fat. It pulls together the work of five contributors who each offer their own work and analysis on ways for resisting anti-fatness, misogyny, and homophobia. Rachele Salvatelli analyzes the very concept of "coming out" as fat, and what this means about the connections between gender and fat. We then turn to a variety of distinctly different time periods and modes of fat activism. First, we get a deep glimpse into the world of U.S. fat activism in the 1970s and 1980s, as fat activist Judith Stein generously shares an interview she did many decades ago with Meridith Lawrence and Susan Stinson, which gives readers a glimpse of creating a fat positive, gender affirming, queer-friendly home and community despite a world that was hostile to it. Then we turn to Mara Mibelli and Chiara Meloni, who recount their own most recent experiences as fat activists within the world of Italian beauty and celebrity culture and offer their explanation for why Italian feminists have been slow to pick up on fat liberation. Rabbi Minna Bromberg illuminates the connections among religion, gender, and fat, as she describes how she is working to liberate fatness and gender in her organization, Fat Torah. And finally, activist and scholar Joy Cox, the author of *Fat Girls in Black Bodies: Creating Communities of Our Own*, exhorts us to find joy in our bodies, refusing to wait until a magical "after" moment when our bodies meet societal standards that, she argues, only work to limit us.

Concluding the book are the words of Substantia Jones, the brilliant artist and creator of the Adiposivity Project, in which she photographs fat people, sometimes clothed, sometimes not, in a joyful celebration of fat possibility. In this final essay, Jones shares the tribute she wrote in memory of Cat Pausé, whom we lost much too soon, in the spring of 2022. In the words that Jones shares about their friendship, about Pausé's joie de vivre, about her unbridled enthusiasm at being an Adiposer herself, we get a powerful glimpse into the wonderful life of Cat Pausé. As the author of *Fat Women Speak* and the editor of both *Queering Fat Embodiment* and the *International Handbook of Fat Studies*, Pausé was an extraordinary thinker in the field of Fat Studies. But she also was a consummate creator of community, hosting the global radio show *Friend of Marilyn*, organizing the extraordinary Fat Studies conferences in New Zealand, and working tirelessly to connect academics, artists, and activists. We are very fortunate to have Pausé's essay collected in this volume as well as Substantia Jones' wonderful memorial to her. This volume is dedicated to Cat.

Using This Volume

When the Routledge Press editor Alexander McGregor first spoke to me about this volume, we envisioned it as part of the *Companion* series, where contributors would clearly define a particular area of research and provide a comprehensive bibliography to help readers understand the full breadth of the field. As work on the volume progressed, some contributors were more interested in sharing their newest research while others maintained their interest in providing a thorough picture of some angle of the interconnected fields of Gender Studies and Fat Studies. We then decided to transition this volume to become a *Reader in Gender and Fat Studies*, one that would offer readers both the chapters that impart an overview of the field and those that push us with their newest research. The result, hopefully, is one that reaches both the reader brand-new to these fields and to those who plan to use these essays to push their own research and thinking.

The grouping of the essays moves from the most overarching and theoretical, in the section on Discourses of Gender and Fat, into many different subtopics (narrative, history, public policy, health, and popular culture) and finally into the last unit on resistance and re-imagination. There are, of course, alternative ways of pairing these chapters and I encourage readers to do just that. All the essays are in conversation with each other. Purkiss' chapter on the history of Black women's anti-fat discourse, for instance, might be contrasted usefully to Lee's chapter on bariatric surgery, as both suggest rather provocatively that fat activists need to be more attentive to and understanding of the reasons why fat women, and fat Black women especially, might choose to engage in weight loss and body modification. To pull from another example, Da'Shaun L. Harrison's essay on antiblack discourse might be paired with many of the essays in the resistance chapter, as he illuminates many of the ways that Black activists have struggled against oppressive structures. For readers particularly interested in the ways scholars and activists are thinking about gender, fat, and Blackness, I would link Harrison's essay with Purkiss' essay on dieting practices among Black women and Breeden and Stewart's essay on the representations of fat Black women in media and popular culture. While I placed Salvatelli's essay on "coming out" as fat in the section on resistance, this is a highly conceptual term that would be usefully used to think about the ways that gendered people claim and resist the identity of fat within almost every context that the other writers in the essay pose. The scenarios that Dark and Stinson explore in their essays on narrative link particularly fruitfully to the frame of "coming out." The three essays in the section on policy might also be paired valuably with the essay by Lind, McPhail, and Mazur in the health section, as their work suggests that the policies that hurt women and children start even prior to birth. And of course, Whitesel's essay on fat gay men's subcultures, Pausé's essay on queer theory, gender, and fat, and Stein's interview on lesbian fat activism might be grouped to think about the ways queer communities have challenged dominant ideas about fat and gender and the ways that fatness itself constructs gender within straight, queer, and trans communities.

I encourage readers to move around the chapters, to see what kinds of connections and oppositions emerge as you pair different essays. Indeed, this book is designed both to provide readers with a comprehensive sense of the literature on gender and fat and to highlight the ways that these categories, gender and fat, never exist on their own but always in relationship to one another and to the complicated contexts in which they reside. Thus, one of the best things that might be done with this text is to mix the essays, to see the kinds of surprising and illuminating connections and questions that these pairings might raise. Mostly, what I hope for readers is that this volume pushes forward the conversation about gender and fat in useful and complex ways, ones that insist on the necessity of intersectionality, ones that resist facile explanations, ones that provide a keen lens to understand how these interconnected phenomena have limited us, and, finally, ones that push us to remember how activists and artists have imagined the liberatory potential of the construction—and deconstruction—of fat and gender.

Bibliography

Albrecht, L. and Rose B. *Bridges of Power: Women's Multicultural Alliances* (Philadelphia, PA: New Society Publishers, 1990).

Beauvoir, S. de. *The Second Sex* (New York: Vintage, 1949).

Bergman, S. B. "Part-Time Fatso" in *Fat Studies Reader*, ed. E. Rothblum and S. Solovay (New York: New York University Press, 2009), 139–142.

Berlant, L. "Slow Death (Sovereignty, Obesity, Lateral Agency)," *Critical Inquiry* 33, no. 4 (June 2007), 754–780.

The Biggest Loser, created by David Broome, Mark Koops, and Ben Silverman, aired October 19, 2004, on NBC (NBCUniversal Television Distribution, 2004).

Bordo, S. *Unbearable Weight: Feminism, Western Culture, and the Body* (Berkeley, CA: University of California Press, 2003).

Brontë, C. *Jane Eyre*, ed. D. Lutz (New York: W.W. Norton & Company, 2016 [1847]).

Butler, J. *Gender Trouble* (New York: Routledge, 1990).

Cameron, L. "Thickening Fat: Fat Bodies, Intersectionality, and Social Justice (book review)," *Fat Studies*, 9, no. 2 (2020), 190–192.

Crenshaw, K. "Mapping the Margins: Intersectionality, Identity Politics, and Violence against Women of Color," *Stanford Law Review*, 43, no. 6 (1991), 1241–1299.

Dark, K. "Big Yoga Student," in *Introduction to Women's, Gender and Sexuality Studies: Interdisciplinary and Intersectional Approaches*, ed. L. Ayu Sarasati, B. Shaw and H. Rellihan (New York: Oxford University Press, 2020), 421–422.

Farrell, A. E. *Fat Shame* (New York: New York University, 2011).

Farrell, A. E. "'In the Position of Fat Women Is Shown the True Position of Woman in Our Society': *Shadow on a Tightrope* and the Centrality of Feminist Independent Publishing," *American Periodicals: A Journal of History and Criticism* 28, no. 2 (2018), 139–152.

Foucault, M. *Archaeology of Knowledge* (New York: Pantheon Books, 1972 [1969]).

Friedman, M., C. Rice., and J. Rinaldi, eds. *Thickening Fat: Fat Bodies, Intersectionality and Social Justice* (New York: Routledge, 2020).

Gilbert, S. and S. Gubar. *The Madwoman in the Attic: The Woman Writer and the Nineteenth-Century Literary Imagination* (Yale University Press, 1979).

Goffman, E. *Stigma: Notes on the Management of Spoiled Identity* (New Jersey: Prentice-Hall, 1963).

Guy-Sheftal, B., ed. *Words of Fire: An Anthology of African-American Feminist Thought* (New York: The New Press, 1995).

Hall, S. "The Work of Representation" in *Representation: Cultural Representation and Signifying Practices*, ed. S. Hall (London: Sage Publications, 1997), 1–59.

Haraway, D. "Situated Knowledges: The Science Question in Feminism and the Privilege of Partial Perspective," *Feminist Studies* 14, no. 3 (1998), 575–599.

Herndon, A. M. *Fat Blame* (Lawrence, KS: University Press of Kansas, 2014).

Johnston, J. and J.Taylor. "Feminist Consumerism and Fat Activists: Grassroots Activism and the Dove 'Real Beauty' Campaign," in *Feminist Frontiers*, ed. V. Taylor, N. Whittier and L. Rupp (Lanham, MD: Rowman & Littlefield, 2019), 115–127.

Khazan, O. "Fat-Shaming Eric Garner," *The Atlantic*, December 4, 2014, www.theatlantic.com/health/archive/2014/12/fat-shaming-eric-garner/383416/.

Kristeva, J. *The Powers of Horror: An Essay on Abjection*, trans. L. Rudiez. (New York: Columbia University Press, 1982).

LeBesco, K. *Revolting Bodies?: The Struggle to Redefine Fat Identity* (Amherst, MA: University of Massachusetts Press, 2003).

LeBesco, K. "On Fatness and Fluidity: A Meditation," in *Queering Fat Embodiment*, ed. C. Pausé, J. Wykes, and S. Murray (Burlington, VT: Ashgate, 2014), 49–60.

Mollow, A. "Unvictimizable: Toward a Fat Black Disability Studies," *African American Review*, 50 no (2) (2017), 105–121.

Moraga, C. and G. Anzaldua., eds., *This Bridge Called My Back: Writings by Radical Women of Color* (New York: Kitchen Table, Women of Color Press, 1983).

Orbach, S. *Fat Is a Feminist Issue: A Self-help Guide for Compulsive Eaters* (New York: Paddington Press, 1978).

Orbach, S. *Fat is a Feminist Issue II: A Pogram to Conquer Compulsive Eating* (New York: Berkeley Books, 1982).

Orbach, S. "Fat Is Still a Feminist Issue," in *Gendered Voices, Feminist Visions*, ed. S. Shaw and J. Lee (New York: Oxford University Press, 2019), 215–217.

Pausé, C. and S.R. Taylor., "Fattening Up Scholarship" in *Routledge International Handbook of Fat Studies*, ed. C. Pausé. and S. R. Taylor (New York: Routledge, 2021), 1–18.

Pausé, C., J. Wykes., and S. Murray, eds. *Queering Fat Embodiment*. (London: Ashgate, 2014).

Rothblum, E. and S. Solovay, eds. *The Fat Studies Reader* (New York: New York University Press, 2009).

Schoenfielder, L. and B. Wieser., eds. *Shadow on a Tightrope: Writings by Women on Fat Oppression* (San Francisco, CA: Aunt Lute Books, 1983).

Shuster, M. and S. Van Dyne. *Women's Place Within the Academy: Transforming the Liberal Arts Curriculum* (London: Roman and Littlefield, 1985).

Stinson, S. *Martha Moody* (Easthampton, MA: Small Beer Press, 2020).

Strings, S. *Fearing the Black Body: The Racial Origins of Fat Phobia* (New York: New York University Press, 2019).

Tillmon, J. "Welfare is a woman's issue," *Ms.*, Spring, (1972) 111.

Tong. R. *Feminist Thought: A More Comprehensive Introduction* (Boulder, CO: Westview Press, 2009).

Truth, S. "Woman's Rights," in *Words of Fire: An Anthology of African-American Feminist Thought*, ed. B. Guy-Sheftal (New York: The New Press, 1995), 36.

Wann, M. *Fat!So?* (Berkeley: Ten Speed Press, 1998).

Weber, S. "The Entwined History of White Supremacy and Fat Hatred," *bitchmedia*, September 7, 2017, www.bitchmedia.org/article/fat-shaming-heather-heyer-white-supremacy.

White, F. R. "The Future of Fat Sex," in *Gendered Voices, Feminist Visions*, ed. S. Shaw. and J. Lee (New York: Oxford University Press, 2019), 328–336.

White, F. R. "Embodying the Fat/Trans Intersection" in *Thickening Fat: Fat Bodies, Intersectionality, and Social Justice*, ed. M. Friedman, C. Rice, and J. Rinaldi (New York: Routledge, 2020), 119.

PART II

Discourses of Gender and Fat

Discourse is a useful term for exploring how culture shapes meaning through the way we talk about, study, and understand particular topics. The chapters in this section each introduce readers to a different discursive approach to thinking through the connections between gender and fat—neoliberalism, hyper(in)visibility, queerness, and antiblackness. Each of these conceptual ways of thinking about gender and fat might usefully be applied to the particular "case studies" in the sections that follow.

DOI: 10.4324/9781003140665-3

2

UNDESIRABLY DIFFERENT

Hyper(in)visibility and the Gendered Fat Body

Jeannine A. Gailey

In this chapter, I discuss the phenomenon of hyper(in)visibility as one way to understand the gendering of fat bodies. I became interested in fat studies when I was in graduate school and learned about a behavior called "hogging" from the local weekly entertainment guide. Hogging, as it was described, is a practice where men, usually in groups, bet about who can have sex with the fattest woman or it is where men will use, and sometimes abuse, fat women for sexual gratification. My colleague and friend, Ariane Prohaska, and I decided shortly thereafter that we had to learn more about this deplorable practice. We launched a small study where we interviewed undergraduate, heterosexual men and conducted a content analysis of blogs and forums. What we learned, in sum, was that the men who engaged in these behaviors were seeking to prove to each other that they were "real men" through sexual conquest and the degradation of fat women and that they thought their actions were justifiable because, in their eyes, fat women are desperate and/or easy (Gailey and Prohaska 2006; Prohaska and Gailey 2010).

Following that research, I began to study the emerging academic field of fat studies and focused my attention specifically on fat women and how they negotiate living in an anti-fat society. I started that research interviewing fat women about their life course, paying particular attention to their sexual and dating histories, but as the interviews progressed, I broadened my focus to capture a more complete picture about how they experience their bodies, lives, and world as fat women. It was through in-depth interviews with 74 women that I conceptualized the phenomenon of hyper(in)visibility (Gailey 2014), a predicament where one is exceptionally visible and invisible, often simultaneously.

In what follows, I present how hyper(in)visibility can help us understand the intersection of gender and fat. My goal for this chapter is twofold: (1) to conceptualize and illustrate the spectrum of visibility and the phenomenon of

DOI: 10.4324/9781003140665-4

hyper(in)visibility; and (2) to demonstrate how the phenomenon of hyper(in) visibility operates by discussing the societal expectations of fat ciswomen, fat cismen, and fat queer people.

The Spectrum of Visibility and the Phenomenon of Hyper(in)visibility

It is through our appearance and bodies that we communicate to others our social location. Social location refers to our social position vis-à-vis our race, ethnicity, gender, age, able-bodiedness, body size, and so forth. The ways these social categories intersect affects how we are perceived by others as well as where we are positioned in the social hierarchy. I contend that human bodies exist on a spectrum of visibility from hypervisible at one extreme and hyperinvisible at the other. We are all visible and invisible at times, but it's how visibility and invisibility function that is a both a consequence of the social hierarchy and simultaneously reinforces that same hierarchy. For example, those who are able-bodied, white, middle or upper class, cisgender, and thin are at the top of the social hierarchy and have the most privilege. They are seen when it benefits them and ignored when it does not.

Contrast this with the way that queer people, those with physical disabilities or disfigurements, and fat persons are treated by strangers. As visible as they appear and feel, they experience invisibility in numerous social settings, to the extent that they're often completely dismissed or erased. Moreover, they notice people's stares, looks of disgust or ridicule, and often have a feeling of being "onstage" (Gailey 2014, 10). Those with privilege are socially invisible. They don't receive the same looks of judgment, ridicule, or contempt that those who are marginalized do. People with privileged bodies are able to slip in and out of visibility and invisibility easily and when it is convenient for them. In contrast, those with marginalized bodies are paid exceptional attention or are exceptionally overlooked, often simultaneously.

Hyper(in)visibility is the phenomenon whereby marginalized bodies are subjected to both an extraordinary amount of attention and scrutiny and are simultaneously completely disregarded and dismissed. I argue that contemporary Western societies relegate fat people to a hyper(in)visible space, an experience that occurs explicitly within institutions (e.g., hidden from view in corporate endeavors that showcase thin women) and implicitly in our interpersonal and imagined worlds (through shunning particular body types in everyday life and the internalization of fat hatred) (Gailey 2021, 2014; Gailey and Harjunen 2019). Fat women and queer people, and increasingly, fat men, are hyperinvisible in that their needs, desires, and lives are grossly disregarded, yet at the same time they are hypervisible because they're the target of a disproportionate amount of critical judgment.

At the extremes, a hyperinvisible person is nearly or totally deprived of recognition, and a hypervisible person will be heavily scrutinized or paid a tremendous amount of attention…I argue that the prefix "hyper" is necessary to understand the process of Othering. Being seen and socially acknowledged means that we exist and that we matter. Yet as Goffman (1963) writes, most people grant strangers in public the courtesy of civil inattention, which simply means that most people will pass strangers on the street or in a public space without commentary or inspection. But this courtesy of civil inattention is often not granted to fat people, particularly fat women, because strangers expect that women, especially when in public, should be accommodating to the male gaze by being attractive (thin). In what follows, I demonstrate how hyper(in)visibility can help us understand the intersection of gender and fat by discussing how it impacts cisgender women, cisgender men, and queer people.

Fat, Gender, and Hyper(in)visibility

Western heteronormative cultural norms dictate that women should be beautiful (thin), and if they aren't they are compelled to at least try to be, which typically means losing weight. In addition, fat represents a challenge to the identification as sexual (Murray 2004) because body size is connected to the heteronormative system of meaning and value that establishes what it means to be masculine and feminine and prioritizes men's pleasure in sex.

Gender is not an inherent quality of an individual, instead it is a performance or a social doing where individuals, through their interactions with others, demonstrate their mastery of either a masculine or feminine presentation (Butler 1993). This takes place in accordance with the societal expectations about the "appropriate" roles for men and women. In the West, the gendered order is typically referred to as "hegemonic masculinity" (Connell 1987), which is the template for the way men should behave *and* look, the goals to which they should aspire, and the type of women they should be attracted to, date, or marry. In this context, hegemonically masculine men dominate women and subordinated men. Women are expected to accommodate the interests and needs of men, a concept known as "emphasized femininity" (Connell 1987), which includes meeting the normative standards of beauty (thinness).

Cisgender Women

Emphasized femininity works to sustain hegemonic masculinity and heteronormativity; in essence, they're two sides of the same coin. Fat women's bodies are typically not considered to align with the feminine ideal because their body symbolizes both domination (due to its size) and resistance to idealized femininity (thinness) (Gailey 2012). Farrell (2009, 261) notes,

> as women gained more political and geographic freedom in the early 20th century, they were increasingly curtailed by a set of body disciplines that

mocked and denigrated all those who did not seem to display proper modes of bodily control.

Women who don't appropriately attend to and "invest" in their bodies are shunned and viewed as deviant. As Dolezal (2015, 110) writes, "a woman's subjectivity is structured by the self-consciousness of being constantly under surveillance and visible as a result of objectification." Hence, women cannot move their bodies freely, as their bodies are always already made known to them by society.

Fat women's bodies uniquely demonstrate characteristics associated with both masculinity and femininity, which at the outset seems paradoxical. Their bodies are masculine because they take up "excess" space and their body is ultra-feminine because it is soft, curvy, and fleshy. Moreover, fat women's bodies are read as simultaneously nonsexual and hypersexual (Braziel 2001; Farrell 2011; Gailey 2014, 2012). However, the fact that fat women are both masculine and feminine and sexual and nonsexual is perpetuated by the phenomenon of hyper(in)visibility.

Fat women regularly have to deal with hypervisibility because they often receive disapproving stares and commentary while exercising (Harjunen 2019), grocery shopping (Gailey 2014), sitting in class (Stevens 2017, eating out (Owen 2012), sitting on public transportation (Huff 2009; Owen 2012), on social media and blogs (Hynnä and Kyrölä 2019; Taylor 2018), in television shows (Taylor and Gailey 2019), shopping for clothes (Jennings 2010) and when interacting with health care professionals (Gailey 2014; Wilson 2009).

In a study with fat college students, Stevens (2017) found that the phenomenon of hyper(in)visibility was made more salient in the types of spaces that exist on college campuses, such as dining areas, recreation centers, classrooms, and predominantly undergraduate bars near the campus. Respondents noted that it is often difficult to fit in the desks in classrooms or easily move down the aisles between the desks, which simultaneously makes them both hypervisible and hyperinvisible because their bodies aren't considered in the design of public spaces.

Similarly, Harjunen's (2019) research on fat women who exercise in public painfully demonstrates the ways in which fat women are publicly castigated and shamed when wearing a swimsuit. Her research reveals that strangers stare, make clearly audible comments about how "she shouldn't be in public in a bathing suit" while simultaneously assuming that she's fat because she doesn't exercise and overeats. Fat women who wish to exercise are hypervisible when they do so in public because they're made into a spectacle and hyperinvisible because they sometimes have difficulty finding swimsuits or workout clothing in their size, and many come to avoid public exercise altogether (Gailey 2014).

This sort of mistreatment and stigmatization happens in nearly all social settings, and sometimes even in places where one would expect to feel safe. Calogero et al. (2018) argue that therapists must employ weight inclusive therapy because of the overwhelming research that shows that fat women are frequently not safe in therapy due to the hyper(in)visibility they experience. The last thing someone needs when they enter therapy is to have their lives and experiences be reduced to their bodies or body size. Both Gailey (2021) and Monaghan (2008b) argue that the obesity epidemic discourse, fat oppression, and marginalization are forms of symbolic violence because the treatment of fat people is so deplorable that it can easily be seen as a form of non-physical violence. Moreover, anti-fat sentiments and the experience of hyper(in)visibility leads many fat people to internalize fat hatred (Gailey 2014).

As Harjunen (2017, 89) writes, "[Women] are actively encouraged to think of self-governance and disciplining the body as sources of empowerment and pleasure." Women who don't find pleasure in body work or who don't engage in intentional weight loss are viewed as deviant and violating one of the most fundamental gender roles for women. When women don't subscribe to the popular cultural demands they are frequently subjected to vitriol and erasure. Unfortunately, fat men are also increasingly judged for having an "unruly" body and, like fat women, are apt to internalize fat hatred and express dissatisfaction and contempt with their body (Tischner 2013).

Cisgender Men

Fat men also violate gender norms, not surprisingly, in a similarly paradoxical manner, which has a significant impact on the way they see themselves and how others see them. Yet, there has been much less theorizing about fat men and boys' bodies. Gilman (2004, 32) expressed this concern nearly 20 years ago, writing

> the scholarship since the 1960s has focused almost entirely on women's bodies and on patriarchy, the body of the fat boy has, in fact, long been a source of "fascination, concern, horror, [and] interest" representing as he does "the outer limits of the performance of masculinity."

Research indicates that men in the United States are increasingly presenting with eating disorders and body dysmorphia, engaging in diets and weight loss behaviors, as well as using cosmetic surgeries and procedures to correct their "uncontrollable" bodies (Monaghan 2008a, 2008b; Mosher 2001; Tischner 2013).

Fat bodies, in most respects, are the opposite of the muscular, hard, and chiseled body prescribed by hegemonic masculinity; the one exception is that fat bodies are large and take up space, which is commonly associated with masculinity. Yet, fat is typically feminized, and femininity is relegated to the marginal position of Other, while masculinity is most closely associated with being human. For men to achieve hegemonic masculinity they must reject any and all things feminine or risk being subordinated. Gilman (2004, 19) writes, "the very notion of a hobbled masculinity seems to be built into the image of the fat man." Monaghan (2008a), one of the first scholars to focus nearly exclusively on fat men, views fat oppression as an emergent process that is directed at both men and women's bodies, though he does acknowledge that it's aimed at bodies that are positioned as feminine regardless of their biological sex. Monaghan (2008b) draws our attention to the fact that the violence associated with the war on obesity is of particular concern to women because they experience fat hatred as a gendered (misogynistic) practice, but men who embody what Connell (1995) conceptualized as "marginalized or subordinated masculinities" also risk humiliation and hyper(in)visibility due to fatphobia.

Bell and McNaughton (2007) state, "fatness has long had threatening implications for men, given the ways it potentially undermines normative forms of masculinity" (127). Fatness has the *potential* to emasculate men, especially if the fat is distributed in the hips or chest. Men with adipose tissue in their chest are often said to have "man boobs" (Bell and McNaughton 2007; Lozano-Sufrategui et al. 2016; Monaghan 2008a). However, one component of hegemonic masculinity is to take up space, which fat bodies do. In this way we can see that fat men aren't held to the same narrow standards regarding their appearance as women, but gendered appearance norms have begun to shift. Men's bodies were historically overlooked because their primary currency was their occupational status and wealth. Yet, as gender and sex roles change, men's bodies have increasingly become sites of contestation. As men become increasingly objectifed we could begin to see more fat men internalize fat hatred and experience discrimination.

Previous research indicates that some men will develop self-protective strategies, such as hiding their bodies from public purview and using humor to cover up that they're hurt or offended by anti-fat comments, i.e., they become hyperinvisible (Lozano-Sufrategui et al. 2016; Monaghan 2008a, 2008b; Tischner 2013). In fact, it's "common knowledge" that fat men are supposed to wear a shirt while swimming because their bodies are deemed unsightly. In fact, onlookers sometimes express disgust quite openly, whereas friends or family might joke about his "man boobs" and protruding belly, rendering him hypervisible. Some fat men have reported being "mothered" or infantilized by women, especially coworkers and friends (Monaghan and Hardey 2009). For instance, in a study of men enrolled in a weight management program some discussed experiencing hyperinvisibility when they're mothered by women because they saw it as a sign that they aren't attractive and aren't manly (Lozano-Sufrategui et al. 2016).

Queer People

Scholarly writing about queer and fat goes back to the late 1990s and early 2000s when fat studies was in its infancy. Charlotte Cooper (2012) began writing on fat and queer activism in the 1990s and scholars like Kathleen LeBesco and Hanne Blank quickly followed. Today there's an increasing number of scholars working on the intersection of queer and fat but it is still sorely understudied. White (2021) argues that trans studies and fat studies share many similar goals, i.e., they're both interdisciplinary, both are oriented toward anti-oppressive goals and they both focus on the theorization of nonnormative embodiments; but there's little research that focuses on trans and fat. White contends that this significantly limits our understanding of the relationship between gender and fat. While my research unfortunately can't fill this gap, I would like to highlight what has been written and illustrate how great the need is for more research on queer and fat, especially fat and transgender and gender nonbinary people.

Queer bodies, in a heteronormative society, are viewed as abject because homosexuality and gender nonconformity are direct repudiations of the hegemonically masculine gendered social order. Fat queer people experience their bodies in ways that cisgendered fat people don't (White 2014). Cisgenderism is a helpful way to think through this.

Cisgenderism (Ansara and Hegarty 2012) is the system of thinking and practice—based on the assumption of a cisgender norm—that invalidates people's own understanding of their genders and bodies, including misgendering, pathologizing, marginalizing, and binarzing people. Examples of cisgender norms include assuming that because someone looks masculine that they were assigned male at birth, calling someone "sir" or "ma'am" on the assumption that everyone is male or female, or asking personal questions about a person's sex life and medical interventions when one finds out that person is transgender. These examples clearly show that queer and/or trans people's adherence to gendered expectations will impact the way they are treated by those within and outside the queer community. Moreover, hyper(in)visibility would provide a useful tool to investigate the processes and mechanisms at place for the lived experiences of queer and trans people.

Allison Taylor (2018) studied queer fat femme blogs and found that fat femmes often experience hyper(in)visibility. Her research demonstrates how queer fat femmes are often erased in the lesbian community because they are feminine and fat, and at the same time they're rejected as feminine because of their body size. Femininity is read as heterosexual, which means that all too often queer fat femmes, as well as queer fat men and those who are fat and gender nonbinary, are invisible in queer communities (White 2014). Koehle's (2022) rhetorical analysis of blogs written by fat trans people found that gender, fatness, and race could not be separated when the bloggers were discussing their ability to pass because femininity is inextricably linked to whiteness and thinness. The trans Black women had a difficult time imagining that they really could be women because of their size—both height and weight—and race. One of the bloggers wrote, "who's ever heard of a 6'2" 320 pound woman" and another writes about having to shop in men's department's due to lack of women's clothing that can accommodate tall fat women (Koehle 2022, 82–83). Many of these bloggers felt exiled from their gender because they couldn't meet the cisgender standards.

Research on gay men has found that their bodies are read as effeminate, which frequently results in stigmatization, subordination, and sometimes violence (Barron and Bradford 2007), as well as the predicament of hyper(in)visibility. Whitesel

(2014) found that gay fat men experienced significant stigmatization, especially when it came to attracting partners. This is consistent with previous research that has found that gay and bisexual men had significantly higher levels of anti-fat attitudes, dislike of fat people, and are more likely to be overly critical and fixated on their bodies (Robinson 2016). It's not uncommon on gay men's dating sites to see users post "no fats, no fems" on their profile, publicly marking that there is no room for fat or effeminate men in the gay dating scene. Fat gay men are marked as hypervisible as their bodies are noted publicly as not belonging (or are fetishized), while simultaneously they're hyperinvisible because they aren't welcome in the online dating community and their feelings and needs are disregarded.

White's (2021, 2019) theorizing on the intersection of trans and fat is probably the most thorough discussion about how trans-fat people create "gender trouble." Most of the research that addresses fat and trans treats them as discrete categories. For instance, trans/fat masculine men are sometimes misgendered because their bodies don't fit the narrow ideal of cis gendered men's bodies (Taylor 2018; White 2014). While fat transwomen sometimes experience misgendering because our society associates femaleness with slenderness, either way they all suffer the predicament of hyper(in)visibility, even though I haven't found the concept used in the trans and fat work. White (2021) asks us to entertain the possibility that fat doesn't cause gender to fail, but rather drives it into a liminal state "between" binary genders. Viewing it in this manner opens up the possibility for the subversion of the gender binary and enables us to think about what fat "does" rather than what it fails to do.

Conclusion

In this chapter, I have introduced and explained how the phenomenon of hyper(in) visibility can be utilized for discussing the intersection of fat and gender. As I've shown, this concept has broad applicability and succinctly illustrates how societal messages and interactions perpetuate the discrimination against fat people, especially because fat complicates and subverts gendered appearance-based norms. In addition, the phenomenon of hyper(in)visibility is incredibly harmful because it contributes to the internalization of fat hatred. Fat women, fat men, and queer and trans fat people all experience the phenomenon of hyper(in)visibility—a predicament that exists in our visually and appearance oriented culture. The increasing prevalence of surveillance technologies, social media, and dependence on virtual spaces means that we are looking at ourselves and each other more than ever. While those with privilege are not immune to the heteronormative pressures that mandate that women, queer people, and increasingly men conform to the narrow beauty strictures, they aren't scrutinized and made into a spectacle nor are they disregarded, which is precisely why the prefix "hyper" is necessary. Fat people often experience, simultaneously, deprivation of recognition and surplus attention in socially and medically significant settings.

Research on gender and fat has focused mainly on cisgender heterosexual women to date and ignored other human bodies that could experience the phenomenon of hyper(in)visibility. Research and theorizing regarding cisgender straight and gay men is increasing and there's been an uptick in research examining the intersection of fat and queer bodies in general, but there is very little research on the experiences of transgender fat people. In addition, future research must examine the way that other social categories, such as race, ethnicity, and social class intersect with gender, sexuality, and fat because we know that their gendered experiences will be different due to racism and classism.

In order to begin dismantling this system of oppression, we must shift our focus away from body weight and normative gender expectations surrounding body size and appearance and instead appreciate the diversity of human bodies. Moreover, as White (2021) asks, let's begin to theorize more about the ways that fat can potentially blur and subvert gendered binaries, as opposed to thinking of it only as something that creates a problem for gender.

References

Ansara, Y. Gavriel and Peter Hegarty. 2012. "Cisgenderism in Psychology: Pathologising and Misgendering Children from 1999 to 2008." *Psychology & Sexuality* 3 (2): 137–160.

Barron, Michael and Simon Bradford. 2007. "Corporeal Controls: Violence, Bodies, and Young Gay Men's Identities." *Youth & Society* 39(2): 232–261. DOI: 10.1177/0044118 X07307767

Bell, Kristin and Darlene McNaughton. 2007. "Feminism and the Invisible Fat Man." *Body & Society* 13(1): 107–131.

Braziel, Jana E. 2001. "Sex and Fat Chics: Deterritorializing the Fat Female Body." In *Bodies Out of Bounds: Fatness and Transgression*, edited by Jana Evans Braziel and Kathleen LeBesco, 231–254. Berkeley: University of California Press.

Butler, Judith. 1993. *Gender Trouble*. London: Routledge.

Calogero, Rachel M., Tracy L. Tylka, Janell L. Mensinger, Angela Meadows, and Sigrun Daníelsdóttir. 2018. "Recognizing the Fundamental Right to be Fat: A Weight-Inclusive Approach to Size Acceptance and Healing from Sizeism." *Women and Therapy* 22–44. DOI: 10.1080/02703149.2018.1524067

Connell, R. W. 1987. *Gender and Power: Society, the Person, and Sexual Politics*. Redwood City, CA: Stanford University Press.

Connell, R. W. 1995. *Masculinities*. Cambridge: Polity.

Cooper, Charlotte. 2012. "A Queer and Trans Fat Activist Timeline: Queering Fat Activist Nationality and Cultural Imperialism." *Fat Studies* 1: 61–74. DOI: 10.1080/21604851.2012.627503

Dolezal, Luna. 2015. *The Body and Shame: Phenomenology, Feminism, and the Socially Shaped Body*. London: Lexington Books.

Farrell, Amy E. 2009. "'The White Man's Burden': Female Sexuality, Tourist Postcards, and the Place of the Fat Woman in Early 20th-Century U.S. Culture." In *The Fat Studies Reader*, edited by Esther Rothblum and Sondra Solovay, 256–262. New York: New York University Press.

Farrell, Amy E. 2011. *Fat Shame: Stigma and the Fat Body in American Culture*. New York: New York University Press.

Gailey, Jeannine A. 2012. "Fat Shame to Fat Pride: Fat Women's Sexual and Dating Experiences." *Fat Studies* 1(1): 114–127.

Gailey, Jeannine A. 2014. *The Hyper(in)visible Fat Woman: Weight and Gender Discourse in Contemporary Society*. New York: Palgrave Macmillan.

Gailey, Jeannine A. 2021. "The Violence of Fat Hatred in the 'Obesity Epidemic'". *Humanity and Society*. DOI: 10.1177/0160597621995501

Gailey, Jeannine A. and Ariane Prohaska. 2006. "'Knocking Off a Fat Girl': An Exploration of Hogging, Male Sexuality, and Neutralizations." *Deviant Behavior* 21: 31–49.

Gailey, Jeannine A. and Hannele Harjunen. 2019. "A Cross-Cultural Examination of Fat Women's Bodies: Stigma and Gender in North American and Finnish Culture." *Feminism & Psychology* 29(3): 374–390. DOI: 10.1177/0959353518819582

Gilman, Sander J. 2004. *Fat Boys: A Slim Book*. Lincoln: University of Nebraska Press.

Goffman, Erving. 1963. *Stigma: Notes on the Management of Spoiled Identity*. Harmondsworth: Penguin.

Harjunen, Hannele. 2019. "Exercising Exclusions: Space, Visibility, and Monitoring of the Exercising Fat Female Body". *Fat Studies* 8(2): 173–186. DOI:10.1080/21604851.2019.1561101

Harjunen, Hannele. 2017. *Neoliberal Bodies and the Gendered Fat Body*. New York: Routledge.

Huff, Joyce. 2009. "Access to the Sky: Airplane Seats and Fat Bodies as Contested Spaces." In *The Fat Studies Reader*, edited by Esther Rothblum and Sondra Solovay, 176–196. New York: New York University Press.

Hynnä, Kaisu and Katriina Kyrölä. 2019. "Feel in your Body: Fat Activists Affect in Blogs." *Social Media and Society*, 1–11. DOI: 10.1177/2056305119879983

Jennings, Laura. 2010. "Where the [Fat Women's] Bodies are Buried: A Sociological Look at Women's Clothing Departments." Paper presented at Popular Culture Association Annual Meeting, April 2, St. Louis, Missouri.

Koehle, Han. 2022. "Gendering the Fat Body: Rhetoric and Personhood in Transition." In *Advancing in Trans Studies: Moving Toward Gender Expression and Trans Hope Advances in Gender Research*, edited by Austin H. Johnson, Baker A. Rogers, and Tiffany Taylor, 77–90. Bingley: Emerald Publishing Limited.

Lozano-Sufrategui, Lorena, David Carless, Andy Pringle, Andrew Sparkes and Jim McKenna 2016. "Sorry Mate, You're Probably a Bit Too Fat to Do Any of These." *International Journal of Men's Health*, 15(1): 4–23.

Monaghan, Lee F. 2008a. *Men and the War on Obesity: A Sociological Study*. Milton Park, UK: Routledge.

Monaghan, Lee F. 2008b. "Men, Physical Activity, and the Obesity Discourse: Critical Understandings from Qualitative Study." *Sociology of Sport Journal* 25: 97–129.

Monaghan, Lee F., and M. Hardey. 2009. "Bodily Sensibility: Vocabularies of the Discredited Male Body." *Critical Public Health* 19(3–4): 341–362.

Mosher, Jerry. 2001. "Setting Free the Bears: Refiguring Fat Men on Television." In *Bodies Out of Bounds: Fatness and Transgression*, edited by Jana Evan Braziel and Kathleen LeBesco, 166–193. Berkeley: University of California Press.

Murray, Samantha. 2004. *The Fat Female Body*. London: Palgrave Macmillan.

Owen, Lesleigh. 2012. "Living Fat in a Thin-Centric World: Effects of Spatial Discrimination on Fat Bodies and Selves." *Feminism & Psychology* 22(3): 290–306.

Prohaska, Ariane and Jeannine A. Gailey. 2010. "Achieving Masculinity through Sexual Predation: The Case of Hogging." *Journal of Gender Studies* 19(1): 13–25.

Robinson, Brandon Andrew. 2016. "The Quantifiable Body Discourse: 'Height-Weight Proportionality' and Gay Men's Bodies in Cyberspace." *Social Currents* 3(2): 172–185.

Stevens, Corey. 2017. "Fat on Campus: Fat College Student's Experiences of Stigma." *Sociological Focus* 50(4): 1–20.

Taylor, Allison. 2018. "Flabulously" Femme: Queer Fat Femme Women's Identities and Experiences." *Journal of Lesbian Studies* 22(4): 459–481. DOI: 10.1080/10894160.2018.1449503

Taylor, Hannah and Jeannine A. Gailey. 2019. "Fiction Meets Reality: A Comparison of *Dietland* and the Experiences of North American Fat Women". *Fat Studies* 10(1): 34–49. DOI: 10.1080/21604851.2019.1644984

Tischner, Irmgard. 2013. *Fat Lives: A Feminist Psychological Explanation*. London: Routledge.

White, Francis Ray. 2014. "Fat/Trans: Queering the Activist Body." *Fat Studies* 3(2): 86–100. DOI: 10.1080/21604851.2014.889489

White, Francis Ray. 2019. "Embodying the Fat/Trans Intersection. In *Thickening Fat: Fat Bodies, Intersectionality, and Social Justice*, edited by May Friedman, Carla Rice and Jen Rinaldi, 110–121. London: Routledge.

White, Frances Ray. 2021. "Fat and Trans: Towards a New Theorization of Gender in Fat Studies." In *The International Handbook of Fat Studies*, edited by Cat Pausé and Sonya Renee Taylor, 78–87. London: Routledge.

Whitesel, Jason. 2014. *Fat Gay Men: Girth, Mirth, and the Politics of Stigma*. New York: New York University Press.

Wilson, Bianca D. M. 2009. "Widening the Dialogue to Narrow the Gap in Health Disparities: Approaches to Fat Black Lesbian and Bisexual Women's Health Promotion." In *The Fat Studies Reader*, edited by Esther Rothblum and Sondra Solovay, 54–64. New York: New York University Press.

3

GENDERED FAT BODIES AS NEOLIBERAL BODIES

Hannele Harjunen

In this chapter, my aim is to shed light on the relationships between neoliberalism, fatness, and postfeminist body politics. I will present the idea that neoliberal thought has had a significant effect on the formation of our present-day body norms. My intention is to investigate some of the ways in which "neoliberal bodies" are constructed. In particular, I am interested in how neoliberal thought motivates the normalization of certain gendered body practices and encourages the exclusion of those bodies that do not fit in.

Neoliberalism, a school of thought in economics that emphasizes freedom and choice in the form of the free market and the deregulation of the economy, has dominated political and economic discourses since the 1980s (Harvey 2007; Ventura 2012). Neoliberal thought has noticeably shaped the structures of society, its institutions, and organizations over its reign. The consequences of the neoliberal orientation are evident in present-day societies, whether we talk about business, governance, education, or social and health care (Ventura 2012; Wrede et al. 2008, 17; Yliaska 2014).

The effects of neoliberalism, however, are not limited to the sociopolitical and economic spheres. Its social and cultural effects are substantial and widespread. It has been argued that neoliberalism has become the leading cultural ethos that guides the way in which we see and interpret the world and ourselves (Gill 2017, 608; Ventura 2012).

In neoliberally attuned societies, economic factors are considered first and foremost. The effectivity, productivity, cost-effectiveness, and measurability of the aforesaid are promoted and valued in all spheres of life. It has also been shown that these "neoliberal norms" have come to govern the so-called intimate sphere, for example, how we eat, move, relax, and rest. Everything from diet and working out to sleep can be programmed, scheduled, counted, and quantified for the best

DOI: 10.4324/9781003140665-5

(or most effective) possible result. Furthermore, the requirement to do so has become commonly adopted and accepted; that is, it has become normalized in the present day, for example, in what is known as the wellness culture (Cederström and Spicer 2015). Neoliberalism as a form of governmentality (Brown 2003; Lemke 2001; Oksala 2013) has arguably come to inform our understanding of socially acceptable bodies: the way in which bodies are perceived, treated, and evaluated as well as the relationship one is supposed to enjoy with one's own body (e.g., Guthman 2009; Harjunen 2017; Sutton 2010). Even the terms used to describe one's relationship with one's body are nowadays imbued with economic rhetoric. The body is increasingly considered "property" (Crawford 2006; Gill 2007); taking care of the body is body "management," and one's appearance is seen as social "capital" that can and should be used to one's advantage (Kukkonen et al. 2019).

Health has been observed as one of the principal arenas in which people are being moulded into neoliberal subjects (Ayo 2012; Cheek 2008; Crawford 2006). The neoliberal body must meet certain, often numeric, and somewhat arbitrary, norms regarding size, diet, and exercise, among other things. This numeric and quantifiable evidence is then taken as a sign of healthiness or lack thereof. The body mass index (BMI) is a prime example of this logic.[1] Other common examples could be the random requirement to take 10,000 steps a day or a diet that allows one to eat for only six hours a day. Furthermore, as the health and normative appearance and attractiveness of the body are regularly conflated, those with non-normative bodies, such as fat bodies, are routinely assumed to be unhealthy solely based on their size and appearance. It has been argued that so-called healthism—a lifestyle that prioritizes the pursuit of health, which it sees as the property and responsibility of the individual and often a matter of one's own will—is a central part of neoliberal governmentality (Crawford 1980, 2006). It effectively individualizes health and ignores the structural factors that contribute to it, such as people's socio-economic position or access to healthcare.

Failing to meet set requirements concerning the body's appearance/health is readily interpreted as a personal failure, a sign of one's bad choices and lack of moral fibre. This kind of logic has been typically applied to fatness and fat people. Fatness has been understood as an individual's problem, one that they have caused and must solve by themselves. In essence, an individual's health, behaviour, virtuousness, and worth are all read off the surface of their body (Harjunen 2017; Sutton 2010). Most importantly, the ability to self-govern is taken as a cue of one's productivity or at least a suitable social performance of it.

As a number of scholars have shown, fat prejudice and fatness as a stigmatized quality are by no means a new phenomenon (Braziel Evans and LeBesco 2001; Rothblum and Solovay 2008). Fatness has been constructed as an unhealthy and socially unacceptable form of embodiment over the course of decades, even centuries (Farrell 2011; LeBesco 2004; Harjunen 2009). However, the fat stigma seems to have intensified in a society and culture dominated by neoliberal norms and values (LeBesco 2010, 2011).

The ideal neoliberal body is, or at least appears to be, always in control, effective, and productive. The appearance of the body is bound to signal that one has internalized the neoliberal ethos. Self-monitoring and the ability to self-govern and make rational and "good choices" are essential qualities of a good neoliberal subject.

In this context, the fat body is regarded as, and fat people appear to be, diseased (i.e., "obese"), expensive, and irresponsible. It could be said that the fat body has been chosen to represent a kind of "anti-neoliberal" body that signifies everything a proper neoliberal body is not: it appears unproductive, ineffective, and unprofitable (Harjunen 2017). This apparent asynchronicity with the dominant ethos could also explain, at least in part, why fatness and fat people have become so vilified over the past two decades. The so-called obesity epidemic discourse, which will be discussed below, has been one of the major constituents in this process (Boero 2012; Campos et al. 2006; Gard and Wright 2005).

The Obesity Epidemic Discourse as a Neoliberal Discourse

Public and academic discussion on fatness has been in flux in the 2000s. Even though fatness has been talked about as a health concern and a medical issue for a long time, the emergence of the so-called obesity epidemic discourse has added volume and intensified both public and academic discussion on fatness. It created a global moral panic, or a "fat panic," which has moulded public opinion on fatness and fat people to a considerable degree (Campos et al. 2006; Oliver 2006). The so-called obesity epidemic discourse has presented fatness as the number one health threat (e.g., Boero 2012; Gard and Wright 2005; Oliver 2006), but it does not end here. The discussion on fatness has been increasingly moralistic in tone and has established fatness and fat people as an overall social and political problem on a global scale.

It has been well recognized in research that the obesity epidemic discourse has enhanced fat stigma (Boero 2012). During the height of the obesity epidemic discussion in the early 2000s, fatness—that is, fat people—were found to be guilty of just about any and all social and political ills of the world. During the past 20 years, fat people have been accused of destroying public economies and healthcare systems as well as contributing to oil price hikes, causing climate change, and being responsible for the problem of starvation, among other things (Harjunen 2017).

What happened is that the obesity epidemic discourse helped transform fatness from an issue that was thought to exist primarily in the personal, medical, and health realms to occupying a prominent place in the global economic and political spheres (Harjunen 2017). Paradoxically enough, and despite this shift, individual fat people continue to be blamed and made to feel guilty for causing a vast array of social problems, while structural problems are being overlooked. The major social and political issues connected to "obesity," such as poverty, food insecurity, disability, access to healthcare, and racism, are rarely considered or discussed in connection with the "obesity epidemic" (Herndon 2005; Strings 2019). It is obvious that correcting these issues is far beyond any individual's control.

The emergence of the obesity epidemic discourse has been linked to the intensifying neoliberal ethos of the 2000s (Harjunen 2017). It is evident that this discourse has never been exclusively about health. It is a medical (Gard and Wright 2005), economic (Harjunen 2017), and moral (Jutel 2005) discourse all at once. It is a great example of biopolitics that has multiple motivations concerning population control (Wright and Harwood 2008). It has somewhat cynically showcased fatness and fat people as an embodied manifestation of the social, economic, and moral degeneration that the neoliberal economy has been responsible for creating. For example, Guthman and DuPuis (2006) have linked the obesity epidemic discourse to the prevailing neoliberal thought, arguing that neoliberalism produces obesity both as a phenomenon and a problem. They see the obesity epidemic as part of the inner logic of neoliberalism, which includes widening differences in income and living standards, the overproduction of foods low in nutritional quality, the growth of the health business/industry, and increased responsibilization of individuals for their own health (healthism). In this sense, the obesity epidemic could be called a "neoliberal epidemic." The obesity epidemic and, consequently, fat people have been scapegoated and used as a way to deal with the wider problems of the neoliberal global economy.

Gender and Neoliberal Care for the Self

Feminist research has shown that women and their bodies have been the target of oppressive body norms and patriarchal social and moral control. Women's bodies are under constant social monitoring and regulation (Bordo 1993; Gill 2007). Body norms, especially the body size norm, are more strictly observed for women than for men. The size norm has become the most central in terms of the female body. Women are taught to routinely monitor their body's appearance, especially size, from an early age. It has been shown that women feel considerable pressure to attain and present a body that looks normative, and therefore, they often use unsafe methods to achieve it (e.g., Bordo 1993; Heywood 1996; Wolf 1991).

As is the case with body norms in general, neoliberal body norms are also gendered and embodied. A number of feminist scholars have discussed neoliberalism as a gendered ideology and have pointed out the manner in which this reflects on gendered bodies. Neoliberal ideas and practices shape our conceptions of both (gendered) bodies and physical bodies (e.g., Harjunen 2017; Sutton 2010; Ventura 2012). The effects of neoliberalism on gendered body norms and body practices can be detected, for instance, in the representations of women in popular culture (Gill 2007), health, sports, fitness culture (Dworkin and Wachs

2009; Heywood 2007), and the mainstream commercial appropriation of the body positivity movement (Puhakka 2018). It should be noted here that most of the feminist research on gendered body norms has focused on heterosexual and cis women, including my own. Other sexual orientations and genders have been clearly under-researched in this respect.

It is well known that the so-called capitalist consumer culture has played a significant role in creating and maintaining normative body norms and that women have been its primary target audience (Bordo 1993). Therefore, how do gendered body norms that draw from neoliberal ideology differ from the body norms that have been previously recognized by feminist scholars (Bartky 1990; Bordo 1993)? A number of differences have been identified. For example, neoliberal body norms seem to combine their ideal of choice and freedom to feminist ideas about self-determination and empowerment. Body norms and the constant requirement of body management have thus become viewed as part of women's own subjectivity and being. Body work has become something that is part and parcel of being a woman (Gill 2007, 2008; Harjunen 2017).

British scholar Rosalind Gill (2007, 164) has claimed that, in the 2000s, the media discourse of popular women's magazines seems to have constructed women as ideal subjects of neoliberalism. According to Gill, an integral part of this has been the post-feminist sensibility, which seems to be in line with neoliberal thought. Gill proposes that instead of interpreting post-feminism as the end of feminism or a new stage in feminism, as it has been sometimes presented, it could be seen as a contemporary "sensibility" that draws from neoliberal thought (Gill 2007, 148). It could be said that postfeminist sensibility is at least partially a product of neoliberal capitalism and consumer culture. The neoliberal discourse on the body has appropriated feminist ideas, and feminist ideas have been infiltrated by neoliberal ideas. This has made possible the rather odd blend of feminist subjects that have adopted the neoliberal body discourse and practices as signs of empowerment and subjectivity.

Gill (2007, 155) has alluded to three ways in which neoliberal culture aims to control women. The first is the requirement of self-surveillance, despite the simultaneous denial that such a requirement exists. Second, the demand for self-surveillance is extended to cover new spheres of life such as one's conduct in the intimate sphere; and third, the expectation to work on oneself is extended to one's interior life, which also needs to be transformed. The whole body and soul are in need of transformation.

All three methods described above are easily detected in the present-day approach to fatness and fat bodies, both in media representations and women's material lives. Women in general, but fat women in particular, are duty bound to self-monitor, discipline, and constantly improve the flawed self and out-of-control body (Harjunen 2009). The omnipresent makeover paradigm that exploits fat bodies aims to produce dutiful and docile subjects who are forever dieting, exercising, and toning in order to achieve the elusive ideal. The numerous dieting makeover shows can be held as a crystallization of the neoliberal approach to the fat body (Ritter 2021). Fat shaming of women is used as a moralizing tool to label them as "bad neoliberal citizens" (Rose Spratt 2021).

Interestingly, as Gill (2007) has maintained, women's body work is often presented in the semblance of something that will make you both look and, thus, feel better. It is marketed as self-improvement, empowerment, and a form of "pampering" or as "taking time for oneself."

Even though body work takes a great deal of time and effort, an appearance of naturalness and effortlessness should prevail (Gill 2007, 155). This ensures that the post-feminist practices of self-governance and discipline become ingrained in one's conduct and, thus, indiscernible from the self.

Neoliberal Health, Gender, and Fatness

The obesity epidemic discourse positioned the fat body as the focus of neoliberal governance (Boero 2012; Wright and Harwood 2008). This discourse can be viewed as a form of neoliberal governmentality (Foucault 1991), one that aims to produce certain types of (normative) bodies and (normative) citizens. In some way, it is logical that fatness and fat people have been targeted. Many of the cultural consequences of neoliberalism have been played out in the arena of health, whether we are talking about conceptions of health, the pursuit of health, health practices, or the organization and accessibility of healthcare. Since fatness has long been understood almost exclusively in the biomedical frame, fat people have been socially stigmatized and morally condemned, and fatness seems like an easy target for neoliberal governance (Gard and Wright 2005).

In the neoliberal context, health is considered a personal matter. It is one's own responsibility and merit. Health is assumed to be a result of one's own actions and correct lifestyle choices (Crawford 1980, 2006). One key expectation of neoliberal health is economic in nature. In neoliberal society, the ideal citizen should not be a financial burden to society; they should not be a cost to society. Paradoxically enough, they are expected to invest their own money to buy health products and services. Consumption is an essential part of doing neoliberal health, for health is constant doing. In the neoliberal economy, certain bodies, such as fat bodies, are readily deemed unhealthy and, thus, expensive, and assumedly lacking in health investment.

One can become a good neoliberal health subject by being controlled, effective, self- responsible, always aiming to make good choices, and investing a great deal of time, money, and energy into one's health. Neoliberal health is visible in the way in which healthcare is organized and the increased responsibilization of individuals for their health and healthcare costs. In countries such as the USA, where universal healthcare does not exist, this has been the case for some time, but in recent years, the trend has also permeated Nordic welfare states in the form of budgetary cuts, privatization, and the outsourcing of healthcare. (Crawford 2006; Harjunen 2017).

Neoliberal body norms are often connected to gendered ideas concerning health and fitness. Healthism also targets women and women's bodies (Dworkin and Wachs 2009; Heywood 2007; Markula 2008). Patriarchal, biomedical/healthist, and neoliberal capitalist expectations are intertwined in today's body norms and are acutely felt by fat people, specifically fat women. These three discourses also play together—they are intertwined and overlap in many contexts, such as in discussions concerning gender and the body, fatness, health, exercise, and diet culture (Dworkin and Wachs 2009; Heywood 2007; Markula 2008). Capitalist beauty, diet, and fitness industries have encouraged women, in particular, to think of and treat their bodies as property and social capital that they need to work on, take care of, and keep normatively sized and ever youthful. Women's bodies are a central part of the neoliberal economy, both as products and consumers.

The post-feminist stance has helped create neoliberal female subjects, with the emphasis being placed on individual responsibility, self-regulation, and free choice in applying femininity to the body. Kauppinen (2012, 96) has observed that while the discourse of post-feminist self-management might appear feminist, it operates according to the logic of neoliberal governmentality. Feminism is exploited to create the entrepreneurial subject of neoliberalism. According to Kauppinen, we are not in fact dealing with feminism so much as gender-specific neoliberal governance.

Consequences of Neoliberal Body Norms

The transgression of body norms often results in social penalties of some kind. Fat people, women especially, are subject to discrimination and are habitually discussed and represented in stereotypical and biased terms. Fatness is generally seen as a temporary phase that one should aim to leave behind. Constant questioning of the validity of fat people's embodied subjectivity has an effect on their sense of agency. As long as fatness is seen as liminal and transient, the fat body cannot be understood as a valid base for subjectivity, and fat people will be stuck in the liminal state (Harjunen 2009; Kyrölä and Harjunen 2017). All this is paradoxical in light of what is known of the success, or failure rate of diets (Sarlio-Lähteenkorva 1999).Considering that neoliberal thought emphasizes freedom and choice, the range of acceptable choices concerning the female body, in particular, is very limited and marked by normative ideas of femininity (Gill 2007). When it comes to bodies and body norms, instead of freedom, neoliberal thought seems to promote increased control, self-discipline, and anxiety, which are not exclusive to women.

The free choice that forms the basis of neoliberal rationale does not extend to freedom to choose one's body size. The only choice that is acceptable is the one that results in a normatively sized body that performs health in a normative manner. Fatness is considered an individual's own choice only in the accusatory sense: the individual has failed in their body's weight management and has chosen not to do anything about it or given up entirely. Fatness is not seen as a valid choice for body size. Fat people who are not seemingly engaging in weight loss (performing health in the acceptable way) are treated as unreliable witnesses of their own experience. It is usually assumed that every fat person would like to lose weight, even when they claim to be happy with their body size. Choosing to be fat has been, until recently, exclusively a stigmatizing choice. By "choosing" a body that does not comply with the norms, one inevitably places oneself outside the norm. The active shaping of the body and its appearance signals progress, goals, and a work ethic.

Especially for women, changes in body size are only socially acceptable if they result in a body that does not transgress the normative boundaries set for the size and shape of the female body. In current neoliberal body culture, women who do not seem to engage in body-shaping practices or exercise that might result in weight loss are not performing health, neither are they performing femininity in the correct way. Being able to perform a normative body size is paramount, even at the expense of health. Even when weight loss is a result of a life-threatening illness, it is applauded.

Weight-loss dieting, which is mostly performed by women, can be seen as part of the neoliberal performance of health and normative femininity. Women's body norms, which were previously thought of as something external, oppressive, and imposed on women, now work through the incorporation of discipline disguised as "free" choice. Self-management and self-discipline are construed as part of female subjectivity. Women become entrepreneurial subjects, and in doing so, body work and performing femininity in a certain way become crucial.

In the 2000s, feminist fat activism has become mainstream in the form of the body positivity movement. For many people, this movement has provided respite from observing the norm of being oppressively thin (Puhakka 2018). Over the last decade, however, the movement has been increasingly appropriated by mainstream commercial culture. It has become a catch-all term that is abundantly used in fashion, wellness, fitness, exercise, and even the diet industries. Curiously, in this brand of marketized body positivity, fat people do not seem to be the target group. In fact, fat bodies seem to be forgotten, or only appropriately sized (smallish) or shaped (hourglass) fat people are represented.

In this context, anything relating to body, be it body shaping by exercise or even dieting, can be deemed body positive. The only requirement seems to be that what one is doing is experienced as empowering by that individual. The vital idea of body positivity to include all kinds and body sizes has effectively been diluted. This kind of body positivity could be called neoliberal and post-feminist, for it seems to repeat their ideas about individual responsibility, doing health, and normative female appearance through the misguided naming of body positivity. Despite attempts to broaden women's body size norms, the thin norm remains dominant. What has changed is that the terms of the normative body seem to follow the logic of neoliberal governmentality (Gill 2008).

Since the 1990s, women's intersectional differences relating to sexuality, class, race, and ability, for example, have become better represented in both academic and popular feminist discourse. It is now well known that the assumed normative female subject of feminism has reflected existing social and political power relations and favoured white, middle class, heterosexual, Western, able-bodied, and thin subjects. This privileged group of women was often also considered the primary and only subject of post-feminism (Gill 2017, 612). In Gill's (2017) article, in which she revisits the concept of post-feminism, she noted that post-feminism had become a hegemonic form of feminism that cut through intersectional differences. Gill did not specifically talk about body size as an intersection, but she discussed how the post-feminist and neoliberal discourse had taken on queer, racialized, or transnational subjects and cultures. The same development has taken place regarding fat people and fat activism or, in the least, the body positivity movement. It has been transformed from a radical political movement to a matter of a neoliberal post-feminist subjectivity construction. One of the biggest challenges that fat activism faces in the post-feminist and neoliberal era is how to maintain focus on social change and strive for social justice for fat people.

Note

1   On criticism of the use of the BMI, see, for example, Harjunen (2017).

References

Ayo, Nike Y. 2012. "Understanding Health Promotion in a Neoliberal Climate and the Making of Health-Conscious Citizens." *Critical Public Health*, 22 (1): 99–105.

Bartky, Sandra. 1990. *Femininity and Domination: Studies in the Phenomenology of Oppression*. New York: Routledge.

Boero, Natalie. 2012. *Killer Fat: Media, Medicine and Morals in the American "Obesity Epidemic."* New Brunswick: Rutgers University Press.

Bordo, Susan. 1993. *Unbearable Weight: Feminism, Western Culture and the Body*. Berkeley: University of California Press.

Braziel Evans, Jana and Kathleen LeBesco. 2001. *Bodies out of Bounds: Fatness and Transgression*. Berkeley: University of California Press.

Brown, Wendy 2003. "Neo-liberalism and the End of Liberal Democracy." *Theory & Event,* 7 (1) [online] Available At: https://muse.jhu.edu/journals/theory_and_event/v007/7.1brown.html [Accessed: 15 August 2021].

Campos, Paul, Abigail Saguy, Paul Ernsberger, Eric Oliver and Glenn Gaesser. 2006. "The Epidemiology of Overweight and Obesity: Public Health Crisis or Moral Panic?" *International Journal of Epidemiology*, 35: 55–60.

Cederström, Carl and Spicer André. 2015. *The Wellness Syndrome*. Cambridge: Polity Press.

Cheek, Julianne. 2008. "Healthism: A New Conservatism?" *Qualitative Health Research*, 18 (7): 974–982.

Crawford, Robert. 1980. "Healthism and the Medicalization of Everyday Life." *International Journal of Health Services*, 10: 365–388.

Crawford, Robert. 2006. "Health as a Meaningful Social Practice." *Health: An Interdisciplinary Journal for the Social Study of Health, Illness and Medicine*, 10 (4): 401–420.

Dworkin, Shari L. and Faye Linda Wachs. 2009. *Body Panic: Gender, Health, and the Selling of Fitness*. New York: New York University Press.

Farrell, Amy. 2011. *Fat Shame: Stigma and the Fat Body in American Culture*. New York: New York University Press.

Foucault, Michel. 1991 [1978]. "Governmentality Lecture at the Collège de France, Feb. 1, 1978." In *The Foucault Effect: Studies in Governmentality*, edited by Graham Burchell, Colin Gordon, and Peter Miller, 87–104. Hemel Hempstead: Harvester Wheatsheaf.

Gard, Michael and Jan Wright. 2005. *The Obesity Epidemic. Science, Morality, and Ideology*. London: Routledge.

Gill, Rosalind. 2007. "Postfeminist Media Culture: Elements of a Sensibility." *European Journal of Cultural Studies*, 10 (147): 147–166.

Gill, Rosalind. 2008. "Culture and Subjectivity in Neoliberal and Postfeminist Times." *Subjectivity*, 25: 432–445.

Gill, Rosalind. 2017. "The Affective, Cultural and Psychic Life of Postfeminism: A Postfeminist Sensibility 10 Years on." *European Journal of Cultural Studies*, 20 (6): 606–626.

Guthman, Julie. 2009. "Teaching the Politics of Obesity: Insights into Neoliberal Embodiment and Contemporary Biopolitics." *Antipode*, 41 (50): 1110–1133.

Guthman, Julie and Melanie DuPuis. 2006. "Embodying Neoliberalism: Economy, Culture, and the Politics of Fat." *Environment and Planning: Society and Space*, 24: 427–448.

Harjunen, Hannele. 2009. *Women and Fat: Approaches to the Social Study of Fatness*. Jyväskylä Studies in Education, Psychology and Social Research no: 379, 2009. The University of Jyväskylä.

Harjunen, Hannele. 2017. *Neoliberal Bodies and the Gendered Fat Body*. London: Routledge.

Harvey, David. 2007. *A Brief History of Neoliberalism*. Oxford: Oxford University Press.

Herndon, April. 2005. "Collateral Damage from Friendly Fire? Race, Nation, Class, and the "War against "Obesity"." *Social Semiotics*, 15 (82): 127–141.

Heywood, Leslie. 1996. *Dedication to Hunger: The Anorexic Aesthetic in Modern Culture*. Berkeley: University of California Press.

Heywood, Leslie. 2007. "Producing Girls: Empire, Sport, and the Neoliberal Body." In *Physical Culture, Power, and the Body*, edited by Jennifer Hargreaves and Patricia Vertinsky, 101–120. New York: Routledge.

Jutel, Annemarie. 2005. "Weighing Health: The Moral Burden of Obesity." *Social Semiotics*, 15 (2): 113–125.

Kauppinen, Kati. 2012. "At an Intersection of Postfeminism and Neoliberalism: A Discourse Analytical View of an International Women's Magazine". *Critical Approaches to Discourse Analysis across Disciplines*, 7 (1): 82–99.

Kukkonen, Ida, Tomi Pajunen, Outi Sarpila, and Erica Åberg. 2019 *Ulkonäköyhteiskunta – Ulkoinen Olemus Pääomana 2000 -Luvun Suomessa*. Helsinki: Into-Kustannus.

Kyrölä, Katariina and Hannele Harjunen. 2017 "Phantom/Liminal Fat and Feminist Theories of the Body". *Feminist Theory*, 18 (2): 99–117.

LeBesco, Kathleen. 2004. *Revolting Bodies. The Struggle to Redefine Fat Identity*. Amherst and Boston: University of Massachusetts Press.

LeBesco, Kathleen. 2010. "Fat Panic and the New Morality." In *Against Health: How Health Became the New Morality*, edited by Jonathan Metz and Anne Kirkland, 72–82. New York: New York University Press.

LeBesco, Kathleen. 2011. "Neoliberalism, Public Health and the Moral Perils of Fatness." *Critical Public Health*, 21 (2): 153–164.

Lemke, Thomas. 2001. "The Birth of Bio-Politics – Michel Foucault's Lecture at the Collège de France on Neo-liberal Governmentality." *Economy and Society*, 30 (2): 1–17.

Markula, Pirjo. 2008. "Governing Obese Bodies in a Control Society." *Junctures: The Journal for Thematic Dialogue*, 11: 53–66.

Oksala, Johanna. 2013. "Feminism and Neoliberal Governmentality." *Foucault Studies*, 16: 32–53.

Oliver, Eric J. 2006. *Fat Politics: The Real Story behind America's Obesity Epidemic*. New York: Oxford University Press.

Puhakka, Anna. 2018. "Can Ambivalence Hold Potential for Fat Activism? An Analysis of Conflicting Discourses on Fatness in the Finnish Column Series Jenny's Life Change." *Fat Studies: An Interdisciplinary Journal of Body Weight and Society*, 8 (1): 60–74.

Ritter, Susanne. 2021. "Control through Compassion: Legitimizations of Surveillance, Dynamics of Power, and the Role of the Expert in the Finnish Makeover TV Shows Jutta and the Super Diet and Jutta and the Half-Year Super Diet." *Fat Studies: An Interdisciplinary Journal of Body Weight and Society*, https://doi.org/10.1080/08038 740.2021.1939782

Rose Spratt Tanisha Jemma.2021. Understanding 'Fat Shaming' in a Neoliberal Era: Performativity, Healthism and the UK's 'Obesity Epidemic.' *Feminist Theory*. https:// doi:10.1177/14647001211048300

Rothblum, Esther and Sondra Solovay, eds. 2008. *The Fat Studies Reader*. New York: New York University Press.

Sarlio-Lähteenkorva, Sirpa. 1999. Losing Weight for Life?: Social, behavioural and health-related factors in obesity and weight loss maintenance. Department of Public Health, University of Helsinki.

Strings, Sabrina. 2019 *Fearing the Black Body: The Racial Origins of Fat Phobia*. New York: New York University Press.

Sutton, Barbara. 2010. *Bodies in Crisis: Culture, Violence and Women's Resistance in Neoliberal Argentina*. New Brunswick: Rutgers University Press.

Ventura, Patricia. 2012. *Neoliberal Culture: Living with American Neoliberalism*. Farnham: Ashgate.

Wolf, Naomi. 1991 [1990]. *The Beauty Myth*. London: Vintage.

Wrede Sirpa, Lea Henriksson, Håkon Host, Stina Johansson, and Betina Dybbroe. 2008. *Care Work in Crisis: Reclaiming the Nordic Ethos of Care*. Lund: Studentlitteratur.

Wright, Jan and Valerie Harwood, eds. 2008 *Biopolitics and the "Obesity Epidemic": Governing Bodies*. London: Routledge.

Yliaska, Ville. 2014. *Tehokkuuden Toiveuni: Uuden Julkishallinnon Historia Suomessa 1970 Luvulta 1990 -Luvulle*. Helsinki: Into Kustannus.

4

TO HAVE AND NOT TO HOLD

Queering Fatness

Cat Pausé

In the introduction to *Queering Fat Embodiment*, co-editor Jackie Wykes defines queering as "a mode of political and critical inquiry which seeks to expose taken-for-granted assumptions, trouble neat categories, and unfix the supposedly fixed alignment of bodies, gender, desire and identities" (2014, 4). In that same edition, Zoë Meleo-Erwin (2014) argues that fat bodies are "queer modes of embodiment in that they elicit great anxiety through the disruption of norms about how bodies are supposed to look and how they are supposed to function" (107). Several years earlier, Elena Levy-Navarro (2009) suggested that fat people were queer because they disrupted the Global North norm to strain for the chalice of youth and prolong life as long as possible; "fat are queer in our culture exactly because they are seen as living life that is 'unhealthy' and thus a life that is presumably defying the imperative to cultivate maximum longevity" (17). A decade later in the *International Handbook of Fat Studies*, Allison Taylor argues that queering fatness is "an important scholarly endeavour … because it has the potential to expand normative notions of fatness and challenges the re/production of fat and other oppressions with and beyond the field of fat studies" (2021, 281).

Queering is a theoretical and methodological tool for disrupting and deconstructing dominant (and usually essentialist) assumptions and discourses (Jagose 1996; Pausé 2014). Queering is a "mode of political and critical inquiry which seeks to expose taken-for granted assumptions, trouble neat categories, and unfix the supposedly fixed alignments of bodies [and] gender" (Wykes 2014, 4). It is especially useful in critiquing heteronormative ideas about body shape and size, as thinness is "too often represented as unremarkable" (Jagose, speaking about heterosexuality, quoted by Longhurst 2014, 22). Without question, queering offers exciting ways to think about fatness, and to be fat.

DOI: 10.4324/9781003140665-6

As a theory, it has a wide range of uses in academia, including within the field of Fat Studies. Using queer theory, Fat Studies scholars trouble the negative associations of fatness and the fat body, un-fixing assumptions about what bodies are desirable, worthy, and worth celebrating. Fat Studies scholars have used queer theory to question the negative assumptions made about fatness and the fat body, to rethink the value in stories of sadness and anger, and to consider new kinds of fat futures. As noted by Wykes, "The potential queerness – and queer potential – of fat has long been an important part of the political project of fat activism and scholarship" (2014, 3). Fat Studies scholars have utilized queer work around performativity, embodiment, shame, and failure, to help make sense of the fat experience.

Fatness and Gender

Fat Studies has an established literature on the relationship between fatness and gender (LeBesco 2001; Gailey 2014; White 2014, 2020; Whitesel 2014). Much of this scholarship has focused on ways that fatness queers gender, destabilizing normative binary categories and presentations and troubling dominant ways of being, doing, and identifying, gender. For cis people, fatness is often a "spoil[er of] gendered identities" (Monaghan and Malson 2013, 316). Fat women are unable to be feminine, due to their fatness; fat men are unable to be masculine, due to their fatness (LeBesco 2001). Kimberly Dark (2014) recounts always having to play the guy in role playing with her teenage friends, because she was the fat one.

> Ask anyone who grew up as a fat girl if she ever got the female lead with thinner girly girls around…We didn't even discuss it – that's just the way it was. Someone had to be Travolta and it was going to be me. I was the biggest of the group, therefore the most convincing guy. Or maybe I was the least convincing Sandra Dee. No discussion was needed.
>
> *(28)*

Jeannine Gailey (2014) argues that for women, fatness illuminates both masculine (taking up space) and feminine (being soft and curvy) characteristics.

When fatness is read by dominant binary gender discourses, it can create spaces for both anxiety and affirmation for queer people (Mulder 2021). This is largely due to the way that fatness can shape a body into having 'breasts' or 'hips' in ways that suggests a gender, without any consideration to the gender identity of the individual. A masculine individual man may develop 'man boobs', denying him the masculinity for which he aspires. A feminine individual may have no discernible difference between her breasts, waist, and hips, denying her the femininity for which she aspires. Depending on how others read the gender of an individual, the individual's fatness may reinforce their gender identification or disrupt it. In his conversation with Jamie Burford, Sam Orchard (2014) reflected that his fatness impacted on gender in different ways across different queer communities,

> Within small gay male communities, I felt as though I had to be super skinny, or super ripped to be attractive to other men. Within transmasculine communities, I felt as though weight was seen as feminine, or, rather, as feminizing, as in: "urgh, look at my curves". Then, as I moved to larger queer communities, with more bear scenes, the discourses around "sexiness" and body weight changed again.
>
> *(63)*

Francis Ray White (2020) suggests this is especially fraught for those who identify as non-binary and trans, as fatness contributes to others projecting a binary gender identification onto them. Some who are non-binary may try to coral this tool of fatness to shape their bodies into a physical representation more closely aligned with their gender identity. The distribution of fat in non-binary and trans bodies is a key consideration for how their gender identity may be perceived, by both themselves and others. As Norman (a non-binary participant in White's research) shared, "I have bulges in all the wrong places" (White 2020, 114). While fatness may spoil gendered identities for cis people, fatness prevents the recognition of gendered identities for trans people (White 2020). Mulder (2021) explored how a group of fat queer people in the United States understood their gender in the contexts of both fatness and queerness by analysing narrative essays and a thread on the *FatshionistaLiveJournal*. Mulder found that trans and non-binary individuals discussed the fear of being misgendered or not 'enough' due to the shape that fatness lent their bodies. "Both internal perception of their gender and fatness, along with a fear of how others will gender their fat body impacts their comfort with their gender identity and presentation" (Mulder 2021, 40).

Queering Fat Scholarship: The Beginning

Eve Sedgewick and Michael Moon are credited with producing the first Queer Fat Studies English text in 1990 (LeBesco 2001; Murray 2009; Taylor 2021). Their work explored the intersections of fatness, gender, queerness, and disability. In their discussions, they consider whether the language and process of identity management used by queer people might provide useful for fat people. Specifically, they considered the role of the closet and the process of coming out. Sedgewick and Moon asked questions as to whether fat people could be in the closet about their fat identities and concluded that this was not available to fat people due to the visibility of the fat body. They also pondered whether the identity management style of 'coming out' is available to fat people. Just as they dismissed the idea of a "closet of size" (305), Sedgewick and Moon asked, "what kind of secret can the body of a fat woman keep?" (305). But they recognized that while fatness could not be hidden, identity management styles adopted by queer peoples could be useful for fat people in their political work. To come out as fat, then, would be to be size-affirming and unashamed of their fatness. "[It] is a way of speaking one's claim to insist on, and participate actively in, a renegotiation of the *representational contract* between one's body and one's world" (2001, 306). Their discussion was reprinted in 2001 within an edited book by Jana Evans Braziel and Kathleen LeBesco, *Bodies Out of Bounds.*

In *Bodies Out of Bounds*, LeBesco (2001) suggests that by queering fat bodies, she can make an argument for them being bodies that matter. Placing LeBesco's work in context is important; it is almost a decade before *The Fat Studies Reader* is published, and exactly a decade before the *Fat Studies Journal* begins production. LeBesco is writing when scholarship about fatness is almost exclusively the purview of medical and health sciences. In her chapter, LeBesco intends to "alter the discourses of fat subjectivity by moving inquiries about fat from medical and scientific discourses to social and cultural ones, offering ... a different way of looking at, and living in, fat" (75). Using language to queer fatness and make fat bodies matter is a critical tool for fat liberation in this context, argues LeBesco. As queer activists have been loud and proud about their so-called perversions, so should fat people. Rhetoric can be used by fat studies scholars and fat activists to challenge assumptions about fatness and speak new ways of seeing and understanding and embodying fatness into being.

LeBesco (2004) returns to issues of queering fatness in her book *Revolting Bodies* a few years later. In this text, she provides a chapter in which she considers the useful parallels between being queer and being fat, and what this might mean for Fat Studies scholars and fat activists. Of these parallels, for example, she includes the search for the gay gene and the fat gene (independent, she points out, of a search for the thin gene and the straight gene), the stigmatization of both groups, and the common charges of gluttony – by gay men for sex, and by fat women for food. Another theme commonly explored by LeBesco is the identification of being out as queer and out as fat. While acknowledging that fatness is visible in a way that being queer is not, LeBesco still argues that fat individuals can be out as a fat. It is in this book that LeBesco suggests that "fatness may be read as a mere subset of queerness", because all fat sex is queer sex (2004, 88). In LeBesco's estimation of fat sex being queer sex, she was not suggesting that all fat people are queer. Rather, she was acknowledging that fat people queer sex because fat people are not supposed to be sexually desirable, or find sexual pleasure in their bodies. LeBesco's early work at queering fat studies is an example of what Allison Taylor identifies as the first branch of Queer Fat Studies.

Branches

Taylor (2021) has argued that Queer Fat Studies scholarship can be separated into five branches; each branch represents a unique approach of queering fatness.

These branches are useful ways to categorize and understand Queer Fat Studies scholarship to date, and how we might envision this scholarship going forward into the future. According to Taylor, the first branch of Queer Fat Studies focused on the similarities and differences between fatness and queerness. Rooted first in queerness, this branch considers which theoretical, methodological, and ontological, tools of queerness and queer studies may be useful for those involved in fat activism and fat studies scholarship (although the latter is not often phrased that way as this is before such a thing was known to exist). "Examining how fatness is un/like queerness, and how queer theory can challenge and offer alternatives to dominant and oppressive concepts of fatness, these scholars identify the significant role queer theory can play in negotiating fat oppression" (Taylor 2021, 275).

The second branch focuses on criticizing fat studies scholarship and activism when it engages in work to normalize fatness within the existing power structures of white supremacy, patriarchy, heteronormativity, and capitalism. This branch moves a step further with Queer Fat Studies, employing queer theories and methodologies to push fat studies and fat activism beyond superficial goals of acceptance and pride.

> This branch of queer fat studies demonstrates how queer theory can be applied to fat studies to critique the ways in which fat studies and activisms may unintentionally re/produce dominant structures of power. Therefore, queer/ing fatness helps to create space for multiple, ambiguous, and contradictory fat embodiments, making for a more inclusive movement.
>
> *(Taylor 2021, 277)*

The third branch of Queer Fat Studies focuses on the intersections between studies and queer studies, often bringing in other disciplines such as disability studies and trans studies. This third branch explores the ways these different disciplines relate to one another; how they are similar, and different, and complicate one another, and complement one another. In a way, it is an extension of the earliest branch, where fat studies and queer studies were first meeting.

> By analyzing how these fields speak to, contradict, support and challenge one another, this branch of queer fat studies rigorously explores and poses critiques of dominant aspects of fat studies and politics. Queer/ing fatness highlights exclusions in fat studies, contributing to more inclusive conceptions of fatness and fat oppression.
>
> *(Taylor 2021, 278)*

Anti-social queer theory sits at the core of the fourth branch, according to Taylor. Anti-social queer theories use queering as a tool to interrogate and disrupt normalcy, comfort, and respectability politics. This approach to Queer Fat Studies opens the door for focusing on the negative aspects of being fat; it allows for a scholarship that focuses on the trauma, the shame, and the oppression of fatness to understand fatness and fat lives. "An anti-social queer/ing of fatness finds potential in embracing the 'negative' aspects of fatness and emphasizing the ways in which fatness challenges mainstream norms of gender, health, and embodiment, among other things" (Taylor 2021, 280). The fourth branch could almost be considered a version of the second, or perhaps a more radical departure from normativity than the second.

The final branch of Queer Fat Studies focuses on temporality; these studies present alternative ways to think about fatness, fat bodies, and fat people, all in relation to time. Rejecting fatness as a state of 'before' (before weight loss, before good health, before full life), Queer Fat Studies consider how the construct of time is used to oppress fat people, and the ways that fat people can push back against this oppression by creating their own relationships with time.

> Queer/ing the ways fat people exist in time, this branch of queer fat studies recuperates fat presents, and futures. Like anti-social approaches to queer/ing fatness, queer/ing fat temporalities involves positing "queer" as a critique of normativity, specifically dominant ways of conceiving of and structuring life and time. Rather than asking fat people to fit in and keep up with normative timelines, queer/ing fat temporalities suggests that there are different timelines that are possible for fat people, thereby challenging fat oppression.
>
> *(Taylor 2021, 280–281)*

Here, Queer, and FAT: Origins

Long before there was Queer Fat Studies scholarship, there was queer fat activism. Within the history of white fat liberation in North America and the United Kingdom, queer people have been at the forefront of the movement[1] (Cooper 2016; Levy-Navarro 2009). Elena Levy-Navarro (2009, 63) argues that queer people are "woven into the history of fat liberation". Queer people such as Judy Freespirit, Judith Stein, and Aldebaran, organized groups such as The Fat Underground and Pretty, Porky, and Pissed Off, to collectively fight for fat liberation. Decades later, queer fat activists Charlotte Cooper and Kay Hyatt strut around in motorcycle jackets to signify their memberships in The Chubsters, a queer fat girl gang.

Fat Black queer women are the "Black superwomen who are meant to sustain [their] communities" (Thomas 2018, para. 4). One of those Black superwomen is Sonya Renee Taylor, the Executive Director of *The Body is Not An Apology*, a multimedia company that amplifies the voices of many, but especially Black queer fats. Taylor's rallying cry, the body is not an apology, is a mantra meant for those with unruly bodies – Black bodies – fat bodies – disabled bodies – queer bodies (Taylor 2018). New ways of thinking and being and queering are the focus of a new podcast, *Unsolicited: Fatties Talk Back*. This podcast is hosted by a group of queer non-white activists: Bryan Guffey, Da'Shaun L. Harrison, Caleb Luna, Marquisele

Mercedes, and Jordan Underwood. In the handful of episodes produced thus far, *Unsolicited* has explored food, fitness, gender, sexuality, class, race, intentional weight loss, and more. In their new book, Da'Shaun L. Harrison's (2021) work on fatness, Blackness, queerness, and desirability exposes the limitations of gender for everyone, but especially for those who are not white, not straight, and not cis.

Adrienne Hill suggests that fat queer women brought "the language, performance media, and identity politics of their communities into their engagements with fat activism" (3). The Fat Underground was started by Judy Freespirit and Aldebaran,[2] two queer Jewish lesbians (Bracha Fishman 1998). The Underground broke away from the National Association to Advance Fat Acceptance, believing the organization to be too interested in social events where fat straight women could find dates. The Underground has a strong underground in the radical therapies of the time, believing that rather than changing the self, the focus should be on changing the society; Freespirit and Aldebaran were also facilitators of the Fat Women's Problem-Solving Group in the Radical Feminist Therapy Collective (Cooper 2016).

The Fat Underground held consciousness raising sessions for its members, wrote position papers that challenged the dominant beliefs about fatness, and held disruptive protests.[3] It was a "dynamic space where fat feminists were able to reflect and act together", and Cooper credits it with engaging in "some of the most vigorous fat activism of the movement to date" (2016, 150–152). One product of the Fat Underground that remains in popular circulation today is the *Fat Liberation Manifesto* (Freespirit and Aldebaran 1979). When the Underground broke apart in the mid-70s, members of the group went to establish other feminist fat activist groups.

Shortly thereafter, Karen Stimson and Aldebaran began the Fat Liberation Front on the east coast of the United States (Stimson 2003). Also, along the coast, Judith Stein and Meridith Lawrence founded Boston Area Fat Liberation.[4] Stein spent much of the late 70s hosting workshops on fatness at various lesbian gatherings, such as the Michigan Womyn's Music Festival. At the same time, Aldebaran founded Fat Liberator Publications, which created a mechanism for publishing fat positive material for distribution purposes. The two groups came together for a series of meetings in 1980 – the Feminist Fat Activist's Working Meeting and The New Haven Fat Women's Health Conference (Cooper 2016). From these meetings came F. A. T. (Fat Activists Together), a predominantly lesbian group, which published *Shadow on a Tightrope: Writings by Women on Fat Oppression* in 1982. This text remains a central text for fat liberation and scholarship (Pausé and Taylor 2021; Farrell 2018). In the same year, the Fat Lip Reader's Theater gave their first performance in Berkeley entitled, "For fat women only" (Stimson 2003).

Across the pond in England, the London Fat Women's Group began in the late 80s by fat working-class lesbians. Through events and discussions, they produced The Fat Dykes Statement and later, the newsletter, *Fat News* (Cooper 2010; Smith 1989). As the '90s began, self-publishing was a popular way for fat activists to share their ideas with one another and raise awareness for others. *FaT GiRL: A Zine for Fat Dykes and the Women Who Want Them* was produced by the FaT GiRL Collection in San Francisco (Simic 2015; Snider 2009). As explained by one of the founding collective members, Max Airborne,

> *FaT GiRL* spread the word among a certain generation of freaky fatties that we can have an alternative society where we are valued, we can have community, sexuality, joy, and full lives as fat queers – without dieting or assimilation or apology.
>
> *(Cooper 2009a, 7)*

FaT GiRL published articles, games, self-help material, and pictures, often explicit pictures, of fat people, striving to present fat queer people as sexual and objects of desire (Simic 2015).

In 1997, NOLOSE (National Organisation of Lesbians of Size Everywhere) was founded by Dot Nelson-Turnier; NOLOSE works to end fat oppression and celebrate fat queer culture. NOLOSE has hosted conferences, fatshion clothing swaps, newsletters, funding grants for regional activity, and more. At the turn of the century, NOLOSE expanded itself to include women and trans folks, and from 2011 it welcomed people of all genders (NOLOSE n.d.). Other one-off events, such as the fat dyke dance rally, Let it All Hang Out, and The Fat of the Land Queer Chub Harvest Festival, offered opportunities for fat queer people to join in community with one another (Cooper 2009b).

The Internet and development of Web 2.0 tools (such as Facebook and YouTube) have allowed for exponential growth in the opportunities for fat activists to create, collaborate, and share their work around the world (Pausé 2014). Fat activists blog, and Tweet, and Tumble, and Insta, and more; "they queer fat embodiment, disrupting the normative obesity discourse and rejecting the demands of the neoliberal system ... they area, in short, doing fatness wrong" (Pausé 2015, 5). One of those sites of queering fatness and gender both was the *FatshionistaLiveJournal*. *FatshionistaLiveJournal* was a website founded in 2004 by Amanda Piasecki as an online space where queer fat femmes could discuss and celebrate fat fashion, or fatshion; many well-known activists began their fat political work in this space (Cooper 2016).

Fatshion

At the intersection of gender, fatness, and the fat activism online is Fatshion, a portmanteau of fashion and fat. Fatshion is a popular form of self-expression and activism online. Fat people with a passion for fatshion share OOTD (outfit of the day) photos, blog about their fatshion experiences, share advice with others, and create communities around the topic, such as *FatshionistaLiveJournal*. In selecting fashion, a purview of thin bodies that function much like hangers in a store, fat people queer fashion (Connell 2012). They reject that fashion is only meant for those who are very slim, while also rejecting the fashion norms that are projected onto fat bodies. Fat bodies can be made visible in new and unexpected ways through fatshion, especially when they break fashion rules and defy normative conventions of taste.

In celebrating fat people's ability to enjoy fashion, fat people are also taking an area of great anxiety and anger for fat people (the ability to find affordable and cute clothes to wear) and allowing it to serve a similar purpose that it does for non-fat people: a way of expressing one's identity and a hobby that can be pleasurable. "Fatshion encourages fat people's creative participation in space where they are usually excluded" (Cooper 2016, 76). This is especially true for fat people of colour. Fat Black fatshionistas such as Stephanie Yeboah, Simone Mariposa, and Lucia Morris reject white supremacist patriarchal ideals of beauty on their platforms, showcasing their fat Black beauty (Yeboah 2017). Amena Azeez in India, Sine Benjaphorn in Thailand, and Latasha Ngwube in Nigeria, are on the fore front of fat activism in their countries, using fatshion as their venue into the public spotlight. And Fat Black queer Instagram influencers like Brandon Stewart, Jervae Anthony, and Dexter Mayfield use the social media venue to push boundaries and queer gender and fashion (when they are not being shadow banned, see Davis 2021).

Cody Charles writes that fatshion allowed them to explore their gender in new ways,

> I allowed myself to interrogate and explore my gender and gender expression by trying out different shades of makeup, a variety of red lipsticks, leggings, and floral cardigans, boots, and shoes with heels all in this Black fat assumed male body. I allowed myself to challenge W.E.B. DuBois' double consciousness and take risks with my Black radical queer voice.
>
> *(Cody 2018 para. 12)*

For Charles, this act of "queering [their] approach to life" allowed them to understand who they were and where they fit in their life; it allowed them to "survive childhood and commit to a more joyous adulthood" by seeing beyond the choices allowed to them under white supremacy and patriarchy (2018 para 12).

Margitte Kristjansson (2016) explored how fatshion queers both what is believed about fat bodies (and who is and who is not allowed to be fashionable) and consumption. Kristjansson presents a brief history of fat fashion in the United States, noting that

> when women's lib found many thin women choosing to buck fashion trends and the cultural imperatives to present themselves in traditionally "beautiful" ways, the fat woman was fighting to be recognized as someone worthy of these things in the first place.
>
> *(138)*

And those fat women, whose desire for fashion outweighs any suggestion that clothing should instead be camouflage, is queering both fashion and consumption. And when fashion producers and companies do not create spaces for such engagement, "today's fa(t)shionistas have developed their own ways to engage with fashion when the industry refuses to recognize them as viable customers" (134). These ways include blogs, community forums like the *FatshionistaLiveJournal*, fatshion zines and shows, and clothing swaps. The Big Fat Flea, for example, was an annual clothing swap/fatshion event hosted by NOLOSE. As noted by Charlotte Cooper (2008) participants of the Big Fat Flea flaunt and subvert normal fashion rules, "squee[zing] into clothes of the 'wrong' size...and play dressing-up for the fun of it" (15). There are no gender rules at such events and disrupting gender binaries are part of the joy to be had alongside fellow fats.

There is not enough space here to present a full review of queer fat activism, but those wanting more should read Charlotte Cooper's 2016 book, *Fat Activism: A Radical Social Movement*. In this text, Cooper writes about how queerness informed and shaped white fat activism in the United States and the United Kingdom. For Cooper, the connections between queerness, fatness, and gender are clear: queers trouble gender, just as fatness troubles gender. And queer fatness troubles it even further.

Limitations and The Future

While this chapter has explored many of the ways that queering fatness had led to new understandings of gender, and the role that gender has played in queering fatness, there are significant gaps in our understanding of these intersections. In their chapter in *Thickening Fat*, Francis Ray White (2020) asserts that Fat Studies scholarship on fatness and gender has been cis-centric. What little work has been done at the intersection of fatness and transness, according to White, has been too reductive or simply comparative. White argues that Fat Studies scholarship at this intersection could be richer if it allowed for an exploration of how "fatness and gender work together in the production of bodies that are then legible as male, female, or both/neither" (110). In addition to being cis-centric spaces, these spaces of fat queerness, whether they be activist spaces or academic spaces, are still largely white spaces (Lind 2020). It is white queer fat bodies who are known as the mothers of fat liberation. It is white queer fat bodies who are most well known as current activists and academics[5] (Lind 2020; Senyonga 2020).

Even with these limitations, queering fatness offers many new possibilities for both activists and scholars alike. Emily R.M. Lind (2020) asserts the utility of applying queer theory concepts to our understanding of fatness; not because fatness is a subset of queerness, as once suggested by LeBesco (2004, 88–89), but because both queerness and fatness "are marginalized by hegemonic gender roles" (185). Queerness and fatness both find themselves positioned as deviant by these gender roles; especially as these states disrupt the normative gender binary. In addition, fat bodies are inherently queer because they thwart the essential normative presentation of a body, which is to be non-fat (Wykes 2014). As a tool, queering is about troubling the distinctions between categories. Applied to fatness and gender, queering allows for a disruption of gender binaries – and more importantly – a disruption of how gender is to be seen and performed. And just as fatness is thought to be a liminal space, so does fatness render gender to be the same. Fatness adds to the fluidity of gender, as it shapes and bends how gendered bodies are perceived. This can be both liberating and restricting.

Queering Fat Studies opens new doors and "means of expanding normative conceptions of fatness and a critique of the broader field of fat studies" (Taylor 2021, 273). Taylor (2021) suggests that the branch of anti-social queer theory is the most useful branch of Queer Fat Studies as it goes past comparing fatness and queerness, or ways that queer theory can be used to understand fatness. Anti-social Queer Fat Studies push past this to employ the methodologies of queer studies to new ways of theorizing and embodying fatness. It rejects any notion of respectability politics, allowing the experience of being fat to be good and bad and everything in between. Taylor concludes,

> Anti-social queer theory therefore offers queer fat studies a theoretical framework for re/valuing a variety of fat embodiments without re/producing the dominant structures of power that work to keep fat bodies in subordinated positions. Anti-social queer theory's potential to critique broader structures of normativity and to re/value and re/imagine multiple ways of being fat position it as the most compelling approach, thus far, to queer/ing fatness.
>
> *(2021, 281)*

Fat activists and scholars alike should look to the utility in Anti-social Queer Fat Studies as a tool of scholarship and liberation.

Notes

1 This may be true in other places around the world, but those histories remain unknown to those in the English-speaking world at present.
2 Aldebaran is also known as Vivian F. Mayer and Sara Golda Bracha Fishman.
3 Around the same time, Girth and Mirth began a social organization for fat gay men (Whitsel and Shuman 2013).
4 Also called Boston Fat Liberation, Boston Area Fat Feminist Liberation, Boston Area Fat Lesbians.
5 The whiteness of the space is a result of many factors. In academia, for example, the white supremacist system means people of colour have enormous barriers to their success and participation in the Ivory Tower. White scholars of Fat Studies, while facing barriers related of their own, at least are accepted as having a place in the academy. It is no wonder, then, that the established scholars in the field are by and large white fat women. (This is not to be confused with who is well known in the public eye for this work, which is most often non-fat white scholars).

Bibliography

Bracha Fishman, Sara Golda. 1998. "Life in the Fat Underground." *Radiance* (Winter) Accessed 1 May 2021, www.radiancemagazine.com/issues/1998/winter_98/fat_underground.html

Burford, Jamie and Orchard, Sam. 2014. "Chubby Boys with Strap-Ons: Queering Fat Transmasculine Embodiment". In *Queering Fat Embodiment*, edited by Cat Pausé, Jackie Wykes, and Samantha Murray, 61–74. Surrey: Ashgate.

Chalkin, Vikki. 2016. "Obstinate Fatties: Fat Activism, Queer Negativity, and the Celebration of 'Obesity'". *Subjectivity* 9, no. 2: 107–125.

Cody, Charles. 2018. "A Pride Story: Choosing to Live My Black Fat Queer Life". *Medium*, 15 June 2018. https://level.medium.com/a-pride-story-choosing-to-live-my-black-fat-queer-life-6413c66edf9e

Connell, Catherine. 2012. "Fashionable Resistance: Queer 'Fa(t)Shion' Blogging as Counterdiscourse". *Women's Studies Quarterly* 41, no.1/2: 209–224.

Cooper, Charlotte. 2008. "What's Fat Activism?" Working Paper WP2008–02. Accessed 1 May 2021. www.ulsites.ul.ie/sociology/sites/default/files/Whats%20Fat%20Activism.pdf

Cooper, Charlotte. 2009a. "Interview: Max Airborne." *Obesity Timebomb!*, 3 November 2009, http://obesitytimebomb.blogspot.com/2009/11/rad-fatty-max-airborne.html

Cooper, Charlotte. 2009b. "Fat Activism in Ten Astonishing, Beguiling, Inspiring, and Beautiful Episodes". In *Fat Studies in the UK*, edited by Corinna Tomrley and Ann Kaloski Naylor, 19–31. England: Raw Nerve Books.

Cooper, Charlotte. 2010. "Revisiting The Fat Dykes Statement." *Obesity Timebomb!*, 28 January 2010, http://obesitytimebomb.blogspot.com/2010/01/lgbt-history-month-fat-dykes-statement.html

Cooper, Charlotte. 2012. "A Queer and Trans Fat Activist Timeline: Queering Fat Activism Nationality and Cultural Imperialism". *Fat Studies* 1, no. 1: 61–74.

Cooper, Charlotte. 2016. *Fat Activism: A Radical Social Movement*. London: HammerOn Press.

Dark, Kimberly. 2014. "Becoming Travolta". In *Queering Fat Embodiment*, edited by Cat Pausé, Jackie Wykes, and Samantha Murray, 27–30. Surrey: Ashgate.

Davis, Cheyenne. M. 2021. "It's Terrible Being a Fat, Black Femme on Instagram". *Input*, 14 October 2021. www.inputmag.com/culture/its-terrible-being-a-fat-black-femme-on-instagram

Farrell, Amy Erdman. 2018. "'In the Position of Fat Women Is Shown the True Position of Woman in Our Society': *Shadow on a Tightrope* and the Centrality of Feminist Independent Publishing". *American Periodicals: A Journal of History and Criticism* 28, no. 2: 139–152.

Freespirit, Judy and Aldebaran. 1979. "Fat Liberation Manifesto." *off our backs* 9, no. 4: 18.

Gailey, Jeannine. 2014. *The Hyper(in)visible Fat Woman*. New York: Palgrave.

Harrison, Da'Shaun. 2021. *Belly of the Beast*. Berkeley: North Atlantic Books.

Hill, Adrienne C. 2009. "Spatial Awarishness: Queer Women and the Politics of Fat Embodiment". Masters Arts Thesis, Bowling Green State University, Ohio.

Jagose, Annamarie. 1996. *Queer Theory*. Dunedin: Otago University Press.

Kristjansson, Margitte. 2016. "Fashion's 'Forgotten Woman': How Fat Bodies Queer Fashion and Consumption". In *Queering Fat Embodiment*, edited by Cat Pausé, Jackie Wykes, and Samantha Murray, 131–146. Surrey: Ashgate.

Kyrölä, Katariina. 2014. *Weight of Images: Affect, Body Image and Fat in the Media*. Surrey: Ashgate.

LeBesco, Kathleen. 2001. "Queering Fat Bodies/Politics". In *Bodies Out Of Bounds*, edited by Jana Evan Braziel and Kathleen LeBesco, 74–90. Berkeley: University of California Press.

LeBesco, Kathleen. 2004. *Revolting Bodies? The Struggle to ReDefine Fat Identity*. Boston: University of Massachusetts Press.

Levy-Navarro, Elena 2009. "Fattening Queer History: Where Does Fat History Go From Here?" In *The Fat Studies Reader*, edited by Esther Rothblum and Sandra Solovay, 15–22. New York: New York University Press.

Lind, Emily R. M. 2020. "Queering Fat Activism: A Study in Whiteness." In *Thickening Fat: Fat Bodies, Intersectionality, and Social Justice*, edited by May Friedman, Carla Rice, and Jen Rinaldi, 183–194. New York: Routledge.

Longhurst, Robyn. 2014. "Queering Body Size and Shape: Performativity, the Closet, Shame, and Orientation". In *Queering Fat Embodiment*, edited by Cat Pausé, Jackie Wykes, and Samantha Murray, 13–26. Surrey: Ashgate.

Meleo-Erwin, Zoe. 2014. "Queering the Linkages and Divergences: The Relationships Between Fatness and Disability and the Hope for a Liveable World". In *Queering Fat Embodiment*, edited by Cat Pausé, Jackie Wykes, and Samantha Murray, 97–114. Surrey: Ashgate.

Monaghan, Lee and Malson, H 2013. "'It's Worse for Women and Girls': Negotiating Embodied Masculinities through Weight-Related Talk". *Critical Public Health* 23, no. 3: 304–319.

Moon, Michael and Eve Kosofsky Sedgwick. 2001. "Divinity: A Dossier, a Performance Piece, a Little-Understood Emotion". In *Bodies Out Of Bounds*, edited by Jana Evan Braziel and Kathleen LeBesco, 292–328. Berkeley: University of California Press.

Mulder, Gabriella Ann. 2021. "Navigating the Fat Queer Body: The Impact of Cultural Discourses on Identity Construction and Belonging". PhD Dissertation, DePaul University.

Murray, Samantha. 2009. "Marked as 'Pathological': 'Fat' Bodies as Virtual Confessors". In *Biopolitics and the Obesity Epidemic: Governing Bodies*, edited by Jan Wright and Valerie Harwood, 78–92. New York: Routledge, 78–92.

NOLOSE. n.d. "About". Accessed 1 May 2021. https://nolose.org/about/

Pausé, Cat. 2014 "Causing a Commotion: Queering Fat in Cyberspace". In *Queering Fat Embodiment*, edited by Cat Pausé, Jackie Wykes, and Samantha Murray, 75–88. Surrey: Ashgate.

Pausé, Cat. 2014. "Express Yourself: Fat Activism in the Web 2.0 Age". In *The Politics of Size: Perspectives From the Fat Acceptance Movement Vol1*, edited by Ragen Chastain, 1–8. Santa Barbara: Praeger Publishing.

Pausé, Cat. 2015. "Rebel Heart: Performing Fatness Wrong Online". *M/C Journal* 18, no. 3. https://doi.org/10.5204/mcj.977

Pausé, Cat and Sonya Renee Taylor. 2021. "Fattening Up Scholarship" In *The Routledge Handbook of Fat Studies*, edited by Cat Pausé and Sonya Renee Taylor, 1–18. London: Routledge.

Senyonga, Mary. 2020. "Reading and Affirming Alternatives in the Academy: Black Fat Queer Femme Embodiment". In *Thickening Fat: Fat Bodies, Intersectionality, and Social Justice*, edited by May Friedman, Carla Rice, and Jen Rinaldi, 219–229. New York: Routledge.

Simic, Zora. 2015. "Fat as a Feminist Issue: A History". In *Fat Sex: New Directions in Theory and Activism*, edited by Helen Hester and Caroline Walters, 15–36. Surrey, England: Ashgate.

Smith, Heather. 1989. "Creating a Politics of Appearance: The National Fat Women's Conference: Report". *Trouble + Strife*, 16 (Summer): 36–41.

Snider, Stefanie. 2009. "Fat Girls and Size Queens: Alternative Publications and the Visualising of Fat and Queer Eroto-Politics in Contemporary American Culture". In *The Fat Studies Reader*, edited by Esther Rothblum and Sandra Solovay, 223–231. New York: New York University Press.

Stimson, Karen. 2003. "Fat Feminist Herstory, 1969–1993: A Personal Memoir". *Largesse* via the WayBack Machine, 23 June 2003. https://web.archive.org/web/20030623021 536/http://largesse.net/Archives/herstory.html

Taylor, Allison. 2021. "What's Queer About Fat Studies Now? A Critical Exploration of Queer/ing Fatness". In *The Routledge International Handbook of Fat Studies*, edited by Cat Pausé and Sonya Renee Taylor, 273–283. London: Routledge.

Taylor, Sonya Renee. 2018. *The Body is Not An Apology*. New York: Random House.

Thomas, Alexandra. 2018. "Fat Black Queer Femmes Are the Fetishized Backbones of Our Communiites – But Who Takes Care of Us?" *The Body Is Not An Apology*, 25 July 2018. https://thebodyisnotanapology.com/magazine/desire-belonging-on-blackn ess-femininity-and-queerness/

White, Francis Ray. 2012. "Fat, Queer, Dead: 'Obesity' and the Death Drive". *Somatechnics* 2: 1–17.

White, Francis Ray. 2013. "No Fat Future? The Uses of Anti-Social Queer Theory for Fat Activism". In *Queer Future: Reconsidering Ethics, Activism, and the Political*, edited by Elahe Haschemi, Yekani, Eveline Killan, and Beatric Michaels, 21–36. Surrey: Ashgate.

White, Francis Ray. 2014. "Fat/Trans: Queering the Activist Body". *Fat Studies* 3, no. 2: 86–100.

White, Francis Ray. 2020. "Embodying the Fat/Trans Intersection". In *Thickening Fat: Fat Bodies, Intersectionality, and Social Justice*, edited by May Friedman, Carla Rice, and Jen Rinaldi, 110–136. New York: Routledge.

Whitesel, Jason. 2014. *Fat Gay Men: Girth, Mirth and the Politics of Stigma*. New York: NYU Press.

Whitesel, Jason and Amy Shuman. 2013. "Normalising Desire: Stigma and the Carnivalesque in Gay Bigmen's Cultural Practices". *Men and Masculinities* 16, no. 4: 478–496.

Wykes, Jackie. 2014. "Introduction: Why Queering Fat Embodiment?" In *Queering Fat Embodiment*, edited by Cat Pausé, Jackie Wykes, and Samantha Murray, 1–12. Surrey: Ashgate.

Yeboah, Stephanie. 2017. Why Are Women of Colour Left Out of Body Positivity? *Elle*, 15 Sept 2017. www.elle.com/uk/fashion/longform/a38300/women-of-colour-left-out-of-body-positivity/

5

ANTIBLACKNESS, GENDER, AND FAT

Da'Shaun L. Harrison

In 2021, I published my debut title *Belly of the Beast: The Politics of Anti-Fatness as Anti-Blackness*. I needed to write something that didn't require me to compartmentalize my identities in an effort to give language to my experiences in the World. It was imperative that Black fat trans/masc folks were able to contextualize their experiences, with their entire Being, and for folks—more generally—to gain clarity on why we must move beyond self-love, beyond Desire/ability, beyond policing, beyond health, beyond abolition, and beyond Gender. And how these varying forms of violence cannot be divorced from the Black fat trans/masc identity. I wrote it as an intervention.

Belly of the Beast seeks to provide clarity on several modes of violence that justify defining antifatness *as* antiblackness. What this means is that antifatness *is* antiblackness—which is to say that it is the condition under which the Black fat—which I use coterminously as/with the Slave—is held captive to and by the World. Antiblackness creates the World and gives meaning to everything in it. This means that antiblackness functions as a schema—an outline or paradigm—of the (il)logical instantiation of Black flesh, Black (as) pain, Black (as) trauma, Black (as) suffering, the Black belly (and/as) beastliness. In other words, antiblack antifatness is the framework by which the Black fat subject is relegated to a bifurcated abject (Hartman 2010, 3–14) human-animal experience; experiencing both the objectification and subjugation of its body and Being; living as the Beast being held captive by the "forced humanization of blackness" through universal humanity. It is the metaphysical/global structure that determines how we are engaged in life and D/death (Patterson 1982), as well as who lives and who dies. In this way, fatness, as with Blackness, is always and already criminalized, penalized, objectified, marginalized, and defined by the libidinal economy (Wilderson 2010, 1–35)—or the collective unconscious.

DOI: 10.4324/9781003140665-7

The (Il)logics and Incoherence of Gender

To borrow from Frank B. Wilderson, III, Black/fatness is coterminous with Slaveness (Wilderson 2021). This is to say that Black flesh is always and already positioned as "nonperson." The Black fat—or the Slave—as a global disposition *has* to exist for the sake of humanity's legibility; or, said differently, the Black fat is an essential paradigm for the maintenance of "the Human"—even and especially as the Black/Slave/Abjected are removed from Humanness. As this is the case, there is no Human without the Slave.

It is my position that "Human"—most simply—is made up of white, thin people; "Black" (and Black fat) is always interchangeable with "Slave." What this means is that the World, or our society, is overdetermined by a Human/Slave dichotomy on which various modes of violence—like Gender—are built.

Gender's rationale is coherent only to the Human, which is to say that the intelligibility of Gender, or its ability to be understood by the Human mind, (seemingly) falls apart at the site and sight of the Slave. In *Becoming Human: Matter and Meaning in an Antiblack World* and *Scenes of Subjection: Terror, Slavery, and Self-Making in Nineteenth-Century America*, however, Zakiyyah Iman Jackson and Saidiya Hartman, respectively, suggest that part of the antiblack violence of "universal humanity" is that it coerces Black(ened) folks into understanding themselves as—and desiring to be—Gendered. This is what Jackson calls "human-animality" and Hartman calls "slave humanity." Additionally, in *Mama's Baby, Papa's Maybe: An American Grammar Book*, Hortense Spillers offers an analysis wherein she excavates, or unearths, the historical ways Black folks are removed from "normative gender" and kinship; she calls this "ungendering," and concludes by arguing that there is a particular radicality in claiming monstrosity as opposed to "joining the ranks" of gender (Spillers 2003, 203–239). I posit that while all Black folks are ungendered, many, if not most, still have a desire to *be* Gender(ed)—whereby I mean Human; I call this in-Human (not inhuman): the (coerced) desire to situate one's ungendered self wholly *inside of* the confines of Humanness without contending with their position as the underbelly of humanity.

Moreover, this desire to be Gender(ed) is about a desire to, at the very least, have your experience understood by the Human psyche. In *Undoing Gender*[1] Judith Butler writes:

> To be oppressed means that you already exist as a subject of some kind, you are there as the visible and oppressed other for the master subject, as a possible or potential subject, but to be unreal is to be something else *again* (emphasis mine). To be oppressed you must first become intelligible.

As stated in a conversation between myself and Northwestern University graduate student, Jordan Mulkey, "blackness is intelligible but only as the violence of intelligibility." This means that the antiblack violence Black folks experience has no logic; it is violence for the sake of hegemonizing Black flesh to sustain whiteness and antiblackness, more particularly. This desire to *be* Gender(ed), I believe, is about a flesh-eating aspiration to be(come) more than just flesh; at least, that is what creates the desire. By this, I am returning, again, to Spillers when she writes in *Mama's Baby, Papa's Maybe*:

> I would make a distinction in this case between "body" and "flesh" and impose that distinction as the central one between captive and liberated subject-positions. In that sense, before the "body" there is "flesh," that zero degree of social conceptualization that does not escape concealment under the brush of discourse, or the reflexes of iconography.

The in-Human desires to have one's experiences recognizable to the captains on water and the masters on land that hold us captive in/on/between the ship, the plantation, the Hold (Sharpe 2016, 68–101)—which is to say, to feel represented even in the wake of our continued unintelligibility. Black folks are browbeaten into believing in Gender because Gender is Human, and Human is power. The in-Human—perhaps even unknowingly—prefers (or is forced) to ascribe to cisness, or even Gendered variants, because it suggests and assigns a logic to the violent experience of living in Black flesh in an antiblack World. We are coerced, through the process by which we go from Beings in flesh to flesh with identities imposed onto our Being, into desiring to be legible / intelligible / unend(ed/ing). But, as Rinaldo Walcott names in *The Long Emancipation: Moving Towards Black Freedom*,[2] we are already living in the time of emancipation—or the afterlife of slavery, to borrow from Hartman—and therefore no amount of representation or attempt at making the master feel the pain you endure will ever amount to freedom. It can't. The appearance of Gender as something (and some Thing) necessarily accessible to and by the Black fat is deceptive in that it does not account for the ways that Gender functions as a nonsensical (sub)structure.

In conversation with scholar, writer, and professor Patrice Douglass, Zakiyyah Iman Jackson states,[3]

> representation is not re-presentation or mimesis. It is *a doing and a making*. And so, I think our understanding of what's at stake with representation shifts *dramatically* when we understand that representation is a doing and a making inside of the realm of ontology.

In *Becoming Human*, she elaborates[4]:

> Regarding re-presentation, in the grammar described, there are "black (maternal) female" figures (or representations) that appear, but they function at the register of myth rather than indexicality and, therefore, reveal that representation *performs* rather than functions *mimetically* as the notion of

"re-presentation" suggests. ... (if "figure" is the appropriate concept here, "portal" is probably more accurate).

This means that the Human—who depends on the making of a/the Black Gendered Being to mold and exploit (because the Human understands Black flesh as prey)—creates itself against the representation of a Black Gendered figure (or portal), to borrow from Jackson, which must exist first so that the Human is what's comprehensible. In this way, Black folks' desire to be represented/seen/understood by forcing their way into a Gender(ed) logic without acknowledging that the (il) logic of antiblackness sustains itself through this desire by the unintelligible to have their deaths made legible.

In an unpublished conversation between myself and a doctoral student in Black geographies, Tea Troutman said:

> If we see a nigga attempting to do a gender—we know niggas are ungendered— the only way we [can] perceive them as a black gendered body is for them to try to make legible their death and suffering in a humanist turn. And the world then needs to construct a black gender as a representationalist logic that they then use to secure the category of the animal and the human over and against the humanity of the black. Like, the black woman and her fatness with the breasts that could [rest] over her shoulder. Or the black brute ... male that is hypersexualized, drawn as larger than life, drawn as animalistic to convey the popular imaginary of black man *as* rapist, black man *as* destructive.

As we have witnessed with hashtag Black Lives Matter, and other forms of hashtag (activism) as Black Death (Harrison 2020), the demand of the movement itself is to make our "death and suffering" legible. It is an attempt to exist, and to exist as intelligible; to position intelligibility *as* freedom as opposed to intelligibility as proof that antiblackness still reigns. To this point, to be ungendered requires the in-Human, and all of us for that matter, to acknowledge that what we are suffering does not have a logical resolution, because it has no epistemological ground. This means, what/if ever there is a solution to the end of our suffering, it cannot and will not be known through our desires and attempts to help sustain Gender and overall antiblack violence.

This is where scholar and author Joy James's work becomes pivotal to understanding how we function in the World. In a lecture at Brown University, James makes clear that antiblack violence is repurposed and mutates with each attempt at preserving blackness and Black life. What James also makes clear, however—in her construction of the captive maternal—is that this violence does not mean that we give up on, or let go of, the community that holds us. She says,[5]

> Every time we stabilize, they build upon that stability and enforce another form of theft—trauma, time theft, loss—for productivity of a state that you find horrific. ... It's an impossible task, but it's one completely worthy of you.

Sticking with James, in her essay *"New Bones" Abolitionism, Communism, and Captive Maternals*,[6] James notes that generative powers stolen from the "captive maternal" can be recovered:

> The Captive Maternal is linked not only to the routine theft of generative powers of the enslaved but also to the inevitable (sporadic) organized revolts against captivity. Black parents and communities labor to keep children and elders and themselves stable and protected. That care can be fueled by fear or love, or loyalty, or a mixture of motivations. Often its labor is used to stabilize the very structures that prey on Black lives and honor in schools, hospitals, jobs, and prisons. Generative powers stolen and repurposed by the state and capital for accumulation can also be stolen back for rebellions.

As I see it, this suggests that our commitment must be to the destruction of the World, as it is parasitic upon Black flesh. This impossible demand through "Black activity" (@_RAWilcox, June 5, 2021) attempts to actualize what is often regarded as "impractical and improbable" (Jackson 2020).

Gender and the Black Fat

This chapter started by defining "antifatness as antiblackness," and moved to defining Gender's incoherence and (il)logics. These were necessary starting points in a chapter about antiblackness, Gender, and fat(ness) because, as explored in chapter six of *Belly of the Beast*, "Meeting Gender's End," I understand Gender to function as a structure that helps to stabilize antifatness—which is to say that Gender functions as an entity that exists solely to preserve and sustain antiblackness and antiblack violence. There is no way to arrive at that conclusion without first knowing how antiblackness is stabilized by Gender and antifatness, but also how each of them help to characterize antiblackness and expand its violence on/in/ through the World.

Now that these concepts and ideas have been defined and expounded upon, it is necessary that I begin to make clear just how interwoven all of these concepts are; to clarify how Black fatness is disrupted by Gender's hold; to draw attention to how Black fat transness can only be defined by the antiblack antifat violence of Gender.

In chapter six of *Belly of the Beast*,[7] I write:

> Fat Black trans people are forced to move to and through gender in a way that makes most evident to me that gender itself is something worth interrogating more closely. In so many ways, fatness functions as a gender of its own. Fatness fails, and therefore disrupts, the foundation on which gender is built. This is why the request is made of fat trans people to lose weight before they can be affirmed in their gender, or why little fat Black boys are often misread as girls, or why fat Black women are often denied access to womanhood in a

way that operates differently than the typical ungendering of Black subjects at large. But gender is birthed from violence, and therefore fatness operating as its own gender is not liberatory so much as it is forced. Fat people are situated in this extension of what is already a prison because fat bodies deviate from—or rather are already positioned outside of—the designated or assigned "look" of gender."

When bodies are sexed at or before the birth of a child, they are also gendered. The (perceived) reproductive organs and (perceived) sexual anatomy of children determine how they are separated into a binary gender—boy or girl. Rarely are they referred to as "male" or "female," and yet the gender they're assigned is thought to provide clarity not only on their organs and anatomy, but also on what roles and attributes they can be expected to fulfill and display as they grow older. This process is intended to make the body, or the flesh, of the child meaningful and intelligible. This constitutes and inaugurates cisness, and a cisgender positionality, as the ultimate power. And, the Slave—meaning someone who is Black—is regarded as no more than property, relegated to a human-animal positionality and unfastened from a Gendered possibility. What this means is that intersex people and/or people who later identify themselves as trans, and Black people more generally, are always *and* already situated outside of the realm of a Gendered experience. So, the sexed gendering of bodies at or before birth is an experience reserved for cisgender white people (or people who have adopted and/or been coerced into their practices). *But. And.* When interrogated further, it becomes clear that this practice is particularly reserved for thin bodies.

In chapter five of *Belly of the Beast*, I walk the reader through the creation of what is referred to as the body mass index (BMI)—created by Belgian mathematician Adolphe Quetelet in the 19th century (Harrison 2021, 69–84). What he also created, through the creation of BMI, was the *l'homme moyen*, loosely interpreted as "the ideal/average/normal man." One of his first published studies was titled "*Recherches sur le poids de l'homme aux différent âges*," or "Research on the weight of man at different ages" (Eknoyan 2007). This study would eventually be published as a book, and would be the first of many published works for Quetelet as a statistician, polymath, and researcher. Through the use of the weights and heights of typical French and Scottish men, Quetelet was able to develop the model of ideal beauty (Kubergovic 2013)—a major contributor to race science and eugenicist projects throughout the West. At the time of the development and spread of *l'homme moyen*, race science was being further developed as Africans continued to be taken by ship across the Atlantic Ocean and traded as capital and property. As detailed by Sabrina Strings in *Fearing the Black Body: The Racial Origins of Fat Phobia*,[8] the 19th century—The Enlightenment era, as well as the era in which Quetelet's index was developed and spread—was also the moment in which fear of and aversions to fatness was developed as a coherent ideology used as a way to further subjugate and objectify the Black body. This was not by coincidence. Antiblackness is (il)logical, but it is also intentional.

What is being clarified by this mapping and chronology is that the sexed gendering of bodies is not only about developing Black transness, but also Black trans fatness as a way to establish power "over and against the humanity of the black." Gender is a structure forged with the purpose of creating and maintaining a class of subjects designed to be inferior to another, but more than that, it is also a structure forged with the intent to ensure the unintelligibility of the Black trans fat. The role of "either" (cis)Gender is achieved through a continued performance. ("Either" is in quotes here because I recognize that there are endless ways that people refer to their gender(s) and genderlessness, and yet, when referring to Gender, it is only ever about Man and Woman).

As I wrote in *Belly of the Beast*:

> These roles—and these performances—are implied, but also explicitly named, characteristics and duties one must fulfill to be "man" or "woman." They are not inherent to us, meaning we are not born as "boys" or as "girls." In basic sociological terms, we are taught immediately after birth through social institutions like family, media, and school what role we must fulfill if we are to hold on to the gender we are assigned at birth. When we start breaking the rules of those assigned roles, and thus falling outside of gender's hold, we become "sissies" or "tomboys"—depending on which role you were assigned to fulfill from birth. As Judith Butler states in her book *Gender Trouble*, our behaviors that are gendered are not innate to us. We learn them, and then we learn to perform them. And this performance is policed and maintained by cisheteronormativity, or the idea that everyone already is—and therefore all things must be seen as—cisgender and heterosexual. In other words, cisheteronormativity is the "law and order" of gender in that it is what determines who is departing from their assigned role and must therefore be punished because of it.

Butler's work highlights the importance of the Performative, or "performative utterance" (Austin 1962, 5–6)—language intended to separate the verbal act of *describing* what one is doing from the act of *doing* what has been verbalized. In *How to Do Things with Words*, J.L. Austin uses "I do"—as stated in marriage ceremonies—as an example of "performative sentence." "I do" is not describing the action of the other individual, it is *creating* a (new) reality: in this case, a legal bond and (oft) public commitment between two people. "I quit" is another example of performative sentence or performative utterance. It is not describing what the employee is doing, but rather the employee is *actually* doing it—yet again, creating a new reality, not only for the employee, but also for their boss and coworkers. So when Butler says that our gendered behaviors are a performance, she means that these behaviors *create* Gender. And similar to the aforementioned examples, Gender performance does not only impact the individual; it impacts everyone around us. In other words, Gender as a "performative" is World-making; it is "a doing and a making." We "do" Gender by ascribing and subscribing to gender(ed) norms and roles established, again, by the libidinal economy.

Returning to *Belly of the Beast*:

> To this point, and to return to Butler, it is not our gender that defines our performance, but rather our performance that is always already defining Gender. In her essay, "Performative Acts and Gender Constitution: An Essay in Phenomenology and Feminist Theory," Butler refers to gender as an illusion and an "object of belief," expanding further by noting that "gender reality is performative which means, quite simply, that it is real only to the extent that it is performed." What "performed" means in this sense is not that one is standing on a stage or pretending to do something for the sake of being lauded, but rather that one is creating the thing by which their life and beinghood is defined through myriad acts and repetitions. So what is gender? It is only what we make it, but what we make it is defined by, in simple terms, the World around us. Hortense Spillers knew this, too, about the Black, in particular, when she wrote "Mama's Baby, Papa's Maybe: An American Grammar Book". In that essay, as we covered earlier in the book, Spillers provides an analysis for what it means for Black subjects to always be "ungendered". This means that gender is lost to the Black—which more directly means that gender reads differently for our bodies and our Being. Ungendered as monstrosity—it is to suggest that we are removed from gender, that we are misaligned with a normative, "coherent" gender, making us Beasts from birth.

This is to say that we cannot situate Black people only in or only outside of Gender, and that it was designed that way intentionally. Gender, and its binary, do not belong to us; we are held captive by it. Black folks were never meant to fit comfortably inside of Gender. This means that all violence projected onto/afflicted upon all Black people—but especially Black people who describe themselves or are perceived as nonbinary/trans/non-cis—can be directly described as Gender(ed) and antifat violence by way of antiblackness. The binary is not ours; it was never intended to be and it will never be.

Gender is defined by Thinness in that for one to settle or be positioned inside of the performance, they must always be pushing away from fatness—as evidenced by the disparity in the cost of gender-affirming surgeries for Black fat trans folks in relation to our thin trans counterparts; as evidenced by the generally understudied, and therefore positioned as anecdotal, fetishization of Black fat trans flesh; as evidenced by the general aesthetic of Black transness that many fat bodies cannot conform to. If shedding oneself of fatness, or altogether removing themselves from fat as an identity, is the only way for one's gender to be affirmed—both socially and surgically—then Gender is a structure that must also be toppled.

Fat trans people are finding it nearly impossible to find binders that feel affirming for them; many are being forced to engage an inherently antiblack antifat medical system that uses body mass index as an indicator for whether or not they deserve to be affirmed in their bodies; we are being engaged as the Other, even in spaces that, in name, were created for our comfort and safety. Gender works in relationship to health and Desire as a means to further ostracize the Black fat, and as this is the case, only one solution will prove to be sufficient enough for our liberation: we must see to Gender's end, which means we must destroy Gender.

Conclusion

Fat Studies—as a whole—must contend with the ways that Gender disrupts any possibility of a fat liberation. As a discipline, it considers the way that Gender(ed) violence affects, particularly, fat white women, but it does not consider—or even acknowledge, for that matter—the way that the antifat violence that fat, non-Black people experience is but the residue of the antiblack violence their (non-Black) bodies help to sustain. The field of Fat Studies must reckon with the way that antifatness further complicates the "human–animality" of Black Gendered figures. In this same vein, Black Studies, largely, must contend with antifat violence. It does not interrogate the ways that antiblackness engenders a particular *type* of violence for the Black fat that necessitates its own distinct naming: the Black fat is not only experiencing abject human–animality but is also traversing a violence in which our corporeal organism is the basis for antifat violence despite the impossibility of Black flesh lending itself to the emblematic structure called "body." In other words, our "bodies" are generally understood as the reason for the violence we endure, but as I referenced from Spillers earlier in the chapter, "the body" is reserved for the Human, which is always, within this framework, not Black.

Black Fat Studies—a discipline specific to researching and teaching on the violence of antiblack antifatness, as well as the historical, political, socio/economic, and cultural implications of existing in/as Black fat flesh—is a necessary step forward. The state of Fat Studies right now, barring a few key texts, is set on self-help texts and memoirs with liberal analyses that keep discourse stagnant and immoveable. Fat liberation activism is limited by notions of self-love and body positivity *as* representational liberatory conceptions. Our organizing efforts must move beyond attempts to stabilize state apparatuses by way of bargaining with the state for rights that, by name, are reserved for the Human; instead, we must be clear about the ways each of these structures function together to maintain antiblack antifat Gender(ed) violence. We must talk of and theorize around Gender *as* (a mode of) violence, or we risk regressing into a liberal logic that posits that the Black must salvage Gender in order to be humanized rather than understanding

Gender as a prop on which antiblackness becomes stabilized. This is an issue for many reasons, but one of the greatest is that the Black fat lives in peril for as long as Gender exists.

Notes

1 Butler, Judith. "Beside Oneself: On The Limits of Sexual Autonomy." Essay. In *Undoing Gender*, 17–39. New York, NY: Routledge, 2009.
2 Walcott, Rinaldo. *The Long Emancipation: Moving Toward Black Freedom*. Durham, NC: Duke University Press, 2021.
3 January Duke on Gender Black Feminism Beyond the Human. *YouTube*, 2021. https://youtu.be/eKlyq3itFSM
4 Jackson, Zakiyyah Iman. "Sense of Things: Empiricism and World in Nalo Hopkinson's *Brown Girl in the Ring*." Chapter. In *Becoming Human: Matter and Meaning in an Antiblack World*, 83–120. New York: New York University Press, 2020.
5 Joy James: The Architects of Abolitionism. *Youtube*, 2019. https://youtu.be/z9rvRsWKDx0
6 James, Joy. "'New Bones' Abolitionism, Communism, and Captive Maternals." Verso, June 4, 2021. www.versobooks.com/blogs/5095-new-bones-abolitionism-communism-and-captive-maternals
7 Harrison, Da'Shaun L. "Meeting Gender's End." Chapter. In *Belly of the Beast: The Politics of Anti-Fatness as Anti-Blackness*, 85–104. Berkeley, CA: North Atlantic Books, 2021.
8 Strings, Sabrina. *Fearing the Black Body: The Racial Origins of Fat Phobia*. New York: New York University Press, 2019.

Bibliography

Austin, J.L. 1962. *How to Do Things with Words: The William James Lectures*. Edited by J.O. Urmson, 5–6. London: Oxford University Press.

Butler, Judith. "Beside Oneself: On The Limits of Sexual Autonomy." Essay. In *Undoing Gender*, 17–39. New York, NY: Routledge, 2009.

Eknoyan, Garabed. "Adolphe Quetelet (1796–1874)-the Average Man and Indices of Obesity." *Nephrology Dialysis Transplantation*, Volume 23, Issue 1, pages 47–51. OUP Academic. Oxford University Press, September 22, 2007. https://doi.org/10.1093/ndt/gfm517

Harrison, Da'Shaun L. "The Hashtag as Black Death." *Wear Your Voice Magazine*, July 14, 2020. www.wyvarchive.com/the-hashtag-as-black-death/

Harrison, Da'Shaun L. "Meeting Gender's End." Essay. In *Belly of the Beast: The Politics of Anti-Fatness as Anti-Blackness*, 85–104. Berkeley, CA: North Atlantic Books, 2021.

Hartman, Saidiya V. "Introduction." In *Scenes of Subjection: Terror, Slavery, and Self-Making in Nineteenth-Century America*, 3–14. New York, NY: Oxford University Press, 2010.

Jackson, Zakiyyah Iman. "Losing Manhood: Plasticity, Animality, and Opacity in the (Neo)Slave Narrative." Essay. In *Becoming Human: Matter and Meaning in an Antiblack World*, 45–82. New York: New York University Press, 2020.

James, Joy. "'New Bones' Abolitionism, Communism, and Captive Maternals." Verso, June 4, 2021. www.versobooks.com/blogs/5095-new-bones-abolitionism-communism-and-captive-maternals.

January Duke on Gender Black Feminism Beyond the Human. *YouTube*, 2021. https://youtu.be/eKlyq3itFSM

Joy James: The Architects of Abolitionism. *Youtube*, 2019. https://youtu.be/z9rvRsWK Dx0

Kubergovic, Erna. "Quetelet, Adolphe." *The Eugenics Archives*, September 2013. http:// eugenicsarchive.ca/discover/connections/5233cb0f5c2ec5000000009c

Patterson, Orlando. 1982. *Slavery and Social Death: A Comparative Study.* Cambridge, MA: Harvard University Press.

Sharpe, Christina. "The Hold." Essay. In *In the Wake: On Blackness and Being*, 68–101. Durham, NC: Duke University Press, 2016.

Sirvent, Roberto, and Zakiyyah Iman Jackson. BAR Book Forum: Zakiyyah Iman Jackson's "Becoming Human". Other. *Black Agenda Report*, 2020.

Spillers, Hortense J. "Mama's Baby, Papa's Maybe: An American Grammar Book." Essay. In *Black, White, and in Color: Essays on American Literature and Culture*, 203–239. Chicago, IL: University of Chicago Press, 2003.

Strings, Sabrina. *Fearing the Black Body: The Racial Origins of Fat Phobia.* New York: New York University Press, 2019.

Walcott, Rinaldo. *The Long Emancipation: Moving Toward Black Freedom.* Durham, NC: Duke University Press, 2021.

Wilcox, RAW. Twitter. Twitter, June 5, 2021. https://twitter.com/_Rawilcox/sta tus/1401253096857255945?s=20

Wilderson, Frank B. *Afropessimism*. Liveright Publishing Corporation, 2021.

Wilderson, III, Frank B. 2010. *Red, White & Black : Cinema and the Structure of U.S. Antagonisms.* Durham, NC: Duke University Press.

PART III

Narrating Gender and Fat

Stories are fundamental to our experience of the world. They are everywhere—on social media, on TV, in novels, in the conversations we hold with others, even within our own heads. Kimberly Dark and Susan Stinson ask us to ponder these stories about gender and fat, including what it means when different people tell them and what it means when they explode our old ways of thinking.

DOI: 10.4324/9781003140665-8

6

EMBODIED NARRATION

Kimberly Dark

When I teach Sociology or Women's Studies classes in person, courses like "Body and Identity," I want students to acknowledge right away that there are *actual bodies* in the room. It sounds ridiculous, but the university classroom erases bodies, sometimes even tries to erase bodily functions like the urge to pee or eat or sleep. I'm guilty of trying to keep from going to the restroom until the break, or agreeing to be in class at an hour when I know I'd be better off horizontal. Our bodies are not important in the university classroom. We're supposed to control them and eradicate their needs—even needs like big enough chairs or a functioning elevator to reach the fourth floor. (Seriously, I once had a semester-long battle about the Americans with Disabilities Act non-compliant practice of having campus police unlock the elevators at 8 a.m., when many classes began at 7:30.)

I have been teaching both online and in person for decades, and when people had a collective freak-out over being forced to switch exclusively to online teaching and learning during the pandemic, part of me thought, well, it's not as if we all brought our bodies into those classrooms anyway. Online teaching and learning presented manifold challenges, but for many, the embodied part was actually easier. The seating in your home, at least, is controlled by you, and you can roll your eyes without being seen.

Why do I push them to acknowledge bodies when most classes forge ahead without doing so? I figure that if we are going to be discussing bodies and identities in immediate and scholarly ways, *and we had those things right there in the room with us*, we might as well see what could be gained from the experience. I suspect it would also be useful in a chemistry or business class too, because our embodiment is a big part of how we perceive one another, assign positive and negative traits. It guides our abilities to communicate and collaborate in ways we never fully explore.

DOI: 10.4324/9781003140665-9

I don't force students to be totally in their own bodies *and* talk about them, of course. That would be going way too far. Even when I do offer a brief meditation at the beginning of class, or other "coming into the body" activities, escape hatches are built in. Nobody should be forced to be embodied and mindful—especially in locations and with company where power imbalances abound. It makes good sense for some people and in some settings, to be only partially present, or to keep ones' guard up (Dark 2018).

I've found it especially useful for students to acknowledge my body, since mine is the one they're obliged to look at during most of the time we're together. Discussion time in my classes doesn't involve the use of electronics, so they really are paying unusual attention to what they can see. Unless they're looking at each other—which would be weird when the person isn't talking—or counting the smudges on the white board, they're looking at my body, at my head, at my mouth moving. They're considering my clothing choices, my mannerisms, my size, and the shape of my body, along with the obvious categories I seem to occupy based on visual confirmation. I am a woman, fat ("well-shaped," but whoa, too large to fit into a desk-chair-combo), old—or maybe middle-aged and maybe used-to-be-pretty—tall, white (unless we're in Britain or Australia and then I'm probably mixed, "half-caste" or maybe just returned from holiday because I'm *sooo* tanned). If they notice my limp, they might consider me disabled and if I reference being queer, they might think they perceive that too: I talk loudly, have a commanding demeanor, a deep voice. (These are traits students have reported when I ask them to reflect on whether they can "see" my queerness.)

My body is definitely "in play" in the room. The professor's body is always a visual spectacle though it's not polite to acknowledge the scrutiny students offer, given the paucity of visual alternatives. In my case, the aspect of my embodiment that likely seems least socially acceptable to acknowledge or discuss is fatness. Not only do we have to consciously bring bodies into the room, I have to construct fatness as a respectable topic of conversation and help them to acknowledge my own fatness in a way that advances our collective aims and also co-constructs my dignity. (Of course, I could just avoid fatness as a topic of study, as most sociology classes do, but in my courses about bodies, we take up the theme.)

"I want you to know that *I know* that *you* know that you have a fat professor."

That's what I say after a brief speech on our general embodiment. And then we have a little laugh and talk about how I am using "fat" as a neutral descriptive term in class, not as an insult word or a marker for pity, as it is used in many places in the world. I ask them to notice how that feels—today, and tomorrow, and the following week. I ask again at the end of the semester, and they report they're also using "fat" as a neutral term—though they realize how strange this seems in conversations with friends and family.

I point out that I'm not just experienced at *being* fat; the internal experience is actually least salient. I am interacting with them as a person who's read widely on the theme and understands how to apply structural thinking regarding social inequality. I am also speaking as a person who has been marginalized, harmed, and degraded by that very social inequality and I'd prefer they don't forget it. They have access to me on this topic during our term of study and I am bringing no small resource. Pun intended.

Gender, of course, comes up later, but not by much. A long time ago, I discovered that just talking about the data on stigmatized bodies makes some students defensive. People like to hold onto the fairytale idea that most people really acknowledge talent and hard work in the workplace, a good heart and kindness in romantic relationships, etc. It helps if I don't argue with students about the gendered nature of fat stigma. They get the lesson very quickly when I ask the following questions—prompting them to reveal (to themselves) what we already collectively know about fat and gender.

"Which is more acceptable if you're a fat woman?" I call out to the class, "A big belly or a big butt?"

"A big butt!" They all call out, though not quite in unison, as they begin to understand that their answers will conform, stunningly.

"How about a fat thighs or fat ankles?"

"Fat thighs," they say together and laugh.

"How about a fat face or fat boobs?"

"Boobs!" They practically sing together, happy to say the word in public, and confident in their knowledge of what it means for fat to be gender-conforming, though they had likely not considered that part of their knowledge set before.

"That last one's a trick question," I say, "because boobs *are* fat. The most acceptable fat on a woman's body!" They all nod knowingly.

"Okay, which is more acceptable if you're a fat man?" I forge ahead. "A big belly or a big butt?"

"A big belly!" They say, with a bit of surprise at the turnaround.

"What about fat boobs or a fat face?"

"Wow," some of them remark. "Definitely not man-boobs." They look at each other, horrified by the image in their minds.

"Fat thighs?" I add.

"No way," they say. Usually someone will add that a fat face isn't good on a man, but it's better than on a woman. And hey, there's really nowhere for a man to be *acceptably* fat other than his belly or shoulders, is there?

"Aha," I say. "So, are there narrower social standards for men in any other ways?"

Some of them know this lesson already. "Yeah, they can't cry or show emotion or wear dresses and skirts, or be anything other than tough…"

"So, a fat body that falls outside of the category 'big-bellied big-guy' is feminizing? And that's still the fastest way for men to lose respect?" They are nodding. "And all of these gender and size and race and age and ability markers are influencing people at once?"

They nod some more.

Now we can discuss intersectionality. No one is just a gender or just a race or just a body type—though white able-bodied maleness opens doors like no other embodiment. Even white men are complex, and individuals occupy many vectors of social identification. (Personalities too, but I'm a Sociologist, so that's not of interest in my class, unless it can be made aggregate as an expression of culture. The "Karen" is one example that brings us closer to seeing how, yes, even personality is often an expression of culture). For instance, fat white men can use race and gender to overcome fatness but only if their fatness is gender-conforming. Sure, fatness is still a stigmatized trait for men. Sure, things like height mitigate the perception of white male efficacy.

We can also begin to discuss being fat and gender-non-conforming because the rules for that embodiment are still being written by our culture and so far, things don't look good for fat non-binary folks.

Fat, Gender, and Their Myriad Intersections

We need stories. Repeating narratives, like the one about my classroom teaching above, help us to rediscover what we know and to claim that knowledge. The tricky thing is that the culture tells us to take our place in a hierarchy of worth and then, to act like we were never told any such thing! Students want to argue about individual tenacity—unless we embed the theories and data in narratives and memories about our own and others' experiences. Then they move more deeply, more quickly. If I ask students about their views on fat and gender, and their myriad intersections, suddenly the standard stories pop up about how people have self-determination and love conquers all and people can improve themselves if they want to. Intersectionality is easier when they recall their actual experiences.

Not surprisingly, more has been written about the compulsory femininity of fat female presentation than about fat and masculinity. Women are more stigmatized by small variations in fatness and there's also so much more nuance to work with since men can only be acceptably fat in very narrow ways. There are so many ways for women to gain and lose social capital and many of those ways depend on gender conformity. Compulsory femininity is a strong standard.

For instance, as a femme dyke, I am well-formed for stigma avoidance—or at least I was in my youth. Did you notice my mention, above, about how students might interpret my embodiment? I'm using the term "well-formed" to mean that I am gender-conforming. Another way to elevate the status of the stigmatized female body is to call it "proportionate," which really means that it looks like a hegemonically slender body, only bigger. When I was younger, I didn't have a pronounced belly. I was thick in the hips, thighs, and calves, but slender again at the ankle. My waistline was pronounced. I'm fatter, post-menopause, and have a much bigger belly. It even announces itself with a bit of a jiggle. No longer "well-formed," or "proportionate."

I wrote a book called *Fat, Pretty and Soon to be Old*, about appearance privilege/stigma; it explores everyday moments in which our appearance markers and identities are intersectional. "Fat" and "old" are almost always said as insults—very different from their euphemisms: curvy, robust, Rubenesque and experienced, wise, seasoned. "Pretty" is an identity marker that can be attained by having certain white-supremacy-approved physical features, or by clothing and coiffing and making oneself up in hegemonically glamorous feminine ways. Though prettiness conveys privilege, it's vain to claim the term for oneself. It must be conferred by others (and approved by the male gaze).

Fat stigma and hatred do not affect everyone in the same way. We know that whiteness can mitigate fatness and that color matters too. In her historical analysis of fat in the United States, Amy Farrell explores the suffrage movement's choice to identify womanhood with pale waifishness, an almost ethereal presence in order not to threaten the systems of earthbound men (Farrell 2011, 82). This past effort to construct appropriate white-femininity still draws a line between white feminists and women of color today—a line that is often invisible to white women, because of privilege. Black women, of course, never fail to see that their embodiment as women is less socially respected. Black and brown women's bodies are associated with myriad forms of degeneracy, death, and disease.

Having a clearer understanding of social inequality, painful though it may be—can be a catalyst for positive change. Afrofuturism (also called Black futurism) is both a cultural aesthetic, and a way of theorizing possible futures without white supremacy at the core of culture. It combines science fiction, history, and fantasy to explore and depict the African American experience. Hunter Ashleigh Shackelford discusses fatness as a form of Black futurism in "When You Are Already Dead." It's a powerful proposition to discuss the ways in which anti-blackness can actually release the body from time. If one is already presumed dead, the possibilities are endless.

> Black fat means surviving mutating, time-altering forms of violence, it means literally defying presumed and prescribed death while surviving more versions of fatality. The afrofuturistic multidimensionality that is required of the Black fat consciousness and Black fat being is a rubric of cyborg divergence, beyond 'human' grammar, beyond the cages of thinness and whiteness.
>
> (Shackelford 2021, 253)

Reaching back and reaching forward, race and class remain salient features of how fat, gender, and race intersect.

Age and disability are also critical aspects of how people narrate fat intersections. Since I developed a limp from arthritis, I have felt a disdain I never experienced as a physically fit young adult. Onlookers assume I limp because I'm fat and lazy. Of course they do. As a fat woman, I have a deficit of cultural capital. Sociologist Pierre Bourdieu extended Marx's idea of capital into the realm of the cultural (Oxford Reference 2021). Marx distinguished capital from money. Money to buy goods or services is just money. Capital is money that is used to buy things in order to sell them again. Capital creates wealth, which is intertwined with social relationship. Appearance privilege and the hierarchy it creates can be understood in similar terms. We gather the favor of onlookers for what it can purchase in the future. I may be accommodated in the moment by a railing or outstretched arm to steady me, but my cultural capital has definitely been diminished by my limp.

Bourdieu refers to the "symbolic" collection of skills, mannerisms, credentials, accent, posture, etc., that comprise the tool kit of privilege, of which we are often unconscious—or perhaps we are only conscious of the vectors of appearance that give us *inordinate* privilege or pain. For instance, some women—especially those with very pale complexions and hair—are aware of the privilege that astute make-up application can provide them. They notice precisely because that hyper-privilege is contingent; without make-up, they may seem overly pale. The privilege of whiteness might go unnoticed because it is always there. It is only when they receive the additional privilege that make-up affords, that the whole bargain becomes noticeable.

The currency of my younger, more capable body was "bankable" because even if someone were judging me poorly for being fat, I could always ameliorate my status by performing—or even referencing the performance of—laudable physical feats. The future is a mushy concept when aging and disability begin to take up more space in daily navigations. Some privileges are no longer attainable, and while they may only live in memory, we claim them out-of-time by resurrecting narratives about athletic and glamorous pasts, as I discuss in "Does this Limp Make Me Look Fat" (Dark 2019, 89).

There is no way to mitigate or ignore the kinds of social sanctions for appearance that Nomonde Mxhalisa discusses in "Desirability as Access: Navigating life at the intersection of fat, Black, dark and female" (2021, 205). Mxhalisa explores the ramifications—both personal and financial—of being judged ugly across various vectors that social norms and standards deem important.

Trans and Non-binary Fat Appearances

The intersections of appearance and identity markers are extremely complex and worthy of the kind of attention this book provides. It's also helpful for us to keep looking for them in our everyday interactions. They may not always be dramatic, but they are profound. For instance, while men have a narrower range of expressions available to them, the generalization that largeness is a positive trait for men is a persistent boon. If we're in a social gathering, and my friend Bob can't remember people's names, his polite default for women is, "Hey Beautiful!" For men, it's "Hey Big Guy!" These compliments are culturally legible regardless of age or race. They still exclude non-binary people.

The current cultural explosion of gender and multiplication of gender identities and ways of discussing and exploring embodiment can be a powerful catalyst for cultural improvement. They are revealing much about the persistent fractures that patriarchy, racism, and misogyny cause in our everyday lives.

A decade ago, my friend Drake reported to me that he had been denied "top surgery"—a gender confirmation surgery that would remove his breasts. Assigned female at birth, my friend is 5'4" and very fat. He receives state-subsidized medical care due to long-term disability. This is worth mentioning because of the additional stigma assigned to people without the means to pay privately for medical care. I have accompanied him to appointments for uterine cysts and other reproductive medical procedures and witnessed firsthand the disdain and dismissal he received because of his weight and size. Or perhaps because of his gender identity? Yes, the intersections would be difficult to tease out without a qualitative study involving linguistic analysis, even though I witnessed the affronts. The specific sanctions he received on those visits *seemed* to target weight. At one point, his doctor said that she would terminate treatment if he didn't "take responsibility" for his health by losing weight. She later did so, and then a subsequent doctor denied his request for top surgery as a component of gender reassignment. "Elective" surgery was deemed inappropriate for someone of his size. When I pressed about the doctor's data about outcomes for this surgery in high weight individuals, none was offered. Rather, I was told to consult "common sense."

Han Koehle's research on access to medical care for transgender people yielded an unplanned data set regarding how "antifatness provides a mechanism for gender policing by which fatness constitutes gendered moral deviancy" (2021). It's important to note that these themes were embedded in narrative, rather than being clearly marked at the outset of the research. As Koehle states, "If you're too fat, you're doing your gender wrong and it's a violation against your community."

Thankfully, the number of first-person narratives available in popular online media is increasing daily. Some of these offer rigorous scholarship in addition to personal accounts. Some are brief, angry, or poorly written. Still others offer literary accounts. Those that regard the intersections of fat and gender, as in Koehle's work, are particularly important for our current cultural understanding. As Francis Ray White points out in "Fat and Trans: Towards a new theorization of gender in Fat Studies" (2021, 78), the majority of first-person scholarly writing in Fat Studies is by trans men. For trans women's perspectives, we need to go to other sources.

In "The Intersection of Fatmisia and Transmisia" (2017), Kivan Bay explores other reasons that top surgery might be denied to a fat patient. An interviewee, "Johnny," described being denied surgery and then quickly being approved by another surgeon. "I was 'overweight and would look weird after surgery if my stomach was bigger than my chest.' Doctor's words." Johnny added, "It seems like a very thinly veiled 'you won't be attractive enough for us to proudly call you our patient.'"

Transgender people face significant barriers to medical transition even when they are slender and beautiful—but of course, beauty privilege (and by beauty, I always mean hegemonic white-supremacist standards of beauty) functions alongside other factors. As more and more people seek to remain non-binary rather than transitioning from one gender to another, the preferences for hyper-conforming gender expectations are laid bare. Gender-transition surgeries such as Caitlyn Jenner's can be held up as impressive in their success at conforming to feminine standards of beauty—including youth. Perhaps it would be more difficult for a surgeon to proudly show photos of an individual whose desired appearance would not be immediately legible to *People Magazine*. And let's not forget that the fat body is still a hated body, even when overlaid with other successful hegemonic attempts at beauty.

To put it bluntly, people who enthusiastically or significantly non-conform are often socially coded as some kind of horror, and trans people of all genders are already highly suspect both to medical professionals and in the media/public. In "Transfat," Sam Orchard explores the experience of loving his fat body as congruent with his gender expression, yet he was also told to lose weight before taking testosterone, and then again before top surgery (2021, 258). Unlike my friend Drake (who never received hormones or surgery), Sam was able to find a private provider for testosterone and accomplish weight loss in advance of surgery.

The language of horror is pervasive in discussing trans and intersex people as "freaks of nature" and in discussing fat bodies as "grotesquely obese." Lesleigh Owen (2015) reclaims the idea of monstrosity in a limited way in "Monstrous freedom: charting fat ambivalence," as she describes the freedom of non-conformity. Trans agency is not immediately respected by the medical industry, in similar ways that the agency of fat people is not respected. Even the ability to seek treatment for bronchitis or psoriasis is questioned by medical staff who would rather we focus on weight loss.

Trans people who refuse to attempt both gender conformity and weight loss are indeed an uppity lot, in the best ways possible. Bay's interviewees were seen as threatening when they were unapologetic about their gender and bodies (Bay 2017). In her academic study, Allison Taylor similarly found that some respondents feared failing to conform to fat expectations of femininity, while others reported a reclamation of space within the title "queer fat femme" to appear in a range of ways (Taylor 2021).

Katelyn Burns reflects on the compulsory prettiness that emerged during her discussions of her male-to-female gender transition with both medical professionals and others in her life. "Among late transitioning trans women that I've met we all share a similar narrative. We were always 'too' something. Too fat, too bald, too ugly, too masculine. This self-hatred comes purely from society's expectations for women's bodies and appearances" (Burns 2016).

As a large person, 6'2" and 320 pounds, Burns reported feeling that she could not succeed at passing as female even before approaching medical personnel. Of course, some who are assigned female at birth are this size, and larger. They are also set up to be pitied or seen as failed specimens of femininity. The profound hatred that our culture adopts for fat women is all the more visible because of its intersection with trans women's choices to transition. Burns explains:

> For transgender women, society's policing of female bodies is especially problematic. The intersection of fat and transphobia is a very dangerous one. If trans women are deemed too manly to be women, it spawns the hateful "man in a dress" trope from society. The ability to pass as a member of the gender she or he is transitioning to is one of the most basic considerations that any pre-transition trans person makes. Passing privilege is safety for a trans person. Safety from harassment and safety in using the correct restroom. Getting clocked as transgender oftentimes leads to abuse or violent confrontation. Visibly trans bodies are considered unworthy of dignity or respect and are marginalized from society in many of the same ways that fat bodies are. Fat people are constantly told that being fat is based on their own irresponsible decisions. Society says to just eat right and exercise and then they'll consider your feelings or respect your bodies. Society demands transgender bodies look like cis bodies and then they'll consider you a "real woman" or a "real man."

Fashions and Expectations

I used to shop at a (sadly) now defunct plus-size clothing resale store in Southern California. They sold clothing made for women. Because my work kept me traveling, pre-pandemic, I became a connoisseur of plus-size resale stores in the cities I visited. This one was by far the largest, and for more than a decade, more than half of my wardrobe came from that store. One day, I was in a fitting room (there were three, in a small alcove) and one of the staff came in loudly twittering, "Well gosh, I'm just so uncomfortable! I may laugh if you put on these dresses! Oh!" She exclaimed, finally considering the possible discomfort of those in the fitting rooms, "There's a man coming through! Oh dear, there's a man in here! Using the fitting room!"

I privately rolled my eyes at the upheaval she was causing, though of course I understand that most patrons likely considered these the "women's fitting rooms" because the store was *for* women. While clothing is obviously not inherently gendered, not everyone shares that interpretation. I mean, I wasn't on the job, but I certainly wasn't going to let this blatant gender kerfuffle pass without comment.

"As long as the fitting rooms are being used as intended, it shouldn't matter who's in them!" I called out over my curtain which separated me from the next patron who was silently trying on clothes adjacent to the man who had just been introduced to us by his gender.

The staff member continued her nervous, seemingly uncontrollable talking, attending to the man as though he needed her presence. She was treating him differently than she would treat either of us already in the fitting rooms. "I know you're just buying this as a costume, but I may laugh at you if I have to see you in a red dress!" She chortled. "You should show me though, to make sure it fits!"

The guy seemed not to enjoy being made a spectacle. "It's for a 'red dress run' so I really just need to see if I can move in it and it's not too tight. It'll be okay."

I've heard of this tradition of the Hash House Harriers, a self-described "drinking club with a running problem." I've known people who run with the group. I felt relieved that this was not a trans woman being publicly skewered by the staff person's cruel ineptitude. He bought his dress and exited before I ever saw him, but I had further words with the staff when I was making my own purchases.

Actually, she brought it up first: "Did that freak you out? That man in there?"

I said, "No, all people should mind their business in dressing rooms; why would gender matter? And furthermore, lots of people who look like 'big guys' to you might want to try and buy these clothes and wouldn't appreciate being laughed at. I don't appreciate them being laughed at around me."

The shop owner overhead me and chimed in, "It's true, lots of transsexuals and transvestites shop here because of the larger sizes."

The woman having the gender–freak-out stared at me for a moment, and then responded, thoughtful, "You know, I hadn't thought of it that way. Because I'm older and that's not been part of my experience, I just never thought of it. I wouldn't want to make anyone uncomfortable or insult people. Thank you so much for pointing that out. I'll try never to do that again."

"No problem," I said, smiling.

If only body and gender acceptance were always that easy. It's helpful to remember that they sometimes can be with the aid of simple intervention. Indeed, the retelling of this narrative here (and elsewhere) may do extra duty apart from the actual event. Most women can place themselves in that dressing room, and explore the various ways they might feel comfort or discomfort about the bodies changing clothes nearby. They can imagine the pain of being thought a "failed woman" in public.

Given the nature of compulsory prettiness for women, and for fat women in particular, and for fat women of color extra-in-particular, fashion is an oft-discussed arena for reform. Learning to dress professionally (read: white and middle-class) is an intersecting pursuit. The reclamation of bright colors, cute girlie-fashions, and horizontal stripes is also a pursuit in which clothing companies have become complicit.

As some of the aforementioned work has explored, appearances and labels create expectations. They also convey information about which assumptions should not be made. This is part of what's tricky about unmet gender expectations as when the man tried on the red dress. "Male" and "female" have been such powerful social organizers that some don't want to let go of their expectations, even if it would be liberating to do so.

In her article for Autostraddle, "Fat Queer Tells All: On Fatness and Gender Flatness," Allie Shyer chronicles her explorations of gender and clothing expression. She has found what McCrossin and others found too:

> There is little precedent for fat androgyny. Generally our androgynous icons are svelte and lacking in secondary sex characteristics. David Bowie, Tilda Swinton, Katherine Hepburn; these small-bodied, predominately white figures of androgyny have created an aesthetic with little room for deviation. This means that for those of us with bodies that do not conform to traditional standards of androgyny, we are often misread and misunderstood, even in queer spaces. Every day I struggle to present my fat queer body in a way that is intentional and binary-defiant. Sometimes this means I don't get what I want.

Shyer goes on to comment on wearing feminine clothing to a particular social gathering and then at the following gathering wearing more masculine clothing. Both group and individual expectations of Shyer seemed to shift in ways that irritated Shyer. Of course we should each be able to express ourselves as we choose, but what of others' expectations? It's easy to state the desire to dress for ourselves—to express our own tastes and interests—but as soon as we come in contact with others, the social pact kicks in. Who you seem to be influences who I may choose to be in that social exchange. I can appreciate Shyer's irritation at not being accepted as a fluid individual and I want to live in a world where I too can have mutable traits and appearances and still maintain respect and dignity. But what if someone specifically attracted to feminine women saw her at the first party and behaved accordingly—with flirtation. That individual might feel confused when no longer attracted at the second gathering. No outward outrage would be warranted, of course, but for someone with a marginalized sexuality, the social exchange may feel all the more vulnerable to begin with.

To put this another way, if someone shows up at my house dressed as a plumber, with a plumber's tool box—and I happen to need my pipes fixed—I'm going to be a lot more attached to that person's appearance-conforming behavior than if I don't need a plumber! I think dating—and other somewhat lower emotional stakes interactions too—are a bit like this. We want to know what to expect just by looking. I might be happy for the plumber who says, "Yeah, well, I used to enjoy plumbing and now I just like the outfit," so long as I didn't think my pipes were getting cleaned. What's at stake on my end? Well, my time and personal anticipation—and perhaps also my performance of excitement, and the role I occupy as householder with cash set aside for a plumber. Potentially, there are expectations on both sides of an appearance-based interaction.

I would agree with Shyer that we have far too many of these anticipation-via-appearance interactions in our culture. They feed unconscious bias—not about plumbers or potential lovers, but perhaps about who's a "thug" or who's a "good

American" if the police pull you over. People who disrupt gender are usefully disrupting the structure by which we judge all interactions.

Claiming Spacious and Compassionate Narratives Based on Already Traveled Terrain

Progress is not linear, but is aided by historical understanding. The more I can focus on—and help students discern—the scaffolding for social inequality and how it's similar across issues, the better. My 30-year-old son recently met up with me in Reykjavik for a few days of vacation before I attended a conference there. I'm grateful that we still enjoy traveling together, and that my frequent flier miles afford us this kind of week-away at times. Near the end of our time exploring the glaciers and volcanic beaches, I was turning my attention toward the conference ahead.

"I need to get a manicure before I get back to work," I said.

"Mom, that totally doesn't matter. So your nail polish is chipped? You're applying standards from a generation that's no longer making the rules in professional settings. Lighten up. You don't *need* a manicure. Maybe you want one, which is fine, but it's not a need."

I considered his comments. I don't feel "put together" without my nails done. Indeed, my mother taught me this. I was born in the 1960s; I've always appreciated a good manicure on people of any gender. My mother taught me a lot of things about appearance and fashion, and I've discarded most of those lessons—or bent them to my own standards. Is it possible that my chipped nail polish wouldn't make people think less of me? I already know it would cause me discomfort, which is the main reason to attend to it. But was my son correct?

Back in the 1990s, I worked for an elementary school district. Openly queer (and any LGBTI) people were not the norm. When I first started working there, and came out to a colleague, the district social worker, she told me to reconsider letting my sexual orientation be known to everyone. "It can define you and limit the work you're able to do," she said.

I was stunned because her views seemed retrograde at the time. Even still though, there are few workplace safeguards for those who come out as queer. One is especially vulnerable when one works with children. Back then, some of the teachers who marched in the annual big city Pride Parade with the GLSEN (Gay, Lesbian, Straight Educators Network) would march with bags over their heads, so tenuous was their acceptance, so fragile their respectability.

I worked in the district office—not directly with children. I am also gender-conforming. That is to say, I don't "look like a dyke." People didn't assume it of me, and before gay marriage became briefly legal in California the first time, few considered the possibility out loud—especially in the workplace. I didn't heed my co-worker's warnings, and I didn't suffer repercussions either. I was well-dressed, a mother, and I was exceptionally good at my job. Sure, I was fat, but in that situation, fatness seemed to somehow support a view of me as parental, rather than sexually deviant. Our visual markers morph and morph again to fit the meanings that people mean to make. (Our linguistic markers shift too—note that the words that feel appropriate to me in these paragraphs range from dyke to queer to lesbian.)

A small group of us—lesbians who worked in the district and the community—began having monthly lunches. Every month, in the small town where we worked, we were a possible spectacle for onlookers as we gathered in various local eateries. At its height, our group numbered eight. Big enough that we were up to something. What did we all have in common? We were from different schools and community agencies. A colleague came by our table to say hello once and remarked, "Well now, this is a meeting of powerful women who are great at their jobs! I don't know what else you all might be doing here together, but I know that!"

It was true. In order to be queer and working with youth—whether publicly queer to all, some, or none—we had each learned that it was vital to be beyond reproach in every other way possible. We didn't so much as steal a paperclip from the office supplies. Whether dressed more feminine, masculine or in-between, we were well-dressed, and if we ever took 20 minutes extra during those lunches, we made up two hours at the end of the day because we were dedicated to our work.

I know what I know about my manicure. My respectability is tenuous because of my fatness now more so than because of my queerness. I do a different kind of work and my aging body is fat in a different way. I don't put on full-femme-drag, but I adhere to the rituals that I enjoy—good nails, lipstick, and hair are among them. I couldn't show up to that conference thin any more than I could show up straight, or male for that matter. Those things would improve my respectability but they're well beyond my control.

As a person who considered my femme identity decades ago, I can report that while I've always understood that acceptable femininity can be used to reduce fat stigma, it's never been enough. At some point in my early thirties, privilege stopped being my aim on most days. I'm more interested in justice, and in cultivating an appearance that feels good, validates my sexuality, and cultivates solidarity with those I find kindred. I've never put full effort into femininity for a few specific reasons: that's not how I want to spend my time, nor do I want others to think hyper-conformity is worthy of my time; I want to be seen as someone who has other things going on, other interests and priorities; I want to be true to my quirky recalcitrance too. I am aware of honoring the artfulness of femme ingenuity in women's history: a path to a kind of power that doesn't play by the official rules.

When it comes to fat and gender—especially gender non-conformity (which, it could be argued, fat people are more likely to be doing, whether queer or not)—we are making our own maps of intersectional social systems. We have to do it because the rules aren't clear. And that means we can make something more compassionate of fat and gender than the models we were given for either of those things alone. Autoethnography, which is considered the realm of narrative expression in many social sciences, is helping to make those maps. Bloggers and activists and other writers are narrating fat and gender too.

The kind of narrative you're reading in this chapter can be described as autoethnography, as can much of my writing. It's social analysis based on personal storytelling. I often explain it this way: Every story is about me, but I'm not the subject. The subject is the culture and how we understand our lives within it, and within our personal choices. I tell you stories from my life in order to illuminate the culture in action, rather than holding it in stasis for the analysis to take place. Each of us is constantly making and responding to culture, after all. Stacy Holman Jones and Dan Harris suggest that we might use autoethnography not just for analysis but also to expand empathy. In their book *Queer Autoethnography* they ask,

> Could our exercise of empathy for the known become a rehearsal for empathy for the unknown, or even the unknowable? What if that empathy gave way to a recognition of the precariousness and vulnerability of the other that allows all of us—animal, vegetable and mineral—to live out the ethical responsibility to not harm one another?
>
> *(2019, 11)*

I hope that my son's generation is capable of respecting anyone wearing chipped nail polish, regardless of the person's body size and shape. I hope today's children grow up feeling greater and greater leniency about appearance hierarchy until the whole pursuit of appearance and identity privilege just feels like nonsense. And that none of us will be able to resurrect oppression based on human hierarchy ever again.

References

Bay, Kivan. 2017. "The Intersection of Fatmisia and Transmisia." *Medium*. September 18, 2017. https://medium.com/@kivabay/the-intersection-of-fatmisia-and-transmisia-78fb10f90551

Burns, Katelyn. 2016. "My Intersection with Being Trans and Fatphobia," *Gender 2.0*. January 17, 2016. https://medium.com/gender-2-0/tagged/fatphobia

Dark, Kimberly. 2018. "When Mindfulness Feels Forced." *Yoga International*. December, 2018.https://yogainternational.com/article/view/when-mindfulness-feels-forced

Dark, Kimberly. 2019. "Does This Limp Make Me Look Fat." In *Fat, Pretty, and Soon to be Old*, 89–93. Chico, CA: AK Press.

Farrell, Amy. 2011. "Feminism, Citizenship, and Fat Stigma." *Fat Shame: Stigma and the Fat Body in American Culture*, 82–116. New York: New York University Press.

Holman Jones, Stacy Linn, and Dan M. Harris. 2019. *Queering Autoethnography*. New York: Routledge, Taylor & Francis Group.

Koehle, Han. 2021. "Gender Is the Opposite of Fat." Filmed April 2021 for UCLA Rise Center's Body Liberation Series. Video, 33:14. www.youtube.com/watch?v=4fXz uaKx5RA

Mxhalisa, Nomonde. 2021. "Desirability as Access: Navigating Life at the Intersection of Fat, Black, Dark and Female." In *The Routledge International Handbook of Fat Studies*, edited by Cat Pausé and Sonya Renee Taylor, 205–209. New York: Routledge.

Orchard, Sam. 2021. "Transfat." In *The Routledge International Handbook of Fat Studies*, edited by Cat Pausé and Sonya Renee Taylor, 258–260. New York: Routledge.

Owen, Lesleigh. 2015. "Monstrous Freedom: Charting Fat Ambivalence." *Fat Studies* 4(1): 1–13. https://doi.org/10.1080/21604851.2014.896186

Oxford Reference. 2021. "cultural capital." Accessed 27 Jul. 2021. www.oxfordreference. com/view/10.1093/oi/authority.20110803095652799.

Shackelford, Hunter Ashleigh. 2021. "When you Are Already Dead." In *The Routledge International Handbook of Fat Studies*, edited by Cat Pausé and Sonya Renee Taylor, 253–257. New York: Routledge.

Shyer, Allie. 2013. May 6. "Fat queer tells all: On fatness and gender Flatness." www. autostraddle.com/fat-queer-tells-all-on-fatness-and-gender-flatness-175110/

Taylor, Allison. 2021. "Fashioning Fat Fem(me)ininities." *Fat Studies*: 1–14. DOI: 10.1080/21604851.2021.1913828

White, Francis Ray. 2021. "Fat and Trans: Towards a New Theorization of Gender in Fat Studies." In *The Routledge International Handbook of Fat Studies*, edited by Cat Pausé and Sonya Renee Taylor, 78–87. New York: Routledge.

7

FAT STORIES

Susan Stinson

A door in my second-floor apartment opens onto a small landing. The doorway is hung with a soft, loose piece of screening. It is translucent. I put rain boots on the sill of the open door to hold down the bottom of the screen, so it doesn't let insects in. On this hot summer afternoon, the screen is billowing. Filled with wind, it curves like a belly or a sail into the room where I am writing, then it flattens and falls as the breeze changes.

I can see through the screen to a box of thyme growing on the landing and, beyond that, to the big maples and a willow across the street. The leaves of the trees are tossing and swaying. The thyme is woody and exuberant, shivering slightly, a sprawl of small leaves and purple flowers. I get up and reach past the screen to run my hand over the thyme as I would over the body of a beloved. This scents my palm. I disturb a bee.

Layers of screen, thyme, and trees blow in messy rhythms like breath. I have been looking at the thyme for years as I tend it; I've been looking at the screen and trees for decades. Their surfaces let my eyes rest in shivers of motion. All three of them – screen, trees, thyme – fill space in ways akin to how my fat body moves: how it salts the air with sweat, strains the fabric of efficiency, how a chair or a limb might crack, how life insists on itself in all its forms. That is a story I find myself recounting as I look up from my computer and gaze out through the screen over the thyme to the trees. The depth and ease with which the shapes and motions of my body are in conversation with the shapes and motions of the nonhuman world is a story that sustains my life.

There is a big story about fatness that goes something like this: a fat person is fat because of a deep inner wound, flaw, or weakness. She is eating her feelings. She has too many feelings, all the wrong ones. (All respect to and solidarity with people who have eating disorders. I am exploring a different story here.) The big

DOI: 10.4324/9781003140665-10

story about fatness affects people of other genders and no gender, but the way I learned it centered on women. Through the scholarship and writing of Sabrina Strings (more on this later), I recognize this story as disciplining white women into trying to fit a narrow, racist, physical, and moral ideal while also marking Black women and other non-white groups (a category with shifting definitions) of women as being inherently less than that ideal through an association with fatness.

I recently attended a Zoom conversation between Da'Shaun L. Harrison and novelist and memoirist Kiese Laymon around the release of Harrison's book *Belly of the Beast: The Politics of Anti-Fatness as Anti-Blackness*. Harrison observed that in Southern culture, Black fat bodies get read as being associated with women. They went on to say that this puts any fat person at greater risk of gendered violence.

A straight, cisgendered male painter once told me that he had been uncomfortable when he had sex with a fat woman because she was bigger than him, and so potentially stronger. Although I was already writing fat characters, I had been so immersed in the story of my fatness as weakness, as representing ill health, and as being inherently unlovely that it took the truth-telling of another artist for me to see that men might be committed to dismissive stories about fat female and femme bodies because of a sense of threat from the power inherent in our size. I had never dreamed of using that strength, or even acknowledging that it was there, but having it brought to my attention changed that. I am a fat, 60-year-old lesbian with chronic illness and mobility issues. I am also physically strong. And I know it.

But that's not the big story about fatness. It goes more like this: The fat person (me and maybe you or someone you are at risk of becoming) would be a walking death wish if she weren't too lazy to walk. If she would turn herself over to diets, discipline, and doctors, if she would only start taking care of herself, she could achieve a normal size and a normal life. She shouldn't expect this to be easy – wanting things to be easy is part of why she is fat – but if she dedicates herself to following a few simple rules, she is good. (I heard this most recently from a nurse who was giving me a mandatory weigh-in before knee replacement surgery: "You've been good." The moral judgment was not medically necessary; it was, in fact, a significant barrier between me and medical care. But it was a familiar part of the story.) Eventually, her body will reflect that goodness by becoming thin. If not, the phrase "morbid obesity" is a judgment, a prediction, and a threat.

There are many wilder, stranger, smarter stories about fatness and gender. Telling such stories means having to fight the tenacious influence of the big story, which tends to mangle and distort any new fat story to get back to familiar, predetermined conclusions. This happens, at least in part, because there are powerful institutions heavily invested in the big story about fatness.

To illustrate what I mean, here is an example from medical research. In "The Obesity Wars and the Education of a Researcher: A Personal Account," Katherine M. Flegal describes what happened when she (a senior scientist at the Center for

Disease Control and Prevention), a CDC colleague, and two expert statisticians from the National Cancer Institute published an article that found that obesity was associated than fewer deaths relative to normal weight than had been previously predicted, and that overweight was associated with slightly fewer deaths than normal weight. She writes, "We were unprepared for the firestorm that followed" (Flegal 2021, 1). In this case, Flegal notes that they were not actually telling a story but presenting data. She adds, "However, some apparently had trouble grasping this…" (Flegal 2021, 4). The details of the "damage control" (Flegal 2021, 2) her group faced from various other scientists and public health organizations is best read in her article, but for the purposes of considering fatness and story, her seemingly modest conclusion is illuminating: "Scientific findings should be evaluated on their merits, not on the basis of whether they fit a desired narrative" (Flegal 2021, 4). This desired narrative is the big story about fatness.

If well-respected researchers working from within powerful institutions are attacked for simply accurately reporting what the data they analyze reflects about fatness and mortality, how can storytellers hope to be heard? But there are writers with the will and craft to explore themes of fatness and gender in ways that let these things acquire and shed meanings; hum with multiple resonances; and/or create new cognitive, emotional, and cultural spaces in which a broader range of fat, gendered experiences might be lived, shared, and told.

Beginning to tell stories about fatness that run counter to "the desired narrative" can be daunting. Language becomes elusive. In the early eighties, I was a member of the Feminist Alliance/Lesbian Caucus student organization at the University of Colorado. When I was in my senior year, our group received a call for writing about fatness for the anthology that became *Shadow on a Tightrope: Writings by Women on Fat Oppression* (Aunt Lute 1983). I stared at the flyer, fascinated and baffled. I was a fat lesbian. I had been taking fiction and poetry workshops and considered writing to be my vocation. I was also deeply engaged in the feminist project of reclaiming language. For example, I freely used the word "dyke." But, at that moment, I couldn't imagine what stories I could possibly tell about fat. I knew that being fat had profoundly shaped my life, but that knowledge evoked experiences of shame, failure, and rejection for me. Having my work published was one of my fiercest ambitions but writing about being fat seemed to risk shutting off my best route out of the cultural stories I was trying to escape. Did I have to bring my stigmatized body with me into my writing life, into the world of my imagination? And wasn't obsession with weight a trivial concern?

In the end, I didn't try to write anything for the fat feminist anthology, but my inability to do so haunted me. I graduated and moved from Colorado to Boston. I got a job and tried to figure out how to be a writer. One thing I knew was that meant I had to write, so, when I wasn't working at a paid job, I did. The first thing I started writing about were experiences of fatness.

The year was 1984, more or less. George Orwell was in the air, and so was Tina Turner. I was sitting on the floor in the basement of New Words, the feminist bookstore in Cambridge, MA, still a little excited that I had taken the subway to get there. This was a staged reading of Judith Stein's *The Purim Megillah*, a feminist retelling of the Book of Esther. A fat woman read the part of beautiful Queen Esther, who speaks bravely to her husband on behalf of her people. The banished Queen Vashti goes to live with a band of women in the desert.

This was the first time I had ever been to a reading featuring the work of an out lesbian. Judith was fat, too. Not only that, but she had an essay in *Shadow on a Tightrope*, which had come out in June 1983. I was in a fat women's discussion group co-facilitated by her partner, Meridith Lawrence, but I had never met Judith. Most people at the reading were sitting in metal folding chairs. I was in the back. As the staged reading went on, I cried, overwhelmed to see that a writer's fatness could be part of her literary choices. That her work was welcome at this feminist bookstore. And that a roomful of women had come to listen. It is hard to capture in 2021 how strange that was, but it was revelatory. It made me believe that I could write poems, essays, and novels as the fat lesbian I was, and that there would be readers for them.

After the reading, I was invited to go with Judith, Meridith, and others to the S&S restaurant across the street. The restaurant was named for how the great grandmother of the owners would greet her customers in Yiddish: "Es and es." Eat and eat. We were a long table full of fat queers. It was a beautiful, unashamed aria of what to eat, how to make friends (etc.), and, since I wasn't Jewish, how to behave when invited to be part of traditions that were not my own. Judith, radiant, came around the table to greet each one of us. It was a profound experience of abundance, boisterousness, and community.

That is how I came to fatness, gender, and story. Telling the story of the evening is a way to honor this tradition and community. Some of people who participated in it have died. The bookstore is also gone. It was fleeting and simple, a reading and dinner with soon-to-be friends, but the story may evoke this moment for others who were not there, who were perhaps not yet born, but who find themselves engaged with the question of how to tell more varied, stranger, more subtle stories of fatness. This is one way it happened in one specific time, place, and community.

The big story about fatness – and, of course, there is more than one – extends to communities, to entire groups of people. In *Fearing the Black Body: The Racial Origins of Fat Phobia*, Sabrina Strings traces the origin of fat hatred to Enlightenment era efforts among Europeans to develop theories of race and white supremacy. Strings writes, "The image of fat black women as 'savage' and 'barbarous' in art, philosophy, and science, and as 'diseased' in medicine has been used to both degrade black women and discipline white women" (Strings 2019, 211). She is clear: "In other words, the fear of the black body was integral to the creation of the slender aesthetic among fashionable white Americans" (Strings 2019, 212).

Within the same paragraph, Strings points out that this connection has been neglected by white feminist scholars and historians. This is true, and it extends to storytellers, too. Within my knowledge and memory, everyone at the beloved table I describe above was white. We were not the same in class, ethnicity, or religion, but we belonged to what Isabel Wilkerson has identified in her book *Caste: The Origins of Our Discontents* as an upper caste in a violently enforced caste system. I wanted to transform the brutal hierarchies we lived within, and I was learning from others who wanted that, too. We identified our practices, communities, and movement as "fat liberation" with the intention of making explicit connections to other liberation struggles. In the introduction to my first book, *Belly Songs: In Celebration of Fat Women*, Elana Dykewomon wrote:

> To have the body of a Jew adds another level to my ambivalence about my body. These imposed body hatreds remind me of Michelle Cliff's Claiming an Identity They Taught Me To Despise, of the intersections of racism and woman-hating. The widespread cultural effects of having so many despised bodies on the landscape are unbelievable (and so, of course, few really take this seriously).
>
> *(Dykewomon 1993, i)*

I saw this, but my craft and imagination were limited/are limited by my caste. In her unflinching book of literary and cultural criticism, *The Origin of Others*, Toni Morrison writes, "The danger of sympathizing with the stranger is the possibility of becoming a stranger. To lose one's racial-ized rank is to lose one's own valued and enshrined difference" (Morrison 2017, 41). The ways that power is distributed and defended in the world make the biases of the upper caste dangerous to everyone. But working within limitations in relation to power and privilege is part of the nature of writing a story.

In *Craft in the Real World: Rethinking Fiction Writing and Workshopping*, Matthew Salesses does a masterful job of challenging accepted models of teaching and talking about story. He describes his overall project like this: "to take craft out of some imaginary vacuum (as if meaning in fiction is separate from meaning in life) and return it to its cultural and historical context" (Salesses 2021, xiii).

In a discussion of the audience, theme, and purpose of a story, he writes:

> You are asked to step into the role of the implied reader, and by figuring out the expectations you should read with, you create an image of the implied author. Craft is about how the words on the page do this: what expectations the writer engages with imply whom both the implied reader and implied author are and what they should believe in and care about, what they need explained and/or named, where they should focus their attention, what meaning to draw from the text.
>
> *(Salesses 2021, 62)*

A story in which both the implied author and reader are fat are rare. Most people who read such a story are spending time in unfamiliar mental territory that they may not have ever tried to imagine. A person who engages honestly with such a story may be changed by it. Or it might create an experience of thought and reflection that opens the possibility of later change. Salesses writes, "Craft is the history of which kind of stories have typically held power – and for whom – so it is also the history of which stories have typically been omitted" (Salesses 2021, 39). He defines tone as an orientation toward the world (Salesses 2021, 50).

In her essay collection *Wow, No Thank You*, Samantha Irby's tone is what a *New York Times* review by Parul Sehgal calls "wildly, seditiously funny" (Sehgal 2020). Sehgal writes, "This is her voice: deadpan, confiding, companionable. It can ascend to high silliness … and then, without any strain, carry us into the darkest rooms in her past" (Sehgal 2020). This tone lets Irby write about poverty, racism, grief, and Crohn's Disease and also light up all kinds of moments with sentences like, "Sure, sex is fun, but have you ever cut your own hair?" (Irby 2020, 132). This is part of a long incantation in an essay called "Lesbian Bed Death." It reminds me of Gertrude Stein's great poem, "Lifting Belly." Irby's tone is an orientation toward the world, for sure, one that took me (and a lot of other people; the book is a bestseller) to the hardest places gasping with laughter instead of terror.

In "Season 1, Episode 1," Irby describes pitching her first book as a television series. Her list of themes includes inflammatory bowel disease. She writes,

> I don't treat my Crohn's like it's an albatross around my neck, like I'm laboring under the weight of this oppressive disease…. It's a serious topic that can be dealt with in a really funny way while also repping for the chronically ill and constantly medicated, like me.
>
> *(Irby 2020, 226–227)*

Irby is explicit that the implied audience for the work includes the "chronically ill and constantly medicated" (Irby 2020, 227). This contrasts with some early writing around fatness in which some authors sought to establish that fatness is not unhealthy. Here, chronic illness and its discontents are fully present. I experience the wit and explicitness about both bodily functions and messy feelings as a relief.

Another theme in the television pitch comes under the heading, "fat people doing fat shit without crying big fat tears about it" (Irby 2020, 228). As a fat reader who has long found most stories about fat characters presented in popular culture to be profoundly unsatisfying and barely related to actual human beings, the tone of Irby's description of this theme makes me feel released, welcomed, and fought for. (*This Is Us*, mentioned below, is a popular television drama that ran for six seasons.)

> I can't watch This Is Us because even though the brothers are hot and the dad is a smoke show, in the first couple episodes the fat girl doesn't get to be much more than "fat," and wow, no thank you! Maybe there are fat people sitting

around silently weeping about being fat every minute of every day, but that is a redemptive arc thin people like to see on television, and it's just not the fucking truth.

(Irby 2020, 228)

Irby could not be clearer that she has stakes in how stories about fat people are told, and that she wants her stories to be different. She moves in her work from performance to essays to stories that became images on television, then back to essays. Amid her pitch about fat themes in her work, she writes, "… sometimes I hate my body not because it's fat, but mostly because I never wake up in the morning to discover it had transformed into a wolf or a shark overnight" (Irby 2020, 228). This wish to cross species is more rewarding to ponder or attempt to embody than the crying of big fat tears. In "Girls Gone Mild," Irby's account of taking up partying again in her late thirties, suddenly her vision sharpens, she can smell every bead of sweat in the club. Then, "I hear the seams of my shirt ripping as my chest broadens, tufts of coarse hair forcing their way out of the collar from of my shirt. I bolt from my seat as I feel my claws split my shoes open" (Irby 2020, 33). The character of Irby in this essay is a werewolf until – "muzzle retracting and haunches reverting to their gelatinous state" (Irby 2020, 33) – she gets home to take a shower and eat chips. It's funny and shocking. In this essay, the character changes dramatically, physically, beyond the rules of bodies as we know them. In the collection as a whole, the world changes to become a place in which Irby's voice shapes popular culture. That change is not fiction, but it is built on story.

In Elizabeth McCracken's dark fairy tale, "Birdsong from the Radio," Leonora is a mother who becomes a monster, many monsters. As with most fairy tales, the heart of it is in the telling. It is a gradual transformation from a story of family life – a mother telling stories, nuzzling her children's necks, taking bites; three children laughing, "Rosa, Marco, Dolly plump loaves of bread, delicious;" (McCracken 2021, 108) a father busy making radios – to layers on layers of loss. As the children get bigger, Leonora bites, demanding love. Once thin, she thickens. "She had gone mad, or was going" (McCracken 2021, 110). She keeps trying to eat her children, who huddle together in the same bed, afraid.

So she had to sneak. The weight of her as she sat on the edge of their beds in the middle of the night was raptorial: ominous yet indistinct. At any moment, the children thought, she might spread her arms and pull them from the sheets through the ceiling and into the sky, the better to harm them elsewhere.

(McCracken 2021, 110)

The weight was raptorial. She is getting fatter, yet she might fly, carrying them to harm. The children decide that they must leave to save themselves. They tell their father, who understands nothing. He takes them to a new house and hires "a nanny, Madeleine, a jug-eared, freckled beauty. A good girl, as her father later described her to the news cameras" (McCracken 2021, 111). The day after her twenty-first birthday, still drunk, she crashed her car on ice after she picks up the children from school. All of them die.

" 'No children,' thought Leonora. She had intended to get herself upright and go looking for them. She should have eaten them when she could" (McCracken 2021, 112).

Now, the story – which has been spent time with the children at a seemly distance and is in Madeleine's thoughts as she dies – stays close to Leonora as she grieves beyond the boundaries of what human society can tolerate. Able to bear it or not is not a question for Leonora. She is too deeply in it. It is of her. She hears the voices of her children on the many family radios. Then the voices of her children are gone, leaving a feral burble she still hears after she turns the radios off.

Things get even more agonizing and extraordinary:

> She felt her torso, where her children would have been, had she managed to eat them.
>
> Not everyone who stops being human turns animal, but Leonora did.
>
> It was time to leave the house. The top of her back grew humped with ursine fat, and she shambled like that, too, bearlike through the aisles of the grocery at the end of the street. She shouldered the upright fridges full of beer; she sniffed the air of the checkout lanes. Panda-eyed and eagle-toed and lion-tailed, with a long braid down her back that snapped as though with muscles and vertebrae. Her insides, too. Animals of the dark and deep. Her kidneys dozing moles; her lungs, folded bats. The organs that had authored her children: jellyfish, jellyfish, eel, eel, manatee.
>
> I am dead. I am operated by animals.
>
> Her wandering took her to the bakery.
>
> *(McCracken 2021, 113)*

This is a fat person deep in grief, but she is far from crying big fat tears about being fat. Instead, her fatness marks her wildness, her animal self – selves! – the voraciousness of both her love and her grief. She begins to frequent the bakery, where she sees the shapes of her children in the challah. She cradles the loaf, then she eats it, every morning. It is a discomfiting act of communion, bread transfigured into beloved flesh. When other mothers of the neighborhood look at her tearing into challah in the bakery, "Leonora could see the rictus of judgment on the mother's face" (McCracken 2021, 115). I am not Leonora and can only nod to her inner beasts, but I have known the rictus of judgment on the faces of many strangers if they should happen to catch sight of me in the fat body I have, let alone see me eating. Having the phrase "the rictus of judgment" allows language for a lifetime of stiffened and stiffening encounters. Leonora is experiencing so much more than this. Still, the phrase is a feast in a realm of experiences for which I am starved for precise and nuanced words.

Five years pass. Leonora – "poisoned, padded, eyes sunk in her face" (McCracken 2021, 116) – is a monument while the deaths of her children are forgotten. Then a man approaches her in the bakery. It is the father of Madeleine, the nanny, come to try to redeem Leonora. The animals in her body roar back to life. She remembers sitting at the back of the church at the funeral for the children: "Nobody spoke to her. She was a mother who'd let her children go, a creature so awful nobody believed in her. She'd had to turn herself into a monster in order to be seen" (McCracken 2021, 118).

Madeleine's father has a dead child, too. Leonora feels his sorrow and guilt "like schools of tiny flicking fish who swim through bone instead of ocean. He was not entirely human anymore either. Indeed, she could hear the barking dog of his heart, wanting an answer. Her heart snarled back, but tentatively" (McCracken 2021, 118).

There is nothing more urgent and riveting than Leonora's feelings in this moment. Her organs are turning in their burrows. "She was thankful to remember that she was a monster. Many monsters. Not a chimera but a vivarium. Her heart snarled, and snarled, and snarled" (McCracken 2021, 119). A vivarium is an enclosure, container or structure adapted or prepared for keeping animals under seminatural conditions for observation or study or as pets. Leonora might do anything.

What she does is offer to buy him a challah. In the last line of the story, she says, "It will be a pleasure to watch you eat" (McCracken 2021, 119). Leonora's pleasure was the last thing I expected to emerge from this moment. The same is true of her thankfulness. These feelings are still burrowing in me as I read and reread the story.

"Eight Bites" by Carmen Maria Machado is also a fairy tale of family, loss, and a kind of haunting that becomes something much bigger. In it, the despised and discarded fat of a woman's body becomes a ghost, a monster, a daughter, something "mothersoft," and an immortal being.

It takes place in a family of women: sisters, mothers, daughters. A woman living on Cape Cod has learned from mother, who is now dead, that eight bites is all she needs to eat at any meal. She tries this but chooses to follow her three sisters into bariatric surgery. Her sisters help her. Her daughter, over the phone, objects. The surgery works. She gets smaller. She can eat just eight bites: "Before, I would have been growling, climbing up the walls from want. Now I feel only slightly empty, and fully content" (Machado 2017, 161).

But she wakes with something small standing over her. At first, she thinks that this is her daughter as a child, but she realizes it can't be her. It has a person-shaped outline, with weight when it sits on her bed. Most of the time, though it hides, breathing audibly, making things creak. When she asks her sisters if they'd felt a presence "after," they all have. One speaks of her joy, another her inner beauty, another her former shame. When she finally finds the being in the basement, it's body-shaped, dripping, and looks like her daughter. Closer, "it smells warm, like toast" (Machado 2017, 165). As the woman gets closer, she is moved to rejection, then violence:

> I kneel down next to it. It is a body with nothing it needs: no stomach or bones or mouth. Just soft indents. I crouch down and stroke its shoulder, or what I think is its shoulder.
>
> It turns and looks at me. It has no eyes, but still, it looks at me. She looks at me. She is awful but honest. She is grotesque but she is real.
>
> I shake my head. "I don't know why I wanted to meet you," I say. "I should have known."
>
> She curls a little tighter. I lean down and whisper where an ear might be.
>
> "You are unwanted," I say. A tremor ripples her mass.
>
> I do not know I am kicking her until I am kicking her. She has nothing and I feel nothing except she seems to solidify before my foot meets her, so every kick is more satisfying than the last. I reach for a broom and I pull a muscle swinging back and in and back and in, and the handle breaks off in her and I kneel down and pull soft handfuls of her body out of herself, and I throw them against the wall, and I do not know I am screaming until I stop, finally.
>
> I find myself wishing she would fight back, but she doesn't. Instead, she sounds like she is being deflated. A hissing, defeated wheeze.
>
> *(Machado 2017, 165)*

She walks away and goes on to live life as a new woman. Sometimes, she can still hear this unloved being in the house. The story moves into future tense as she describes the last time she sees the being, which will be the day of her death. She will wake, anticipating a visit from her daughter and granddaughter, feeling a great pressure on her chest. "Arms will lift me from my bed – her arms. They will be mother-soft, like dough and moss" (Machado 2017, 167). The woman will start to ask a question, then realize that she knows this:

> by loving me when I did not love her, by being abandoned by me, she has become immortal. She will outlive me by a hundred million years; more, even. She will outlive my daughter, and my daughter's daughter, and the earth will teem with her and her kind, their inscrutable forms and unknowable destinies.
>
> *(Machado 2017, 167)*

The body – the soft, indented, fat life force – will bear her away like an angel of death or a god as the woman whispers apologies. These are well-deserved apologies, although most likely irrelevant to the inscrutable, immortal being – one of many – that her rejected and attacked fatness has become. These immortal beings will inherit the earth in ways that those who have tried to control their bodies through manipulations and deprivations in service to gendered cultural imperatives cannot begin to understand. Still, there is connection between the woman and her rejected fatness that lasts for her entire human lifetime. Even she will see it and be sorry in the end as the being made by her rejection – this organless body – will gently and without accusation help her leave her life when the time for her death comes.

On the previous page, the woman in "Eight Bites," narrating beach summers as a new woman, says, "If you're brave, you'll turn your body over to this water that is practically an animal, and so much larger than yourself" (Machado 2017, 166). Samantha Irby, Elizabeth McCracken, and Carmen Maria Machado have all written stories and essays that risk turning the imagination over to fatness in ways that enter water that might be an animal or many animals, but, for all its salt, is something much bigger and wilder than big fat tears. Reading them and engaging with the monsters in this work is like the moment I first understood that physical strength could come with my fatness, when I understood that strength could be a kind of power that looked nothing like what I had been trained to recognize or desire. Fatness, monsters, and power are not containable, simple, or pretty. These stories about them by Irby, McCracken and Machado are nothing like the neat insistence of the big story about fatness, the big lie.

I write about these stories in the bathtub, with a wooden tray resting on the edges to hold my notebook. This tray has slats like a bridge. The water is like skin with my body beneath. Air is the skin of the world with water, bodies, trees, screens, and thyme within. A story is a wave. It's a rustle in the wind. It's the fat of my belly rising under the water, falling to rest on my thighs. A story is a fat, middle-aged woman who may become a beast. Deeply imagined stories of fatness and gender fill out the body of the world.

Bibliography

Dykewomon, Elana. 1993. "Introduction." In *Belly Songs: In Celebration of Fat Women*, by Susan Stinson, i–iii. Northampton, Massachusetts: Orogeny Press.

Flegal, Katherine M. 2021. "The Obesity Wars and the Education of a Researcher: A Personal Account." *Progress in Cardiovascular Diseases*, June. https://doi.org/10.1016/j.pcad.2021.06.009

Harrison, Da'Shaun. 2021. *Belly of the Beast: The Politics of Anti-Fatness as Anti-Blackness*. Berkeley, California: North Atlantic Books.

Irby, Samantha. 2020. *Wow, No Thank You: Essays*. New York: Vintage Books.

Machado, Carmen Maria. 2017. "Eight Bites." In *Her Body and Other Parties: Stories*, 149–168. Minneapolis, Minnesota: Graywolf Press.

McCracken, Elizabeth. 2021. "Birdsong from the Radio." *The Souvenir Museum: Stories*. First edition. 107–119. New York: Ecco.

Morrison, Toni. 2017. *The Origin of Others*. The Charles Eliot Norton Lectures, 2016. Cambridge, Massachusetts: Harvard University Press.

Salesses, Matthew. 2021. *Craft in the Real World: Rethinking Fiction Writing and Workshopping*. New York: Catapult.

Schoenfielder, Lisa, and Barb Wieser, eds. 1983. *Shadow on a Tightrope: Writings by Women on Fat Oppression*. 1st ed. Iowa City, Iowa: Aunt Lute Books.

Sehgal, Parul. 2020. "The Wildly Funny Samantha Irby Is Back, Not a Moment Too Soon." Review of *Wow, No Thank You: Essays* by Samantha Irby of *New York Times*, April 1, 2020. www.nytimes.com/2020/04/01/books/review-samantha-irby-wow-no-thank-you.html

Stein, Gertrude, and Richard Kostelanetz. 1980. *The Yale Gertrude Stein: Selections*. New Haven: Yale University Press.

Stein, Judith. 1986. *The Purim Megillah: A Feminist Retelling*. Cambridge, Massachusetts: Bobbeh Meisehs Press.

Strings, Sabrina. 2019. *Fearing the Black Body: The Racial Origins of Fat Phobia*. New York, NY: New York University Press.

Wilkerson, Isabel. 2020. *Caste: The Origins of Our Discontents*. First edition. New York: Random House.

PART IV

Historicizing Fatness

Gender and fat have not always had the same meaning. It has changed over time, and not always in a linear fashion. These two writers ask us to think about the importance of time period when we consider gender and fat in two very different contexts. Hill pushes us to think about historiography itself—in other words, the ways that the contemporary thinking of historians shapes the scholarship they do, including our ways of thinking about ancient representations of fatness. Purkiss challenges us to think critically about why African American women would choose to engage in anti-fat practices.

DOI: 10.4324/9781003140665-11

8

THE POLITICS OF FAT AND GENDER IN THE ANCIENT WORLD

Susan E. Hill

Despite what one might see in the media, no discussion of fat—in any of its multiple forms—is ever simple or straightforward. Fat, as a substance, is, as Christopher Forth points out, "mutable and ambiguous" because it can be solid or liquid; fat's variability as matter is also reflected in its multiple cultural meanings: "the sensuous qualities of fat do not exist separately from culturally shaped perceptions and discourses that make sense of them (Forth 2019, 23; 36).[1] Fat, however, is not simply materially or culturally slippery: scientific discourse also seems challenged to characterize it appropriately. Ole Mouritsen notes that fat is fundamental to human life, as important as "proteins and genes" (Mouritsen 2015, 1). Yet, he argues that fats are given less attention by scientists because they fail to adhere to the "central dogma that molecular structure controls function (Mouritsen 2015, 1). Instead of exhibiting "clear structure and *order*," which would indicate their functional value, fats are instead characterized by "*disorder* and a lack of any obvious structural elements" (Mouritsen 2015, 16). Together, the scientific bias for order and structure along with fat's malleability and variability reflects the challenges of elucidating its social and cultural meanings, as well as its scientific significance. Fat is indeed what I have previously called a "cultural trickster," sometimes associated with life, sometimes with death: good or bad, depending on time, writer/creator, and context (Hill 2011, 13).

Sometimes, fat is perceived to be beneficial. Fat is not only "the most important part of our brain and the second most important of all other soft tissue" in the human body (Mouritsen 2015, 1), "fat"—as in "oil" or "grease" or fat that is ingested—is fundamental to many aspects of cooking. Samin Nosrat, author of *Salt, Fat, Acid, Heat: Mastering the Elements of Good Cooking,* notes that "fat is essential for achieving the full spectrum of flavors and textures of good cooking, and that it is responsible for "five distinct textures: crisp, creamy, flaky, tender, and

DOI: 10.4324/9781003140665-12

light" that "excite our palates" (Nosrat 2017). Particularly good acting roles that offer opportunities for an actor to show their skills have been described as "full of fat lines," and, at least since biblical times, the phrase "the fat of the land" has always been a reference to the best possible earth that grows the most abundant, most nourishing food (OED online 2021).

Yet, even when fat is perceived to be good, it seems that negative societal perceptions of fat must be acknowledged: even Mouritsen concedes that the typical perspective on fat is as "something vicious" that is "dangerous to our health and well-being" (Mouritsen 2015, 1). Perhaps paying homage to the wickedness of fat will make his argument that the ingestion of fat was necessary for the expansion of brain volume that led to "emergence of modern humans" more palatable to his readers (Forth 2019, 17). The plethora of recipes that contain fat substitutes are legion. And, it might be fine for the land to be fat, but it is not fine for you and me to be fat.

Indeed, having a fat body—at least in the modern, Western world—is never perceived to be good, hence the \$78 billion dollar weight loss industry (Research and Markets 2021), which continues to balloon despite the evidence that around 80% of people who diet fail to maintain their weight loss for 12 months (Engber 2020). The media shows us every moment of every day that thin is beautiful and fat is ugly, always interpreted as undesirable, inevitably conjuring ideas of excess, gluttony, laziness, and stupidity.

The meanings of fat are rendered even more complex when we add historical and cultural perceptions of gender into the mix. In the ancient Western world, fat has a variety of diverse, sometimes contrary, meanings. The fat, male body can be a sign of wealth and power and/or overindulgence and weakness. If a fat male body is portrayed in a negative light, it may be characterized as immoral, excessive, and inappropriately feminine. Fat male bodies are often found in satire, used to make fun of cultural situations and practices. If a male athlete has a fat or gluttonous body, it may be primarily an indication of his strength and ability "to beat one's opponents and thus to demonstrate one's place in the social hierarchy" (Bažant 1982, 131). Fat female bodies have been associated with fertility and abundance. As with masculine fat bodies, the fat female body can also be used as a vehicle for humor or satire. On rare occasions, the fat female body may also indicate power and strength.

Despite any variations in the meaning of the fat body in the ancient world, what is abundantly clear is that most discussions about it are tinged with contemporary scorn for the fat body: it seems that ancient fat bodies are inevitably morally depraved, examples of the grotesque, eminently laughable or, in some rare instances, explained away as not actually fat at all. Whatever we can say about fat bodies in the ancient world—no matter how complicated the conversations are to begin with—what we often end up with is simply a recitation of the disdain and derision we find in contemporary views. Ancient fat bodies are a perfect example of the truism that "however remote in time the events there recounted may seem to be, the history in reality refers to present needs and present situations wherein those events vibrate" (Croce 1941, 19).

Here, I offer examples of contemporary understandings of the interplay between fat and gender in the ancient Western world, focusing on ideas of fertility and leadership. Though these examples are not comprehensive (how could they be?!), they are representative of the ways that the complex and varied relationships between fat and gender have been consistently articulated by present-day interpreters. My approach is thus primarily historiographical in the sense that I am interested in attempting to understand both how fatness was perceived by people in the ancient world and how ancient fat bodies are understood by those attempting to make sense of them from contemporary perspectives. In examining the ways that we understand ancient ideas of fertility and leadership, two things are certain: the contemporary disdain for the fat body inevitably shapes discussions of what ancient fat bodies can mean. If, however, we can recognize, and set aside, the overwhelmingly negative cultural messages we constantly receive about fat bodies today, we discover that the meanings of fat bodies in the ancient world are multiple, often contradictory, distinctly contextual, and fascinating.

Must Ancient Female Figurines Always Be About Fertility?

In her article, "Fertility and Gender in the Ancient Near East," Stephanie Budin criticizes the prevailing "fertility = female" paradigm that seems to guide the interpretation of female images throughout history (Budin 2015, 30). She argues that the contemporary understanding of the female role in fertility and reproduction has been imposed on the past, thus eliding an understanding of any connections between males and fertility. She notes that there is a growing interest in examining the ways that women in the ancient world are associated with ideas other than fertility, and in the ways masculinity is also associated with fertility. Alas, she notes that, "perhaps oddly, there is a general tendency in scholarship to divide notions of fertility along gendered lines: One studies female fertility (or not), or masculine fertility, but not the combined contributions of both" (Budin 2015, 31). One might make a similar critique of discussions of fertility and fatness: one might study ancient fat bodies (which may or may not have to do with fertility) or one might study fertility; rarely is an ancient image of a fat female body examined outside of the parameters of fat female = fertility. Moreover, images of ancient fat male bodies that are interpreted as relating to fertility are also marked as feminine, since they, too, have large breasts and bellies.

The most apparent link between fat and fertility in the ancient world centers on a group of around 200 small, female figurines dated to the Upper Paleolithic or Late Stone Age (approx. 50,000–10,000 BCE) found across Europe and Eurasia. The most famous of these is the Venus of Willendorf, which was found in 1908 in Austria. Some of these figurines, like the Willendorf, are fat; others are not, though many of them have exaggerated genitalia, breasts, or buttocks. In their early interpretations of these figurines, male scholars assumed that they were made by males for males, and that their nudity signaled their purpose as sexual or erotic items (Nelson 1990, 17). The assumption—that any female nude is inevitably sexual—is problematized by their fatness, which sits uneasily with their purported sexual purpose:

> In spite of being naked, however, it would seem that the fat figurines have little sex appeal to modern male scholars. This has called forth various explanations, ranging from assertions that they are stylized, to a suggestion that you cannot tell *what* might have turned on those prehistoric men (you can almost see the shrug and the wink), to a rejection of the erotic argument on the grounds that the figurines are simply too grotesque!
>
> *(Nelson 1990, 17)*

Fat female bodies must represent sexuality, and therefore, fertility, because they can represent nothing else.

When anthropologist Maria Gimbutas began publishing her analysis of these figurines, she also argued that they represent fertility and sexuality, though she interpreted them in a much more positive light. For her, these are figurines that represent mother goddesses and harken back to an egalitarian, matrilineal, and peaceful time, before the advent of the patriarchy, which ushered in war and hierarchy (Steinfels 1990). But, as feminist anthropologists have pointed out, these figurines could have numerous other meanings, as well. Soffer et.al. point out that many of these figurines, including the Willendorf, appear to be decorated or clothed, revealing the importance of plant-based weaving and basket-making in Upper Paleolithic cultures. They speculate that the products produced through this labor were highly valued because they were reproduced on objects carved out of ivory, bone, and stone: "Simply put, we suggest that being depicted wearing such garments associated the wearer and by extension, the maker of them with a marked position of prestige" Soffer et.al. 2000, 524). And, Patricia Rice argues that, taking into account the wide variety of figurines found, their focus is not merely on fertility, but on all of the stages of womanhood. Given this, Rice suggests that the figurines "represent some combination of secular pragmatism and sacred mysteriousness, rather than either exclusively" (Rice 1981, 412).

What is interesting about all of this speculation is that, if these figurines are not solely about fertility, and their fatness is not (only) about pregnancy, why are many of them fat? To explain this, LeRoy McDermott speculates that they are actually not fat. Instead, their fat bodies are simply the result of what happens when a woman looks down at her own body and recreates it in a carving (McDermott 1996, 231). If these are self-created figurines, McDermott speculates that, instead of being "embarrassingly obese," they are not fat at all because "what has actually been seen as evidence of obesity or adiposity is actually the foreshortening effect of self-inspection" (McDermott 1996, 228, 245). Agreeing with Rice, McDermott concludes that the figurines are representations of female development over time. And, their fatness is simply a side effect of self-creation without mirrors. From McDermott's perspective, there is no reason to pay attention to the fatness of these figurines.

Although McDermott's thesis has been widely criticized, at least it suggests agency on the part of Upper Paleolithic women, who were carving figures of their own bodies (McDermott 1996, 248ff). What remains challenging about these figurines in the context of thinking about gender and fat is that if their fatness means anything, it must be about fertility. There is no room to envision these figurines as symbols of beauty, desirability, or as an aspirational body type. Such speculation is simply beyond the imagination of contemporary interpreters of the ancient past. Indeed, readings of ancient statues that may or may not be about female fertility are as conceptually slippery as some material forms of fat.

If discussions of fat female figurines focus primarily on reproductive fertility, discussions of male fertility figures tend to focus not on their bodies, but on their activities (Budin 2015, 32; Roth 2016, 190). There certainly are many gods in the ancient world who are involved in deeds that fall under the broad category of "fertility." Most of these deities' acts, however, are not about reproductive creation, but rather about world creation. In these contexts, the only feature of the god's body that may be important is the penis, which, if represented, is often portrayed as exceedingly large in comparison to the rest of the god's body. A good example of this is the Greek god, Priapus, who is a fertility deity associated with vegetation, gardens, sexuality, and male genitalia, and is always represented with a huge erection, even though he is often depicted as "dwarfish" (Theoi.com 2021).

There is one ancient Near Eastern fertility deity who is definitely fat: Hapi, the Egyptian god of the Nile. What is interesting about representations of Hapi and other fecundity figures in Egypt, is that they are predominantly male, and are depicted with "long pendulous breasts" that are "distinguished from those of normal or fat women by their pendulous character" and stomachs that "spill over their belts and continue down to the groin" (Baines 1985, 93; 95). Although John Baines, who has studied the iconography of fecundity figures in Egypt extensively, argues that these figures are male and fat, other descriptions of these figures suggest that we know that Hapi is a fertility god because of his "female breasts" (El-Sawi 1983, 7) or because he "was depicted as a man with long hair and heavy breasts of an old woman, combining both the male and female life producing forces" (Almasri and Mustafa 2019, 64). It seems that the fertility of the Nile cannot be represented by a male deity because any figure with large breasts must be female and must represent fertility.

The contemporary tendency to interpret these ancient representations of fat females only as fertility figures, and the propensity to interpret fat male deities as fertility figures precisely because they look like fat females, suggests that, when confronted by anomalous or ambiguous figures that challenge our ideas of sex and gender, modern interpreters tend to fall back on contemporary understandings.

This is not surprising, but does suggest that the fat female = fertility and fat male = femininity reading of ancient figures is well-entrenched in the contemporary imagination. But, what if the fat, male body is not a feminized body? What if the fat female body is not about fertility? Refusing to engage alternative interpretations may not only undermine our ability to get a clear understanding of the meanings of the fat body, it may also undercut our capacity to recognize complex understandings of gender in the ancient Western world that may expand our awareness beyond binary categories (Robb and Harris 2017, 134). Expanding our scholarly perspectives on what fat bodies might mean could open up new avenues of exploration for understanding the meanings and importance of fat in the ancient world.

Can a Fat Man Be a Good Leader?

Lazy, self-indulgent, unintelligent: these are common perceptions of the fat body in the contemporary Western world. How and why were these connections made? Have fat people always been stigmatized? In the ancient Western world, people did believe that virtue and vice were written on the physical body. The pseudoscience of physiognomy carefully delineated how body features—physique, proportion, hair, eyes, voice, and so on—reveal a person's character. Indeed, Gian Franco Chiai notes that there is so much evidence in ancient literary, archeological, and biographical sources of connections between bodily appearance and moral character that he proposes the idea of "a 'common sense physiognomics' to refer to a shared common knowledge and perception of human physiognomy by ordinary people" (Chiai 2019, 204).

Yet, when we look more carefully at the ways in which physiognomy was used to judge character in the ancient world, we see that connections between appearance and character are always already full of contradictions and inconsistencies: it may be, for example, that the fat body is sometimes seen as evidence of immoral action, but there are other situations in which it represents power, status, and military prowess. In other words, however intently people may want to read the ancient fat body as evidence of some kind of moral failing, it is difficult to make a solid case. Given that fat bodies continue to be perceived as a reflection of moral failure, it may be instructive to explore how and where these ideas may have originated.

Physiognomy is certainly a possible source of ideas that connect fat and immorality. As George Boys-Stone argues, physiognomy is a likely outcome of ancient philosophical questions regarding what it meant to be a "well-functioning individual" (Boys-Stone 2007, 19). Philosophical examination of what it meant to be happy or to live a good life was frequently couched in a nature/nurture debate: how do we explain how one person succeeds in living a happy, virtuous life and another person does not? Is bad behavior simply the result of social and cultural influences? Or is there something innate about an individual leads them in that direction? (Boys-Stone 2007, 19). Since most ancient philosophers believed that there was an active connection between the soul (which controls human action) and the body, it seemed reasonable to assume that "one could, in principle at least, tell what a person is like from the way he or she looks" (Boys-Stone 2007, 19). The acceptance of this idea was widespread: there are major physiognomic treatises in Greek, Latin, and Arabic, and we can see physiognomic thinking in numerous ancient texts, including medical treatises, biographies, histories, and the philosophies of two of the founding fathers of Western philosophy, Plato and Aristotle (Swain 2007, 1–16).

An example of physiognomic assumptions and inconsistencies can be seen in Plato's dialogue, *Timaeus*. Although this dialogue is not widely read today, it was "regarded as the definitive expression" of Plato's philosophy until the Middle Ages (Zeyl 2000, xiv). The *Timaeus* is Plato's creation story: it explains how the universe was formed and how it is ordered, and it culminates with the creation of humans.[2] In his discussion of health and disease, Plato turns to diseases of the soul. He states, "now all that is good is beautiful, and what is beautiful is not ill-proportioned. Hence we must take it that if a living thing is to be in good condition, it will be well-proportioned" (Plato, 87c). He is clear that "health and disease" as well as "virtue and vice" are determined by the correct or erroneous balance of body and soul (Plato, 87d). Plato does, however, admit that "we can perceive the less important proportions and do some figuring about them, but the more important proportions, which are of the greatest consequence, we are unable to figure out" (Plato, 87c). He goes on to discuss situations in which a person's body is out of proportion with the soul and vice versa, and how in these situations either the body becomes diseased or the mind "wears the body out" (Plato 88a). In other words, a beautiful, well-proportioned body gives evidence of a properly proportioned soul, but when a body or soul is not properly proportioned, we are not certain exactly what is out of proportion or in what way. In this scenario, the only way that we would know if a person has a properly proportioned soul and body is if they were virtuous and beautiful. It is unlikely that the vast majority of people would fit this description.

Moreover, when we note that the *Timaeus* also articulates how human bodies and minds are gendered, we can see why men are always going to be in a position of privilege: for Plato, the mind is rational, masculine, and human, and the body is irrational, feminine, and animalistic (Hill 2011, 48). This gendered dichotomy translates into real world features of men and women, where men are gifted with "austerity and self-control," skills required of good leaders, and women are perceived to be lustful and self-indulgent, making them unsuited for public positions (Dench 1998, 121).

The physiognomic ideas of Plato and others are lurking in the work of Roman historian, Suetonius (b. ~70 CE), whose most famous work, *Lives of the Caesars*, was written during the time of the reign of Hadrian (117–138 CE). In his biographies of 12 successive Roman rulers, Suetonius carefully describes the bodily features of each of his subjects—the first biographer to do so—using language that suggests his familiarity with physiognomy.[3]

Emperor Augustus (r. 27 BCE–CE 14), for instance, is clearly a good leader: he is just, caring, and succeeds at his military pursuits. He is a generous and attentive host, and his own habits of eating and drinking reflect his seriousness and discipline. His body confirms his positive actions:

> His appearance was striking and he remained exceedingly graceful all through his life, though he cared nothing for adorning himself. [….] The expression of his face, whether he was speaking or silent, was so calm and serene…His eyes were clear and bright; he liked it to be thought that they revealed a godlike power and was pleased if someone who regarded him closely then lowered their gaze, as though from the sun's force. [….] He was short of stature…but did not appear so because his limbs were well made and well-proportioned so that one only noticed his height by comparison when someone taller was standing next to him.
>
> *(Suetonius, "Deified Augustus," 79)*

Augustus checks all of the physiognomic boxes for good proportions and characteristics.

In contrast, we have Nero (r. 54–68 CE), who has serious character flaws: he is cruel, self-indulgent, and extravagant, putting in place laws and practices that benefit only him. He avoids his duties, preferring to spend time at the theater. He dines sumptuously but is not a good host. All of these flaws are, indeed, written on his body: "He was of good height but his body was blotchy and ill smelling. His hair was fairish, his face handsome rather than attractive, his eyes bluish-grey and dull, his neck thick, his stomach protruding, his legs very thin…" (Suetonius "Nero," 51). All of Nero's defects are summarized in this description, including the lack of proportionality, especially marked by the contrast between his very thin legs and "protruding" stomach. Nero is a fat man who was not a good leader.

While Augustus is a good, well-proportioned leader, and Nero is neither, there are also portraits of people whose bodies do not seem to match their characters. Chiai calls these "paradoxical portraits" (Chiai 2019, 204). Emperor Otho (r. 69 CE) is such an example. Having been tricked into defeat in battle, Otho is determined to take his own life. Directly after the description of his death, Suetonius describes Otho's body:

> Otho's appearance and manner did not suggest a spirit of such greatness. He was apparently of modest stature, with crooked feet and bandy legs, while in the care of his person he was almost feminine, plucking out his body hair and, as his hair was thinning, wearing a kind of wig fitted closely and carefully to his head so no one would notice it.
>
> *(Suetonius, "Otho," 11)*

Otho was certainly not well-proportioned, though he is not described as fat, and his habits suggested femininity: neither of these aspects of his character suggests that he could be a good leader, even though he showed extraordinary courage in taking his own life. This "paradoxical portrait" seems to reveal that how a leader looks may not, in fact, tell us much about his character at all; even Suetonius realizes this.

Indeed, literary descriptions of rulers like those we find in Suetonius, have little in common with "the positive associations of corpulence in Hellenistic state iconography" that we see in coinage and portraiture (Bradley 2011, 24). For example, Roman coins regularly depicted emperors—Otho is one of them—with a "stout neck, heavily modelled rolls of flesh and protruding brows," so that they would be "instantly recognizable to his subjects as a strong, sturdy military commander who was a force to be reckoned with" (Bradley 2011, 33). In the influential *Physiognomy* of Polemon, masculinity is defined by, among other things, "a large head, a broad forehead, overhanging eyebrows, hollow and bluish-black eyes, a thick nose, a spacious jaw and mouth, [and] a thick neck" irrespective of proportionality (Polemon 2007, 395). Polemon's descriptions of masculinity and femininity are based, respectively, on features of the lion and the leopard. Polemon is clear that, "in masculinity there is femininity, and in femininity there is masculinity, and the name (of male or female) falls to whichever has precedence" (Polemon 2007, 393). Nonetheless, anyone interpreting physiognomic signs should "know that the male is in every respect more powerful, more obviously bold, less shameful, and more enduring of adversities that befall him than the female" (Polemon 2007, 395). Coins that represent fat leaders thus follow physiognomic signs of strength, leadership, and wealth, signs of masculinity and military courage. Even though Suetonius does not describe Otho as fat, he is portrayed as such on coins.

Bradley also points out that that there are many female portraits of Roman women

> where the fat neck, pendulous chin, jowly cheeks, expressive piercing eyes and arching muscled brows point to seniority, intelligence, and *gravitas*— no-nonsense high-society matrons with masculine faces who could pack a punch and hold their own alongside their male peers.
>
> *(Bradley 2011, 27)*

Only if a woman is represented with masculine characteristics, she, too, can be perceived to have the qualities of a leader.

So, can a fat man be a good leader? Who knows? Suetonius might say no, while numismatic images and other kinds of visual portraits of those same leaders may beg to differ. While physiognomy is used extensively in ancient Greek and Roman texts as ways to characterize the moral character of men and women, physiognomic meanings were themselves multilayered and fluid, dependent on interpretations that take into account combinations of physical features that could be combined in hundreds of different ways. What is certain is that in the ancient world's texts and artifacts that address questions of leadership, we are confronted with a complex set of meanings where, at the very least, conflicting ideas, including wealth, power, indulgence, excess, self-control, beauty, proportion, strength, weakness, courage, and cruelty are at play.

Conclusion

When we look for possible sources of the persistent idea that fatness is evidence of moral turpitude, we discover that the very same challenges we have today are evident in ancient texts and artifacts. Conceptually, the fat body is remarkably slippery, defying definite interpretations and meanings. Moreover, there are layers upon layers of interpretive difficulties: there are significant challenges in reading the ancient fat body in a positive way, no matter how clear it is that a favorable reading may be warranted, precisely because the equation fat = bad is so expected and common. Add to this the intricacies of mixing fat and gender, and the complexities multiply exponentially. All this is to say that, in many cases, reading the ancient fat body as anything other than fertile, undesirable, and debauched is an act of resistance against the politics of then—and now.

Notes

1 I am indebted to Forth's book for emphasizing the relationship between the material forms of fat and the "culturally shaped perceptions and discourses that make sense of them" (36).
2 I rely here on, and expand, my previous reading of Plato's *Timaeus* in *Eating to Excess*, 43–55.
3 There is much scholarly debate on the extent to which Suetonius relied on actual physiognomic handbooks to write his biographies, or whether he was simply familiar with the cultural understanding of physiognomic assumptions. A summary of these arguments can be found in Gian Franco Chiai, "Good Emperors, Bad Emperors," 210–215. For my purposes, the accuracy of Suetonius's physiognomic descriptions are less important than the assumptions that he and his contemporary readers make about the connections between bodily features and the acts of his subjects.

Bibliography

Almasri, Eyad, and Mairna Mustafa. 2019. "Nabataean Fertility Myth, Place, Time, Rituals and Actors based on Archaeological Evidence." *Mediterranean Archaeology and Archaeometry* 19, no. 2: 63–79. https://link.gale.com/apps/doc/A600672464/AONE?u=uni_rodit&sid=bookmark-AONE&xid=72fec739
Baines, John. 1985. *Fecundity Figures: Egyptian Personification and the Iconology of a Genre.* Warminster: Aris & Phillips.
Bažant, Jan. 1982. "On the Gluttony of Ancient Greek Athletes." *Listy Filologické / Folia Philologica* 105, no. 3: 129–131. www.jstor.org/stable/23464560
Boys-Stones, George. 2007. "Physiognomy and Ancient Psychological Theory," in *Seeing the Face, Seeing the Soul: Polemon's Physiognomy from Classical Antiquity to Medieval Islam*, edited by Simon Swain, 19–124. Oxford: Oxford University Press.

Bradley, Mark. 2011. "Obesity, Corpulence and Emaciation in Roman Art." *Papers of the British School at Rome* 79: 1–41. www.jstor.org/stable/41725302

Budin, Stephanie Lynn. 2015. "Fertility and Gender in the Ancient Near East," in *Sex in Antiquity: Exploring Gender and Sexuality in the Ancient World,* edited by Mark Masterson, Nancy Sorkin Rabinowitz and James Robson. 30–49. New York: Routledge.

Chiai, Gian Franco. 2019. "Good Emperors, Bad Emperors: The Function of Physiognomic Representation in Suetonius' De vita Caesarum and Common Sense Physiognomics," in *Visualizing the Invisible with the Human Body: Physiognomy and Ekphrasis in the Ancient World,* edited by J. Cale Johnson and Alessandro Stavru, 203–226. Berlin, Boston: De Gruyter. https://doi.org/10.1515/9783110642698-010

Croce, Benedetto. 1941. *History as the Story of Liberty.* Translated by Sylvia Sprigge. New York: W.W. Norton & Co.

Dench, Emma. 1998. "Austerity, Excess, Success, and Failure in Hellenistic and Early Imperial Italy," in *Parchments of Gender: Deciphering the Bodies of Antiquity,* edited by Maria Wyke, 121–146. Oxford: Clarendon Press.

El-Sawi, Ahmed. 1983. "The Nile-God. An Unusual Representation in the Temple of Sety 1 at Abydos." *Egitto e Vicino Oriente* 6: 7–13. www.jstor.org/stable/24232650

Engber, Daniel. 2020. "Unexpected Clues Emerge About Why Diets Fail." *Scientific American,* January 13, 2020. www.scientificamerican.com/article/unexpected-clues-emerge-about-why-diets-fail/

Forth, Christopher E. 2019. *Fat: A Cultural History of the Stuff of Life.* London: Reaktion Books.

Hill, Susan E. 2011. *Eating to Excess: The Meaning of Gluttony and the Fat Body in the Ancient World.* Santa Barbara: Praeger Publishers.

McDermott, LeRoy. 1996. "Self-Representation in Upper Paleolithic Female Figurines." *Current Anthropology* 37, no. 2: 227–275. www.jstor.org/stable/2744349

Mouritsen, Ole G. 2015. *Life—As a Matter of Fat: The Emerging Science of Lipidomics,* 2nd ed. Berlin: Springer-Verlag.

Nelson, Sarah M. 1990. "Diversity of the Upper Paleolithic 'Venus' Figurines and Archeological Mythology." *Archaeological Papers of the American Anthropological Association* 2, no. 1: 11–22. https://doi.org/10.1525/ap3a.1990.2.11

Nosrat, Samin. 2017. Netflix website for the series, "Salt, Fat, Acid, Heat," Accessed September 12, 2021. www.saltfatacidheat.com/fat

Oxford English Dictionary (OED) online. 2021. s.v. "fat, adj. and n.2," accessed September 14, 2021. www-oed-com.proxy.lib.uni.edu/view/Entry/68474?rskey=CsopJq&result=3&isAdvanced=false

Plato. 2000. *Timaeus.* Translated by Donald J. Zeyl. Indianapolis: Hackett Publishing Company.

Polemon. 2007. "*The Leiden Polemon.* Translated with an Introduction by Robert Hoyland," in *Seeing the Face, Seeing the Soul: Polemon's Physiognomy from Classical Antiquity to Medieval Islam,* edited by Simon Swain, 329–463. Oxford: Oxford University Press.

Research and Markets. 2021. *The U.S. Weight Loss & Diet Control Market.* Accessed September 12, 2021. www.researchandmarkets.com/reports/5313560/the-u-s-weight-loss-and-diet-control-market?w=4&utm_source=BW&utm_medium=PressRelease&utm_code=qm2gts

Rice, Patricia C. 1981. "Prehistoric Venuses: Symbols of Motherhood or Womanhood?" *Journal of Anthropological Research* 37, no. 4: 402–414. www.jstor.org/stable/3629836

Robb, John and Oliver J.T. Harris. 2017. "Becoming Gendered in European Prehistory: Was Neolithic Gender Fundamentally Different?" *American Antiquity* 83, no. 1: 128–147. https://doi:10.1017/aaq.2017.54

Roth, Ann Macy. 2016. "Father Earth, Mother Sky: Ancient Egyptian Beliefs about Conception and Fertility," in *Reading the Body: Representations and Remains in the Archaeological Record*, edited by Alison E Rautman, 187–201. Philadelphia: University of Pennsylvania Press. https://doi.org/10.9783/9781512806830

Soffer, Olga, James M. Adovasio, and David C. Hyland. 2000. "The 'Venus' Figurines: Textiles, Basketry, Gender, and Status in the Upper Paleolithic." *Current Anthropology* 41, no. 4: 511–537.

Steinfels, Peter. 1990. "Idyllic Theory of Goddesses Creates Storm," *New York Times* Feb. 13, 1990, Section C, page 1. Accessed October 23, 2021. www.nytimes.com/1990/02/13/science/idyllic-theory-of-goddesses-creates-storm.html

Suetonius. 2000. *Lives of the Caesars*. Translated with an Introduction and Notes by Catherine Edwards. New York: Oxford University Press.

Swain, Simon, ed. 2007. *Seeing the Face, Seeing the Soul: Polemon's Physiognomy from Classical Antiquity to Medieval Islam*. Oxford: Oxford University Press.

Theoi.com. 2021. "Priapus." Accessed October 29, 2021. www.theoi.com/Georgikos/Priapos.html.

Zeyl, Donald J. 2000. *Introduction to the Timaeus*, by Plato. Indianapolis, IN: Hackett Publishing.

9

HISTORICIZING BLACK WOMEN'S ANTI-FATNESS

Ava Purkiss

In 1951, Hazel Garland, an editorial staff member and columnist for the African American newspaper the *Pittsburg Courier*, confessed her struggles with weight on the front page of the paper (Garland 1951, 1). In her "Things to Talk About" column, Garland had written about events in Pittsburgh, including campaigns led by the National Association for the Advancement of Colored People, commemorations of "Negro History Week," plays about decolonization efforts abroad, as well as more lighthearted wedding anniversary announcements, festivals, and banquets. But Garland turned to more personal matters for the *Courier's* feature on its 30-day diet plan. She admitted that she had once weighed 130 pounds but gained 37 pounds over the past two years and credited her weight gain to her inability to "resist food." She was determined to do something about her expanding waistline.

Garland recounted the moment she decided to begin dieting. While attending a party, she overheard acquaintances comparing her to a woman who weighed over 200 pounds. The partygoers joked, "There goes Hazel back to the table. Wouldn't you think she had enough? She used to be attractive, but now she is getting so large she'll soon be looking like Mrs.—" (Garland 1951, 1). Garland's acquaintances then had a good laugh at her expense. After the embarrassing encounter, Garland vowed to slim down and prove to her friends that she could, in her words, "stick to a diet." After her doctor refused to prescribe her weight loss pills, she began the *Courier* diet and found success, initially losing ten pounds in a little over three weeks.

At 167 pounds, Garland considered herself overweight and in need of an intervention (and her social circle seemed to agree). In other articles she authored, she advocated diets of less than 1200 calories per day, proposed salads as an alternative to regular meals, and wrote of the "ugly fat" one gains during the winter season, implicating herself in the latter (Garland 1957, A11). Why would

DOI: 10.4324/9781003140665-13

Garland promote these stringent weight-loss tactics to Black readers and harbor such an unforgiving stance on her own body? How do we square her anti-fat attitudes with prevailing notions about Black fat acceptance and body positivity? How should we interpret those attitudes within the larger history of American fat stigma?

Garland is not a singular figure of Black fat condemnation but is part of a long history of intraracial fat shaming, bodily surveillance, and weight-loss seeking among African American women. Beginning in the early twentieth century, many Black women, particularly those of the middle class, denigrated fatness. Some African American women engaged in physical exercise, resorted to calorie-restrictive diets, and bought into weight loss gimmicks in order to slim down. They cited fatness as a "menace" to health, as perilous to beauty, and as threats to their struggle for citizenship (Purkiss 2017, 14–37). Middle-class Black women preferred a thin, sleek physique that seemingly projected health, attractiveness, and upward mobility. This preference was not necessarily a form of white assimilation or admiration for a white aesthetic but a complicated aspiration for Black social, political, and civic respect that has eluded the Fat Studies literature.

Black Women, History, and Fat Studies

Over the past two decades, the field of Fat Studies has examined the harm inflicted by weightism, fat stigma, and the diet industrial complex. In concert with Feminist Studies, Fat Studies has developed theoretical frameworks for scholars to interrogate taken-for-granted norms about fatness and bodies, especially as these norms inform assumptions about health and beauty. In her groundbreaking *Revolting Bodies*, Kathleen LeBesco offered an early and incisive analysis of fatness as a social (as opposed to a medical) construct that proved formative to Fat Studies scholarship (LeBesco 2003). LeBesco not only examined the fat-condemning milieu in which Americans live but also called for a shift in the political landscape that demeans and disregards fat people—a call that has become a cornerstone of the field. As Esther Rothblum and Sondra Solovay explain, Fat Studies is characterized by an "aggressive, consistent, rigorous critique of the negative assumptions, stereotypes, and stigma placed on fat and the fat body" (Rothblum and Solovay 2009, 2). Fat Studies is both a critical field of inquiry and an important site of social justice activism.

Despite its critical and activist framework, Fat Studies has been steeped in an epistemology that relies on white women as the primary scholars, activists, and subjects of analysis for our understanding of fat animus (Farrell 2019, 29–39). Black women have often served as objects of analysis but not as subjects who inform how fatness operates historically and contemporarily. Blackness is assumed to "neutralize" fatness, as feminist writer Sesali Bowen contends, and Black women are marginalized as both victims of intraracial fat-shaming and thoughtful contributors to the fat acceptance movement (Bowen 2021, 10). Because Black people are assumed to be content with bigger bodies, Fat Studies and other cognate fields have not fully explored the problems, burdens, and complexities of fatness for people of African descent.

The long history of fat stigma, shame, and avoidance is usually theorized outside of the experiences of Black people. Scholars firmly within and adjacent to Fat Studies tend to discuss African Americans' interest in weight loss and thinness-seeking as a recent development. Historian Shelley McKenzie, for instance, asserts that "black media outlets did not begin to cover exercise as part of a healthy lifestyle until the 1970s" (McKenzie 2013, 10). Moving the timeline even further into the twentieth century, feminist philosopher Susan Bordo notes that only in the 1990s did "features on diet, exercise, and body image problems" appear prominently in Black print culture, whereas middle-class, heterosexual white women's "obsessive relations with food" have been longstanding in print media (Bordo 2004, 103). Similarly, historian Peter Stearns claims that for most of the twentieth century, Black people lacked the "ethical demands" to participate in diet culture (Stearns 2002, 90). Even when scholars accurately historicize weightism among Black people, this weight consciousness is racialized as white. Historian Elizabeth M. Matelski cites excellent evidence of Black dieting in the 1950s but frames this weight-loss behavior as a desire for white body ideals and not a distinctly Black bodily aspiration (Matelski 2017, 108–28). More commonly, conventional histories of dieting, exercise, and general aversions to fatness either omit or make passing references to African Americans (Black 2013; Dworkin and Wachs 2009; Schwartz 1990; Todd 1999).

In an effort to expand traditional Fat Studies frameworks, recent scholarship has added a critical racial analysis to concepts of fatness and fat stigma. Sociologist Sabrina Strings traces the key historical developments that created an inextricable relationship between Blackness and fatness, arguing that the transatlantic slave trade and tropes of "greedy" Africans shaped the modern disdain for fat bodies. (Strings 2019). Writer and activist Da'Shaun L. Harrison argues that anti-fatness *is* antiblackness and that desire politics, notions of health, and state-sanctioned violence are grounded in a tangled relationship between race and body size (Harrison 2021). Other works have interrogated how Blackness and fatness intersect and have shown that an analysis of fatness, without other categories of analysis, is incomplete (Bass 2001, 219–30; Friedman, Rice and Renaldi 2019; Patterson-Faye 2016, 926–44; Sanders 2019, 287–304; Shaw 2006; Strings 2015, 107–30). This exciting trend in the scholarship, however, does not represent a majority of the Fat Studies literature. Moreover, these newer inquiries primarily concern contemporary versions of weightism and generate questions about historical manifestations of Black fat subjectivity and fat shame.

In this chapter, I posit that to fully understand the complexity of race, gender, and fat denigration, we must first historicize intraracial antifatness. Focusing on the first half of the twentieth century, I show that Black women have a long history of dieting and exercising for weight loss that precedes most scholarly periodizations of African American weight consciousness. This historicization allows for a better grasp of how fat avoidance (not fat acceptance) intersected with Black movements for citizenship and dignity. Fat Studies and fat activism have allowed us to recognize fat acceptance as a social movement in and of itself, but we have missed how fat liberation posed specific barriers to Black women—a demographic that had fatness, and its attendant "negative" implications, constitutively attached to their bodies and beings. The politics of representation, racial pride, and the stakes of citizenship appeared too high for most African American women to accommodate fat acceptance. When we look at the forms of fat animus African Americans levied on themselves and each other, a complicated story emerges that nuances traditional Fat Studies understandings of the history of fat oppression.

"Warning! Fat Is Dangerous!": Black Women's Citizenship, Racial Pride, and Self-Discipline

Race, gender, and embodiment, among other qualities, were closely tied to notions of citizenship in the twentieth century (Brown 2008; Greer 2019; Mckiernan-González 2012; Molina 2006; Ngai 2014; Russell 2011; Shah 2012). Black women, who were perceived to be outside of the category of "good" citizens, found themselves with a limited set of tools to demonstrate their social and civic value. Their bodies served as an important measure of their corporal and moral "fitness." Black women thought critically about the size, shape, and movement of their bodies and developed their own culture of fat avoidance. Several social and political forces informed this culture. On a national level, Americans began to seek out intentional physical exercise in the late nineteenth and early twentieth centuries as the country shifted from an agrarian society to a more industrial one, and physical activity became more difficult to achieve through work. Americans regarded those who exercised as healthy, industrious, and commendable members of society. At the same time, fat individuals, once considered upstanding, were now deemed lazy, gluttonous, and deviant as fatness lost its cachet.

The politics of citizenship and racial uplift influenced body ideals for African Americans in the Progressive Era and beyond. Racial uplift ideologues favored racial representatives with respectable, refined bodies that confounded widespread ideas about Black weakness, laziness, and greed. In writing about Black bodies at the end of the nineteenth century, W. E. B. Du Bois asserted:

> we must rapidly come to the place where the man all brain and no muscle is looked upon as almost a big fool as the man all muscle and no brain; and when the young woman who cannot walk a couple of good country miles will have few proposals of marriage.

> *(Du Bois 1897, 184)*

Black women, in particular, avoided fatness for its association with the persistent mammy trope. Despite their class, size, or profession, this trope positioned African American women as fat servants to white desires—women with no civic or political aspirations for themselves. Black women worked mightily to distance themselves from this caricature by shaping their bodies in ways that contrasted with the subservient and excessive "mammy." One Black newspaper in 1914 resorted to hosting a beauty contest for the explicit purpose of "counteract[ing] the world's conception of the American Negro woman based on the caricatures and exaggerations published in the comic weeklies" (*New York Age* 1914, 1). Some African Americans perceived linkages between their actual selves and this imagined figure as real threats to their struggle for civic respect.

African Americans of various political and religious stripes condemned fatness in the 1920s and 1930s. The *Negro World*, the official newspaper of the Universal Negro Improvement Association (UNIA), often promoted "wholesome" eating and exercise while trafficking in anti-fat discourse. The print outlet advertised numerous reducing products in the 1920s, one of which bore the alarmist headline, "Warning! Fat is Dangerous!" (*Negro World* 1923, 8). As a Black nationalist organization, the UNIA advocated the "blending of all Negroes into one strong healthy race," racial honor, and Black separatism. The Association tied its health advice and weight-loss advocacy to larger objectives of racial strength and Black flourishing. In the 1930s, the Women of the Allah Temple of Islam (ATOI) were strongly advised to maintain a slim physique, as the organization perceived fatness as both a moral and racial failure. The ATOI, a precursor to the Nation of Islam, was also a Black nationalist organization that attached abstemiousness and thinness to good health and beauty in distinctly Black ways. One prominent Black woman reformer of the ATOI suggested that thinness was the natural state of Black people and that whites caused excess weight in people of African descent (Taylor 2017). Members of organizations like the UNIA and ATOI avoided fatness as both an act of Black nationalist pride and a rejection of whiteness.

In the mid-twentieth century, African Americans used print media to present Black people as respectable, self-disciplined, and upwardly mobile citizens who could make smart food choices. Black newspapers, magazines, advice books, and even cookbooks counseled Black readers on avoiding extra calories and attaining a slim figure. Proving to be more than a mere volume of sumptuous recipes, Freda De Knight's 1948 cookbook, *A Date with a Dish: A Cook Book of American Negro Recipes*, also offered readers diet advice. De Knight explained:

> A well-balanced diet is a 'must' in your daily routine. And if you want to keep your weight down along with your doctor's advice, eat regularly, wisely and well. Eat sparingly of starches, sugar and fats…. That plate of vegetables should be green. Not potatoes, macaroni, rice and spaghetti.
>
> *(De Knight 1948, 8)*

De Knight transformed a "negro" cookbook, which should have celebrated the pleasures of food and eating, into a forum on moderation. Old, lingering stereotypes likely influenced this seemingly odd dieting imperative. Described as a "slender, bright-eyed, and charming young woman with a fine zest for living" as well as a "cultivated Negro woman" in the book's foreword, De Knight's thin body and gentility served as a challenge to prevalent ideas about Black women's character and corporality. Even in the late 1940s, when the cookbook was published, Black women cooks could not escape the image of the overweight, unsophisticated, and edacious "mammy," and De Knight sought to reframe Black women's relationship to food and cookery. African American women's eating habits, bodies, and characters coalesced in ways that prompted De Knight to engage in Black pro-diet and anti-fat discourse.

Depictions of Black abstemiousness reflected Black women's actual dieting behaviors in the postwar era. Middle-class Black women like De Knight were especially interested, and able, to resort to dieting as a weight-loss tactic. In *Black Bourgeoisie*, E. Franklin Frazier's 1957 analysis of the Black middle-class, Frazier painted Black "society" women as prone to dieting: "The idle, overfed women among the black bourgeoisie. . . . are forever dieting and reducing only to put on more weight (which is usually the result of the food that they consume at their club meetings)" (Frazier 1957, 183; Witt 1999). Although Frazier imbued his study with deep-seated hostility toward Black elites, and his work has been duly critiqued since its publication, his observations of dieting and weight consciousness among Black middle-class women were plausible. Black models, celebrities, professionals, college students, and homemakers did engage in calorie-restrictive and "fad" diets in the 1950s and 1960s. Famous Black women like Lena Horne confessed in *Ebony* magazine that before she performed on stage, she liked to eat beef, lamb chops, or "foreign foods." Horne cautioned, however, that she could not eat with abandon and had to "watch her diet" lest she gained weight (*Ebony* 1947, 9–14). *Ebony* described Horne as "voluptuous," although she weighed 118 pounds with body measurements of 34-26-36 (*Ebony* 1947). Middle and aspiring-class Black female readers of the magazine, who hoped to emulate women like Lena Horne, likely noticed the relationship between her careful eating habits and extraordinarily thin body.

Other Black women and girls, perhaps less comfortably middle-class, turned to their local YWCA or Black newspapers for guidance on food, calories, and fitness in the mid-twentieth century. Y leaders provided this guidance by monitoring the diets of their charges. For example, the Harriet Tubman branch of the YWCA in Durham, North Carolina hosted summer camps for its young African American members and restricted confections during the weeklong retreat. Camp organizers advised its 1956 attendees:

We get Grade-A pasteurized milk and plenty of wholesome food, so ask your folks not to send you any cakes or candy. (You won't need them, because Mrs. Benton and Mrs. Stewart will be there to fix good, tasty food).

(*"The Y-Teens of Durham"* 1956)

The young YWCA members likely preferred candy and cake to milk and "wholesome" fare, but these food limitations became intrinsic to Black disciplining practices that instructed girls and adolescents to develop "appropriate" appetites. These practices required reinforcement as girls matured into women. In 1959, one Black YMCA in Chicago offered courses in which Black women were encouraged to learn the principles of "physical fitness, menu planning, [and] calorie counting" as well as "how to take [one's] weight off and keep it off" (*Chicago Defender* 1959, 15). Organizers branded the courses as "diet club classes" and offered them in January so that members could become "slim by spring." The courses drew so much interest that they necessitated waitlists. As segregated institutions, the YWCA and YMCA provided spaces for Black women and girls to come together in pursuit of recreation, racial belonging, and, unfortunately, body surveillance. These pursuits could not be easily disentangled.

While summer camps and weight-loss courses at the Y allowed African Americans to engage in collective weight and food monitoring, some preferred to diet independently. Black people could easily consult Black newspapers for information on calories, foods to avoid, and self-directed diet instruction in the 1950s. The Black press created their own diets, like the aforementioned "Courier 30-Day Diet" by the *Pittsburgh Courier*, or advocated other calorie-restrictive diets like the Harper's Bazaar 9-Day Diet, the Florida Citrus Reducing Diet, the 800-Calorie Reducing Diet, and the simply titled "Reducing Diet" (Schalk-Johnson 1947, 8; *Chicago Defender* 1953, 17; *The Crisis* 1950, 190–94; *Los Angeles Sentinel* 1953, A4). African Americans challenged the idea that they lacked self-discipline through extreme diet plans, "reducing" success stories, and before-and-after weight loss photographs printed in Black newspapers. The ability to demonstrate self-restraint and moderation through dieting and other slimming practices registered as an important capacity for African Americans, especially in the context of the struggle for full-fledged citizenship during the civil rights era. Narratives of discipline and self-control showed that Black people, particularly African American women, could be rational, self-sacrificing, and "fit" citizens.

Ambivalent Approaches to Black Women's Anti-Fatness

Various Black historical actors, from W. E. B. Du Bois in the 1890s, to Black newspaper editors in the 1950s, believed that physical activity and moderation in eating produced desirable Black bodies and character. Celebrations of Black exercise, dieting, thinness, and weight loss took place at the same time that white media outlets portrayed Black women as overweight mammies and as questions about African Americans' physical and moral fitness for citizenship loomed large. This history, rooted in anti-fatness on the one hand and objections to racist ideas of Black embodiment on the other, does not fit neatly into a traditional Fat Studies framework. While intraracial Black fat stigma supported the status quo, hierarchized Black bodies, and ensconced Black women in interminable diet and exercise cycles, it also functioned as a form of protest. This complex history lives somewhere between fat oppression and resistance to racialized, weight-based stereotypes of Black women.

Black women found themselves mired in interconnected politics of bodily self-determination, health seeking, activism, *and* fat avoidance. Fat Studies has not yet provided a sufficient historical and analytical space for these women. To recount the words of Rothblum and Solovay, Fat Studies is invested in the rigorous critique of the negative assumptions placed on fat. Indeed, the field has trained us to denounce all forms of anti-fatness, but for Black women during the period under study, that denouncement is incomplete when it is not accompanied by a rebuke of the racist forces that led Black women to avoid fatness in the first place.

Given the limited bodily freedoms African Americans possessed, we might pause to consider the full social and political risks of fat acceptance for Black women while mounting our critiques of their anti-fatness. Although out of accordance with the spirit of Fat Studies, we might benefit from resisting an immediate castigation of African American women's anti-fat strategies and cultivating a more ambivalent stance that accounts for how racism and sexism constrained their potential for fat liberation. As Fat Studies adopts a more intersectional approach, scholars within the field now have the opportunity to historicize the full political stakes of fat embodiment for women of color and examine how anti-fatness became paradoxically entangled with efforts for racial justice, pride, and respect.

Bibliography

Primary Sources

De Knight, Freda. *A Date with a Dish: A Cook Book of American Negro Recipes*. New York: Hermitage Press, 1948.

Du Bois, W. E. B. "The Problem of Amusement." *Southern Workman* 27, September 1897: 181–85.

Frazier, E. Franklin. *Black Bourgeoisie: The Rise of a New Middle Class*. New York: Free Press, 1957.

Garland, Hazel. "Courier 30-Day Diet Actually Cuts Down Fat." *Pittsburgh Courier*, February 24, 1951, 1.

———. Slim for Summer: First Week's Diet Should See Reduction in Weight." *Pittsburgh Courier*, June 1, 1957, A11.

———. "Slim for Summer: Get that Figure in Trim for Warm Weather Fashions." *Pittsburgh Courier*, May 25, 1957, B7.

"Give Thought to Balanced Meals." *Chicago Defender*, October 17, 1953, 17.

"Health Hints: Weight Control." *The Crisis*, March 1950, 190–94.

"Meet the Real Lena Horne." *Ebony*, November 1947, 9–14.

"More Interest in Race Beauty." *New York Age*, August 20, 1914, 1.

"New Reducing Diet." *Los Angeles Sentinel*, March 26, 1953, A4.

Schalk-Johnson, Toki. "'You Can Lose Weight,' Says Busy Pittsburgher." *Pittsburgh Courier*, September 13, 1947, 8.

"Warning! Fat is Dangerous!" *Negro World*, April 28, 1923, 8.

"YMCA 'Slim by Spring' Class Opens." *Chicago Defender,* January 6, 1959, 15.

YWCA. "Girls 9 to 18 Summer Camp: Harriet Tubman Branch, July 22—August 4, 1956." YWCA Records, box 13, David M. Rubenstein Rare Book and Manuscript Library, Duke University, Durham, NC.

Secondary Sources

Bass, Margaret K. "On Being a Fat Black Girl in a Fat-Hating Culture." In *Recovering the Black Female Body: Self-Representations by African American Women,* edited by Michael Bennett and Vanessa D. Dickerson, 219–30. New Brunswick: Rutgers University Press, 2001.

Black, Jonathan. *Making the American Body: The Remarkable Saga of the Men and Women Whose Feats, Feuds, and Passions Shaped Fitness History.* Lincoln: University of Nebraska Press, 2013.

Bordo, Susan. *Unbearable Weight: Feminism, Western Culture, and the Body.* Berkeley: University of California Press, 2004.

Bowen, Sesali. "Stop Excluding Black Women from Fat Acceptance Movements." Accessed July 1, 2021. http://feministing.com/2015/09/18/we-need-to-center-not-exclude-black-women-in-fat-acceptance-movements/

Brown, Jayna. *Babylon Girls: Black Women Performers and the Shaping of the Modern.* Durham: Duke University Press, 2008.

Dworkin, Shari L. and Faye Linda Wachs. *Body Panic: Gender, Health, and the Selling of Fitness.* New York: New York University Press, 2009.

Farrell, Amy. "Origin Stories: Thickening Fat and the Problem of Historiography." In *Thickening Fat: Fat Bodies, Intersectionality, and Social Justice,* edited by May Friedman, Carla Rice, and Jen Rinaldi, 29–39. New York: Routledge, 2019.

Friedman, May, Carla Rice, and Jen Rinaldi, eds. *Thickening Fat: Fat Bodies, Intersectionality, and Social Justice.* New York: Routledge, 2019.

Greer, Brenna Wynn. *Represented: The Black Imagemakers Who Reimagined African American Citizenship.* Philadelphia: University of Pennsylvania Press, 2019.

Harrison, Da'Shaun L. *Belly of the Beast: The Politics of Anti-Fatness as Anti-Blackness.* Berkeley: North Atlantic Books, 2021.

LeBesco, Kathleen. *Revolting Bodies?: The Struggle to Redefine Fat Identity.* Amherst: University of Massachusetts Press, 2003.

Matelski, Elizabeth M. *Reducing Bodies: Mass Culture and the Female Figure in Postwar America.* New York: Routledge, 2017.

McKenzie, Shelly. *Getting Physical: The Rise of Fitness Culture in America.* Lawrence: University Press of Kansas, 2013.

Mckiernan-González, John. *Fevered Measures: Public Health and Race at the Texas-Mexico Border, 1848–1942.* Durham: Duke University Press, 2012.

Molina, Natalia. *Fit to Be Citizens?: Public Health and Race in Los Angeles, 1879–1939.* Berkeley: University of California Press, 2006.

Ngai, Mae M. *Impossible Subjects: Illegal Aliens and the Making of Modern America.* Princeton: Princeton University Press, 2014.

Patterson-Faye, Courtney J. "'I like the Way You Move': Theorizing Fat, Black and Sexy." *Sexualities* 19, no. 8 (2016): 926–44.

Purkiss, Ava. "'Beauty Secrets: Fight Fat': Black Women's Aesthetics, Exercise, and Fat Stigma, 1900–1930s." *Journal of Women's History* 29, no. 2 (2017): 14–37.

Rothblum, Esther D. and Sondra Solovay. *The Fat Studies Reader.* New York: New York University Press, 2009.

Russell, Emily. *Reading Embodied Citizenship: Disability, Narrative, and the Body Politic.* New Brunswick: Rutgers University Press, 2011.

Sanders, Rachel. "The Color of Fat: Racializing Obesity, Recuperating Whiteness, and Reproducing Injustice." *Politics, Groups, and Identities* 7, no. 2 (2019): 287–304.

Schwartz, Hillel. *Never Satisfied: A Cultural History of Diets, Fantasies, and Fat.* New York: Doubleday, 1990.

Shah, Nayan. *Stranger Intimacy: Contesting Race, Sexuality and the Law in the North American West.* Berkeley: University of California Press, 2012.

Shaw, Andrea Elizabeth. *The Embodiment of Disobedience: Fat Black Women's Unruly Political Bodies.* Lanham: Lexington Books, 2006.

Stearns, Peter N. *Fat History: Bodies and Beauty in the Modern West.* New York: New York University Press, 2002.

Strings, Sabrina. *Fearing the Black Body: The Racial Origins of Fat Phobia.* New York: New York University Press, 2019.

———. "Obese Black Women as 'Social Dead Weight': Reinventing the 'Diseased Black Woman.'" *Signs* 41, no. 1 (2015): 107–30.

Taylor, Ula Yvette. *The Promise of Patriarchy: Women and the Nation of Islam.* Chapel Hill: University of North Carolina Press, 2017.

Todd, Jan. *Physical Culture & The Body Beautiful: Purposive Exercise in the Lives of American Women, 1800–1875.* Macon: Mercer University Press, 1999.

Witt, Doris. *Black Hunger: Food and the Politics of U.S. Identity.* New York: Oxford University Press, 1999.

PART V

Gender and Fat in Institutions and Public Policy

Ideas about gender and fat are not just personal preferences but are embedded in the institutions that make up society and in the policies that govern these institutions. The authors in this section explore three different arenas of public policy, from immigration policy to parental rights to educational systems, to study how anti-fat stigma and misogyny particularly hurt women and children.

DOI: 10.4324/9781003140665-14

10

PUBLIC POLICY AND THE REPERCUSSIONS OF FAT STIGMA ON WOMEN AND CHILDREN

April Michelle Herndon

My mom took me to Weight Watchers for the first time in 1979. I was seven, and I had just understood that my fatness was a problem. Just the year before, I'd been bragging about wearing a six 6X in little girl's clothing and telling people I was going to play football when I grew up. But then they started weighing us at school. I wish I could say that things have gotten better for fat children, fat women, and mothers of fat children today, but I can't say that with any confidence. I actually worry that they've gotten worse, and I often think that I'm glad that I grew up in the early 70s when the worst I faced was an unhappy team leader at Weight Watchers who was trying to create a diet plan for me. Since that time, there's been a significant historical shift, with children's fatness becoming more than an issue within their families or with their pediatricians. In today's climate, both mothers and children may find themselves justifiably worried that a child's weight may trigger public shaming and even legal action.

The "war against obesity" has spawned a particularly fraught conversation about fatness in our society, especially around the bodies of women and children, and has birthed public policies that are arguably detrimental. Our former First Lady, Michele Obama, took up childhood obesity as one of her signature causes, and she used her platform to make it clear that thinness was desirable and achievable if kids would just move. In today's world, if diet and exercise don't work, children and teens can access bariatric surgery for weight loss. Fat women, too, can readily access bariatric surgeries or any part of the weight loss industry and are sometimes expected to do so in order to receive fertility treatment because weight is considered a contributor to poor success rates. But these "options" and what appear to be "choices" have been born out of a toxic environment and the rhetoric of war against fat women, fat children, and that environment increasingly affects all women and all children. It's an environment that encourages us to think

DOI: 10.4324/9781003140665-15

of fat bodies as undeserving, unproductive, greedy, dangerous, and even a national security threat. Increasingly, as Michael Gard and Jan Wright have pointed out, we are, in fact, encouraged to see all bodies as potentially fat, especially where children are concerned, rendering almost everyone's body a lurking threat (2005, 60). And is so often the case, the notion of the threat and the responsibility for curbing the danger isn't equally distributed. Fat women and children who are also marginalized via race and class, for example, are more often the targets of interventions around fatness and expected to change their bodies to assuage the nation's fears.

In this chapter, I'll examine the repercussions of public policies around fatness, which I'm defining as a set social codes around which informal and formal practices and policies—such as funding decisions, medical regulations, and laws—are based, looking particularly at how women's and children's lives in the United States are negatively affected by many policies said to be well-meaning. In doing so, I'll focus on fat women and fat children, but I'll also show how fatphobia resonates in the lives of all women and all children. I'll examine how the framing of "obesity"[1] within policies as an individual failing affects how blame for "the obesity epidemic" is distributed. In the end, I'll argue that framing fatness as an individual choice and/or pointing to certain groups as making those supposed poor choices more often has put some groups of people under more scrutiny and their bodies and lives more subject to troubling interventions. As feminist bioethicist Alison Reiheld argues,

> It is [her] abiding ethical concern that those most vulnerable to obesity, as it is framed in health and public health, are those least able to rectify it. Individualization of responsibility is thus an ethically bad idea: it burdens the already burdened.
>
> *(2015, 239)*

I will also point out that fatness itself comes in degrees and that fat women and children may also be more or less affected by these public policies based on their size. As Aubrey Gordon points out, there are "scales of fatness" used in the Fat Studies community, with the understanding that those who are "small fat" benefit from their proximity to thinness while those who are "superfat" or "infinifat" likely face a very different set of challenges and kinds of discrimination (2020, 9). The closer someone is to what is considered "normal" or "ideal" weight, the more privilege they are likely to have where fatphobia is concerned. Still, throughout my analysis, I will maintain that to be a woman,[2] especially a woman seeking to have a child or already mothering a child, or to be a child in the United States today, means to be negatively affected—to one degree or another—by harmful discourse and public policies born out of a fear of fatness and not just the current size of one's body.

Embodying the Future: The "War on Obesity" and Pregnant Bodies

The "war on obesity" started in December of 2001 when Surgeon Generals David Satcher, C. Everett Koop, and then Secretary of Defense Tommy Thompson declared that the "war on obesity" was underway (Doherty 2001). Originally positioned as a war for the health of the nation, in the 20 years since, scholars have argued that "the war on obesity" shaped up to be a moral rather than a health crusade (Herndon 2005; Gard and Wright 2005; Biltekoff 2007; LeBesco 2010; Dame-Griff 2016; Gordon 2020). Kathleen LeBesco, for example, has argued that the "'war on obesity' has transcended a public health initiative and has transformed into a full moral panic" (qtd. in Gordon 2020, 41). The result of that "full moral panic" has, arguably, been that fat people are thought to be responsible for their fatness, marking someone's body weight as wholly volitional. As Hannele Harjunen notes, within our current neoliberal frameworks, that sense of personal responsibility means that those "individuals/groups of people who are believed (or assumed) to take risks 'willingly' or seen as somehow 'choosing' to make themselves ill by their irresponsible behavior do not get much sympathy" (2021, 71). She goes on to note that this process displaces all responsibility on to the individual so that, rather than the reliance on the state to care for the individual, the individual should care for him or herself and also care for the state (2021, 71). In the United States, in particular, that individual responsibility is framed as responsibility to one's nation (Herndon 2005; Biltekoff 2007; Dame-Griff 2016), making fatness seem especially dangerous—not just to the individual but to all current and future citizens.

In this atmospheric mix of moral panic, nationalism, the personal responsibility of neoliberalism, and the casting of fatness as a disease, we've seen the rise of "healthism," a term "coined by Robert Crawford in 1980" defined as a "preoccupation with personal health as a primary—often the primary—focus for the definition and achievement of well-being [...]." Further, this process leads to "elevating health to a super value a metaphor for all that is good in life, healthism reinforces the privatization of the struggle for generalized well-being" (Gordon 2020, 10). Feminist bioethicist Reiheld, citing Rebecca Kukla's work on motherhood, makes the argument that those most often expected to engage in this "struggle" are women and mothers because they are "a crucial layer in health care systems, especially in the United States" (2015, 234). Women and/or mothers are most often the people doing the shopping for the house, preparing food, seeing to personal care and medical needs, and so forth. Because so much of the language around the obesity epidemic and healthism focuses on personal choices, and in particular food choices, it's women who are often positioned as having the responsibility for keeping people in their family units and their social groups thin.

Individual women, then, may pursue weight loss through dieting and bariatric surgeries simply because the standards of thinness are more harshly applied to women and the stigma around fatness, especially for women, is well-studied and well-known to exist in our healthcare and judicial systems and in our work lives (Judge and Cable 2011; Schvey et al. 2013; Ciciurkaite and Perry 2017; Mensigner, Tylka, and Calamari 2018; Alberga et al. 2019). Significantly, though, women of childbearing age who wish to have children may pursue weight loss in particular because medical discourse increasingly presents fatness among those who can bear children as a danger to pregnancies and to any resulting children. Women are now warned of "fetal overnutrition," which is the idea that women—by virtue of their own fatness, which is assumed to be caused from a surplus of nutrition—are actually overfeeding the developing fetus. As I wrote about recently, "a PubMed search of the term 'fetal overnutrition' reveals that in the last ten years, over 2500 articles have been written on the subject" (Herndon 2018, 37). This "fattening" of fetal rights, as I've argued, "reveals how the fetal rights discourse trades in fear to legitimize monitoring and controlling women's bodies—and the bodies of fat women in particular—under the guise of creating a healthier generation of Americans" (Herndon 2018, 36). The concerns about "fetal overnutrition" has caused some practitioners suggesting that women *not* gain weight in pregnancy, leading some doctors to push back and note that "during pregnancy, a time when *most* women gain weight, the impacts of stigma and bias are particularly complicated [emphasis mine]" (Hurst et al. 2021, 2). Megan Davidson and Sarah Lewin trace much of this concern around women's weight during pregnancy to fears of what are now called "big babies:" "Anxieties around 'big babies' reached have reached new levels" even though some studies suggest that "four out of every five people who are warned that they may be having a big baby (over four thousand grams) give birth to babies who are not big" (2018, 49). Davidson and Lewin go on to bluntly declare that "the current guidelines for monitoring and managing weight in pregnancy are not making people healthier" (2018, 55).

Weighting to Conceive: BMI, IVF, and Complications

Women who wish to conceive but need help to do so face a whole other set of challenges and policies that seem to try to delineate who is and is not "fit" to be a mother. In particular, the medical policies around In Vitro Fertilization (IVF) and Body Mass Index (BMI) regularly require that women have a BMI under 40, and many IVF clinic websites include their own BMI calculator, suggesting that women check their BMI before considering IVF. Currently, while there's no overarching position statement or policy to govern fertility procedures in the United States, there are sets of practices that have coalesced into standard reasons for denying care, with women's body weight being one of the key criteria on which treatment is denied or postponed.[3]

While many of the clinics following these policies claim they deny women with a BMI over 40 because of failure rates of the procedures, other experts say that denying women IVF based on their BMI penalizes women for one attribute when there are multiple factors that influence outcomes of fertility treatments, many of which are environmental and not within an individual's control. Either way, using BMI as a qualifying tool means some women readily get to become mothers and others don't. Gatekeeping around IVF treatment must also be acknowledged as a process during which some women face more scrutiny than others. Using BMI as a tool for such gatekeeping is especially worrisome because BMI is not, in fact, a neutral measuring tool but is, rather, racially loaded. As scholars such as Sabrina Strings have pointed out, the BMI was developed using European bodies as a standard (2019, 202). Adding further complications with using BMI as a measure of health is that it also fails to take into account any other social factors, such as discrimination and environmental racism, that may lead to poor pregnancy or poor health outcomes, a fact acknowledged by the US government on its *Healthy People 2030* site (United States Department of Health and Human Services, n.d.). Further, scholars from various fields have pointed out that the fat body itself is both historically and contemporarily racialized, as fatness has become synonymous with bodies of color (Herndon 2005; Dame-Griff 2016; Strings 2019; Gordon 2020, 48–49; Lind 2020, 190). What all of these confounding factors mean is that women with high BMIs are being denied medical procedures, and they are likely denied even more often if they are women of color.

Perhaps even more disturbing, the data about losing weight prior to IVF treatment improving outcomes is not as clear as one might think. As Robert Norman and William Mol write, "[…] it is increasingly hard to justify the logical but increasingly impractical view that women should lose a substantial amount of weight before treatment" (2018, 584). As I've written about previously, because it's so difficult to lose weight and then maintain the loss, many fat women "time out" of IVF treatment via age before they're able to meet the prescribed BMI (Herndon 2018), which leaves open an ethical question about denying treatment based on BMI. Norman and Mol also point out—despite most current policies—clinical trials suggest there is "no effect of introducing a lifestyle intervention before IVF versus starting immediate fertility treatment" and that the "medical and ethical opinions may now favor moving to fertility treatment earlier than originally recommended for patients who are overweight or obese" (2018, 581). As other feminist and/or Fat Studies scholars have pointed out, to choose only one characteristic and suggest the factor alone is responsible for poor outcomes is to cherry pick among a vast field of influences while also ignoring any positive influences that could be added to ensure better outcomes (Roberts 1998; Herndon 2014). For example, Norman and Mol also note that emotional support is also thought to positively affect IVF outcomes (2018, 584). The need for that kind of support—the addition of social support rather than the taking away of body weight via dieting or bariatric surgery—is succinctly called for by one woman in McPhail and Mazur's study of women seeking help to become pregnant. Noting that all bodies are different, she says, "So just work with us instead of making our lives so difficult" (2020, 134). Writing about Gina Balzano, a fat woman who sought fertility treatments and ultimately had bariatric surgery so she could meet BMI requirements, journalist Sole-Smith notes that "[Balzano and her husband] see [bariatric surgery] as [Gina's] required sacrifice" (2019). This, in spite of the fact that at least one large, systematic meta-review showed that men with a BMI over 30 may also have reduced fertility (Sermondade et al. 2012), all of which emphasizes the undue burden on women and the overvaluing of BMI as a predictor of outcomes.

It's worth noting, however, that women who undergo some weight loss surgeries and then become pregnant may experience other problems with their own health and the health of their fetus. Many weight loss surgeries are designed to prompt malnutrition, and researchers have pointed out that it's possible that women who become pregnant postoperatively may risk malnutrition for themselves and for their fetus (Pelizzo et al. 2014; Tobah 2020). For example, in their meta-review, Zainab Akhter and colleagues surveyed all available data and determined that neural tube defects in the fetus, iron deficiency that may prompt preterm delivery, and calcium deficiencies and low birth weights were all associated with pregnancies post malabsorptive procedures (2019). Weight loss surgery is not, then, a neutral choice—much less a positive choice—as it's often presented to women hoping to conceive.

Mother Blame: Your Child Is Your Problem (and Everyone Else's)

Women are also expected, if they do bear children, to keep those children thin. Much of this responsibility has been created through the individualizing of weight as a personal issue related to diet, and particularly to food choice and preparation. As Reiheld notes, around the globe, "food preparation is surprisingly consistently feminized" (2015, 232), and some groups are disproportionately targeted as collections of irresponsible individuals who need better mothers to help them make better choices. One high-visibility initiative in the United States that has made this clear is former First Lady Michele Obama's "Let's Move!" campaign. I've written in the past about my issues with the Let's Move! campaign and its focus on large children, especially children from certain racialized communities who she describers as threatening the fiscal health and security of the nation:

> The Let's Move! website emphasizes that childhood obesity is more prevalent in African American and Hispanic Communities. At the launch of the campaign, the First Lady noted that, because of childhood obesity, "the physical and emotional health of an entire generation and the economic health and security of our nation is at stake." Rhetorically, she's asked that people care about children in these communities not because all people deserve access as a human right but because they're unhealthy and about to bankrupt the country.
>
> *(Herndon 2012)*

Writing about her concerns with Obama's campaign, E. Cassandra Dame-Griff argues that Obama uses her "mantle of the public mother" in order to "lay claim to children who do not belong to [her] in the name of determining standards of acceptable childhoods" (2016, 157). In this role, Dame-Griff asserts that Obama's public comments about childhood obesity have the effect of "indicting Latina/o parents, whose parental failure is demonstrated through their children's bodies" (2016, 159). Fat Studies scholars have noted, as Dame-Griff also asserts, that "acceptable childhoods" are often racially defined in ways that mean parents of color and their children are often defined as outside of normal or desirable citizens (Herndon 2005, 2014; Dame-Griff 2016, 102). Dame-Griff goes on to note that in one set of comments, Obama

> calls extra attention to what are often interpreted as "traditional" Latino foods such as "tres leches" cake, "tortillas," and "arroz con pollo," suggesting that it is the presence of these foods in the households and diets of Latina/o children that lead to Latina/o childhood "obesity."
>
> *(2016, 161)*

Thus, children's bodies come to symbolize not only individuals' parenting abilities but also a whole culture's problematic foods that set them apart and construct them, as Dame-Griff argues, as "racially different or foreign, making [them] 'incompatible with the body politic of the citizenry'" (2016, 162).

Ruling on Appropriate Parenting: Courts and Fat Children

The question of parental fitness has also been taken up by the courts. In the early 2000s there were several high-profile legal cases where children were taken out of homes because their weight was understood to be a sign of neglect. In several of these, the mothers' bodies were also put on trial because they, too, were fat. In the cases of children from separate homes known in the court records as D.K., Brittany T., and Liza T., the court documents make multiple mentions of their mothers' weights as a kind of "evidence" of inability to appropriately parent (*In re* L.T.; *In re* D.K.; *In re* Brittany T.). In the case of Brittany T., her mother, Mrs. T (also named Shawna T. in the court documents), is described as "very obese" and her weight is mentioned as being tracked at the nutrition clinic the family court ordered them to attend (*In re* Brittany T.). Throughout the court opinion, Mrs. T. is positioned as being responsible for Brittany T's weight in spite of it being a two-parent home. At one point, a doctor, who testified on the case, noted that Brittany's weight resulted from "poor parental modeling and control of food intake" (*In re* Brittany T.), yet it's only Brittany's mother's weight and eating habits that are present in the court documents, making her the "responsible parent" in the eyes of the legal system and reaffirming the expectation that women keep themselves and their children thin lest their bodies be read as a kind of resistance to both cultural norms and legal standards for appropriate parenting.[4]

Legal scholar Sondra Solovay argues that such cases often showcase the way fatness is seen as *the* problem to be solved, regardless of other health and/ or psychological issues children might have. Commenting on the case of Liza T, a teenager removed from her parents' home, Solovay notes "Liza's physicians diagnosed her as having severe infantile personality disorder and a problem with morbid obesity caused by overeating as a method of coping with the strife between her parents" (2000, 74). Solovay goes on to point out that the court's written opinion on the case contained 17 mentions of Liza's body weight with only 11 mentions of the psychological issues said to cause her weight (2000, 75). The court record showed that Liza went from 290 to 266 pounds during the month she was out of her parents' house, but there was no mention of progress or treatment for the psychological issues she was facing (*In re* L.T.). Ultimately, she was treated for what looked like, at most, a secondary health concern, and if her weight was caused by overeating due to psychological issues, she was not given treatment for the underlying cause; she was also not made thin by being removed from her home.

The "treatment" of being removed from the home not only doesn't produce thin children, it's also likely to cause psychological problems and more stress for children. One of the most widely publicized cases of a child being removed from a home was that of Anamarie Regino, a three-year-old Mexican American girl who was removed from her family's home in September of 2000 because she was having health problems believed to be directly tied to her weight (Herndon 2014, 1). After spending months away from her parents and then being returned, Anamarie never became the thin child the authorities had hoped for (Galvan 2011). In the decade following her removal from her home, several high-profile publications in the medical field advocated for understanding childhood obesity as an issue of medical neglect (Varness et al. 2009; Murtagh and Ludwig 2011), and the influence of these discussions became apparent in countries like Australia and the United States as children were removed from homes to "treat" their obesity because their parents were believed to be part of the problem. Anamarie, who is one of the only children to speak publicly about having been removed from her home, referred to it as "hell" (Harris and Conley 2011). In addition to the psychological harm Anamarie felt, children removed from homes often failed to lose weight or gained back any weight that was lost. This was, perhaps, part of why there appeared to be a lull in conversations about removing children from homes and a brief period when courts seemed reluctant to do so.

Recently, the threat of removing children from homes became real again as two teenagers from West Sussex County in the UK were placed in foster care after social service workers and a judge determined that their parents were at fault for not providing evidence from the children's FitBits of physical activity or documentation that they'd attended Weight Watchers (Badshah 2021). For anyone raising fat children, but perhaps especially for women who may also be marginalized in any other way, the threat of state intervention for a child's weight became all too real once again. Perhaps most concerning is that the judge specifically noted that this was an otherwise "loving family" where the children had clearly had "some very good parenting" (Badshah 2021). This rhetoric showcases body weight as *the* defining trait of a child and *the* defining litmus test of one's ability to parent, all of which suggests that the stakes for having a fat child are quite high, especially for people already targeted by public health campaigns and/or marginalized by race, class or other social locations deemed to put one "at risk" of obesity. As the conversation about "globesity"[5] expands, what happens in one country increasingly influences conversations and policies in others, prompting concern in the United States as I saw many Fat Studies groups and listservs post the story of these two teenagers and express trepidation that the United States would go down this path again.

Cut It Out!: Fat Children, Bullying, and Bariatric Surgeries

Arguably the most extreme interventions in children's and teens' lives and on their bodies are weight loss surgeries. These surgeries can involve anything from a gastric band to procedures such as Roux-en-Y, which involves severing a part of the stomach and bypassing feet of intestines in an effort to curtail food consumption and to limit the amount of nutrients that can be absorbed from the food that is consumed (American Society of Metabolic and Bariatric Surgery 2021). Currently, in the United States the guidelines for surgeries on those under 18 specify that they must be 14 for girls or 15 for boys, have tried other means of losing weight, must be able to weigh the costs and benefits of the surgery, and must be willing to commit to a lifelong regimen of necessary vitamin supplements (Cleveland Clinic 2018). The Cleveland Clinic site also acknowledges that "the long term effects of this surgery are not known, and weight loss surgery does not guarantee that an adolescent will lose all the excess weight and keep it off for a long time" (2018). Despite these warnings, many teens are opting for these surgeries. One comprehensive study that examined available data about children and adolescents undergoing bariatric procedures from 2012 to 2016 found that "about 73% of [metabolic and bariatric surgery] patients were female, half were ages of 17 or 18, and half were non-Hispanic white" (Jenco 2019). We might expect to see more since The American Academy of Pediatrics recently published a piece whose authors write that "metabolic and bariatric surgery are existing but underused treatment options for pediatric patients with severe obesity" (Bolling et al. 2019). The data, however, about the long-term efficacy of these surgeries for weight loss is acknowledged as being a challenge, with the Mayo Clinic, which regularly performs bariatric procedures on teens, noting that "weight gain remains a challenge in adolescent and adults, and therefore close follow-up is necessary to achieve long-term efficacy" (2016).

Notably, the Public Education Committee of the American Society for Metabolic and Bariatric Surgery includes a Q and A section about children. In answering the question "How does obesity affect children?" they respond: "First, a child is more likely to have health issues early on in life. Second, children also face weight bias and bullying" (2021). Thus, children's bodies—rather than what are called obesogenic environments or any of the other social factors, such as bullying, that might contribute to poor health—are the targets for drastic intervention. This extension of blame and responsibility—even for the actions of others—to individual children offers a profound example of how public discussions and policies around "the obesity epidemic" gesture toward the environment as a problem but ultimately intervene at the level of individual bodies.

In the United States this emphasis on individual action—even from young children—means that the medical system has increasingly allowed younger children to undergo surgeries. For example, it's common for children as young as 14 in the United States to be able to undergo procedures at surgery centers like the one at Texas Children's Hospital, whose policies state that adolescents who are 14 and "have reached physical and psychological maturity" (n.d.). The implication here is that 14 is the age at which an adolescent would be able to consent to such a procedure, but there's ample evidence that adults often don't understand how much their lives will be changed post-bariatric surgery and issues with ongoing compliance as a result.[6] In spite of this data, some countries have moved to performing weight loss procedures on much younger children. Most extreme cases of weight loss surgeries are arguably abroad with a five-year-old in Saudi Arabia receiving a weight loss surgery at the age of five and a sleeve gastrectomy being done on a two-and-a-half-year-old by surgeons in Saudi Arabia (Mohaidly, Suliman, and Malawi 2013). As is often the case with conversations about obesity in today's world, however, conversations, practices, and policies around the globe influence one another, so there's good reason to worry about international standards in the time of "globesity."

All Women Are Being Drafted into the "War Against Obesity"

Because of what Karen Zivi calls "maternal ideology," even women who don't plan to become mothers are expected to monitor their weight in the off chance that they might become pregnant, making all women's bodies subject to scrutiny and interventions (2005, 350). Similarly, Martha Fineman claims that

all women should care about the social and cultural presentation of the concepts of motherhood that are part of the process that constructs and perpetuates a unitary, essentialist social understanding of women. "Mother" is so interwoven with that notion of what it means to be a woman in our culture that it will continue to have an impact on individual women's lives.

(1991, 276)

In fact, the maternal ideology around "the obesity epidemic" is so powerful that it's caused some medical experts who are particularly worried about women passing obesity along to their children to suggest that all women be counseled about their weight. Willing to go even further, John Kral argued in his *Pediatrics* article that even the youngest girls should be counseled about their weight. According to Megan Warin and her coauthors, "[Kral] argues that all women, even 'newborn girls,' have the potential to become doubly damaging" and that "the only way to curb the obesity epidemic is to 'urgently' target girls and young women: 'from birth to menarche, behavior modification in mothers and children should be the first choice' in obesity prevention" (2012, 11). The rhetoric of the "obesity epidemic" can at first seem like a mismatch given its usually contagious diseases that are described as epidemics, but the worry that women are passing obesity on to their children—through their very bodies and/or their parenting practices—has made the language of an "epidemic" seem all too logical to those waging the "war against obesity."

The notion of what is often called "intergenerational obesity" has become a driving force in the idea that the place to intervene is in the family and in the lives and bodies of women. John Kral and his coauthors write about "intergenerational transmission of obesity" in a way that highlights its focus on preventing the existence of fat people in the first place through what are arguably claims that sound like they could be published in a eugenics pamphlet. They write that we must "prevent pregnancy in those already obese and severely obese" and suggest that one way to do so might be through prosecutions of those who are fat but still become pregnant. They opine: "If Society [sic] is willing to prosecute drug-abusing mothers, and warn of alcohol and tobacco use during pregnancy, should we not be serious about preventing obese pregnancies?" (2012, 255). As feminist scholars such as Dorothy Roberts and Susan Bordo have pointed out in their groundbreaking works, we now know that the influence of drug use—or other behaviors by the mother—during pregnancy is often no more important to children's development than environmental factors like living in poverty or being exposed to lead paint (1991, 1420; 1993, 78). Thinking critically about which mothers were prosecuted for what drug use, Krista Stone-Manista points out that there are deep inequities in drug prosecutions of pregnant women, namely that women of color and/or poor women were often prosecuted for using crack even though tobacco appears to be just as dangerous (2009, 836). Likewise, it would likely be the case that similar inequities would appear for women being prosecuted for "obese pregnancies" given what we know about the rates of obesity in communities of color and among poor and working-class women.

While there may be some increasing pressure on men to also be thin in order to protect future generations, especially as more data from the field of epigenetics (and the Overkalix study in particular) suggests that men may also have a role to play in determining children's body types and weights, it remains that women are treated as what legal scholars like Nancy Kubasek refer to as a "special case," where responsibility is unfairly placed on to one individual or group. Thinking through fetal abuse laws, Kubasek argues that "by failing to treat all individuals similarly, fetal-abuse prosecutions violate the equal protection clause" (1999, 177). Kubasek and other legal scholars are often writing about prosecutions for drug use while pregnant, for example, but their core assertion—that to only prosecute women given all the other possible and relevant influences on fetuses—makes women into a "special case," which is unjust and unfair. As I've argued elsewhere, the war on drugs and the war on obesity share significant territory in their investment in monitoring and prosecuting women even though environmental issues like lead paint, poverty, and lack of access to clean water are just as likely to influence a fetus. While the obesity epidemic is often traced back to what is now called an "obesogenic environment," the "war against obesity" is being battled in the lives and on the bodies of women and children.

One of the most disturbing developments in the discourse of bariatric surgeries is that they're now referred to as Metabolic and Bariatric Surgeries and becoming options for "small fat" people, especially women. Long-time promoters of weight loss surgeries in the medical field, such as Henry Buchwald, argue that bariatric surgery was always metabolic surgery (2014, 1126) while other advocates of the procedures, such as Blaine T. Phillips and Scott A. Shikora, argue that "metabolic and bariatric surgeries is now a better descriptor" of the surgeries (2018, 97). In rebranding the surgery as "metabolic," practitioners have opened up space to treat even more patients, as metabolic surgery is increasingly written about as appropriate for those who have a BMI between 30 and 35, which would likely be between 50 and 75 lbs. over what's considered ideal body weight. Acknowledging that diets and every other intervention have failed to promote and maintain weight loss, some practitioners position "metabolic surgery" as a brave new cure for everything from type 2 diabetes to hyperlipidemia (Celio and Pories 2016, 656). One doctor, writing in his article about knowing the difference between metabolic and bariatric surgery, laid bare who these newly labeled "metabolic surgeries" and their proponents will likely target: "Women who are in their 40s are the major candidates for metabolic surgery. The advantage is also that it improves their esthetics which further increases follow-up and thereby success rate" (Payal 2020). Thus, doctors and surgeons promoting these procedures know full well that they are taking advantage of a fatphobic culture where women are more often the victims of that fatphobia even when they, as Gordon might describe them, are "small fat." A 2015 study pointed out that while obesity rates in the United States are fairly equal between men and women, 80 percent of those currently undergoing bariatric procedures are women (Fuchs et al. 2015). Policies that allow for what are arguably drastic measures to lose weight that are well-understood as having a gendered dynamic seem to encourage more and more women to undergo these procedures.

Reflecting Back on Moving Forward

When I was a child, there was pressure to be thin, and my mother was pressured to keep her own body and my body thin. Yet, no one referred to me as an "obesity time bomb"[7] or waged rhetorical and physical "war" against kids who looked like me; no one ever thought I'd be taken away from my home because I was fat, and no one suggested I undergo a surgery because other children called me "fat." Mothers and children today can't really make those claims, especially if they're marginalized in other ways. Instead, they're living in the middle of a war where they are perceived as and constructed as the enemy, as threats to the country's fiscal and physical future. As is so often the case in the United States, battles against what is seen as "foreign" or "risky" are most frequently directed against those who are already marginalized via race and class. The "war on obesity" proves no different. Like "the war on drugs" and "the war on poverty" before it, the "war on obesity" claims to be against a threatening enemy to people and the nation but exacts its toll on the bodies and the lives of those it claims to want to help. There is no data to suggest that stigma and fat shaming help people become thin or better parents; in fact, the data suggests that living under this kind of scrutiny, filled with microaggressions from settings in healthcare, education, housing, wages—all the places we would expect to see discrimination against marginalized groups—makes people more unhealthy.[8] For fat people, in particular, this makes it very difficult to sort through whether any health problems are caused by body weight or by the stress of everyday living in a fatphobic society. One thing is for certain, however, the "war on obesity"—with its intense focus on women and children—is not making their lives nor our nation any better.

Notes

1 I use "obesity" in scare quotes here to show that it's a debated label and diagnosis. It may appear elsewhere without those quotation marks because it's being used in healthcare publications or policies in which it isn't being questioned.

2 I want to acknowledge here that there are people who may not identify using terms such as "woman" or "women" yet who may be capable of giving birth. Because most of the sources cited here around IVF policies and such use "woman," I've chosen to use that terminology in the writing for the chapter.

3 A simple Google search reveals hundreds of results from IVF clinics stating their positions on IVF and BMI. Many of the clinic sites also contain BMI calculators as educational tools for women seeking IVF treatment.

4 A more detailed examination of these cases can be found in my book *Fat Blame: How the War on Obesity Victimizes Women and Children*.

5 The World Health Organization uses the term "globesity" as a shorthand to discuss what they describe as the "global obesity epidemic." See www.who.int/activities/cont rolling-the-global-obesity-epidemic

6 Mayo Clinic, as I cite in another part of this chapter, acknowledges problems with compliance. A PubMed search for "bariatric surgery and compliance" also reveals over 600 articles discussing problems with compliance ranging from a failure to take required vitamins to avoiding simple carbohydrates to avoid dumping syndrome. A longer discussion of these issues is in my book *Fat Blame*.

7   This reference is from a cartoon that featured a doctor holding a newborn and telling the parents, "Congratulations! It's an Obesity Time Bomb." See my book *Fat Blame* for a longer discussion of the rhetoric of the "war on obesity" and how children's bodies are described.
8   For more discussion of these issues, see Puhl, Rebecca M., and Chelsea A. Heuer. 2010. "Obesity Stigma: Important Considerations for Public Health." *American Journal of Public Health* 100, no. 6: 1019–1028.

Bibliography

Akhter, Zainab, Judith Rankin, Dries Ceulemans, Lem Ngongalah, Roger Ackroyd, Roland Devlieger, Rute Vieira, and Nicola Heslehurst. 2019. "Pregnancy After Bariatric Surgery and Adverse Perinatal Outcomes: A Systematic Review and Meta-Analysis." *PLOS Medicine* 16, no. 8: 1–20.

Alberga, Angela S., Iyoma Y. Edache, Mary Forhan, and Shelly Russell-Mayhew. 2019. "Weight Bias and Health Care Utilization: A Scoping Review." *Primary Health Care Research & Development* 20 (E116): 1–14.

American Academy of Bariatric and Metabolic Surgery. 2021. "Bariatric Surgery Procedures." Last updated May 2021. https://asmbs.org/patients/bariatric-surgery-pro cedures

Badshah, Nadeem. 2021. "Two Teenagers Placed in Foster Care After Weight Loss Plan Fails." *The Guardian*. March 11, 2021. www.theguardian.com/society/2021/mar/10/ two-teenagers-placed-in-foster-care-after-weight-loss-plan-fails

Biltekoff, Charlotte. 2007. "The Terror within: Obesity in post 9/11 US Life." *American Studies* 48, no. 3: 29–48.

Blanchette, Sarah. 2020. "Critiquing the *DSM-V* Narrative of 'Obesity' as a 'Mental Illness'." In *Thickening Fat: Fat Bodies, Intersectionality, and Social Justice*, edited by May Friedman, Carla Rice, and Jen Rinaldi, 79–90. New York: Routledge.

Boero, Natalie. 2009. "Fat Kids, Working Moms and the 'Epidemic of Obesity': Race, Class and Mother Blame." In *Fat Studies Reader*, edited by Esther Rothblum and Sondra Solovay, 113–19. New York: New York University Press.

Bolling, Christopher F., Sarah C. Armstrong, Kirk W. Reichard, and Marc P. Michalsky. 2019. "Metabolic and Bariatric Surgery for Pediatric Patients with Severe Obesity." *Pediatrics* 144, no. 6: 1–10.

Bordo, Susan. 1993. *Unbearable Weight: Feminism, Western Culture, and the Body*. Berkeley, CA: University of California Press.

Brown, Heather and April Herndon. 2020. "No Bad Fatties Allowed?: Negotiating the Power and Meaning of the Mutable Body." In *Thickening Fat: Fat Bodies, Intersectionality, and Social Justice*, edited by May Friedman, Carla Rice, and Jen Rinaldi, 139–149. New York: Routledge.

Buchwald, Henry. 2014. "The Evolution of Metabolic/Bariatric Surgery." *Obesity Surgery* 24, no. 8: 1126–35.

Celio, Adam C. and Walter J. Pories. 2016. "A History of Bariatric Surgery: The Maturation of a Medical Discipline." *Surgical Clinics of North America* 96, no. 4: 656–67.

Ciciurkaite, Gabriel and Brea L. Perry. 2017. "Body Weight, Perceived Weight Stigma and Mental Health Among Women at the Intersections of Race/Ethnicity and Socioeconomic Status: Insights from the Modified Labeling Approach." *Sociology of Health and Illness* 40, no. 1: 18–37.

Cleveland Clinic. 2018. "Weight Loss Surgery for Adolescents with Severe Obesity." Last reviewed May 29, 2018. https://my.clevelandclinic.org/health/treatments/17859-wei ght-loss-surgery-for-adolescents-with-severe-obesity

Dame-Griff, E. Cassandra. 2016. "He's Not Heavy, He's an Anchor Baby: Fat Children, Failed Futures, and the Threat of Latina/o Excess." *Fat Studies* 5, no. 2: 156–71.

Davidson, Megan and Sarah Lewin. 2018. "Eating for Two: The Fear and Threat of Fatness in Pregnancy." In *Heavy Burdens: Stories of Motherhood and Fatness*, edited by Judy Verseghy and Sam Abel, 45–60. Ontario: Demeter Press.

Doherty, Brian. 2001. "Fatwa on Fat: The Surgeon General Snoops into Private Health." *Reason Magazine*. December 19, 2001. Accessed March 25, 2003. https://reason. com/2001/12/19/fatwa-on-fat/

Fineman, Martha L. 1991. "Images of Mothers in Poverty Discourses." *Duke Law Journal* 92: 274–95.

Fuchs, Hans F., Ryan C. Broderick, Cristina R. Harnsberger, David C. Chang, Bryan J. Sandler, Garth R. Jacobsen, and Santiago Horgan. 2015. "Benefits of Bariatric Surgery Do Not Reach Obese Men." *Journal of Laparoendoscopic & Advanced Surgical Techniques* 25, no. 3: 196–201.

Galvan, Astrid. 2011. "Teen Taken from Parents as a Child Coping with Loss." *Albuquerque Journal* (syndicated in *Deseret News*). October 14, 2011. www.deseret. com/2011/10/14/20222975/teen-taken-from-parents-as-child-coping-with-loss

Gard, Michael, and Jan Wright. 2005. *The Obesity Epidemic: Science, Morality, and Ideology.* New York: Routledge.

Gordon, Aubrey. 2020. *What We Don't Talk About When We Talk About Fat.* Boston: Beacon Press.

Harjunen, Hannale. 2021. "Fatness and Consequences of Neoliberalism." In *The Routledge International Handbook of Fat Studies*, edited by Cat Pausé and Sonya Renee Taylor, 68–77. New York: Routledge.

Harris, Dan, and Mikaela Conley. 2011. "Childhood Obesity: A Call for Parents to Lose Custody." *ABC News.* July 14, 2011. https://abcnews.go.com/Health/childhood-obes ity-call-parents-lose-custody/story?id=14068280

Herndon, April Michelle. 2005. "Collateral Damage from Friendly Fire?: Race, Nation, Class and the 'War Against Obesity'." *Social Semiotics* 15, no. 2: 127–41.

———. 2012. "My Beef with Michelle Obama's Let's Move! Campaign: What Every Child Deserves Regardless of Weight." *Dry Land Fish, Perspectives from the Misplaced.* April 25, 2012. Accessed June 20, 2021. www.psychologytoday.com/us/blog/dry-land-fish/201204/my-beef-michelle-obamas-lets-move-campaign

———. 2014. *Fat Blame: How the War on Obesity Victimizes Women and Children.* Lawrence, KS: University of Kansas Press.

———. 2018. "Overfeeding the Floating Fetus and Future Citizen: The 'War on Obesity' and the Expansion of Fetal Rights." In *Heavy Burdens: Stories of Motherhood and Fatness*, edited by Judy Verseghy and Sam Abel, 35–44. Ontario: Demeter Press.

Hurst, Danielle J., Nicholas B. Schmuhl, Corrine I. Voils, and Kathleen M. Antony. 2021. "Prenatal Care Experiences Among Pregnant Women with Obesity in Wisconsin, United States: A Qualitative Quality Improvement Assessment." *BMC Pregnancy and Childbirth* 21, no. 1: 1–13.

In Interest of L.T., 494 N.W.2d 450 (Iowa Ct. App. 1992).

In re D.K., 2002 WL 31968992, 58 Pa.D. & C. 4th 353 (Pa. Com.Pl. 2002).

In the Matter of Brittany T., 15 Misc. 3d 606, 835 N.Y.S.2d 829 (Fam. Ct. 2007).

Jenco, Melissa. "Study: More Children Having Metabolic and Bariatric Surgery." 2019. *American Academy of Pediatrics News.* August 16, 2019. www.aappublications.org/news/2019/08/16/bariatricsurgery081619

Judge, Timothy A., and Daniel M. Cable. 2011. "When It Comes to Pay, Do the Thin Win? The Effect of Weight on Pay for Men and Women." *Journal of Applied Psychology* 96, no. 1: 95–112.

Kral, John G., Ruth A. Kava, Patrick M. Catalano, and Barbara J. Moore. 2012. "Severe Obesity: The Neglected Epidemic." *European Journal of Obesity* 5, no. 2: 254–69.

Kubasek, Nancy. 1999. "Case Against Prosecutions for Prenatal Drug Abuse." *Texas Journal of Women and the Law* 8, no. 2 (Spring): 167–82.

LeBesco, Kathleen. 2010. "Fat Panic and the New Morality." In *Against Health: How Health Became the New Morality,* edited by Jonathan Metzel and Anna Kirkland, 72–82. New York: New York University Press.

Lee, Jennifer A. and Cat J. Pausé. 2016. "Stigma in Practice: Barriers to Health for Fat Women." *Frontiers in Psychology* 7: 2063.

Lind, Emily R. M. 2020. "Queering Fat Activism: A Study in Whiteness." In *Thickening Fat: Fat Bodies, Intersectionality, and Social Justice,* edited by May Friedman, Carla Rice, and Jen Rinaldi, 183–94. New York: Routledge.

Mayo Clinic. 2016 "Bariatric Surgery in Adolescents." Last updated May 7, 2016. www.mayoclinic.org/medical-professionals/endocrinology/news/bariatric-surgery-in-adolescents/mac-20429497

McPhail, Deborah and Lindsey Mazur. 2020. "Medicalization, Maternity, and the Materiality of Resistance: 'Maternal Obesity' and Experiences of Reproductive Care." In *Thickening Fat: Fat Bodies, Intersectionality, and Social Justice,* edited by May Friedman, Carla Rice, and Jen Rinaldi, 122–36. New York: Routledge.

Mensinger, Janell L., Tracy L. Tylka, and Margaret E. Calamari. 2018. "Mechanisms Underlying Weight Status and Healthcare Avoidance in Women: A Study of Weight Stigma, Body-Related Shame and Guilt, and Healthcare Stress." *Body Image* 25: 139–47.

Mohaidly, Mohammed Al, Ahmed Suliman, Horia Malawi. 2013. "Laparoscopic Sleeve Gastrectomy for a Two-and Half Year Old Morbidly Obese Child." *International Journal of Surgery Case Reports* 4, no. 11: 1057–60.

Murtagh, Lindsey and David S. Ludwig. 2011. "State Intervention in Life-Threatening Childhood Obesity." *Journal of the American Medical Association* 306, no. 2: 206–7.

Norman, Robert J. and Willem J. Mol. 2018. "Successful Weight Loss Interventions Before In Vitro Fertilization: Fat Chance?" *Fertility and Sterility* 110, no. 4: 581–86.

Payal, Ashish. 2020. "Know the Difference Between Bariatric Surgery and Metabolic Surgery." *Medlife.* March 5, 2020. Accessed May 4, 2020. www.medlife.com/blog/difference-between-bariatric-and-metabolic-surgery/

Pelizzo, Gloria, Valeria Calcaterra, Mario Fusillo, Ghassan Nakib, Antonio Maria Ierullo, Alessandro Alfei, Arsenio Spinillo, Mauro Stronati, and Hellas Cena. 2014. "Malnutrition in Pregnancy Following Bariatric Surgery: Three Clinical Cases of Neural Defects." *Nutritional Journal* 13, no. 59: 1–6.

Phillips, Blaine T. and Scott A. Shikora. 2018. "The History of Metabolic and Bariatric Surgery: Development of Standards for Patient Safety and Efficacy." *Metabolism* 79: 97–107.

Pratt, Janey S.A. et al. 2018. "ASMBS Pediatric Metabolic and Bariatric Surgery Guidelines, 2018." *Surgery for Obesity and Related Diseases.* 14: 882–901.

Public Education Committee, American Society for Metabolic and Bariatric Surgery. 2021. "Childhood and Adolescent Obesity." Last updated February 2021. https://asmbs.org/patients/adolescent-obesity

Reiheld, Alison. 2015. "With All Due Caution: Global Anti-Obesity Campaigns and the Individualization of Responsibility." *International Journal of Feminist Approaches to Bioethics* 8, no. 2: 226–49.

Roberts, Dorothy E. 1991. "Punishing Drug Addicts Who Have Babies: Women of Color, Equality, and the Right of Privacy." *Harvard Law Review* 104, no. 7 (May): 1419–82.

———. 1998. *Killing the Black Body: Race, Reproduction, and the Meaning of Liberty.* New York: Vintage.

Schvey, N. A., R. M. Puhl, K. A. Levandoski, and K. D. Brownell. 2013. "The Influence of a Defendant's Body Weight on Perceptions of Guilt." *International Journal of Obesity* 37, no. 9: 1275–81.

Sermondade, Nathalie, Céline Faure, Léopold Fezeu, Rachel Lévy, and Sébastien Czernichow. 2012. "Obesity and Increased Risk for Oliogozoospermia and Azoospermia." *Archives of Internal Medicine* 175, no. 2: 440–42.

Sole-Smith, Virginia. 2019. "When You're Told You're Too Fat to Get Pregnant." *New York Times Magazine.* June 18, 2019. www.nytimes.com/2019/06/18/magazine/fertility-weight-obesity-ivf.html

Solovay, Sandra. 2000. *Tipping the Scales of Justice: Fighting Weight-Based Discrimination.* Amherst, NY: Prometheus Books.

Stone-Manista, Krista. 2009. "Protecting Pregnant Women: A Guide to Successfully Challenging Criminal Abuse Prosecutions of Pregnant Drug Addicts." *Journal of Criminal Law and Criminology* 99, no. 3: 823–56.

Strings, Sabrina. 2019. *Fearing the Black Body: The Racial Origins of Fat Phobia.* New York: New York University Press.

Texas Children's Hospital. n.d. "Bariatric Surgery Program." Accessed June 20, 2021. www.texaschildrens.org/departments/bariatric-surgery

Tobah, Yvonne Butler. 2020. "Pregnancy After Gastric Bypass: Is It Safe?" *Mayo Clinic.* Updated June 23, 2020. www.mayoclinic.org/healthy-lifestyle/getting-pregnant/expert-answers/pregnancy-after-gastric-bypass/faq-20058409

United States Department of Health and Human Services, Office of Disease Prevention and Health Promotion. "Social Determinants of Health." *Healthy People 2030.* Accessed June 20, 2021. https://health.gov/healthypeople/objectives-and-data/social-determinants-health

Varness, Todd, David B. Allen, Aaron L. Carrel, and Norman Fost. 2009. "Childhood Obesity and Medical Neglect." *Pediatrics* 123, no. 1: 399–406.

Warin, Megan, Tanya Zivkovic, Vivienne Moore, and Michael Davies. 2012. "Mothers as Smoking Guns: Fetal Overnutrition and the Reproduction of Obesity." *Feminism & Psychology* 22, no. 3: 360–75.

Zivi, Karen. 2005. "Contesting Motherhood in the Age of AIDS: Maternal Ideology in the Debate Over Mandatory HIV Testing." *Feminist Studies* 31, no. 2: 347–74.

11

HISTORIES OF EXCESS

Overlaps Between Anti-Fat and Anti-Latina Public Discourse

E. Cassandra Dame-Griff

At the turn of the millennium, Fat Studies scholars and Fat Activists alike expressed alarm and dismay at a story that would quickly garner national attention. This was the case of then toddler-aged Anamarie Regino, a Mexican-American girl who was removed from her parents' care due to her weight and her parents' perceived inability to care for their daughter. Writing in 2001 in *The New York Times Magazine*, Lisa Belkin noted that throughout the Regino family's fight for unfettered custody of their daughter, "Ana was transformed from a little girl to a cause," in two particular ways. First—as Belkin wrote—Ana became "a cause célèbre for the National Association to Advance Fat Acceptance, which sees her case as a 'threat to all the parents of fat children'" (Belkin 2001). Second, Ana's case also highlighted the dangers of state overreach into families, particularly families for whom the historical relationship between the family and the state has been marked by family disruption by the state supported by and indeed caused by racist and sexist ideologies of families of Color as pathological. In particular, Ana's case raised red flags regarding Latina mothers and motherhood, as her mother Adela Martinez-Regino (who died in 2011) took center stage as both her staunchest advocate as well as a scapegoat for both state agencies and the media who blamed Adela for overfeeding, cosseting, and ultimately harming her child by not enforcing weight loss (Galvan 2011).

In this chapter, I explore this overlap between anti-fatness and specifically anti-Latina/o/x discourse and how it simultaneously reflects and reinforces racialized and gendered policies around immigration, child-rearing, and parenting, in particular, motherhood. For Latina women in the United States, the intersection of misogyny, racism, and anti-fat attitudes have not only threatened our presence in the United States but also shaped governmental policy and associated discussions by narrating Latinas as unfit mothers through a discursive framing of excess.

DOI: 10.4324/9781003140665-16

This discourse frames Latina women and mothers as physically and culturally embodying excess, as well as being the bearers of excess bodies, both their own and those of their children. This excess, often symbolized through fatness, overeating, or eating the "wrong" types of food, is then wielded as "evidence" of their cultural pathology and unfitness to mother—accusations that shape public sentiment and resulting policies about immigration in general, and specifically Latina women.

To begin, I examine how scholars working at the intersections of Fat Studies, Latina/o/x Studies, Immigration Studies, and Gender Studies grapple with the interplay between anti-fatness and misogynist anti-Latina/anti-immigrant discourse around Latina motherhood. I begin looking at historical representations of Latina—particularly Mexican-American—motherhood as excessive, mapping the ways this mischaracterization of non-white cooking, eating, and feeding practices has merged with anti-fat discourse in the contemporary moment. In this section, I also locate notions of excessive and therefore pathological motherhood in historical context, connecting negative characterizations of Latina motherhood to examples within other marginalized racial and ethnic groups. I then shift to focus on the place of anti-fatness and the so-called "War on Obesity" within debates surrounding immigration, wherein anti-immigration pundits present Latina women and mothers as greedy, often monstrous reproducers—or potential reproducers—who harm not only their own children but the children of (white) others. Finally, drawing on the work of Mae Ngai, April Herndon, and others, I consider the historical and discursive antecedents that shaped notions of deviant femininity and how they exist in the current moment of anti-fat/anti-Latina public discourse. Throughout this chapter, I historically contextualize contemporary conversations at the intersections of anti-fat and anti-Latina discourse, underscoring the precedents set at different historical moments and for other communities and women of Color.

Excessive M(other)hood and Saviorhood

In his 1995 history of Mexican-American acculturation and assimilation in the United States in the first half of the twentieth century, historian George J. Sánchez argued that food—preparation, consumption, and types of food eaten— was a central aspect of Americanization programs of the early 1900s. Bearing "assimilationist goals," Americanization programs zeroed in on Mexican women, understanding wives and mothers as the avenue for teaching Mexican-American families proper American cultural mores, particularly those "concerning diet and health" (Sánchez 1995, 101–2). For American reformers, diet was considered a central space of intervention not only because it offered an opportunity to teach American foodways, but also because it was understood as a cornerstone of health. Importantly and unsurprisingly, "American" foods and foodways (preparations, varieties, mealtimes, etc.) were deemed more healthful than those of Mexicans or, indeed, most other "foreigners" and immigrants. For example"[m]alnourishment in Mexican families was not blamed on lack of food or resources but rather on 'not having the right varieties of foods containing constituents favorable to growth and development'" (Sánchez 1995, 102). Therefore, it was a combination of the food itself (seen as undernutritious) and the behaviors surrounding its preparation and consumption (a lack of variability) that was flagged as unhealthy and thereby a target for reformers.

Interestingly, much of the curriculum surrounding food and foodways was based on a presupposition not of excess but lack, since staving off hunger and indeed malnourishment was a central goal of these Americanization programs. As Sánchez points out, "[t]eaching immigrant women proper food values became a route to keeping the head of the family out of jail and the rest of the family off charity," lest dangerously unfulfilling Mexican foods like tortillas lead children (understood as future adults) to engage in thievery of the more fulfilling lunches of white children (1995, 102).

Paradoxically (and somewhat perplexingly), reformers' concern with malnourishment led them to push removing nutritionally valuable staple foods, such as tortillas and rice and beans, from Mexican-Americans' diets in order to replace them with American staples like bread and lettuce. Thus, Mexican-American malnourishment "was not blamed on lack of food or resources" but on an over-reliance on Mexican foods and foodways, which reformers sought to replace with foods whose value, I argue, was defined not nutritionally but culturally. Still, even in these early renderings of ethnic food as pathological, there lurked a concern about excess, particularly the idea that Mexican-American eating habits leaned toward *over*consumption of "wrong" foods. Thus, "[r]eformers encouraged Mexican *women* to give up their penchant for fried foods [and] their all too frequent consumption of rice and beans" (1995, 102, emphasis mine). Mothers—seen as the sole purveyors of both food and culture—were targeted by reformers, largely due to perceptions of heteronormative, patriarchal gender ideologies and roles in Mexican families. Men and fathers were seen as part of the public sphere as laborers, whereas women and mothers resided in largely domestic spaces and therefore "[t]eaching immigrant *women* proper food values" remained central to reformers' tactics (1995, 102).

While this characterization of Mexican food, and Latina/o/x ethnic foods by extension, as pathological seems to cycle between fears of undernourishment and overnourishment in the early twentieth century, by the latter half of the century into the 2000s, ethnic food is firmly situated in the camp of fattening or "obesogenic," and its disparagement shifts accordingly. What does not change, however, is the general association of ethnic motherhood as the site for intervention, with Mexican-American and Latina mothers remaining as the primary target for various aspects of nutritional "reform"—that further characterize Latina motherhood as excessive and culpable targets in the "War on Obesity." Writing in 2005, April Herndon points back to the 2000 case of

Mexican-American child Anamarie Regino who, as a toddler, was removed from her parents' care because of her weight and her parents'—specifically her mother Adela's—presumed inability to feed her correctly. Even in the somewhat even-handed public coverage of Anamarie, her family, and the decisions that led to her removal, her mother Adela emerges as a central figure of maternal failure, first in terms of her own body (*New York Times* writer Lisa Belkin, whom I mentioned above, describes Adela as a "fleshy, worried woman") but also in her inability or outright refusal to control her daughter's "horrifyingly obese" body (Belkin 2001). While "[m]others' abilities to ensure that their children consume properly and to teach them disciplined freedom in consumption is, however, always dubious and open to surveillance," the Regino case offers additional insight into *which* mothers are more likely to be subject to surveillance and intervention (Power 2016, 60). This case, which has been of interest to Fat Studies, Gender Studies, and Latina/o/x Studies scholars, highlighted for many the intersection of body size with narratives of maternal blame in which "Latino ethnicity [is] taken as further evidence of [Anamarie's] parents' ignorance and inability to care for her" (Saguy and Gruys 2010, 248). Often held up as a somewhat shocking example of institutional overreach into the family based on specious associations of childhood fatness with child abuse, the Anamarie Regino case provides one of the clearest examples of the interplay among anti-fatness and ethnic chauvinism.

However, when placed in the context of Americanization and assimilationist ideology, the case of Anamarie Regino is far *less* shocking and indeed becomes a foregone conclusion. In particular, I argue, it actually falls in line with other historic (and contemporary) examples of invoking excess to justify state intervention into the lives of non-white families and children in the United States. As Margaret D. Jacobs writes in her work on the removal of Native and Indigenous children from their families during the Indian Adoption Era (1958–1967), "[t]he IAP's [Indian Adoption Program's] benevolent rhetoric of saving Indian children echoed common refrains from the turn-of-the-twentieth century assimilation era" (Jacobs 2014, 49). In particular, the IAP repeats American assimilationist frameworks of the "suffering" non-white child whose well-being and indeed, life, can only be saved by benevolent whites. As Jacobs notes, the IAP and other benevolent associations relied on preconceived notions of white cultural supremacy that painted Indian families and communities as "unfit" for reasons of both poverty but also cultural and racial differences. Central to this pathological rendering of Indian families was the "figure of the 'unmarried Indian mother,' whom authorities manufactured as an unfit parent" (2014, 52). Although scarcity was an oft cited justification for removing Native and Indigenous children from families—that is, saving them from poverty—characterizations of excess also shaped attitudes toward Indian mothers.

Social workers highlighted unwed Indian mothers' sexual excess, as they were unwilling or unable (due to imagined or presumed psychological defect) to engage in proper marital practices and sexual relationships within the boundaries of monogamous, Christian marriages (2014, 52–3). This imagined sexualized excess, seen as outside the boundaries of "American social norms [which] exalted the middle-class nuclear family and the containment of women's sexuality within it" simultaneously created the specter of the promiscuous unwed Indian mother *and* the so-called "forgotten Indian child" who must be removed and saved through fostering or adoption by white, middle-class families (2014, 53–4).

For both Mexican-American mothers and Native and Indigenous mothers, therefore, characterizations of unfit motherhood follow a similar logic: uncontrolled or excessive aspects of the mother lead to charges of insufficiency, lack, and damage to the child that therefore require intervention from simultaneously benevolent and culturally "superior" saviors. In other words, within the ideological confines of contemporary anti-fatness, childhood fatness or "obesity" is constructed via a duality of lack *and* excess. In terms of lack, ethnically and racially marked motherhood is defined as a paucity of parental fitness, parental understanding of "correct" eating and feeding, parental supervision, and discipline. Acts as simple as feeding a child and responding to their needs are recategorized as excessive (i.e. "coddling" or "over-indulgent") under reigning anti-fat ideologies. As even Anamarie's Mexican-American doctor Javier Aceves suggested in press coverage of Anamarie's story, the "problem" of Anamarie is a situation in which children are "raised in a family where food was equated with love" (Belkin 2001).

What makes the charges levied against Adela Martinez-Regino unique, though, is how Anamarie's supposed embodied excess is taken as an indicator of racialized maternal pathology. While bodily excess or what in the contemporary moment is deemed "obesity" has long been imagined as a marker of racial, ethnic, and cultural difference and deviance in the United States, constructing it as a consequence of parental and specifically maternal failure reflects the ways anti-fat ideologies have solidified and proliferated in a growing number of social and legal realms. Simply put, while anti-fat attitudes and ideologies are by no means new, they have been so firmly entrenched in the social, political, and now legal realms that they present a new subset of tools by which mothers of Color may be targeted by the state.

The ubiquity of anti-fatness and a widespread cultural acceptance of the framework that fatness is bad, dangerous, and in need of rectification has allowed "obesity" to perform the same functions in discourses about poor parenting as undernourishment and poverty did in the early-to-mid twentieth century. Childhood "obesity," I argue, now acts as a similar cultural touchpoint, a universally understood and feared example of, at minimum, parental failure, up to child neglect or malicious, intentional abuse. As a contemporary cultural boogeyman, it becomes fodder for both specious claims that immigrant and non-white bodies weaken the nation-state *and* a call for benevolent intervention into their lives and communities—for both their sake and the sake of the nation-state. The figure of the pathological mother remains at the core of this handwringing and outright fear of childhood "obesity." In the case of women of Color, assumptions of pathology are enmeshed with beliefs about ethnic, racial, and cultural difference that posit mothers of Color as both conduits of failed personhood and the means by which children of Color can be "saved."

As was the case with social workers, adoption agencies, and white prospective adoptive families seeking to "save" Native and Indigenous children from mothers and other caregivers deemed inept, Latina/o/x children have also been positioned as in need of saving and protection from child-rearing practices that might lead to "obesity." While the case of Anamarie Regino certainly bears this out on a singular scale, this was also true on the national stage as initiatives such as the *Let's Move!* campaign and the Goya-backed *MiPlato* sought to target Latina/o parents as the means to protect Latina/o/x children from "obesity." Both of these initiatives were central to Michelle Obama's positioning as both First Lady and an ideal mother, offering "empowerment" to other families—particularly Latina/o/x families—in the battle against childhood "obesity." Furthermore, these initiatives also served to reinforce narratives of the "War on Obesity," as evidenced by a United States Department of Agriculture press release that stated "[i]n support of the First Lady's initiative, Goya created an army of resources to help fight childhood obesity" (Larson 2017). Thus, Michelle Obama and Goya emerged as partners—Goya as a "national strategic partner"—in the fight against fatness.

As I argued in 2016, the rise of anti-obesity efforts as a supposed social, moral, and public good merged with the First Lady's public service work to produce projects that reinforced narratives of fatness as a national crisis. In the case of her Latina/o/x-specific outreach, this community was described as one in crisis, as "the Hispanic community in particular faces unique challenges: While one in three American children is overweight or obese, in the Hispanic community it's nearly two in five." In offering "assistance" to this group and with justifications rooted in fears not simply of a general childhood obesity crisis but one that "uniquely" impacts Latina/o/x children, *Let's Move!* reinforced narratives of ethnic and cultural pathology that posited Latina/ox parents as unable to correctly feed their children and therefore in need of state (and corporate) intervention (Dame-Griff 2016). In her speeches, particularly to the National Council of La Raza in 2013, Obama reproduced all too familiar narratives of maternal blame in which Latina women's presumed pathological relationship to food—ethnically marked food in particular—led them to feed their children "to death." Ethnically marked foods in both Latina/o/x and Black communities—*arroz con pollo, tres leches cake*, macaroni, and cheese—were singled out as unhealthy foods that should be consumed only sparingly and on special occasions. Using the language of "balanced diets," Obama repeats a similar line of logic as American reformers of the early twentieth century—ethnic foods are not "healthy enough" or "nutritious enough" to be included as staples of the American diet. While Obama's work with *Let's Move!* has largely remained in the public memory as an example of a well-meaning and indeed benevolent example of First Lady activism, it is also an example of a longer American trajectory of parental and particularly maternal blame narratives being used to justify interventions into the lives of communities and individuals of Color.

This simultaneously gendered and racialized assignment of blame is in no way novel in U.S. history, as Latina mothers and Black mothers still bear the brunt of both public discourse and the policies that stem from these ever-present conversations. Notably, fathers are largely left out of these conversations, as evidenced by the hyperfocus on pathological mothering practices. Fatherhood appears only tangential to questions of the family, effectively made invisible and therefore untouchable in critiques of families of Color. In part, this is achieved through pathologization of fathers—particularly Black fathers—as simply absent (with very little understanding regarding the social, economic, and political reasons for these often exaggerated levels of absence). Additionally, I argue, fathers and fatherhood escape this scrutiny due to American ideologies regarding gendered divisions of labor in which men function in the public sphere and women in the private, domestic realm of the home. Deviance from this norm is, of course, seen as potentially harmful to children, but for women of Color, adherence or the expectation of adherence proves equally damning. By performing domesticity with some degree of faithfulness—in this case, feeding children—situates women and mothers as the guilty party when feeding practices themselves are deemed suspect.

Mother Monster and Endangering the Nation-State

In the case of Black and Latina mothers from the mid-twentieth century to the present, public discourse decries their supposedly pathological motherhood practices as a much broader threat to not only their children, but to the children of others and the nation-state as a whole. In the case of Black women, the 1965 Moynihan Report solidified narratives of Black familial life as pathological precisely *because* it was headed by Black women. The report placed much of the blame for poverty and poor educational prospects in Black communities on what white scholars understood as "reversed roles for husband and wife" or matriarchal family systems (Moynihan 1965, 30). This discourse continued and shifted into the realm of policy by the mid-1970s, as the trope of the "Welfare Queen" further demonized Black mothers with the added bonus of now arguing that they were not only harming their children but draining the economy, ultimately threatening the financial stability of the nation-state.

Public discourse and policy following the popularization of these dually racist and sexist depictions also served to reinforce deeply antiblack tropes of excess physicality, emotionality, reproductive capacity (the "Overly Fertile welfare mother"), and laziness, which for some—as Ange-Marie Hancock notes—coalesced into assertions of fatness (Hancock 2004, 73). In 2004's *The Politics of Disgust: The Public Identity of the Welfare Queen*, Hancock argues that reinvigorations of tropes in which "AFDC [Aid to Families with Dependent

Children] recipients were described has having become fat, lazy, and exploitative" contributed to a "backlash" characterized by disdain and indeed, disgust, as the book's title suggests (2004, 50). I argue this question of disgust is one where Fat Studies scholarship and scholarship centering race, ethnicity and their intersections with gender can find clear common ground, particularly because— as Hancock explains in the introduction to her book—disgust functions in part as "social judgement" in which discourses and beliefs around responsibility and blame come to play. Disgust, I suggest, is part of the neoliberal framework in which racism and anti-fatness are both embedded, wherein embodied difference is seen as both pathological and chosen. As Xandi McMahon writes regarding the Jezebel archetype, "[t]hese were affective stereotypes: they primarily attacked Black women by implying they had *too much* emotion," which suggested they needed to be reined in and controlled for their own well-being and that of others (emphasis mine). Similarly, in the case of fatness, bodies marked by their "too-"ness are not simply the object of concern for the sake of the fat individual (despite the familiar trope of concern-trolling or worry about one's "health"). Rather, those identified as overweight and/or obese are seen too as in need of control, lest their excess spill beyond the boundaries of the individual and into the collective. The "Welfare Queen" as object of disgust, scorn, and subject to control by outside agents, including the state, is a necessary stereotype and set of discursive tropes to understand when examining the relationship between anti-fatness and the demonization of non-white motherhood.

For Latina mothers, the tropes that have maligned Black women both past and present—particularly accusations of excess that poses a threat to the nation-state—have transferred in a similar manner. While we see some of this evidence in the Americanization projects as discussed above, this is also true in more recent conservative and right-wing extremist renderings of Latina mothers as neglectful and willing to harm their own children in pursuit of life in the United States. As sociologist Mary Romero has argued in her work on extremist, nativist group Mothers Against Illegal Immigration (MAIA), groups such as these construct Mexican immigrant women as " 'bad' immigrant mothers" who use and abuse their own children to access citizenship (Romero 2011, 57). Citing the case of Elvira Arrenado, a lightning rod for conservative calls for more restrictive immigration and deportation laws, MAIA representatives in fact reproduce the Welfare Queen trope, calling Arrenado "the 'QUEEN' of opportunity." Furthermore, Romero argues, MAIA spokeswomen depict Mexican immigrant mothers as "a serious danger," first by characterizing them as "inferior mothers" and then by asserting that their poor motherhood skills—caused by their Mexican Catholicism and sexual deviance—pose certain ruin to the nation-state.

Importantly, much of this hand-wringing about the presence of Mexican-American children retreads familiar themes of cultural excess, in which Mexican and non-white women and children are imagined as excessive both in their presence and in their consumption of American goods, services, and even food.

As Romero notes, MAIA missives reproduce fears common in population control discourse in which immigrants and citizens of Color are perceived as numerical threats to the primacy of white Americans. MAIA representatives connect overpopulation to a fear of resource scarcity, stating "[Mexicans] are breeding like rabbits! Then they go on food sta[mps] and welfare, and Americans have to pay for that" (2011, 58). Within this discourse, Latina mothers and the children they bear are characterized as both lazy and greedy, a horde of hungry mouths who threaten to further strain American resources, including the supply of food. Indeed, as Romero demonstrates, MAIA makes repeated use of the threat of Latina/o/x overconsumption, suggesting that the children of immigrants are "used by a mother to 'steal' from the mouths of 'legal children' in the USA" and that these mothers "should be charged with child abuse for attempting to benefit from their crime and profiting from additional actions while within the interior of the USA" (2011, 60). While it is unclear in this example if MAIA is suggesting that the children of Latina mothers are somehow the injured party by dint of being assured food, what is clear is that "MAIA argues that the immigrant mothers of U.S. citizens are engaged in child abuse *toward* the children of U.S. citizens" (2011, 60 emphasis added). Within this nativist framework, simply feeding one's own child (of Color) is imagined as detrimental to the presumably white children of others. Here, MAIA defines food through an imagined lens of scarcity that renders the "other" an always/already overconsumer whose sheer presence functions as demographic excess. Thus, Latina/o/x children and the mothers who feed them are rendered guilty of a dangerous, even violent gluttony with the potential to starve "innocent" children.

As other scholars in Latina/o/x Studies have noted, this discourse of overpopulation and resource scarcity has been central to constructions of Latinas/os/xs as a simultaneously excessive and burdensome population. For example, Otto Santa Ana's work on the role of metaphor in immigration and anti-immigration discourse sheds light on the role of both quantitative excess (there are too many) and qualitative excess (they are too different, too "ethnic," etc.) in shaping the language used to debate the place of Latina/o/x immigrants (and non-immigrants) in the United States.

In *Brown Tide Rising*, he argues that the "dominant metaphor" present in discussions of immigration and Latina/o immigration in particular is characterized by two subcategories with the first being "volume, which emphasizes the relative numbers of immigrants" (Santa Ana 2002, 73). This emphasis on numbers functions to "transform aggregates of individuals into an undifferentiated mass quantity," a mass "that is not human" (Santa Ana 2002, 76). Santa Ana's breakdown of this metaphor demonstrates the ways in which fears of numerical or quantitative excess combine with American xenophobia to shape modern discourses about immigration. Similarly, as rhetoric about Latina/o/x immigration characterizes Latinas/os/xs as being "too many," it also relies on the idea that Latina/o/x bodies *themselves* are excessive, or "too much" to belong.

Couched within contemporary anti-obesity rhetoric, "concerns" about Latinas/os/xs' supposed proclivity to fatness reflects the ways in which the ideological construction of problematic or dangerous excess centers the body weights and sizes of racial and ethnic Others. Thus, excess in the form of bodily excess understood as "overweight" or "obesity," becomes central to the rhetorical project of determining which bodies can and cannot belong to the nation-state as well as which bodies pose a threat to national well-being.

Deviant Femininity, Undesirability, and Immigration Law and Policy

As I wrote in 2020, anti-fat discourse poses a unique threat to Latina/o/x immigrants and their communities, as designations of fatness as illness, moral fault, and a drain on the economy collude to produce the figure of the "undesirable immigrant." In 2015, this phenomenon was particularly virulent and found a target in immigrant rights activist Gaby Pacheco, who was an audience member during a May 2015 episode of *AMERICA With Jorge Ramos* featuring "conservative commentator" Ann Coulter. While the interaction between the two women was brief, with Pacheco asking to hug Coulter and Coulter refusing due to having recently had the flu, the backlash against Pacheco herself was swift and sat squarely at the intersection among anti-fatness, anti-Latina, and anti-immigrant sentiment, and sexism.

Soon after the interview aired, *Breitbart News* quoted an e-mail by Coulter in which she promised "[w]hen I'm in charge of immigration (after our 10 year moratorium), I will not admit overweight girls" (Boyle 2015). Commenters on the story responded with a number of jokes about Pacheco's weight, including some that reiterated presumed linkages between body size and ethnic/racial origin, and suggested that Pacheco's body posed a unique threat due to her size. As one commenter stated, "[t]hat fat cow is already invading our space by being here illegally," to which another retorted "[s]he's taking up at least two spaces," with a final commenter adding "[w]ith an option on a third." Other commenters reiterated right-wing fears regarding a conspiracy geared toward the "browning" of the United States, in which undocumented or "illegal" immigrants like Pacheco are believed to play a part. Still others condemn Pacheco in gendered and racialized terms, suggesting readers should "[c]ompare the Nordic beauty and intelligence of Ann (tall, slender, oval faced and blue eyes) with the revoltingly mouthy, obese, greasy hispanic invader."

What is clear in both Coulter's own response and those of her supporters in *Breitbart*'s comment section is that among those who understand Latinas/os/xs as unnecessary, unworthy, and ultimately undesirable immigrants, the ideology of anti-fatness appears to pair seamlessly with nativist and racist frameworks. Indeed, this pairing aligns with restrictive immigration policies originating in the late nineteenth and early twentieth century with the passing of "numerical restrictions" (quotas) which, in addition to setting numerical limits on immigration from nation-states outside the United States, also "embodied certain hierarchies of race and nationality" (Ngai 2014, 23). As Ngai argues, the Johnson-Reed Act of 1924 and its precursors were highly nativist and reflected a growing "nationalism based on race," in which the "quota system distinguished persons of the 'colored race' from 'white' persons from 'white' countries" (Ngai 2014, 23, 27). Embedded in this racially inflected immigration legislation were also notions of "unassimilability" and "racial inferiority," both of which acted as demerits against possible immigrants and nation-states from which immigrants might hail (2014, 24). Additionally, early twentieth century immigration policy included restrictions against those deemed "liable to become a public charge at time of entry," or "LPC" which agencies applied both broadly and heavily to exclude potential immigrants, especially women "who committed minor crimes or violated norms of sexual morality, such as bearing children out of wedlock" (2014, 77).

In retracing this history of racialized exclusionary policies in early immigration law, I suggest that—again—it should not be particularly surprising that responses to a fat Latina immigrant's presence in the United States should be met with such vehement responses linking her presence to invasion, non-belonging, and a reiteration of racialized inferiority. In fact, Coulter's response to *Breitbart* bears this out, as she indirectly invokes the spirit of the "liable to become a public charge at time of entry" provision by highlighting that if she were in charge of immigration, she would use weight as an excluding factor for potential immigrants. *Breitbart* writer Matthew Boyle completes the link between being "overweight" and the LPC provision, writing "[s]he's got a point: Shouldn't the United States be picking the most desirable immigrants to bring into the United States, truly the best and brightest?" (2015). In this formulation, anti-fatness and nativism collude to present Pacheco (and presumably other "overweight [immigrant] girls") as wholly undesirable to the building and maintenance of a white United States.

While neither Coulter, Boyle, nor the commentators are presumably "in charge of immigration," their comments both reflect and reinforce the legislative and policy history that has shaped the United States. As April Herndon argues, "[e]nveloped in the 'war against obesity' are growing concerns about competition for scarce health care dollars and a sense of panic and judgment about who might and might not deserve available resources" (2005, 129). Although this "panic and judgment" certainly has been reinvigorated in the contemporary moment with anti-fat attitudes and policies, I insist that in order to truly understand its potential impact on people of Color and Latina women in particular, we must approach it not as a new phenomenon but as a continuation of discourses, policies, and legislation that target those deemed Other. Indeed, "although the war on obesity might be relatively new, government concern about obesity and immigrants is long standing" (2005, 138) and policies of removing Native and Indigenous children from their mothers and families, attacks on recipients of public aid, and explicitly nativist and racist immigration legislation provide a roadmap of where we have been, and where we may be headed, as anti-fatness becomes weaponized against women of Color.

References

Belkin, Lisa. 2001. "Watching Her Weight." *The New York Times Magazine*, July 8, 2001. www.nytimes.com/2001/07/08/magazine/watching-her-weight.html

Boyle, Matthew. 2015. "Illegal Alien V. Ann Coulter on Jorge Ramos' Fusion: Illegal Reveals Desire to Limit Americans' Free Speech Rights." *Breitbart*. May 28, 2015. www.breitbart.com/politics/2015/05/28/illegal-alien-v-ann-coulter-on-jorge-ramos-fusion-illegal-reveals-desire-to-limit-americans-free-speech-rights/

Dame-Griff, E Cassandra. 2016. "'He's Not Heavy, He's an Anchor Baby': Fat Children, Failed Futures, and the Threat of Latina/o Excess." *Fat Studies* 5, no. 2: 156–71.

Galvan, Astrid. 2011. "Teen Taken From Parents as Child Coping with Loss." *Deseret News*, October 14, 2011. www.deseret.com/2011/10/14/20222975/teen-taken-from-parents-as-child-coping-with-loss

Hancock, Ange-Marie. 2004. *The Politics of Disgust: The Public Identity of the Welfare Queen*. New York: NYU Press.

Herndon, April Michelle. 2005. "Collateral Damage from Friendly Fire?: Race, Nation, Class and the 'War against Obesity.'" *Social Semiotics* 15, no. 2: 127–41.

Jacobs, Margaret D. 2014. *A Generation Removed: The Fostering and Adoption of Indigenous Children in the Postwar World*. Lincoln, NE: University of Nebraska Press.

Larson, Jessica. 2017. "Being all you can Bean with Goya." *U.S. Department of Agriculture*, February 21, 2017. www.usda.gov/media/blog/2012/06/25/being-all-you-can-bean-goya

Moynihan, Daniel Patrick. 1965. *The Negro Family: The Case for National Action*. Washington, DC: US Government Printing Office.

Ngai, Mae M. 2014. *Impossible Subjects*. Princeton, NJ: Princeton University Press.

Power, Elaine. 2016. "Fat Children, Failed (Future) Consumer-Citizens, and Mothers' Duties in Neoliberal Consumer Society." In *Neoliberal Governance and Health: Duties, Risks, and Vulnerabilities*, edited by Power, Elaine and Jessica Polzer, 43–65. Montreal, QC: McGill-Queen's Press.

Romero, Mary. 2011. "Constructing Mexican Immigrant Women as a Threat to American Families." *International Journal of Sociology of the Family* 37, no. 1 (Spring): 49–68.

Saguy, Abigail and Gruys, Kjerstin. 2010. "Morality and Health: News Media Constructions of Overweight and Eating Disorders." *Social Problems* 57, no 2: 231–250.

Sánchez, George J. 1995. *Becoming Mexican American: Ethnicity, Culture, and Identity in Chicano Los Angeles, 1900–1945*. Oxford, UK: Oxford University Press.

Santa Ana, Otto. 2002. *Brown Tide Rising: Metaphors of Latinos in Contemporary American Public Discourse*. Austin: University of Texas Press.

12

FATNESS, GENDER, AND ACADEMIC ACHIEVEMENT IN SECONDARY AND POSTSECONDARY EDUCATION

Heather A. Brown

Since the mid-1960s, researchers have studied the intersections between weight and academic achievement. While most of the research has focused on students ages 3–18 and their test scores or grade point averages, there has been some research that has focused on the impact of fatness on high school graduation rates and subsequent enrollment in and graduation from four-year colleges and universities. Additional research has explored the education levels attained by individuals who were fat children and who are now adults.

Moreover, while the data show either a positive or neutral correlation between heaviness and academic outcomes for male learners, for fat girls and women, the data are clear. There is a strong correlation between fatness and poor academic achievement among fat female learners. Fat girls in the United States were twice as likely to consider themselves to be poor students than their "normal" weight peers; in addition, they are far more likely to be held back a grade level than fat boys or "normal" weight girls (Falkner et al. 2001). Girls ages 14–17 who are "overweight" or "obese" have significantly lower grade point averages than "normal" weight girls (Sabia 2007). Girls who are "obese" in secondary school – no matter their race or socioeconomic status – are significantly less likely to attend or complete college than any other group, including fat boys (Crosnoe 2007; Crosnoe and Muller 2004). Indeed, a systemic review by Hill, Rodriguez Lopez, and Caterson (2018) found that 56% of studies that explored the connections between postsecondary education and "obesity" found negative correlations between higher weights and academic achievement in fat women.

The problems persist into the postsecondary level. Fat women, in addition to thinking of themselves as poor students who are not likely to complete secondary education or enroll in postsecondary education, also were found to be less likely than "normal" weight individuals to even want to pursue postsecondary

DOI: 10.4324/9781003140665-17

education; among those heavy women who attended postsecondary education, almost half believed they could not finish (Ball, Crawford, and Kenardy 2004). Indeed, research indicates that heavy women learners are less likely to obtain their college degrees (Fowler-Brown et al. 2010). Despite this, very little research has been conducted on why this correlation happens, and what research has been done is problematic in multiple ways explored later in this chapter.

Here, I explore the connections (or lack thereof) in the peer-reviewed research on fatness and academic achievement at the postsecondary levels, discuss the implications of the research, and provide insight to the limitations of the research. Given that the research on the connections between weight and academic achievement at the postsecondary level is "scarce and seriously lacking," I also explore the research on the connections between weight and academic achievement at the secondary level to establish a framework for understanding the research (Aimé et al. 2017, 168).

An Overview of the Literature

The earliest research to examine the connections between weight and academic achievement did so by first looking at the elite college acceptance rate of fat, middle class, suburban, mostly white high school students. Fewer fat students from these schools were attending college than should be, especially among fat female students, even though "obesity" and academic performance were not correlated; fat students and "normal" weight students showed similar academic performance patterns. Fat students also did not miss more days of school than other students, and they had similar intentions of pursuing a college education (Canning and Mayer 1966, 1967).

The idea that fatness somehow affects learners' chances of being accepted to or enrolling in postsecondary education was further studied in the 1980s and 1990s. Benson et al. (1980) found that "obese" learners, particularly girls, are discriminated against and discouraged from pursuing advanced education because of their weight, while Crandall (1991, 1995) found that, on average, college-enrolled students of both genders tended to be thinner than individuals who were not enrolled in college. In addition, fatter women were more likely to be paying their own way through college no matter the political orientation of their families, although the same effect was not found for fat men (Crandall 1995). This lack of support can translate into lowered academic attainment by fat women. Gortmaker et al. (1993) found that "overweight" women in the United States had 0.3 years less schooling than did "normal" weight women. A similar effect was not found among overweight men or among "normal" weight individuals who had long-term health conditions. Longitudinal studies in Great Britain showed a slightly different pattern, however. Sargent and Blanchflower (1994) concluded that, when surveyed at age 23, both men and women who were "obese" as teenagers had fewer years of postsecondary education than individuals who were not obese at 16. However, girls who were "obese" at ages 7, 11, and 16 performed far more poorly on math and reading tests and earned 7.4%–11.4% less than "normal" weight women, depending on the level of their "obesity" (Sargent and Blanchflower 1994).

The amount of research published on the connections between weight and academic achievement increased globally in the early 2000s, not uncoincidentally correlated with the start of the "War on Obesity" at that time (Mokdad et al. 2004). In addition, the types of questions researchers ask in their studies have changed. Whereas earlier researchers worked to discover if there was any correlation between weight and academic achievement, more recent research has included a new focus on issues of causation and directionality. For example, researchers began to ask whether being fat caused lower academic achievement or whether lower intelligence and/or academic achievement led to obesity and whether lower achievement was a perception (of learner or, to a more limited extent, the educator) or an actuality.

The study by Falkner et al. (2001) was one of the first to show a shift in thinking from a focus on discrimination as an explanation for lowered academic achievement by fat learners to a musing that the bodies of fat learners ought to be changed in order to help them achieve better academic experiences. Falkner et al. (2001) found that fat girls were 1.51 times more likely to be held back a grade and just over two times more likely to consider themselves poor students. Fat boys, on the other hand, were not as likely as fat girls to be held back a grade, yet they also felt they were poor students and were 2.18 times more likely than "normal" weight students to expect that they would not complete high school (Falkner et al. 2001).

Fat girls and women, in addition to thinking of themselves as poor students who are not likely to complete secondary education, were also found to be less likely than "normal" weight individuals to even want to pursue advanced education (Ball, Crawford, and Kenardy 2004). Using data collected on 7,865 Australian women, ages 18–23, Ball, Crawford, and Kenardy (2004) concluded that fat women were "40% more likely to expect not to finish college than those in the healthy weight range" (1020). This finding is a sharp turn from data collected by Canning and Mayer (1966, 1967) suggesting that fat girls had similar expectations of and desires to attend postsecondary education.

A majority of the research since 2000 has found that fat individuals, and especially fat girls and women, believe that they are poor students, that they will not finish their education, and that they have few expectations of pursuing postsecondary education. Are these perceptions born out in actuality?

Sabia (2007) found that for white high school girls, there was a significant causal relationship between fatness and lower grade point average. A similar relationship was not found for white males or males and females of other ethnic and racial groups. Okunade, Hussey, and Karakus (2009) found similar results, with "overweight" and "obese" white and Asian American girls experiencing delays in high school graduation. Fat, white girls' grades were not affected by low self-esteem, depression, or discrimination but rather the strong correlation between poor academic achievement and weight is a result of a shared lack of discipline since "the least disciplined individuals are most likely to become obese and to achieve less in school" (Sabia 2007, 873).

Kobayashi (2009) explored the relationship between fatness, grade point average, and cheeseburgers. Using data on Japanese and American college students, Kobayashi (2009) found that American students with high body mass indices (BMIs) who eat a lot of fast food tended to have lower grade point averages, while Japanese students who ate a lot of fast food also tended to have lower grade point averages but they were not as likely to have a high BMI. The correlation between lower grade point average and high fast food intake was especially true among Japanese women.

The effect of childhood and/or adolescent weight on actual educational achievement of adults also was an area of key interest to researchers during 2000–2010. Research found that "obesity" was correlated with lower educational attainment, at least for some groups in some situations. Viner and Cole (2005) determined that being "obese" in childhood did not appear to affect the number of years of education earned by adults by age 30, but only if they were no longer "obese." Lawlor et al. (2006) found that there was a connection between childhood-measured intelligence, educational attainment, and weight but what they found was not the relationship they expected. Using the Aberdeen Children of the 1950s cohort study, Lawlor et al. (2006) found that rather than weight affecting educational attainment, childhood intelligence and the number of years of school completed affected adult weight, especially among adult women. "We found that the effects of both childhood intelligence and educational attainment on future BMI were greater in females compared to males, with evidence of a statistical interaction between sex and education but not between sex and childhood intelligence" (Lawlor et al. 2006, 1763). In other words, for women, the higher they tested on childhood IQ tests and the more years of compulsory schooling they completed, the more likely they were to have lower BMIs as adults.

One study found that girls who are obese in secondary school – no matter their race or socioeconomic status – are far less likely to attend or complete college than any other group, including fat boys (Crosnoe 2007). This held true unless the girls also attended high schools in which a higher percentage of the population was also fat; at schools where being fat was the "norm," fat girls were just as likely to pursue a college education as "normal" weight girls (Crosnoe 2007). Fowler-Brown et al. (2010), however, found that the effect of childhood and/or adolescent "obesity" on adult educational attainment depended on the generation surveyed. Using data from the National Longitudinal Survey of Youth, Fowler-Brown et al. (2010) looked at two groups who had been ages 14–18 in either 1979 or 1997. Both levels of "obesity" and college degree attainment were higher in the 1997 cohort than in the 1979 cohort. However, among the 1979 cohort, being fat did not impact the rate at which cohort members earned college degrees. In the 1997 cohort, "normal" weight adolescents were twice as likely to have graduated from college as their fat peers (Fowler-Brown et al. 2010). Odlaug et al. (2015), Martin et al. (2014), Booth et al. (2014), and Anderson and Good (2017) also found connections between negative correlations between fatness and academic achievement, including grade point averages and final grades, with women showing slightly more negative correlations between higher body weights and academic outcomes, while Cheng (2014) found that both sexes were negatively affected almost equally. Aimé et al. (2017), however, found clear connections between higher body weights and lowered grade point averages in college women.

Discussion

Where the research finds definitive, adverse relationships between fatness and academic achievement, fat girls and women are affected more often than fat boys and men are, at least in those studies that looked at data for both sexes. Canning and Mayer (1966, 1967) found that fat girls were more likely than other groups to not attend college despite a desire to do so, while other research suggested this was the case because fat girls had more difficulty paying for college as their families were less likely to support them financially while they were in school (Crandall, 1991, 1995). Ball, Crawford, and Kenardy (2004) focused their own study on fat learners' aspirations on women "because it has been suggested that female obesity may be more discouraged and penalized than male obesity," an assertion borne out by their data (1020). Crosnoe (2007) also asserted that girls face more stigma for "obesity" than boys and are more negatively impacted by this stigma.

Weight bias and discrimination[1] against fat learners are two primary reasons hypothesized by researchers to explain connections between fatness and lower academic achievement. For example, Crosnoe (2007), Crosnoe and Muller (2004), and Ding and Bornhop (2005) explained fat girls' lower academic achievement by suggesting that it involved a vicious cycle that starts when students and teachers react negatively to fat learners, causing fat learners to see themselves as unworthy, which then, in turn, negatively impacts their ability to perform well academically. Palermo and Dowd (2012) and MacCann and Roberts (2012) also argued that discrimination plays a role in lowered academic achievement at the postsecondary level.

However, entire avenues of analysis related to race and ethnicity are either downplayed or missing entirely in the research. While several studies statistically analyze the correlations between weight, academic achievement, and racial or ethnic demographics, that is usually the stopping point, when it should be a starting point for analysis. Simply reporting on whether a certain racial or ethnic group has a particular relationship to academic achievement, college completion, or grade point average ignores not only the magnifying effects of intersectional bias

(Himmelstein, Puhl, and Quinn 2017; Reece 2019) but also the racist foundations of modern weight science (Strings 2019).

The Hidden Curriculum

Discriminatory beliefs and attitudes may be transmitted to learners, particularly girls and women, through the hidden curriculum of the educational system. In her qualitative study of identity formation in fat girls, Rice (2007) concluded that women's sense of who they are as women is developed in childhood, and in the case of fat girls, that single characteristic becomes the "dominating identity they have carried throughout their lives" (167). This development trajectory was painful and destructive for many of the women, because being fat is "a powerful visual symbol of devalued identity that positions girls as deficiently different" (Rice 2007, 170). Rice (2007) also found that while many girls were told outright by family members, teachers, or peers that they were fat and that fat was bad, the message that being a fat girl was a bad thing was reinforced by the hidden curriculum of the school environment.

> These were conveyed through school furniture and dress codes, playground and classroom interactions, popular physical education pedagogies such as fitness tests and team selection, as well as classroom organizing practices of seating arrangements, line ups, and student placement in class pictures.
>
> *(Rice 2007, 165)*

For many students, however, "blame for any discomfort rests solely with fat students" and not with the desk itself or with a social context that requires all students to be able to fit in a certain sized area in order to participate in formal education (Hetrick and Attig 2009, 202).

In the case of fat female learners, the hidden curriculum of gender presentation also impacts their experience of learning. For example, undergraduate women in my own research (Brown 2012) feared that unless they presented a perfectly groomed body with specific markers of traditional femininity, any mistake they made or wrong answer they gave would allow their peers and teachers to judge them harshly. They believed that they could recapture at least some of the size privilege they were lacking by presenting an ideal "feminine" presentation (perfectly coifed, makeup). For study participants, this also played out in their focus on clothing and fashion. A majority of participants felt that wearing attractive, age-appropriate, "girly" clothing was critical to their success on campus. By presenting themselves in fashionable clothing, they claimed the power of ideal femininity and tried to regain some sense of size privilege rather than bowing to cultural stereotypes of fat women as "slobs" who do not care about themselves or their education.

Limitations of Existing Research

There are several overarching limitations of the literature presented here that could provide direction for future research efforts. First, there is no common definition of what counts as academic achievement. Can a learner be labeled a good academic achiever if they get a high-grade point average, or are scores on IQ or standardized tests more important? Is graduation from high school required or must they earn a postsecondary degree? Moreover, a continued focus on graduation from a four-year college or university ignores what may be a mitigating circumstance for many fat learners: fatness is associated with a lower socioeconomic status than thinness, and individuals who come from low socioeconomic status backgrounds are among the least likely groups to enroll in and graduate from institutions of postsecondary education is (Ernsberger 2009; Sobal 1991; Sobal and Stunkard 1989). Expanding the research to explore other avenues of academic achievement may provide a deeper picture of what it means to succeed academically while fat.

Second, while large, nationally representative surveys provide researchers with access to incredible amounts of data, the data may not actually be able to answer the questions researchers are asking. Crosnoe (2007), in particular, discusses the limitations of using currently available survey instruments to study the topic of weight and academic achievement. The currently available survey instruments also appear unable to provide data that could answer the questions researchers seem to want to ask, the questions of why there appears to be a relationship between fatness and poor academic achievement, especially among girls; if girls perceive their weight as a psychological or physiological construct that affects their academic experiences negatively or positively; or how fat learners perceive the interaction between their weight and the social context of the classroom and the effect of that interaction on their academic achievement.

Third, the published research structures the relationship between fatness and academic achievement as inherently problematic. Although each study grounds itself in a review of the extant literature, the literature is not reviewed critically; researchers simply accept the literature as is and work to find ever more subtle relationships between variables that "prove" a negative relationship between fatness and academic achievement, rather than examine previous research for deficits in theoretical framework, methodology, or analysis. The result is that the literature on weight and academic achievement has become an exemplar of confirmation bias; it is a self-contained system that uncritically perpetuates the idea that fat learners, especially fat female learners, will not and cannot be academically successful, even when the data suggest a new understanding is needed. Kaestner and Grossman (2009) provide an example. Their manuscript starts with pithy and problematic statements about the "obesity epidemic," states that fatness is an obvious health problem and that weight must cause other problems as well, provides an uncritical literature review on the negative correlations between fatness and educational achievement, presents data that fat children actually have similar test scores to nonfat children, and then concludes that their findings show that size discrimination cannot possibly be a cause of poor educational outcomes by "obese" children, while suggesting that the core limitations of their research are that the data they used that generated the finding is sorely lacking, throwing the validity of their own finding into question.

Fourth, there is a critical need for more qualitative research on fatness and academic achievement. The voices of fat people and their understandings of their own experiences are almost entirely absent from the peer-reviewed research, which is primarily quantitative in nature.

Finally, demographic characteristics are neither interrogated nor problematized in the existing research. For example, the concept of gender is presented simply as biological sex, leaving trans- and gender-fluid learners out of the data collection and, thus, the analysis of the correlations between weight and learning.

Conclusion

Because the relationship of fatness and academic achievement ought to have everything to do with the field of education and data on the topic could be used to develop programming that would enhance the academic achievement of fat learners, it is problematic that most of the research on the topic is not published in journals targeted to educators. Most of the articles are published in obesity-related journals or in economics journals, which has the effect of either treating academic achievement by fat learners as a medical problem that needs a medical solution or frames it as an economic indicator in which the fat learner is portrayed as a poor investment. Both portrayals argue for the elimination of obesity as the core "solution" to improved academic performance by the fat learner, situating the problem (if it exists at all) as an issue solely of personal responsibility and ignoring the social context in which the fat learner acts as a learner.

Unfortunately, colleges and universities have been encouraged to promote weight loss among heavy learners without peer-reviewed research that suggests such an approach would promote positive academic achievement in this population. This is problematic for several reasons. The first is that researchers still do not fully understand the connections between educational outcomes and weight. Evidence that being fat makes you less intelligent or biologically impedes the ability to learn is lacking, so why should educational institutions focus intervention efforts on weight loss if there is no data to support the success of the intervention? Second, the causes of body size are complex and involve a number of factors, including lower socioeconomic status, that also may negatively affect enrollment in and completion of postsecondary education.

The research suggests there is a problematic connection between fatness and academic achievement, specifically among girls and women. Instead of solving a problem we do not yet truly understand with a solution that fails more than 95% of the time (Bacon and Aphramor 2011; Bacon et al. 2005; Fildes et al. 2015;

Hunger, Smith, and Tomiyama 2020; Mann et al. 2007; Tomiyama et al. 2016; Tylka et al. 2014), it is critical to expand the research and explore the problem with a critical theoretical framework and eye toward equity in education. Fat girls and women deserve to pursue the best possible education to the best of their abilities in the bodies in which they currently exist.

Note

1   See Nutter et al. (2019) for a systemic literature review on weight bias in education.

References

Aimé, Annie, Aude Villatte, Caroline Cyr, and Diane Marcotte. "Can Weight Predict Academic Performance in College Students? An Analysis of College Women's Self-Efficacy, Absenteeism, and Depressive Symptoms as Mediators." *Journal of American College Health* 65, no. 3 (2017): 168–76. https://doi.org/10.1080/07448481.2016.1266 639

Anderson, Angela S., and Deborah J. Good. "Increased Body Weight Affects Academic Performance in University Students." *Preventive Medicine Reports* 5 (2017): 220–23. https://doi.org/10.1016/j.pmedr.2016.12.020

Bacon, Linda, Judith S. Stern, Marta D. Van Loan, and Nancy L. Keim. "Size Acceptance and Intuitive Eating Improve Health for Obese, Female Chronic Dieters." *Journal of the American Dietetic Association* 105, no. 6 (2005): 929–36. https://doi.org/10.1016/j.jada.2005.03.011

Bacon, Linda, and Lucy Aphramor. "Weight Science: Evaluating the Evidence for a Paradigm Shift." *Nutrition Journal* 10, no. 1 (2011). https://doi.org/10.1186/1475-2891-10-9

Ball, Kylie, David Crawford, and Justin Kenardy. "Longitudinal Relationships among Overweight, Life Satisfaction, and Aspirations in Young Women." *Obesity Research* 12, no. 6 (2004): 1019–30. https://doi.org/10.1038/oby.2004.125

Benson, Peter L., Drew Severs, John Tatgenhorst, and Nancy Loddengaard. "The Social Costs of Obesity: A Non-Reactive Field Study." *Social Behavior and Personality* 8, no. 1 (1980): 91–96. https://doi.org/10.2224/sbp.1980.8.1.91.

Booth, J N, P D Tomporowski, J M Boyle, A R Ness, C Joinson, S D Leary, and J J Reilly. "Obesity Impairs Academic Attainment in Adolescence: Findings from ALSPAC, a UK Cohort." *International Journal of Obesity* 38, no. 10 (2014): 1335–42. https://doi.org/10.1038/ijo.2014.40.

Brown, Heather. "Fashioning a Self from Which to Thrive: Negotiating Size Privilege as a Fat Woman Learner at a Small Liberal Arts College in the Midwest." PhD diss., Northern Illinois University, 2012.

Canning, Helen, and Jean Mayer. "Obesity—Its Possible Effect on College Acceptance." *New England Journal of Medicine* 275, no. 21 (1966): 1172–74. https://doi.org/10.1056/nejm196611242752107

Canning, Helen, and Jean Mayer. "Obesity: An Influence on High School Performance?" *The American Journal of Clinical Nutrition* 20, no. 4 (1967): 352–54. https://doi.org/10.1093/ajcn/20.4.352

Cheng, Yen-hsin Alice. "Longer Exposure to Obesity, Slimmer Chance of College? Body Weight Trajectories, Non-Cognitive Skills, and College Completion." *Youth & Society* 49, no. 2 (2014): 203–27. https://doi.org/10.1177/0044118x14540183

Crandall, Christian S. "Do Heavy-Weight Students Have More Difficulty Paying for College?" *Personality and Social Psychology Bulletin* 17, no. 6 (1991): 606–11. https://doi.org/10.1177/0146167291176002

Crandall, Christian S. "Do Parents Discriminate against Their Heavyweight Daughters?" *Personality and Social Psychology Bulletin* 21, no. 7 (1995): 724–35. https://doi.org/10.1177/0146167295217007

Crosnoe, Robert. "Gender, Obesity, and Education." *Sociology of Education* 80, no. 3 (2007): 241–60. https://doi.org/10.1177/003804070708000303

Crosnoe, Robert, and Chandra Muller. "Body Mass Index, Academic Achievement, and School Context: Examining the Educational Experiences of Adolescents at Risk of Obesity." *Journal of Health and Social Behavior* 45, no. 4 (2004): 393–407. https://doi.org/10.1177/002214650404500403

Ding, Cody, and Jason Bornhop. "Overweight and School: Are There Any Perceived Achievement Consequences of Overweight among American Youth?" *Journal of Social Sciences* 1, no. 2 (2005): 118–25. https://doi.org/10.3844/jssp.2005.118.125

Ernsberger, Paul. "Does Social Class Explain the Connection between Weight and Health? In *The Fat Studies Reader*, edited by Esther Rothblum and Sandra Solovay, 25–36. New York: New York University Press, 2009.

Falkner, Nicole H., Dianne Neumark-Sztainer, Mary Story, Robert W. Jeffery, Trish Beuhring, and Michael D. Resnick. "Social, Educational, and Psychological Correlates of Weight Status in Adolescents." *Obesity Research* 9, no. 1 (2001): 32–42. https://doi.org/10.1038/oby.2001.5

Fildes, Alison, Judith Charlton, Caroline Rudisill, Peter Littlejohns, A. Toby Prevost, and Martin C. Gulliford. "Probability of an Obese Person Attaining Normal Body Weight: Cohort Study Using Electronic Health Records." *American Journal of Public Health* 105, no. 9 (2015). https://doi.org/10.2105/ajph.2015.302773

Fowler-Brown, Angela G., Long H. Ngo, Russell S. Phillips, and Christina C. Wee. "Adolescent Obesity and Future College Degree Attainment." *Obesity* 18, no. 6 (2010): 1235–41. https://doi.org/10.1038/oby.2009.463

Gortmaker, Steven L., Aviva Must, James M. Perrin, Arthur M. Sobol, and William H. Dietz. "Social and Economic Consequences of Overweight in Adolescence and Young Adulthood." *New England Journal of Medicine* 329, no. 14 (1993): 1008–12. https://doi.org/10.1056/nejm199309303291406

Hetrick, A., and Attig, D. "Sitting Pretty: Fat Bodies, Classroom Desks, and Academic Excess." In *The Fat Studies Reader*, edited by Esther Rothblum and Sandra Solovay, 197–204. New York: New York University Press, 2009.

Hill, Andrew J., Rocio Rodriguez Lopez, and Ian D. Caterson. "The Relationship between Obesity and Tertiary Education Outcomes: A Systematic Review." *International Journal of Obesity* 43, no. 11 (2018): 2125–33. https://doi.org/10.1038/s41366-018-0256-1

Himmelstein, Mary S., Rebecca M. Puhl, and Diane M. Quinn. "Intersectionality: An Understudied Framework for Addressing Weight Stigma." *American Journal of Preventive Medicine* 53, no. 4 (2017): 421–31.

Hunger, Jeffrey M., Joslyn P. Smith, and A. Janet Tomiyama. "An Evidence-Based Rationale for Adopting Weight-Inclusive Health Policy." *Social Issues and Policy Review* 14, no. 1 (2020): 73–107. https://doi.org/10.1111/sipr.12062

Kaestner, Robert, and Michael Grossman. "Effects of Weight on Children's Educational Achievement." *Economics of Education Review* 28, no. 6 (2009): 651–61. https://doi.org/10.1016/j.econedurev.2009.03.002

Kobayashi, Futoshi. "Academic Achievement, BMI, and Fast Food Intake of American and Japanese College Students." *Nutrition & Food Science* 39, no. 5 (2009): 555–66. https://doi.org/10.1108/00346650910992213

Lawlor, D A, H Clark, G Davey Smith, and D A Leon. "Childhood Intelligence, Educational Attainment and Adult Body Mass Index: Findings from a Prospective Cohort and within Sibling-Pairs Analysis." *International Journal of Obesity* 30, no. 12 (2006): 1758–65. https://doi.org/10.1038/sj.ijo.0803330

MacCann, C, and R D Roberts. "Just as Smart but Not as Successful: Obese Students Obtain Lower School Grades but Equivalent Test Scores to Nonobese Students." *International Journal of Obesity* 37, no. 1 (2012): 40–6. https://doi.org/10.1038/ijo.2012.47

Mann, Traci, A. Janet Tomiyama, Erika Westling, Ann-Marie Lew, Barbra Samuels, and Jason Chatman. "Medicare's Search for Effective Obesity Treatments: Diets Are Not the Answer." *American Psychologist* 62, no. 3 (2007): 220–33. https://doi.org/10.1037/0003-066x.62.3.220

Martin, Anne, David H Saunders, Susan D. Shenkin, and John Sproule. "Lifestyle Intervention for Improving School Achievement in Overweight or Obese Children and Adolescents." *Cochrane Database of Systematic Reviews*, 2014. https://doi.org/10.1002/14651858.cd009728.pub2

Mokdad, Ali H, James S. Marks, Donna F. Stroup, and Julie L. Gerberding. "Actual Causes of Death in the United States, 2000." *JAMA* 291, no. 10 (2004): 1238. https://doi.org/10.1001/jama.291.10.1238

Nutter, Sarah, Alana Ireland, Angela S. Alberga, Isabel Brun, Danielle Lefebvre, K. Alix Hayden, and Shelly Russell-Mayhew. "Weight Bias in Educational Settings: A Systematic Review." *Current Obesity Reports* 8, no. 2 (2019): 185–200. https://doi.org/10.1007/s13679-019-00330-8

Odlaug, Brian L., Katherine Lust, Cathrine L. Wimmelmann, Samuel R. Chamberlain, Erik L. Mortensen, Katherine Derbyshire, Gary Christenson, and Jon E. Grant. "Prevalence and Correlates of Being Overweight or Obese in College." *Psychiatry Research* 227, no. 1 (2015): 58–64. https://doi.org/10.1016/j.psychres.2015.01.029

Okunade, Albert A., Andrew J. Hussey, and Mustafa C. Karakus. "Overweight Adolescents and On-Time High School Graduation: Racial and Gender Disparities." *Atlantic Economic Journal* 37, no. 3 (2009): 225–42. https://doi.org/10.1007/s11293-009-9181-y

Palermo, Tia M., and Jennifer B. Dowd. "Childhood Obesity and Human Capital Accumulation." *Social Science & Medicine* 75, no. 11 (2012): 1989–98. https://doi.org/10.1016/j.socscimed.2012.08.004

Reece, Robert L. "Coloring Weight Stigma: On Race, Colorism, Weight Stigma, and the Failure of Additive Intersectionality." *Sociology of Race and Ethnicity* 5, no. 3 (2019): 388–400.

Rice, Carla. "Becoming 'The Fat Girl': Acquisition of an Unfit Identity." *Women's Studies International Forum* 30, no. 2 (2007): 158–74. https://doi.org/10.1016/j.wsif.2007.01.001

Sabia, Joseph J. "The Effect of Body Weight on Adolescent Academic Performance." *Southern Economic Journal* 73, no. 4 (2007): 871–900. https://doi.org/10.1002/j.2325-8012.2007.tb00809.x

Sargent, James D., and David G. Blanchflower. "Obesity and Stature in Adolescence and Earnings in Young Adulthood." *Archives of Pediatrics & Adolescent Medicine* 148, no. 7 (1994): 681–87. https://doi.org/10.1001/archpedi.1994.02170070019003

Sobal, Jeffery. "Obesity and Socioeconomic Status: A Framework for Examining Relationships between Physical and Social Variables." *Medical Anthropology* 13, no. 3 (1991): 231–47. https://doi.org/10.1080/01459740.1991.9966050

Sobal, Jeffery, and Albert J. Stunkard. "Socioeconomic Status and Obesity: A Review of the Literature." *Psychological Bulletin* 105, no. 2 (1989): 260–75. https://doi.org/10.1037/0033-2909.105.2.260

Strings, Sabrina. *Fearing the Black Body.* New York University Press, 2019.

Tomiyama, A J, J M Hunger, J Nguyen-Cuu, and C Wells. "Misclassification of Cardiometabolic Health When Using Body Mass Index Categories in Nhanes 2005–2012." *International Journal of Obesity* 40, no. 5 (2016): 883–86. https://doi.org/10.1038/ijo.2016.17

Tylka, Tracy L., Rachel A. Annunziato, Deb Burgard, Sigrún Daníelsdóttir, Ellen Shuman, Chad Davis, and Rachel M. Calogero. "The Weight-Inclusive versus Weight-Normative Approach to Health: Evaluating the Evidence for Prioritizing Well-Being over Weight Loss." *Journal of Obesity* 2014 (2014): 1–18. https://doi.org/10.1155/2014/983495

Viner, Russell M, and Tim J Cole. "Adult Socioeconomic, Educational, Social, and Psychological Outcomes of Childhood Obesity: A National Birth Cohort Study." *BMJ* 330, no. 7504 (2005): 1354. https://doi.org/10.1136/bmj.38453.422049.e0

PART VI

Gender and Fat in Health and Medicine

There is a knee-jerk reaction in contemporary culture that fat is unhealthy. Much fat activism and scholarship has focused usefully on challenging this limiting and stigmatizing perspective. The chapters in this section push our thinking on the connections between gender and fat within health care settings, from the treatment of eating disorders to the decisions people make to undergo bariatric (or weight loss) surgery to the difficulties fat people have in securing reproductive health care.

DOI: 10.4324/9781003140665-18

13

EATING DISORDERS, GENDER, AND FAT

Theorizing the Fat Body in Feminist Theories of Eating Disorders

Erin N. Harrop

Eating disorders are complex illnesses that result in a plethora of negative impacts for patients. Eating disorders involve a combination of disordered eating behaviors (e.g., self-starvation, self-induced vomiting, excessive exercise, laxative/diet pill abuse, binge behaviors, among others), disordered cognitions (e.g., fear of fat, fear of gaining weight, obsession with body weight or calories), and other bizarre behaviors or experiences ("body checking," obsessive weighing or measuring, involved food rituals), and physical symptoms and consequences (low heart rate, electrolyte disruption, stomach discomfort, esophagus damage, weight changes, headaches, low body temperature, sleep disruption). Some of these symptoms can become life threatening (Arcelus et al. 2011), making eating disorders one of the mental health illnesses with highest mortality (Chesney, Goodwin, and Fazel 2014).

Within the study of eating disorders, anorexia nervosa and bulimia nervosa are the most commonly studied. With anorexia, patients engage in self-starvation, experience significant weight loss, experience fear of fat and weight gain, and experience distortions in their body image and/or how serious their condition is (American Psychiatric Association 2013). Anorexia can also occur in higher weight bodies (e.g., atypical anorexia); additionally, patients with anorexia frequently also struggle with bingeing, purging, and/or compulsive exercise. With bulimia, patients engage in cycles of bingeing and purging (e.g., self-induced vomiting, laxative abuse, overexercise, or fasting), and (similarly to anorexia) experience fear of weight gain, while "over-valuing" their body size and shape (American Psychiatric Association 2013). Other eating disorders include binge eating disorder (in which individuals experience frequent binge eating), among others (American Psychiatric Association 2013).

DOI: 10.4324/9781003140665-19

Eating disorders are inherently gendered experiences that disproportionately affect women, with studies estimating cisgender women experience eating disorders ten times as often as cis men (American Psychiatric Association 2013). Transgender and nonbinary populations are estimated to experience eating disorders twice as often as cisgender females (Mitchison et al. 2020). While women are at increased risk for eating disorders compared to men (Smink, Van Hoeken, and Hoek 2012; Hudson et al. 2007), all genders suffer with eating disorders, and gender minorities (trans and nonbinary populations) may face additional eating disorder risk factors specific to their unique experiences.

Feminist Discourse in Eating Disorders

Since eating disorders have been traditionally thought of as "women's problems," much of eating disorder research (particularly research dealing with the origin of eating disorders) has drawn from feminist scholars, who focused on feminine ideals of beauty and the ever-present pressures of diet culture as risk factors for eating disorder development (Fallon, Katzman, and Wooley 1994). Feminist scholars have explored gender roles and changing beauty ideals to explain why women are disproportionately impacted by eating disorders, how socialization and social environment contribute to these disorders, and how gender may moderate the experience of these social environments.

Within early feminist theories of eating disorders, most authors centered the experiences of cis women. However, in recent years multiple scholars (particularly in adolescent health) have emphasized the need for eating disorder research to explore trans and nonbinary experiences as well (Parker and Harriger 2020; Avila, Golden, and Aye 2019; Avila 2020; Guss et al. 2016; Diemer et al. 2018; Coelho et al. 2019; Jones et al. 2016; Hartman-Munick et al. 2021).

Feminist thought on eating disorders has evolved significantly over the past several decades. Fallon, Katzman, and Wooley's (1994) important work, *Feminist Perspectives on Eating Disorders*, was one of the first books to compile leading feminist theorists' ideas on the origin and treatment of eating disorders and examine these works through a gendered lens. Among the theories explored in this work, the authors primarily focused on the historical context of eating disorders as a response to the male gaze and control (e.g., how males observe, police, and control female bodies), the influence of media and sociocultural trends toward a deepening thin-centric diet culture, and proposals for various feminist lenses in treatment modalities. Since this work, others have published additional scholarship on feminist approaches to eating disorders, including key books by Garrett (1998), Hepworth (1999), Reindl (2001), Gremillion (2003), Bordo (2004), MacSween (2013), and Lester (2019).

The publication of *Critical Feminist Approaches to Eating Disorders*, edited by Malson and Burns (2009a), marked an important shift in feminist theorizing. This work critiqued earlier feminist thought and shifted focus to new key issues: the need for theories to address eating disorders in non-Western nations, the need for decentering white-female-cisgender experiences, a critical reflection of potentially problematic and vague terms such as "disorder" and "recovery," an explicit focus on how technological advances (e.g., social media, online communities) affect the landscape of eating disorders, and the need to address and include issues of fatness in the study of eating disorders.

The Current Chapter

This chapter reviews these and other recent ideas in feminist thought on eating disorders, in order to synthesize some of the main developments in feminist thought over the past two decades. Further, this chapter integrates a lens of fat liberation and weight stigma while reviewing this literature. In the following sections, I briefly examine six of the major tensions in this literature: (1) fat acceptance as integral to vs. adjunctive to feminist approaches to eating disorders, (2) anti-fat messaging as health promotion or as a trigger for eating disorders, (3) the need for vs. harm in categorizing, diagnosing, and pathologizing eating problems, (4) eating disorders in non-Western cultures vs. centering white Western experiences, (5) pro-ana and pro-mia sites as spaces of resistance vs. subjugation, and (6) body dysmorphia vs. gender dysphoria and other challenges facing trans eating disorder patients.

Tension 1

Fat Acceptance as Integral to vs. Adjunctive to Feminist Approaches to Eating Disorders

While issues of fatness and fat acceptance may seem to go hand in hand with eating disorders (due to the common focuses on bodies and body image concerns), fatness has largely been ignored in mainstream feminist thought. Generally, eating disorder discourse around fatness has been limited to discussions related to "obesity" or binge eating disorder; similarly, fatness has not been conceived as pertaining to discussions of anorexia, bulimia, or other "restrictive" eating disorders.[1] In traditional eating disorder research, fatness is not believed to be a "problem" for people with anorexia or bulimia (who are presumed to be emaciated or have a "normal weight"), except as in relation to experiences of body dysmorphia (in which patients are presumed to be thin, yet believe themselves to be fat).

Within this viewpoint, body size tends to be viewed as a proxy for eating disorder behaviors, with thin people assumed to restrict and purge (e.g., force themselves to vomit, abuse laxatives, and/or engage in compulsive exercise), and fatter people assumed to uncontrollably eat large amounts of unhealthy food (e.g., a binge) and avoid physical activity. Thus, discussions of fat oppression are (for the most part) thought of as adjunctive or unnecessary to discussions of eating disorders, because eating disorder patients are assumed to be thin. These discourses ignore the fact that many higher weight people with eating disorders restrict what they eat (e.g., engage in self-starvation), purge, and engage in compulsive exercise. Sadly, body dysmorphia impacts people throughout the weight spectrum (da Luz et al. 2018; Darby et al. 2009; Ekeroth et al. 2013; Dousti et al. 2021), such that fat and thin people alike may see their bodies in distorted ways. These assumptions explain how "obesity" and fatness are understood as important, but separate eating disorder experiences—apart from the "traditional" eating disorder experiences of anorexia and bulimia.

Discussions of fatness are not absent from the eating disorder field. However, these conversations are often riddled with stereotypes and problematic assumptions. For example, in Zerbe's book on eating disorders (1993), discussion of fatness is mostly limited to a chapter near the end on obesity and binge eating disorder, in which she recommends that "obese" people stop "pay[ing] only lip service to the idea of eating less" and stop "deny[ing] what is actually eaten while searching for easy solutions" and instead limit their caloric intake to 1200 calories/day, in three meals and two snacks (311). Not only does this rhetoric further stigmatize those with elevated body mass indices (e.g., people considered "overweight" or "obese" by the medical industry), it also limits discussions of higher weight people with eating disorders to only binge eating disorder, while prescribing behaviors that would be considered problematic in thinner people (Rothblum and Solovay 2009).

Others have attempted to integrate discussions of fat oppression into an understanding of eating disorders (Lebesco 2009), but have struggled with how to integrate the two fields, pointing out their "many points of intersection" but concluding that anorexia and weight stigma ultimately go in "somewhat different directions" (152). Ultimately, as the fields of gender and fat studies continue to explore their role in the study of eating disorders, we have started to see greater integration of these fields, with some arguing for the necessity of all these perspectives when studying eating disorders. For example, some have argued that addressing fat oppression is critical to meaningfully addressing the social problem of eating disorders (Rothblum 1994; Harrop 2018; Harrop 2020) and that feminist lenses are needed to effectively address weight stigma (Calogero, Tylka, and Mensinger 2016).

Though feminist literature has attempted in some ways to integrate issues of fat-acceptance into eating disorder theory (though some resist this), this issue needs to be taken up more fully. For example, addressing fat oppression through the lens of eating disorders draws together two (apparently divergent) streams of feminist thought: (1) the problematic nature of weight stigma (lens of "obesity"), and (2) the problematic nature of eating disorders (lens of the thin ideal). Within these conversations, ethically addressing fat-oppression cannot occur solely in the contexts of "obesity prevention" or discussions of "binge eating disorder" as these conversations inaccurately confound weight with health, and obesity with bingeing, further stigmatizing fatter individuals. Greater awareness that restriction patterns are evident in all eating disorders, regardless of body size, could serve to alleviate some of this stigma.

Fat oppression and fat acceptance are especially salient aspects of feminist theory when considering eating disorders. Eating disorder patients, by definition, experience distress related to body weight, body image, fear of gaining weight, or fear of "fatness." Eating disorder patients who are in higher weight bodies are likely to experience dual discriminations: stigma due to having an eating disorder and stigma due to living in a larger body. One could further argue for the existence of a third stigma: that of having an eating disorder that is likely not recognized (as eating disorder patients are often expected to be thin) or having to defend or explain their diagnosis if it is recognized (Harrop 2018). Beyond these sources of societal discrimination, eating disorder patients also face high levels of *internalized* weight stigma, as they internalize the messages of society about fat bodies (Mensinger, Calogero, and Tylka 2016; Romano, Heron, and Henson 2021). Thus, a weight stigma perspective should be integral to an understanding of the origins (and likely treatment) of eating disorders.

Tension 2

Anti-Fat Messaging as Health Promotion or as a Trigger for Eating Disorders

One overlap between these fields includes research that highlights how anti-obesity rhetoric ameliorates or contributes to the development of eating disorders (Mensinger, Cox, and Henretty 2021). While the "war on obesity" was launched as health promotion, this approach has been widely critiqued by fat scholars and eating disorders scholars alike (O'Hara and Taylor 2018; Bristow et al. 2020; Psalios 2020). Rice (2009) highlights a connection between obesity prevention frameworks and eating disorders, arguing that attempts to reduce obesity may result in disordered eating habits for some girls. She argues that a better approach would be to "adopt a body equity approach that would advocate for greater acceptance of diverse bodies" (107). Similarly, Mensinger and colleagues demonstrate how a significant number of eating disorder patients attributed the onset of their illnesses to anti-fat messaging, and those patients presented with greater symptom severity. This quantitative work has been supported by qualitative patient interviews that report medical messaging around "obesity" and weight loss as triggers for both initiation of eating disorder behaviors and relapses to eating disorders following periods of remission (Harrop 2020).

While some advocate for combined "obesity" and eating disorder prevention programs (Leme et al. 2020), other scholars argue that such approaches are paradoxical, with "obesity prevention" programs necessarily problematizing weight, increasing body dissatisfaction for higher weight populations, increasing fear of fatness, and increasing weight stigma and risk for eating disorders (O'Hara and Taylor 2018), all of which are contraindicated in eating disorder treatment.

Tension 3

The Need for vs. Harm in Categorizing, Diagnosing, and Pathologizing Eating Problems

Feminist scholars are particularly concerned with the power of language, the examination of meaning, and the critical consideration of discriminatory categories (what they are and who gets to make them). Whether reflecting on what "counts" as feminist theory (Ahmed 2000; King 2001) or interrogating the construction of gender and who "counts" as "women" (De Lauretis 1987), this attention to classification and language is integral to critical feminist approaches. Within eating disorders, language and classification can be especially tricky, as eating disorders (i.e., the "pathological") can be conceptualized as excessive or unbalanced extensions of culturally normative behaviors (e.g., dieting, exercise, body image issues). Thus, drawing a line between what may be *normative* (albeit, arguably dysfunctional) and *pathological* is tricky. To wit, Garland-Thomson (2002) argues that anorexia could be viewed as an "exaggerate[d] normative gender role," such that women with anorexia may be simply living into the feminine ideal of being thin, delicate, and self-controlled. In addition, she warns against the potential for over-medicalization of "disabilities" centering on the female body (89), particularly when they interact with cultural gender ideals.

Bordo (1992) similarly laments the "description, classification, and elaboration of 'pathology' [that] has been the motor of virtually all research" (197). Amid other concerns regarding categorization is the potential for placing too much focus on the "pathological individual" as opposed to the systemic regimes that oppress people around food and weight. Similarly, Hepworth (1999) argues against the "dominant psychiatric definition of anorexia" instead favoring an understanding of anorexia that is "socially constructed through discourse" (3). Malson and Burns (2009a) summarize this debate, saying the following:

> The seemingly categorical divide between the normal and the pathological is disrupted and shown to be illusory, such that within critical feminist perspectives "eating disorders" are not so much viewed as individual pathological responses to patriarchal cultures. Rather, eating dis/orders are theorized here as (multiply) constituted within and by the always-gendered discursive contexts in which we live: (individual) "disorder" is re-theorized as part and parcel of the (culturally normative) order of things.
>
> *(2)*

While some authors more strongly resist the pathologizing and false dichotomies of imperfect categorization, other authors recognize a certain utilitarian ethic in labeling. For instance, though Garrett (1998) seemingly prefers the term "eating problems" (vs. "anorexia" which she finds problematic, pathologizing, and narrow), she elects to use the term "anorexia" because it has become engendered with popular, conventionally understood meanings. She further explains that it is important not to do away with diagnostic language altogether as it facilitates treatment access. However, she warns against viewing this term too narrowly at the expense of excluding voices whose experiences deviate from more "typical" anorexia presentations. Her intention is to broaden "anorexia" to include a greater heterogeneity of meaningful experiences (Garrett 1998).

In a health equity and fat liberation lens, categories inherently define who is "in" and who is "out," facilitating access to services and providers for the "in group," and creating barriers for the "out group." Thus, those with formal diagnoses of anorexia and bulimia, for instance, have greater access to treatment compared to those without formal diagnoses. To the extent that the "in" and "out" groups also mirror privileged identities in society (e.g., eating disorder categories that tend to be populated by thin, white, young, upper-class, cis people), these diagnostic categories could further deepen structural inequities in health care.

This attention to language is also important in describing the phenomena commonly described as "recovery" or "remission" processes (Garrett 1998; Tchanturia and Baillie 2015; Espindola and Blay 2013; Bardone-Cone et al. 2010). Here again, feminist scholars challenge the common label of "recovery" insofar as it is predicated on a disease framework (Garrett 1998) and defined differently in different contexts, disciplines, and by different authors (e.g., physicians, therapists, caregivers, patients; Bardone-Cone et al. 2010). Recovery skeptics have also questioned the extent to which concepts of recovery capture meaningful changes in health and quality of life, versus simply reflecting a lessening of eating disorder symptoms, or taking on a more "palatable" and "reassuring" appearance (Engel et al. 2009; Bardone-Cone et al. 2010; Ackard et al. 2014). "Recovery" is also critiqued for its overemphasis on individual effort and choice, at the risk of ignoring the integral elements of social and systemic processes.

Though eating disorder researchers have struggled with how to best define eating disorders, the DSM-5 made important strides in categorizing several symptom profiles that had previously confounded researchers. Prior to the DSM-5 (i.e., a guide book which describes the symptoms and presentation of various psychiatric disorders), up to 75% of eating disorders were assigned the residual eating disorder diagnosis, which signifies disorders that do not neatly fit a preestablished category (Machado et al. 2007; Machado, Gonçalves, and Hoek 2013; Kjelsås, Bjørnstrøm, and Götestam 2004). By establishing binge eating disorder as its own diagnosis, and creating the categories of atypical anorexia and purging disorder (among others), the DSM-5 significantly reduced those in the residual category (Machado, Gonçalves, and Hoek 2013) and created more awareness of "atypical" eating disorders.

The growing recognition of higher weight individuals with eating disorders (Billings, Lebow, and Sim 2013; Lebow, Sim, and Kransdorf 2015; Kennedy et al. 2017; Darby et al. 2009) has caused increasing debates as to what eating disorders actually look like in the population at large. Additionally, this discussion has pushed an important question to the surface. Which is more salient when defining an eating disorder: an individual's *weight* or their *beliefs, cognitions, emotions, and behaviors*? Such a question has important implications for treatment modalities, both for those with typical disorders and those presenting atypically.

Currently, anorexia is the only psychiatric condition in the DSM-5 that relies on weight for a diagnosis. This dogged insistence on the importance of weight is at the expense of ignoring impairing clinical syndromes in people at higher weights and may point to a level of weight bias in the eating disorders field which could impact bias in research and/or clinical care. Asserting that behaviors are more problematic than weight shifts interventions from a weight-focus to a behavioral focus; similarly, "recovery" definitions shift as well, with remission being characterized by new normalized behaviors and emotions (rather than simply weight restoration or body weight status). An explicit inclusion of higher weight individuals within traditional eating disorders has the potential to expand conceptualizations of what eating disorder illness and remission processes look like, beyond the narrow, more homogenous presentations typically reflected in eating disorder literature.

Tension 4

Eating Disorders in Non-Western Cultures vs. Centering White Western Experiences

The vast majority of research on eating disorders has focused on white, Western, female, cisgender experiences of eating disorders (Bobila 2013). This has led to understandings of eating disorders being primarily focused on white Western culture, contexts, and beliefs, and feminist theories primarily focused on how gendered power imbalances contribute to the development of eating disorders. Similarly, by studying those who present for treatment in Western settings, studies often end up predominated by white, upper-class samples who have more access to treatment resources (Bordo 2013). Indeed, it was previously believed that anorexia was a disease pertaining to *only* upper-class and middle-class white girls, when in fact, it is simply more likely that these women were the most visible patients for society to identify (Bordo 2013). Bordo (2013) explains that the first paradigms for understanding eating problems were "based on populations that were extremely skewed, both in terms of race and in class" (47). These samples were often highly visible, desperate cases that appeared quite salient in their shocking refusal to eat amidst a culture of plenty (Bordo 2013).

Indeed, Malson and Burns (2009b) point out that eating disorders are now a global phenomenon, though they also note that "the expressions of distress are local and nuanced, reflecting the world's ever shifting traditional and modern cultures" (xix). Gremillion (2008) also points out that eating disorder research has been disproportionately focused on gendered differences of power, while lacking an intersectional lens to other identities. She warns that "if we fail to acknowledge that categories of privilege and of marginality are always mutually constructed, then we risk the Othering of underprivileged social groups" (232). Thompson (1994) summarizes these arguments saying that "the feminist framework is limited, however, by race- and class-specific assertions about female socialization; the privileging of sexism over other oppressions" (358).

Within feminist writing, Lee and Katzman (2002) have pointed out how a cross-cultural feminist approach to eating disorders can deepen conceptualizations of these illnesses. These authors argue that the previous believed

> portrait of disordered eating as an appearance disorder incurred by young women lost in the world of caloric restricting is a belittling stereotype that not only camouflages women's real worries, but also misses the universal power of food refusal as a means of proclaiming needs for self-control.
>
> *(263)*

They go on to argue that accounting for the variety in anorexia presentations is important in order to achieve "polythetic definitions that transcend local variations in the context of the anorexic illness" (263). Here, Lee and Katzman are specifically referencing the need to have "fear of fat" excluded from diagnostic criteria, as this diagnostic criterion is less prevalent transnationally; however, their argument could also apply to the need to expand eating disorder conceptualizations to also include those at higher weights with the same sequelae of symptoms, and those across the weight spectrum presenting with other eating disorder presentations.

This tension about the importance of transnational perspectives highlights the need for eating disorder research to be more inclusive of diverse experiences. Inclusivity should not be limited to only different geographic areas, as these authors also argue for greater attention to racial, ethnic, and class differences *within* countries. This need for diversity should also include a diversity of body presentations, which will necessarily intersect with other marginalized identities, with poorer people and certain racial groups being more likely to have higher body mass indices (Freedman et al. 2006; Ernsberger 2009). The focus on thin white bodies in eating disorders inadvertently elevates the experiences of white upper-class women, who are already multiply-privileged in Western society. This results in measures, treatment modalities, and theories of eating disorder development that privilege Western, white, thin, female, cisgendered experiences, which at best produce interventions that may only benefit a slim portion of anorexia sufferers, and at worst, further stigmatize and marginalize the experiences of other populations.

Tension 5

Pro-Ana and Pro-Mia Sites as Spaces of Resistance vs. Subjugation

With the advent of the technological era, internet spaces have become increasingly a subject of debate in feminist literature. Drawing on the themes of other cyberfeminist studies, feminist eating disorder scholars have begun to explore pro-ana and pro-mia sites as spaces of both resistance and subjugation for those with eating disorders. Pro-ana and pro-mia sites are social media spaces wherein those with anorexia (pro-ana sites) and bulimia (pro-mia sites), who are usually young females, meet to support each other with their experiences of their eating disorders. These spaces are explicitly not treatment-focused, with the community belief that anorexia and bulimia are lifestyle choices and eating disorder patients should have full autonomy to continue engaging in the behaviors if they so choose.

These sites are seen by some as especially dangerous, because the targets of these groups (usually adolescent girls) are viewed as particularly vulnerable (Dohnt and Tiggemann 2006; Stice, Spangler, and Agras 2001; Griffin and Berry 2003; Christodoulou 2012). Others have argued against this situation of young girls as weak, passive, and victimized (Holmes 2016a, 2016b). Though there has been significant public outcry about the harm (assumed to be) inherent in these spaces, some feminist scholars have celebrated them as sites of embodiment, resistance, autonomy, and support. Others have identified them as a place of further subjugation. These debates have gained increasing relevance in current events due to allegations that Facebook systematically promotes these groups to young people to increase social media engagement.

In her examination of online spaces as sites of resistance, Daniels (2009) argues that pro-ana women engage "with internet technologies in ways that are both motivated by and confirm (extremely thin) embodiment" (113). She argues that these women go online not to "avoid corporeality but rather to engage with others about their bodies via text and image" (113). While I would argue instead that these people advocate for "body-focus" rather than "embodiment," since pro-ana participants actively encourage each other to disconnect from their bodies (i.e., ignoring hunger cues, masking bodily discomforts, promoting a dualist mind/ body approach), Daniels highlights attempts of the pro-ana community to affirm some embodied experiences.

Others have pointed out how pro-ana and pro-mia sites can be sites of support and coping, of meeting folks with eating disorders where they are, without necessarily increasing levels of harm or disorder (Mulveen and Hepworth 2006; Dias 2013; Brotsky and Giles 2007). Dias (2013) argues that pro-ana sites are important "safer" places where people with anorexia can "find sanctuary from the surveillance of the public sphere" (31). Similarly, Ferreday (2003) asserts that public outcry against pro-ana groups indicates attempts at bodily censorship, while pro-ana and pro-mia site users are actively resisting censorship and claiming their rights to bodily autonomy and difference.

In general, support for pro-ana and pro-mia sites is generally low; most argue against the representation of pro-ana spaces as sites of resistance, autonomy, support, or empowerment. Boero and Pascoe (2012) argue that rather than being spaces which resist surveillance, pro-ana sites actively perpetuate a culture of body-policing and surveillance through posting body pictures and detailed accounts of their eating disorder behaviors. These researchers point out that pro-ana sites are "particularly fraught because of tensions over claims to authenticity," because members cannot easily *see* other members to confirm their eligibility for the group (27). While one could hope that these groups would reduce barriers for those in larger bodies to access eating disorder supports, giving them the chance to interact with eating disordered peers without having to "validate" their diagnosis with physical emaciation, pro-ana groups actively discourage membership of higher weight individuals. Pro-ana and pro-mia groups demonstrate frequent anxiety over the "threat of 'wannarexics,'" or individuals who aspire toward the thinness and beauty of people with anorexia, without wholeheartedly adopting the pro-ana lifestyle and "achieving emaciation" (Boero and Pascoe 2012).

To combat the unwanted intrusions of wannarexics, pro-ana sites engage in self-surveillance and policing of each other's bodies (e.g., pressuring members to post pictures of their starving bodies to prove emaciation) in attempts to defend these online "safe spaces" (Boero and Pascoe 2012). Thus, pro-ana sites can be seen to embody the same surveillance and policing they espouse to flout. Similarly, Riley, Rodham and Gavin (2009) argue that pro-ana communities may attempt to reframe disordered behaviors as more normative "health/appearance concerns." However, body-related discourse on these sites shows instead that pro-ana sites are "(re)produce[ing] eating disorder identities" (348) instead. Ironically, these authors argue that this occurs both in pro-ana spaces and in pro-recovery spaces. Within this context, rather than feeling particularly welcomed or at ease in online pro-ana and pro-mia spaces, higher weight patients with eating disorders may rather experience increased levels of social ostracization due to their higher weights.

However, the inclusion of higher weight "wannarexics" in discussions of pro-ana sites highlights the problems associated with the body-policing and surveillance techniques employed by members of these online communities. In their attempts to ward off "wannarexics," pro-ana and pro-mia communities ward off those with legitimate eating disorders, who do not present in typical or expected ways. For example, by claiming that a patient with atypical anorexia (with a larger body) is a "wannarexic" and not a "*real* anorexic," members of these sites further stigmatize higher weight eating disorder patients and contribute to the further isolation and marginalization of atypically presenting individuals. Further, the rhetoric around "wannarexics" harkens back to debates on "how thin is thin enough" (see Tension 3, this chapter), which perpetuates harm, competition, and hierarchy within the eating disorder community.

Tension 6

Body Dysmorphia vs. Gender Dysphoria and Other Challenges Facing Trans Eating Disorder Patients

No discussion of critical feminist approaches to eating disorders would be complete without an examination of how eating problems manifest in trans and nonbinary populations. As was noted earlier, trans populations often present with higher prevalence of eating disorders compared to their cisgender peers (Coelho et al. 2019). While an in-depth examination of this topic is beyond the scope of this chapter, it is important to note the tension between the body dysmorphia that is often characteristic of eating disorders and the gender dysphoria many trans people experience.

Many trans youth engage in eating disorder behaviors as a means of coping with gender dysphoria, staving off puberty, and manipulating secondary sex characteristics which increase gendered body presentations, from a binary, gender essentialist view (Zamantakis and Lackey 2021; Coelho et al. 2019). In the case of larger-bodied patients with eating disorders, these efforts to suppress gendered sex characteristics may be even more salient, particularly given the thin aesthetic of many agender, nonbinary, androgynous, and genderqueer communities. This overlap of symptoms, behaviors, and motivations makes treating these distressing experiences challenging.

For more androgynous individuals, fatness is often perceived as a barrier to being read as androgynous or genderqueer, leading many to pursue more dangerous dieting and eating disordered behaviors. Author Da'Shawn Harrison, a fat, Black, nonbinary person, interviewed seven other fat, Black, trans and nonbinary persons in their recent book, *Belly of the Beast: The Politics of Anti-Fatness as Anti-Blackness* (Harrison 2021). Within this work, Harrison explains how fatness and antiblackness function to disrupt gender. One interviewee explained simply, "Being fat meant I couldn't be nonbinary" (93). Another echoed this sentiment, "As a fat 'woman' it often feels like androgyny … is denied to you" (95). Thus, dieting and eating disorders (while striving for femininity, masculinity, or androgyny) can become a tool for gender expression within a gendered, binary society. Harrison summarizes these poignant examples as follows, while integrating a racial lens here:

> In so many ways, fatness functions as a gender of its own. Fatness fails, and therefore disrupts, the foundation on which gender is built. This is why the request is made of fat trans people to lose weight before they can be affirmed in their gender, or why little fat boys are often misread as girls, or why fat Black women are often denied access to womanhood.
>
> *(102)*

While body dysmorphia, body dissatisfaction, and gender dysphoria can be difficult to disentangle, addressing each of these issues is important for trans mental health (Zamantakis and Lackey 2021). Within therapeutic interventions for gender dysphoria, gender-affirming treatment (including hormonal and surgical affirmation treatment) has been found to reduce mental distress and produce improved long-term outcomes (Almazan and Keuroghlian 2021; Bränström and Pachankis 2020). However, these treatments are often refused to trans and nonbinary people in fat bodies, with some physicians insisting that patients lose weight prior to receiving care. In so doing, the medical community often unwittingly contributes to disordered eating behaviors in trans and nonbinary patients, by withholding treatment until weight loss. Patients desperate for gender affirmation treatment often fall into eating disorders in an attempt to lose weight quickly and qualify for surgery (Brownstone et al. 2021). Harrison summarizes this unfortunate situation as follows, "Fat trans people … are being forced to engage an inherently anti-Black and anti-fat medical system that uses body mass index as an indicator for whether or not they deserve to be affirmed in their bodies" (103–104).

While some have argued that body dissatisfaction, eating disorder behaviors, and body dysmorphia should be addressed prior to gender-affirming medical care (including hormones, puberty blockers, gender-affirming surgery), Giordano cautions against delaying these potentially life-saving interventions (2017). Similarly, Bray (2015) argues that providers must engage in critical self-reflection to explore why some methods of "body modification" are considered ethically appropriate in trans health care (e.g., gender-affirming surgery, hormones), while other body modification processes (e.g., eating disorder behaviors) are deemed "pathological." Due to the culture's understanding of gendered bodies, gender diverse bodies are constantly under threat of attack (as are fat bodies). Thus, it is unclear why promoting body modification for some is considered "healthy" while for others, body modification is considered "unhealthy." In Harrison's work, they argue that ultimately concepts of gender serve to "further ostracize the Black fat" to such a degree that the only liberatory solution is to "destroy gender" (104). To carry this metaphor further, perhaps the liberatory societal steps include "destroying body ideals" in addition to concepts of gender.

Conclusion: Fattening Feminist Discourses on Eating Disorders

In this chapter I have provided a very brief overview of six of the major tensions in critical feminist and critical fat studies regarding theorizing around eating disorders. Examining higher weight patients with eating disorders brings together the seemingly disparate fields of fat acceptance and eating disorders, showing how these issues cannot, in fact, stay separate. If higher weight individuals are to receive equitable treatment—both in medical settings and society—eating disorders must be studied through an interdisciplinary, intersectional, liberatory lens that integrates weight stigma literature. Societal inequities (e.g., race, ethnicity, gender, class, size, among others) are regularly reproduced in the experiences of diverse patients with eating disorders. By examining these inequities directly, I hope that multidisciplinary scholars can help to expand the study of eating disorders to be more inclusive of the diverse presentations of eating disorders that present within multiple national (and indeed global) settings.

Though largely unexplored in feminist literature, theorizing about higher weight eating disorders adds to the richness of eating disorder theorizing in multiple ways. It deepens discussions regarding diagnostic cut-offs and the harm (or utility) in categorizations. Conversations about higher weight eating disorder experiences highlight the need for continued focus on the diversity of eating disorder presentations—within various genders, races, ethnicities, nations, and body sizes.

Additionally, explorations of the functions (both therapeutic and disordered) of pro-ana (and other online) spaces could be augmented by exploring how larger-bodied individuals successfully navigate (or not) these spaces. Finally, by exploring the meaning and experiences of gender for higher weight trans eating disorder patients, we gain new insight into how concepts of gender, femininity, masculinity, and androgyny are entangled with issues of body ideals and body image.

As we anticipate more critical feminist theorizing of eating disorders, pressing new issues include: integrating aspects of size diversity and fat politics into eating disorder conceptualization, the exploration of trans and nonbinary experiences, examining nondominant eating disorder discourses (e.g., voices of Black, Indigenous, and people of color, disabled, neurodiverse, fat, queer, older, and non-Western voices), the incorporation of intersectional approaches (Crenshaw 1991), the eating disorder consequences of the growing popularity of weight-loss surgeries, and the treatment and prevention needs facing increasingly diverse eating disorder patient populations.[2]

In closing, the interdisciplinary scholarly community studying eating disorders must come to recognize the reality of higher weight persons struggling with eating disorders if we are to continue to expand and be fully inclusive of all eating disorder experiences. Rather than centering thin, cis, feminine experiences of eating disorders, we must reckon with the need to "fatten" our feminist discourses around eating disorders in order to strive for liberation of all bodies. We can begin this theoretical work by situating higher weight bodies with eating disorders within each of these debates, as I have outlined throughout this chapter. This integration of body and size diversity will necessarily deepen our understanding of eating disorders as gendered experiences, while also lending a greater liberatory, intersectional lens.

Notes

1 "Restrictive eating disorder" has been argued to be a misleading term, as it typically refers to anorexia nervosa and bulimia, while excluding binge eating disorder. However, most eating disorder experts agree that restriction tends to be an important behavioral symptom of all of these disorders (though often overlooked in larger-bodied patients).
2 Please note that it is unclear if more people with marginalized identities are getting eating disorders or if researchers are simply getting better at measuring them (or both).

References

Ackard, Diann M., Sara A. Richter, Amber M. Egan, and Catherine L. Cronemeyer. 2014. "What does remission tell us about women with eating disorders? Investigating applications of various remission definitions and their associations with quality of life." *Journal of Psychosomatic Research* 76 (1): 12–18. https://doi.org/10.1016/j.jpsycho res.2013.10.002

Ahmed, Sara. 2000. "Whose counting?" *Feminist Theory* 1 (1): 97–103. https://doi. org/10.1177/14647000022229083.

Almazan, Anthony N., and Alex S. Keuroghlian. 2021. "Association between gender-affirming surgeries and mental health outcomes." *JAMA Surgery* 156 (7): 611–618.

American Psychiatric Association. 2013. *Diagnostic and Statistical Manual of Mental Disorders: DSM-5.* Edited by Association American Psychiatric and D. S. M. Task Force American Psychiatric Association. Fifth edition. *DSM-5.* Arlington, VA: American Psychiatric Association.

Arcelus, Jon, Alex J Mitchell, Jackie Wales, and Søren Nielsen. 2011. "Mortality rates in patients with anorexia nervosa and other eating disorders: A meta-analysis of 36 studies." *Archives of General Psychiatry* 68 (7): 724–731.

Avila, Jonathan. 2020. "6.10 eating disorders in transgender youth." *Journal of the American Academy of Child and Adolescent Psychiatry* 59 (10): S135. https://doi.org/10.1016/j. jaac.2020.07.527

Avila, Jonathan T., Neville H. Golden, and Tandy Aye. 2019. "Eating disorder screening in transgender youth." *Journal of Adolescent Health* 65 (6): 815–817. https://doi. org/10.1016/j.jadohealth.2019.06.011

Bardone-Cone, Anna M., Megan B. Harney, Christine R. Maldonado, Melissa A. Lawson, D. Paul Robinson, Roma Smith, and Aneesh Tosh. 2010. "Defining recovery from an eating disorder: Conceptualization, validation, and examination of psychosocial functioning and psychiatric comorbidity." *Behaviour Research and Therapy* 48 (3): 194–202. https://doi.org/10.1016/j.brat.2009.11.001

Billings, Marcie, Jocelyn Lebow, and Leslie A. Sim. 2013. "Eating disorders in adolescents with a history of obesity." *Pediatrics* 132 (4): e1026. https://doi.org/10.1542/peds.2012-3940

Bobila, Samantha. 2013. "The transcultural feminist model: Lived experiences, intersectionality, and eating disorders." Doctoral Dissertation, Rutgers University.

Boero, Natalie, and Cheri Jo Pascoe. 2012. "Pro-anorexia communities and online interaction: Bringing the pro-ana body online." *Body & Society* 18 (2): 27–57.

Bordo, Susan. 1992. "Eating disorders: The feminist challenge to the concept of pathology." In D. Leter's (Ed.), *The body in medical thought and practice*, 197–213. Massachusetts: Springer.

Bordo, Susan. 2004. *Unbearable weight: Feminism, Western culture, and the body.* California: University of California Press.

Bordo, Susan. 2009. "Not just 'a white girl's thing': The changing face of food and body image problems." In Malson & M. Burns' (Eds.), *Critical feminist approaches to eating dis/orders*, 68–82. New York, NY: Routledge.

Bränström, Richard, and John E Pachankis. 2020. "Reduction in mental health treatment utilization among transgender individuals after gender-affirming surgeries: A total population study." *American Journal of Psychiatry* 177 (8): 727–734.

Bray, Sean. 2015. "Gender dysphoria, body dysmorphia, and the problematic of body modification." *The Journal of Speculative Philosophy* 29 (3): 424–436. https://doi. org/10.5325/jspecphil.29.3.0424

Bristow, Claire, Capella Meurer, Janette Simmonds, and Tristan Snell. 2020. "Anti-obesity public health messages and risk factors for disordered eating: A systematic review." *Health Promotion International* 35 (6): 1551–1569. https://doi.org/10.1093/hea pro/daaa018

Brotsky, Sarah R, and David Giles. 2007. "Inside the 'pro-ana' community: A covert online participant observation." *Eating Disorders* 15 (2): 93–109.

Brownstone, Lisa M., Jaclyn DeRieux, Devin A. Kelly, Lanie J. Sumlin, and Jennifer L. Gaudiani. 2021. "Body mass index requirements for gender-affirming surgeries are not empirically based." *Transgender Health* 6 (3): 121–124. https://doi.org/10.1089/trgh.2020.0068

Calogero, Rachel M., Tracy L. Tylka, and Janell L. Mensinger. 2016. "Scientific weightism: A view of mainstream weight stigma research through a feminist lens." In T. Roberts, N. Curtin, L. E. Duncan, & L. M. Cortina's (Eds.), *Feminist perspectives on building a better psychological science of gender,* 9–28. Switzerland: Springer International.

Chesney, Edward, Guy M. Goodwin, and Seena Fazel. 2014. "Risks of all-cause and suicide mortality in mental disorders: A meta-review." *World Psychiatry* 13 (2): 153–160. https://doi.org/10.1002/wps.20128

Christodoulou, Mario. 2012. "Pro-anorexia websites pose public health challenge." *The Lancet (British Edition)* 379 (9811): 110–110. https://doi.org/10.1016/S0140-6736(12)60048-8

Coelho, Jennifer S., Janet Suen, Beth A. Clark, Sheila K. Marshall, Josie Geller, and Pei-Yoong Lam. 2019. "Eating disorder diagnoses and symptom presentation in transgender youth: A scoping review." *Current Psychiatry Reports* 21 (11): 1–10. https://doi.org/10.1007/s11920-019-1097-x

Crenshaw, Kimberle. 1991. "Mapping the margins: Intersectionality, identity politics, and violence against women of color." *Stanford Law Review* 43: 1241–1299.

da Luz, Felipe Q., Amanda Sainsbury, Haider Mannan, Stephen Touyz, Deborah Mitchison, Federico Girosi, and Phillipa Hay. 2018. "An investigation of relationships between disordered eating behaviors, weight/shape overvaluation and mood in the general population." *Appetite* 129: 19–24. https://doi.org/10.1016/j.appet.2018.06.029

Daniels, Jessie. 2009. "Rethinking cyberfeminism (s): Race, gender, and embodiment." *WSQ: Women's Studies Quarterly* 37 (1): 101–124.

Darby, Anita, Phillipa Hay, Jonathan Mond, Frances Quirk, Petra Buttner, and Lee Kennedy. 2009. "The rising prevalence of comorbid obesity and eating disorder behaviors from 1995 to 2005." *The International Journal of Eating Disorders* 42 (2): 104–108. https://doi.org/10.1002/eat.20601

De Lauretis, Teresa. 1987. *Technologies of gender: Essays on theory, film, and fiction.* Bloomington: Indiana University Press.

Dias, Karen. 2013. "The ana sanctuary: Women's pro-anorexia narratives in cyberspace." *Journal of International Women's Studies* 4 (2): 31–45.

Diemer, Elizabeth W., Jaclyn M. White Hughto, Allegra R. Gordon, Carly Guss, S. Bryn Austin, and Sari L. Reisner. 2018. "Beyond the binary: Differences in eating disorder prevalence by gender identity in a transgender sample." *Transgender Health* 3 (1): 17–23. https://doi.org/10.1089/trgh.2017.0043

Dohnt, Hayley, and Marika Tiggemann. 2006. "The contribution of peer and media influences to the development of body satisfaction and self-esteem in young girls: A prospective study." *Developmental Psychology* 42 (5): 929.

Dousti, Peyman, Narges Hosseininia, Shabnam Dousti, and Pegah Dousti. 2021. "Online group therapy based on acceptance and commitment on body dysmorphic and fear of body image in overweight people." *Rooyesh-e-Ravanshenasi Journal (RRJ)* 10 (4): 25–32.

Ekeroth, Kerstin, David Clinton, Claes Norring, and Andreas Birgegård. 2013. "Clinical characteristics and distinctiveness of DSM-5 eating disorder diagnoses: Findings from a large naturalistic clinical database." *Journal of Eating Disorders* 1 (1): 31. https://doi.org/ 10.1186/2050-2974-1-31

Engel, Scott G., Carol E. Adair, Carlota Las Hayas, and Suzanne Abraham. 2009. "Health-related quality of life and eating disorders: A review and update." *The International Journal of Eating Disorders* 42 (2): 179–187. https://doi.org/10.1002/eat.20602

Ernsberger, Paul. 2009. "Does social class explain the connection between weight and health." In E. Rothblum, M. Wann, & S. Solovay's (Eds.), *The fat studies reader*: 25–36. New York, NY: New York University Press.

Espindola, Cybele R, and Sergio L Blay. 2013. "Long term remission of anorexia nervosa: Factors involved in the outcome of female patients." *PloS one* 8 (2): e56275.

Fallon, Patricia, Melanie Katzman, and Susan Wooley. 1994. *Feminist perspectives on eating disorders*. New York: Guilford Press.

Ferreday, Debra. 2003. "Unspeakable bodies: Erasure, embodiment and the pro-ana community." *International Journal of Cultural Studies* 6 (3): 277–295.

Freedman, David S, Laura Kettel Khan, Mary K Serdula, Cynthia L Ogden, and William H Dietz. 2006. "Racial and ethnic differences in secular trends for childhood BMI, weight, and height." *Obesity* 14 (2): 301–308.

Garland-Thomson, Rosemarie. 2002. "Integrating disability, transforming feminist theory." *NWSA Journal* 14 (3): 1–32.

Garrett, Catherine. 1998. *Beyond anorexia: Narrative, spirituality and recovery*. Cambridge, UK: Cambridge University Press.

Giordano, Simona. 2017. "Eating yourself away: Reflections on the 'comorbidity' of eating disorders and gender dysphoria." *Clinical Ethics* 12 (1): 45–53.

Gremillion, H. 2003. *Feeding anorexia: Gender and power at a treatment center*. North Carolina: Duke University Press.

Gremillion, Helen. 2008. "The race and class politics of anorexia nervosa: Unravelling white, middle-class standards in representations of eating problems." In K. A. Teghtsoonian & P. Moss (Eds.), *Contesting illness: Processes and practices*: 218–238. Toronto: University of Toronto Press.

Griffin, J, and EM Berry. 2003. "A modern day holy anorexia? Religious language in advertising and anorexia nervosa in the West." *European Journal of Clinical Nutrition* 57 (1): 43.

Guss, Carly E., David N. Williams, Sari L. Reisner, S. Bryn Austin, and Sabra L. Katz-Wise. 2016. "Disordered weight management behaviors, nonprescription steroid use, and weight perception in transgender youth." *Journal of Adolescent Health* 60 (1): 17–22. https://doi.org/10.1016/j.jadohealth.2016.08.027

Harrison, Da'Shaun L. 2021. *Belly of the beast: The politics of anti-fatness as anti-blackness*. Berkeley, CA: North Atlantic Books.

Harrop, Erin N. 2018. "Typical-atypical interactions: One patient's experience of weight bias in an inpatient eating disorder treatment setting." *Women & Therapy* 42 (1-2): 1–14. https://doi.org/10.1080/02703149.2018.1524068

Harrop, Erin. 2020. "'Maybe I really am too fat to have an eating disorder': A mixed methods study of weight stigma and healthcare experiences in a diverse sample of patients with atypical anorexia." Doctoral Dissertation, University of Washington.

Hartman-Munick, Sydney M., Scout Silverstein, Carly E. Guss, Ethan Lopez, Jerel P. Calzo, and Allegra R. Gordon. 2021. "Eating disorder screening and treatment experiences in transgender and gender diverse young adults." *Eating Behaviors: An International Journal* 41: 101517. https://doi.org/10.1016/j.eatbeh.2021.101517

Hepworth, Julie. 1999. *The social construction of anorexia nervosa*. Los Angeles, CA: Sage.

Holmes, Su. 2016a. "Between feminism and anorexia: An autoethnography." *International Journal of Cultural Studies* 19 (2): 193–207. https://doi.org/10.1177/1367877914561831

Holmes, Su. 2016b. "(Un) twisted: Talking back to media representations of eating disorders." *Journal of Gender Studies* 27 (2): 1–16.

Hudson, James I, Eva Hiripi, Harrison G Pope, and Ronald C Kessler. 2007. "The prevalence and correlates of eating disorders in the National Comorbidity Survey Replication." *Biological Psychiatry* 61 (3): 348–358.

Jones, Bethany Alice, Emma Haycraft, Sarah Murjan, and Jon Arcelus. 2016. "Body dissatisfaction and disordered eating in trans people: A systematic review of the literature." *International Review of Psychiatry (Abingdon, England)* 28 (1): 81–94. https://doi.org/10.3109/09540261.2015.1089217

Kennedy, Grace A., Sara F. Forman, Elizabeth R. Woods, Albert C. Hergenroeder, Kathleen A. Mammel, Martin M. Fisher, Rollyn M. Ornstein, S. Todd Callahan, Neville H. Golden, Cynthia J. Kapphahn, Andrea K. Garber, Ellen S. Rome, and Tracy K. Richmond. 2017. "History of overweight/obesity as predictor of care received at 1-year follow-up in adolescents with anorexia nervosa or atypical anorexia nervosa." *Journal of Adolescent Health* 60 (6): 674–679. https://doi.org/10.1016/j.jadohealth.2017.01.001

King, K. 2001. "Productive agencies of feminist theory: The work it does." *Feminist Theory* 2 (1): 94–98. https://doi.org/10.1177/14647000122229406

Kjelsås, Einar, Christian Bjørnstrøm, and K Gunnar Götestam. 2004. "Prevalence of eating disorders in female and male adolescents (14–15 years)." *Eating Behaviors* 5 (1): 13–25.

Lebesco, Kathleen. 2009. "Weight management, good health and the will to normality." In Malson & M. Burns' (Eds), *Critical feminist approaches to eating dis/orders*, 146. New York, NY: Routledge.

Lebow, Jocelyn, Leslie A. Sim, and Lisa N. Kransdorf. 2015. "Prevalence of a history of overweight and obesity in adolescents with restrictive eating disorders." *Journal of Adolescent Health* 56 (1): 19–24. https://doi.org/10.1016/j.jadohealth.2014.06.005

Lee, Sing, and Melanie A Katzman. 2002. "Cross-cultural perspectives on eating disorders." In C. G. Fairburn & K. D. Brownell's (Ed.), *Eating disorders and obesity: A comprehensive handbook*: 260–264. New York, NY: The Guilford Press.

Leme, Ana Carolina B., Jess Haines, Lisa Tang, Karin L. L. Dunker, Sonia T. Philippi, Mauro Fisberg, Gerson L. Ferrari, and Regina M. Fisberg. 2020. "Impact of strategies for preventing obesity and risk factors for eating disorders among adolescents: A systematic review." *Nutrients* 12 (10): 3134. https://doi.org/10.3390/nu12103134

Lester, Rebecca J. 2019. *Famished: Eating disorders and failed care in America*. Oakland, CA: University of California Press.

Machado, Paulo P. P., Sónia Gonçalves, and Hans W. Hoek. 2013. "DSM-5 reduces the proportion of EDNOS cases: Evidence from community samples." *International Journal of Eating Disorders* 46 (1): 60–65. https://doi.org/10.1002/eat.22040

Machado, Paulo P. P., Barbara C Machado, Sónia Gonçalves, and Hans W Hoek. 2007. "The prevalence of eating disorders not otherwise specified." *International Journal of Eating Disorders* 40 (3): 212–217.

Malson, Helen, and Maree Burns. 2009a. "Re-theorising the slash of dis/order." In H. Malson & M. Burns' (Eds.), *Critical feminist approaches to eating dis/orders*: 1. New York, NY: Routledge.

Malson, Helen, and Maree Burns (Eds). 2009b. *Critical feminist approaches to eating dis/orders.* New York, NY: Routledge.

Mensinger, Janell L., Rachel M. Calogero, and Tracy L. Tylka. 2016. "Internalized weight stigma moderates eating behavior outcomes in women with high BMI participating in a healthy living program." *Appetite* 102: 32–43. https://doi.org/10.1016/j. appet.2016.01.033

Mensinger, Janell L., Shelbi A. Cox, and Jennifer R. Henretty. 2021. "Treatment outcomes and trajectories of change in patients attributing their eating disorder onset to anti-obesity messaging." *Psychosomatic Medicine* 83 (7): 777–786. https://doi.org/10.1097/PSY.0000000000000962

Mitchison, Deborah, Jonathan Mond, Kay Bussey, Scott Griffiths, Nora Trompeter, Alexandra Lonergan, Kathleen M. Pike, Stuart B. Murray, and Phillipa Hay. 2020. "DSM-5 full syndrome, other specified, and unspecified eating disorders in Australian adolescents: Prevalence and clinical significance." *Psychological Medicine* 50 (6): 981–990. https://doi.org/10.1017/S0033291719000898

Mulveen, Ruaidhri, and Julie Hepworth. 2006. "An interpretative phenomenological analysis of participation in a pro-anorexia internet site and its relationship with disordered eating." *Journal of Health Psychology* 11 (2): 283–296.

O'Hara, Lily, and Jane Taylor. 2018. "What's wrong with the 'war on obesity?' A narrative review of the weight-centered health paradigm and development of the 3C framework to build critical competency for a paradigm shift." *SAGE Open* 8 (2): 215824401877288. https://doi.org/10.1177/2158244018772888

Parker, Lacie L., and Jennifer A. Harriger. 2020. "Eating disorders and disordered eating behaviors in the LGBT population: A review of the literature." *Journal of Eating Disorders* 8 (1): 1–51. https://doi.org/10.1186/s40337-020-00327-y

Psalios, Susanna. 2020. "Collateral damage of the 'war on obesity': The Australian anti-obesity campaign: From fat Stigma to eating disorders." Doctoral Dissertation, La Trobe University.

Reindl, Sheila M. 2001. *Sensing the self: Women's recovery from bulimia.* Cambridge, MA: Harvard University Press.

Rice, Carla. 2009. "How big girls become fat girls: The cultural production of problem eating and physical inactivity." In H. Malson & M. Burns' (Eds.), *Critical feminist approaches to eating dis/orders*: 97–109. New York, NY: Routledge.

Riley, Sarah, Karen Rodham, and Jeff Gavin. 2009. "Doing weight: Pro-ana and recovery identities in cyberspace." *Journal of Community & Applied Social Psychology* 19 (5): 348–359.

Romano, Kelly A, Kristin E Heron, and James M Henson. 2021. "Examining associations among weight stigma, weight bias internalization, body dissatisfaction, and eating disorder symptoms: Does weight status matter?" *Body Image* 37: 38–49.

Rothblum, Esther D. 1994. "'I'll die for the revolution but don't ask me not to diet'": Feminism and the continuing stigmatization of obesity." In P. Fallon, M. A. Katzman, & S. C. Wooley's (Eds.), *Feminist perspectives on eating disorders*: 53–76. New York, NY: Guilford Press.

Rothblum, Esther D., and Sondra Solovay. 2009. *The fat studies reader.* New York: New York University Press.

Smink, Frédérique RE, Daphne Van Hoeken, and Hans W Hoek. 2012. "Epidemiology of eating disorders: Incidence, prevalence and mortality rates." *Current Psychiatry Reports* 14 (4): 406–414.

Stice, Eric, Diane Spangler, and W Stewart Agras. 2001. "Exposure to media-portrayed thin-ideal images adversely affects vulnerable girls: A longitudinal experiment." *Journal of Social and Clinical Psychology* 20 (3): 270–288.

Tchanturia, Kate, and Claire Baillie. 2015. "Recovery/discovery oriented group." In K. Tchantura's (Ed.), *Brief group psychotherapy for eating disorders: Inpatient protocols*: 198–231. New York, NY: Routledge.

Thompson, Becky. 1994. "Food, bodies, and growing up female: Childhood lessons about culture, race, and class." In P. Fallon, M. A. Katzman, & S. C. Wooley's (Eds.), *Feminist perspectives on eating disorders*: 355–378. New York, NY: Guilford Press.

Zamantakis, Alithia, and Dresden Lackey. 2021. "Dying to be (A) gendered: An exploratory content analysis of trans/nonbinary people's experiences with eating disorders." *Sociological Inquiry* 92: 870–893.

Zerbe, Kathryn J. 1993. *The body betrayed: Women, eating disorders, and treatment.* Washington, DC: American Psychiatric Press.

14

IMMOVABLE SUBJECTS, UNSTOPPABLE FORCES

Bariatric Surgery, Gender, and the Body

Nikkolette Lee

The quest to "solve" the "problem" of fatness through medical techniques goes much further back than the futuristic medical procedures of the 21st century. In fact, some historians, and more notably, obesity scientists claim that medical treatments for obesity can be traced as far back as the 10th century AD. King Sancho I of León, also known as Sancho the Fat, took the Spanish throne in 958 AD – however, during his reign he became so fat that "he could not walk, ride a horse, or pick up a sword," leading to calls for his deposition for the crime of being too fat to lead (Faria 2017, 90). Despised by nobles and commoners alike for his perceived incompetence in matters of both war and peace, his grandmother, Queen Toda of the neighboring Kingdom of Navarre, called on the famous and well-respected physician Hasdai ibn Shaprut to remedy Sancho's "massive obesity" (Baltasar 2004, 1138). King Sancho was then carried 800 kilometers to the royal court in Cordoba, where Hasdai ibn Shaprut served, to receive treatment. Hasdai's treatment to cure Sancho's "super-super-obesity" consisted of sewing Sancho's lips shut and subsequently tube-feeding him for six months (Baltasar 2004, 1138). The exact and complete details of his diet have been lost to history, but apparently included an ancient panacea known as *theriaca*[1]: a mélange of herbs, animal products, minerals and "above all opium," often administered along with water, wine, or oil (Serracino-Inglott 1986, 31). After six months under Hasdai ibn Shaprut's regimen, Sancho the Fat reportedly lost half his weight and triumphantly returned to León on a horse to reclaim his throne. It is unclear if King Sancho ever gained the weight back, but his dramatic weight loss is cited as part of the grand strategy that brought (temporary) peace to the warring kingdoms of Spain (Hopkins and Lehmann 1995, 452). However, less than ten years later in 966 AD, King Sancho the (formerly) Fat was assassinated by one of his own nobles with a poisoned apple (Gargantilla Madera and Arroyo Pardo 2016, 101).

DOI: 10.4324/9781003140665-20

Western medical knowledge has evolved and improved exponentially over the last one thousand years; the tireless pursuit of eradicating fatness, however, remains unchanged (if not intensified) for many physicians. Myriad medical interventions ranging from strict diets to jaw wiring have been developed and expanded upon since Sancho the Fat's time, and fatness has only become increasingly medicalized since. There are a whole host of other methods of medically removing, lessening, or altering fat, but here I'll be focusing on the relatively modern phenomenon of bariatric surgery and its unique peculiarities. Of particular relevance are the tense connections between weight loss surgery and gender; this essay additionally aims to highlight these dynamics. Work in Fat Studies has shown that gender and the weight loss and diet industries are intimately connected, and this is no different for weight loss surgery.

Before going any further, I would like to clarify my rationale regarding terminology in this piece. When discussing this topic, I am purposeful in how I use the terms "fat," "overweight," and "obese." The terms "obese" and "overweight" carry a distinctly clinical, pathological connotation, and I employ the terms when discussing excess fat in the context of medical and scientific discourse. Conversely, I use the word "fat" to describe the social, embodied experience of "being big," and to better capture the socially and historically contingent fluidity, subjectivity, and ambiguousness that comes with existing in a larger body (Cooper 2010, 1020–21).

As a secondary aside, I'd also like to discuss my purpose in writing this piece. As a sociologist by trade, I am open about how my identity and personal experiences inform my research. Most relevant to this piece is my own fatness, and my own experience as a fat person within the same society that I primarily study. By extension, I possess a whole host of personal opinions about the topics that I study: fatness, fatphobia, medicine, the body, among other things. I do not subscribe to an ideal of pure objectivity and neutrality in my research; our positionalities often inform our worldviews, philosophies, and approaches toward theory and research. However, my goal in this (brief) exploration of bariatric surgery is not to give a treatise of my personal opinions of the surgery. More accurately, I hope to instead present the varying institutional, factional, and personal positions of those involved in the discourses around the surgery. Part of my personal ethos as a social scientist and researcher is the belief that research is primarily about the participants and the social issues that affect them; in this case, that population would be the people who choose to receive bariatric surgery. I am not interested in either demonizing or valorizing these people or their personal logic regarding the procedure(s), nor is my goal to demonize or valorize the surgery itself, regardless of my feelings on the subject.

What Is Bariatric Surgery?

Bariatric surgery encompasses a group of operations that help people lose weight by making changes to the digestive system (National Institute of Diabetes and

Digestive and Kidney Diseases [NIDDK] 2021 CE: 2020). Some procedures reduce the size of the stomach, physically limiting a person's food intake; others alter the small intestine, purposely inducing nutrition malabsorption. Altering the digestive system can also impact hormone production and intestinal flora, potentially reducing feelings of hunger and "improv[ing] how the body metabolizes fat and makes use of insulin" (NIDDK 2021). Currently, the most common bariatric procedure is the sleeve gastrectomy, followed by the Roux-en-Y gastric bypass (American Society for Metabolic and Bariatric Surgery [ASMBS] 2018). Regardless of the specific procedure done, they have the same goal: to aid in curing "morbid obesity." Officially classified as a disease by the World Health Organization (WHO) in 1978, obesity is defined as "a disease in which excess fat is accumulated to an extent that health may be adversely affected" (Buchwald 2005, 594). Obesity and morbid obesity are both listed as diseases by the National Center for Health Statistics and the Centers for Medicare and Medicaid Services, along with a clinical modification code in the International Classification of Diseases. This alone speaks to the incredible amount of medicalization of the fat body over the last half-century, though this process has been in motion for much longer (see Gard and Wright 2005; Murray 2008).

Scientific research on bariatric surgery has proliferated as the procedure becomes more financially lucrative and medically significant. Studies on bariatric surgery's effectiveness, safety, and outcomes have historically produced mixed results, but lean toward general support of the procedure as a legitimate weight loss technique for fat people. The National Institutes of Health (NIH) themselves have expressed emphatic support for bariatric surgery as a solution to morbid obesity (The National Institutes of Health Consensus Statement Online 1985), and research on the topic frequently characterizes the surgery as the "most effective" therapy for "morbid obesity" (Buchwald 2005, 594). Of course, bariatric surgery can also produce negative results; patients often report postoperative symptoms such as pain from excess skin or digestive problems like dumping syndrome (Vogel 2018, 515). Furthermore, medical research indicates that post-surgery patients are at a higher risk for anemia, malnutrition, disordered eating, alcohol addiction, or even death (Ackerman 1999; Ertelt et al. 2008; Kalarchian et al. 2007; Throsby 2007). However, in the words of Karen Throsby, despite the risks, bariatric surgery "is premised on a risk calculation that relies upon the unacceptability of the fat body and the equation of fatness with mortally dangerous ill-health" (Throsby 2007, 1563).

The modern incarnation of bariatric surgery begins in the mid-20th century. In 1952, Swedish physician Viktor Henrikson published a case report regarding his surgical treatment for obesity, making him the first surgeon to officially perform an abdominal bariatric surgery. Henrikson detailed his patient, a 32-year-old woman purportedly suffering from "obesity, constipation, something that slowed her metabolism (without myxedema)" and failed attempts at weight loss ([1952] 1994, 54). His solution entailed a 105 cm (3.5 ft) resecting of the woman's small intestine, which he had also performed on two other women. Reportedly, the surgery was generally unsuccessful, with the patient weighing more at the 14-month postoperative mark than she did before the procedure. Henrikson did report some "subjective" improvements in the patient's quality of life, including "feeling healthy and energetic" (54). It should be noted, however, that failure was not uncommon during the nascent stages of bariatric surgery's history.

A year later, Dr. Richard Varco quickly followed in Henrikson's footsteps, performing the first intestinal (jejunoileal) bypass on a human being at the University of Minnesota. While Varco never officially published any reports about the procedure, he is still recognized as one of the earlier pioneers of bariatric surgery (Buchwald 2008, S1). Nevertheless, the literature indicates that, generally, Kremen, Linner, and Nelson are regarded as the official progenitors of modern metabolic bariatric surgery, having published their seminal article "An Experimental Evaluation of the Nutritional Importance of Proximal and Distal Small Intestine" in 1954. Their article details a series of extensive intestinal surgeries performed on dogs, complete with thorough experimentation and observation regarding the dogs' postoperative weight, nutritional absorption, and mortality (Kremen, Linner, and Nelson 1954). While Richard Varco may or may not have performed the jejunoileal bypass first, it was Arnold Kremer, John Linner, and Charles Nelson who brought it to the full attention of the medical community.

Dr. John Linner later published a short retrospective of his career as one of the first bariatric specialists, in which he detailed the process of performing the jejunoileal bypass on a human being for the first time, also in 1954. The patient in question, a fat, Minnesotan woman named Ruth Dvork, complained "bitterly that her main problem was that she was much too fat and, although she could lose weight, she could never keep it off" (Linner 2007, 570). Despite Linner's open concession that the surgery had never been performed on a person before, Dvork expressed excitement at the results of the dog study and "strongly urged that [Linner and his colleagues] … proceed with the surgery no matter what" (570). With the absence of an institutional review board at the time, the enthusiastic consent of the patient, and the support of Kremen, he went ahead with the surgery. While the bypass surgery itself was initially successful, Dvork experienced multiple bouts of intestinal hemorrhaging requiring additional surgery. Furthermore, Dvork expressed discontent with the amount of weight lost, prompting Linner to perform a more extensive bypass 17 years later in 1971. This second surgery brought her weight down between 170 lb. and 190 lb., "resulting in a very happy and satisfied patient" (570).

The jejunoileal bypass was indeed successful at causing significant weight loss and was lauded as a grand success in the fight against morbid obesity. By the 1960s and 70s, though, it proved to be an overall dangerous procedure, frequently leading to complications varying from persistent diarrhea to irreversible hepatic cirrhosis of the liver, which was fatal (Salameh 2006, 194). This prompted physicians and researchers to go back to the drawing board, triggering a boom in bariatric surgical research, technology, and techniques. Possibly the most well-known of these developments was Dr. Edward Mason's Roux-en-Y gastric bypass (RYGB) from 1967, a surgical technique still used today. Mason conceived of the procedure after noticing that women who had undergone "partial gastrectomy [a procedure with similar stomach modification] for peptic ulcer disease had difficulty achieving weight gain" post-surgery (195). After performing the RYGB on other obese women, he determined that the procedure had serious worth. It is worth noting that Mason specifically stated the gender of these early gastric bypass patients, and I could not find any obvious scientific explanation as to why he did this or if the procedure affected men differently. As it currently stands, RYGB can be and has been performed on people of any gender or sex, so the mystery remains as to whether his observation was just a case of scientific specificity or a reflection of the greater weight loss pressure women experience. In the next four decades, scientists created, developed, and streamlined the commonplace bariatric procedures (RYGB, Sleeve Gastrectomy, Gastric Band, Biliopancreatic Diversion with Duodenal Switch, and Single Anastomosis Duodenal-Ileal Bypass with Sleeve Gastrectomy) that exist today. The history of these surgeries themselves are fascinating, certainly in terms of the medical science alone, but also in terms of the social and physical ramifications that result from them, and the views on gender, the body, and fatness the doctors and researchers who pioneered these procedures possessed.

How Did We Get Here?

As we have seen, bariatric surgery's history easily stretches back over half a century, and the ASMBS, the central organization for physicians specializing in the field, was formed in 1983 (American Society for Metabolic and Bariatric Surgery n.d.). Curiously though, it wasn't until the 1990s that bariatric surgery seemed to gain widespread notoriety, both in terms of surgery rates and social relevance. A notable example of the increased fear of fat comes from Natalie Boero's (2007) analysis of the *New York Times*, featuring an article series from 2000 called "Fat Epidemic," focusing on "one of the United States' worst public health problems" (48). However, the *New York Times* had been soliciting the medical opinions of the ASMBS for articles since the late 70s, highlighting just how long public health anxiety around fatness has been proliferating (*New York Times* 1977). Sociologists and psychologists were discussing fat stigma in academic literature as early as 1968 (Cahnman 1968).

To best contextualize the prevalence of bariatric surgery in the United States, the public statistics, logic, and math regarding fatness as a whole ought to be addressed. The CDC's National Center for Health Statistics reports that in 2018 about 74% of all Americans between the ages of 20 and 74 were overweight or obese – compare this to about 45% of the population in 1962 (Fryar, Carroll, and Afful 2020).

The categories for "overweight" and "obese" are currently defined by the body mass index (BMI), a mathematical formula of body weight (kilograms) divided by height squared (meters) (Nuttall 2015, 119). The BMI was a quickly accepted replacement for the earlier diagnostic, Metropolitan Life Insurance Company's simplistic and dated weight divided by height formula (Wt/Ht) (118). The Wt/Ht formula's simple mathematics, however, did not take the physiological build of human beings into account, leading to an inaccurate picture of what the "average weight" of a person looks like (119). The BMI, for its relative improvement in the science of determining health through basic arithmetic, was also subject to several shifts, reorganizations, and updates, complicating these obesity statistics. In 1995, the WHO published a technical report with the intent of establishing uniform categories of the BMI; they decided on a quartile system, comprised of "underweight, normal, overweight, and obese" (WHO Expert Committee on Physical Status: the Use and Interpretation of Anthropometry). This report also determined that a BMI of 20.0 to 24.9 fell into the "normal" category, while 25.0 to 29.9 indicated overweight. At this time, the NIH was using a BMI of 27.8 or 27.3 (men and women, respectively) as the cutoff for overweight, but by 1998 had adopted the WHO's new, lower, standardized BMI scale (Kuczmarski and Flegal 2000, 1078). This is significant because this one decision immediately reclassified thousands of formerly "normal" sized Americans as "overweight," further fanning the flames of public health panic around the emerging "obesity epidemic." The history of the BMI and weight classification in the United States is a topic complex enough to merit its own paper, but for the purposes of this exploration of weight loss surgery and gender, it should provide sufficient context on the shifting scientific views around fatness at the turn of the millennium.

During the early 1990s, at the nascent stages of the "obesity epidemic," and its rhetoric, bariatric surgery remained relatively niche. According to the ASMBS (2018), in 1993, surgeons completed around 8,500 bariatric surgeries in the United States. By 2018, these numbers skyrocketed to a total of 252,000 (American Society for Metabolic and Bariatric Surgery 2018). This information illuminates certain trends. The first is that the number of fat Americans has almost doubled in 60 years, though how much of that increase is due to actual weight gain and how much is due to the various changes in weight diagnostic formulas is up for debate. Secondly, the number of bariatric surgeries in the United States has increased at an exponentially higher rate over a significantly shorter time span. Given the sheer number of overweight and obese people in the United States, an incredibly small fraction of these people in the United States have ever actually gotten any kind of bariatric surgery. Despite this, the statistics also indicate an undeniable and exponential increase in the incidence of these surgeries.

When it comes to gender and bariatric surgery, the data depicts a decidedly stark dynamic. The incidence of obesity itself is generally equal between men and women, if not slightly higher for men during some years. Male patients in the bariatric surgery population also had higher proportions of "moderate, major, and extreme severity" of illness and higher rates of comorbid conditions such as type 2 diabetes, hypertension, or liver disease (Young, Phelan, and Nguyen 2016, 227).[2] Notwithstanding this, the vast majority of bariatric surgeries are performed on women. A ten year study between 2001 and 2010 by Young, Phelan, and Nguyen indicates out of a cumulative 810,999 patients, 19.3% were male and 80.7% were female (227); an additional study by Fuchs et al. (2015) indicates similar trends, with 81.3% of bariatric patients between 1998 and 2010 being female. It is apparent that the statistics paint a heavily gendered picture of bariatric surgery, with women making up the overwhelming majority of patients. Both social and medical scientists have posited an assortment of reasons as to why this is, some of which will be explored here.

Social Attitudes Regarding Bariatric Surgery

Bariatric surgery has become a topic of research in multiple disciplines, from the hard sciences to the humanities. Naturally, this has led to a wide variety of theoretical approaches, research methodologies, and attitudes toward bariatric surgery as a weight loss method as well as the concept itself. Some see bariatric surgery as a positive tool to reduce obesity and/or improve quality of life, citing its health benefits and swift weight loss as obvious selling points. Meanwhile, others view it as an inherently violent procedure, physically and psychologically harming and alienating fat people.

More data is needed, but it appears that by and large, most bariatric surgery researchers have not undergone a bariatric procedure themselves. Given the low statistics, this is unsurprising. While my interest in the topic is related to my own experiences as a fat person and social scientist, I also have never had a bariatric procedure. Not undergoing weight loss surgery, of course, does not negate the body of empirical research or even one's opinion on the topic, but when considering who controls and creates the dominant narratives regarding this surgery, it is worth noting. Therefore, in addition to analyzing the broader discourses around the topic, it is also important to consider the experiences of this relatively small population of people. The people who choose to get these surgeries are not a monolith, and research in multiple areas has shown that there is a multitude of external factors and internal motives that go into the decision. Furthermore, the fact that most bariatric patients are women complicates these narratives, inviting further questions about the gendered body, fatness, and bodily autonomy.

"The Apotheosis of Fat Hatred:" Bariatric Surgery as Fat Antagonism

Research in both the social and medical sciences overwhelmingly confirm the existence of prejudice against fat people.[3] In a social landscape where fatphobia and anti-fat attitudes remain solidly and deeply entrenched, the mere concept of bariatric surgery manifests as a salient phenomenon. Bariatric surgery, by its very nature, is a particularly visceral cadre of medical procedures. While the specific techniques vary, these surgeries constrict, rearrange, bypass, and in most cases, irreversibly manipulate the digestive system, a series of organs responsible for one of our most basic human needs: eating food.

Fat activist Marilyn Wann describes bariatric surgery as "a mutilation of healthy body parts," likening the surgery to an act of symbolic and literal violence against the self (1998, 41). Lindo Bacon, physiologist, nutritionist, and pioneer of the Health at Every Size movement characterizes bariatric surgery as a "high-risk disease-inducing cosmetic surgery [more] than a health-enhancing procedure" (Bacon 2010, 41). The National Association for the Advancement of Fat Acceptance (NAAFA) takes an anti-bariatric surgery stance, citing the "tremendous number of deaths and severe complications" linked to weight loss surgery, but "does not reject anyone supportive of their goals as an organization" (National Association for the Advancement of Fat Acceptance n.d.). These harsh critiques of the surgery are not unfounded by any means. Empirical research, including some cited in my initial discussion of bariatric surgery above, highlights the large host of surgical risk and long-term side effects associated with bariatric surgery. Even some of those who willingly underwent the procedure have expressed dissatisfaction with the results of the procedure and regret about agreeing to the surgery at all.

Some researchers in support of weight loss surgery have conceded that the procedures present a large number of potentially negative side effects and complications. In addition, research continues to unearth new information about the science of obesity, complicating the simplistic public health narrative positing that fatness is illness and thinness is health. This is often the case with science in general; as research progresses, new information is constantly unearthed and integrated into the already existing corpus of knowledge. Sometimes, that new information contradicts the narratives scientists emphatically supported previously, disrupting the trust normally afforded to scientists and medical professionals. Sociologist Thomas Gieryn refers to this negotiation of information and ideology by scientific researchers and professionals as "boundary-work." Scientific boundary-work aims to maintain "professional authority and resources," expand authority into "domains claimed by other professions or occupations," and separate experts from "rival" groups by characterizing them as "deviant, pseudo-, or 'amateur'" (Gieryn 1983, 791–792). It would be reductive to claim that obesity scientists utilize boundary-work for purely altruistic or nefarious reasons, or that they conceptualize their duties of interfacing with the public as boundary-work at all. However, I posit that as fat activism becomes increasingly accepted as a legitimate social movement and framework, the adversarial nature of boundary-work encourages the discrediting of fat activists' critiques toward dominant scientific discourses regarding obesity, and in this case, weight loss surgery. Fat activists and Fat Studies scholars, on a fundamental level, are critical toward the dominant discourses regarding fatness, including the active pathologizing and medicalization of the fat body. In the words of bariatric surgery researcher Karen Throsby, bariatric surgery is often framed as "the apotheosis of fat hatred" by those most critical of it, the ultimate act of physical and symbolic violence against fat people (Throsby 2012b, 107).

Using Gieryn's logic of boundary-work, it is in the interest of scientific professionals to cast doubt on the ardent criticism and apprehension that fat activists, and fat people at large, express about bariatric surgery. While scientists and medical professionals may not announce their disdain or distrust of fat people, the discrediting of fat activists and fat people's understandings of science can be observed in a multitude of ways. Medical professionals have been documented as holding the same stereotypical views of fat people as the lay population, seeing them as lazy, dishonest, stupid, and even hostile (see Bombak, McPhail, and Ward 2016; Puhl, Andreyeva, and Brownell 2008; Puhl, Luedicke, and Grilo 2014; Sabin, Marini, and Nosek 2012; Schwartz et al. 2003). Anecdotally, fat activists also tend to be characterized as easily offended, emotional, and sensitive, engaging in pseudoscience to justify their "unhealthy" lifestyles, and incorrect in their assertion that fatphobia is a significant form of discrimination. While more empirical work is needed to study this type of anti-fatness, I believe that there is some credence to these observations, and that we should take the experiences and analysis of fat organizers seriously. I cite them as further examples of the discrediting of fat people's understanding of obesity science and of their own bodies.

Despite this, fat activists and critical weight researchers continue to express doubt about the legitimacy and efficacy of weight loss surgery, citing factors such as the profit motives behind the costly surgeries and the (often blatant) fatphobic attitudes held by physicians and scientists as confounding variables in the simplistic, implicitly causal narrative supporting bariatric surgery as a solution to the problem of fatness.[4] Furthermore, bariatric surgery does nothing to address the prevalence of fatphobia, which even ardent surgery advocates acknowledge as a significant social issue. This fatphobia manifests so strongly that even those who have gotten bariatric surgery and successfully lost weight, in theory "shedding" their social designation as fat, still experience stigma for ever having been fat enough to need weight loss surgery in the first place (Fee and Nusbaumer 2012; Hansen and Dye 2018). Even from a less radical standpoint, it can also be argued that bariatric surgery also fundamentally ignores the socioeconomic sources of obesity, such as access to healthy food or space to exercise.

Steven Epstein, in his research on AIDS and social movements, describes the phenomenon of credibility struggle. Stemming from Weberian analyses of power, Epstein conceptualizes credibility as a system of cultural authority, a combination of "power, dependence, legitimation, trust, and persuasion," culminating in any one actor's capacity to offer what can be taken as truth (Epstein 1995, 411). Credibility struggle in the world of science, then, defines the consistent attempts of various players to "rephrase the definition of 'science'" to give efficacy to their own forms of credibility (Epstein 1996, 19). Bariatric surgery functions as a significant "boundary object" between the worlds of fat activists and obesity professionals, a phenomenon that cuts between two social worlds, understood differently depending on the "social standpoint from which it is viewed" (18). It follows that bariatric surgery holds prominent political stakes for many fat activists. The surgery itself is subject to its own scientific debates regarding its efficacy and safety, but it also invites opportunity for political action and agitation from those critical of it. The phenomenon of bariatric surgery, a surgery that evokes a sense of barbarism in its crude but effective methods, presents fertile ground for critical interrogation, connecting to broader critiques of fatphobia within society at large.

Importantly, we must return to the fact that most people who choose to undergo bariatric surgery are women. Additionally, many prominent fat activists, such as Marilyn Wann, Charlotte Cooper, Sonya Renee Taylor, and Aubrey Gordon (also known as Your Fat Friend) also identify as women.[5] The overlap in fat stigma and misogyny is no doubt significant; bariatric surgery is yet another example of this intersection. Thus, the already complex social battlefield between mainstream scientists and fat activists is also complicated by the heavily gendered dynamics of bariatric surgery. While gender disparity in medicine has been slowly decreasing over time, about two thirds of practicing physicians in the United States are men (Association of American Medical Colleges 2021). The field of bariatrics presents a notably starker picture; using the membership statistics of the ASMBS as a metric, only 17% of bariatric practitioners are women (American Society for Metabolic and Bariatric Surgeons 2021). Given the male-skewed statistics of the medical field and the female-skewed statistics of bariatric patients, we are presented with a uniquely gendered struggle for power and credibility that will be explored in further detail in next section.

In terms of the repudiation of bariatric surgery by activists, individuals express varying degrees of sympathy toward those who choose to undergo it. Activists such as Wann and Bacon offer their understanding, although with the assertion that bariatric patients often acquiesce to the procedure under coercive circumstances. For example, some well-intentioned fat people get the surgery because of a life's worth of fatphobia crushing their spirits, or perhaps under the influence of the "slick sales pitch[es]" of bariatric surgeons and doctors (Wann 1998, 41). Conversely, some activists paint bariatric surgery as a traitorous act to the cause of fat acceptance, an admission of self-hatred. I find that these thorny debates, both within fat positive circles and between scientists and activists, at the core, boil down to a question of agency, power, and the body. Are the women who choose these surgeries folding under an oppressive pressure and subsequently relinquishing control over their fat body? Or are they reclaiming bodily agency after many years of alienation and shame? Could it be something else, or perhaps a combination of the two?

Self/Control: Embodiment, Agency, and Bariatric Surgery

Depending on your positionality toward the topic, it is appealing to paint bariatric surgery as purely exploitative or purely beneficial for fat people. However, the findings seen throughout the literature depict a decidedly more complicated picture, fraught with various tensions both between and within the individuals involved.

For many of those who opt for weight loss surgery, the process is not necessarily informed by the wide-reaching political stakes held by activists, though it certainly is for some. For many, getting weight loss surgery is a series of individual-scale relationships, interactions, and exchanges of power. The choice to get bariatric surgery is also often informed by the personal experiences of any given patient, of their self and self-concept. The social dynamics inherent to the bariatric surgery experience are varied and complex, involving many actors: nutritionists, psychologists, primary care physicians, surgeons, patients. What is notable about these fat women[6] is their ability to negotiate and navigate new power dynamics, often subverting the socially accepted, unidirectional flow of power between medical professions and fat patients, given the former group's high amount of credibility.

While the bulk of this chapter will focus on the experiences of women who undergo bariatric surgery, I would like to take some time to discuss bariatric surgery in relation to those who aren't (cisgender) women, namely cisgender men as well as transgender and/or nonbinary individuals. In this analysis I informally use terms such as "men" and "women" to discuss patients receiving bariatric surgery. Additionally, I generally apply statistics referring to "males" and "females" seen in the literature to "men" and "women" as groups. Of course, gender is an expansive and complex part of one's identity, and realistically cannot be distilled into the simple categories of "male," "female," "man," and "woman." However, much of the literature focuses on cisgender individuals exclusively or does not delineate between transgender and cisgender subjects. This is especially the case for many of the biology, medicine, and/or surgical journal articles I source many statistics from. With this acknowledgment, in general, when I apply "male" and "female" traits or statistics, I am careful not to ideologically conflate biological sex and gender.

Furthermore, on a related note, research regarding transgender people who receive bariatric surgery is extremely limited and would benefit greatly from additional study. As such, in addition to cisgender men, I will also give a brief and incomplete analysis of transgender, nonbinary, and gender nonconforming individuals and their experiences with weight loss surgery. As detailed above, we have seen that the vast majority of bariatric patients are women, but what about the minority? In general, there is a dearth of research focusing on the experiences of men/male and transgender bariatric patients, but there is a slowly increasing body of work.

In the words of one man who received bariatric surgery, "even though it's the same surgery for a man as it is for a woman, it's almost like it's two different worlds" (Newhook, Gregory, and Twells 2015, 653). Men who pursue bariatric surgery frequently are aware of and acknowledge the heavily gendered nature of weight loss surgery. Additionally, men often expressed feelings of alienation or discomfort with these gender dynamics, both regarding the surgery and of fatness itself, culturally. When discussing their bodies, women are more likely to conceptualize their fatness as part of their identity or having a "profound effect on their sense of self" in some way, while men avoided describing their bodies as "fat," instead opting to lean into masculine descriptors such as "tough," "robust," or "strong" (Newhook, Gregory, and Twells 2015, 657). To invoke Goffman, simply having a bigger body did not necessarily "spoil" a masculine identity (Monaghan 2007, 587). This speaks to the conflicting cultural coding of fatness; thinness is associated with a sense of disciplined femininity, yet the quality of fatness is itself also seen as feminine (Newhook, Gregory, and Twells 2015, 658). The bariatric surgery process, at its core, forces patients of all genders to navigate and contend with multiple gendered, embodied meanings.

However, bariatric surgery, much like narratives around weight loss, is firmly imbued with messaging geared toward feminine fat bodies. Furthermore, the primary supporters of the surgery are women, regardless of whether they are the one getting the surgery or not. Men are more likely to be both less likely to choose to get surgery as well as more likely to discourage others from getting it. Weight loss support groups were also mainly populated by women. This phenomenon could be linked to the masculine inclinations to eschew emotional openness and maintain independence by denying assistance from others. Men struggle with the tenuous position of self-control and self-management while maintaining a "discourse of dominant masculinity that repudiates self-care" (Brenton and Elliott 2014, 103).

Connell uses the term "hegemonic masculinity" to conceptualize what constitutes a "real man," with traits such as "power, success, strength, stoicism, and self-sufficiency" (R.W. Connell 1995 cited in Groven, Galdas, and Solbrække 2015). Men who get bariatric surgery are opting for an extreme measure in order to seize control of their own bodies, to finally build the ideal male body: "healthy, well-functioning …, able to complete tasks and fulfill normative roles (e.g. father, worker, mate, etc.)" (McCreary, Saucier, and Courtenay 2005, 90). Hegemonic masculinity not only requires physical discipline, but moral discipline as well. The state of having a fat body represents a "weakness of the physical body-self" (Robertson, Sheikh, and Moore 2010, 702).

Dieting and exercise, as heavily gendered practices, provides an additional point of contention for male patients. The act of controlled and restrictive eating is at odds with the masculine ideal of the hearty, huge appetite. In order to minimize this kind of discomfort, many men instead emphasized their relationship to exercise, using their newfound thinness to participate in new and/or challenging activities, like physically rigorous jobs or playing sports (Natvik et al. 2015). Relatedly, the other reoccurring theme was one of sexuality, heterosexuality in particular. Both single and partnered fat men often expressed negative feelings and personal experiences regarding their bodies, their sexuality, and their perceived virility. Instead of inspiring feelings of happiness or excitement, some fat men started to see sex as a tiring, physically uncomfortable, and embarrassing activity, putting strain on their sexual and romantic relationships. The scientific literature also focused on the impacts of obesity on the male reproductive system, warning of hormonal and physical abnormalities of decreased testosterone, hypogonadism, and erectile dysfunction that could impair their ability to reproduce as well as maintain a healthy sexual appetite (Granero-Molina et al. 2020, 4263). Men who pursue bariatric surgery find themselves in a heavily gendered space, oftentimes finding themselves navigating a new and radically different way to conceptualize their bodies.

Transgender people represent a third and much smaller subpopulation of bariatric patients. This is worth noting, as transgender adults in the United States are more likely to be obese or overweight than the general population (van der Sluis et al. 2021, 1). Given the complicated relationships between body fat, hormone therapy, and gender reassignment surgery, there is relatively little research investigating the experiences of fat transgender people and bariatric surgery. Fatness is often referenced as an impediment to appropriate gender affirming care. Excess fat is often claimed to lower the quality of top surgery procedures for transgender men, with many doctors refusing to perform mastectomies to patients above a BMI >35. The upper BMI limit for vaginoplasty is even lower, at 30 (van der Sluis et. al 2021, 4). High BMI is seen as an impediment to multiple genital assignment surgeries, making weight especially salient for trans people. These limits are even more restricting for those undergoing hormone replacement therapy, whose weight may be more difficult to control due to hormonal imbalances. Hormone therapy can also produce side effects that can reduce the safety of bariatric surgery, such as cardiovascular disease or polycythemia (Hecht et al. 2019, 3367). Conversely, post-weight loss surgery trans people can often experience unexpected and extreme hormonal or endocrine side effects from the procedure.

Importantly, transgender individuals are also more likely to suffer from substance abuse, physical and emotional abuse, self-harm, and/or mental illness, making access to quality healthcare precarious and gender affirming procedures difficult to attain (Hecht et al. 2019, 3366). However, it is worth nothing that transgender people are more likely to be open about past abuse compared to the general population (3366). These intersecting phenomena make navigating the fundamentally gendered experience of physical transition an exceptionally complex medical experience. The subject of transgender bariatric patients is still seriously lacking, and additional research could further elucidate more about the topic in the future.

In this next section, I will be focusing on women again, setting out to further theorize the effects of the disciplining power society exerts on fat women, and how fat women resist these forces, specifically in the realm of bariatric surgery and the interactions with medical professionals that comes with it. In his theoretical framework, Foucault conceived what he called the "microphysics of power," asserting that power is not a simply a tool used by those with privilege, but a system of relationships "constantly in tension" with each other (Foucault 1995, 26). Power is exercised strategically by multiple parties at any given time, creating a webwork of relationships "constantly in tension," likening power to a "perpetual battle" as opposed to a "transaction … or the conquest of a territory" (26). Furthermore, he stresses that these innumerable power relations are not necessarily absolute or well-defined. The microphysics of power present ample opportunities for regular conflict, struggle, instability, and even "temporary inversion of the power relations" at hand (27). In the previous section, I attempted to define the macro-level dynamics of power within the field (to use a Bourdieusian term) of bariatric surgery, of patients, scientists, doctors, and activists. Here, using Foucault's microphysics of power, I now move down to the everyday micro-level "battles" for power, particularly in the form of knowledge production and the acquisition of credibility, to conceptualize the individual experiences of women who undergo bariatric surgery.

Additionally, I employ Foucault's disciplinary power in my analysis to describe how bariatric patients and their bodies are categorized. Disciplinary power aims to render individual subjects "docile" through the production of certain forms of knowledge, such as positivistic human sciences such as medicine and biology, and through the emergence of disciplinary techniques such as surveillance and examination, which facilitates the process of attaining knowledge about individuals. This acquisition of knowledge creates dividing practices, ways in which bodies can be placed in dichotomies that dictate standards of normality; sane or insane, legal or illegal, healthy or ill. Fatness, at least in the eyes of the dominant discourses of health, is a deviant position, and thus subject to multiple forms of discipline. The deviance of fatness renders fat bodies as docile bodies, able to be "subjected, used, transformed, and improved" (136).

While the literature on bariatric surgery and fatness engages with a wide range of theory, Foucauldian analysis remains one of the most common theoretical frameworks used to analyze the experiences of bariatric patients. Fat Studies scholar Samantha Murray describes the fat subject as a "failed body project," seen as morally weak and unwilling to change themselves or adopt a "healthy" lifestyle (2005, 155). In her words, to be seen as fully human, the fat body is "expected to engage in a continual process of transformation, of becoming and indeed, *un*becoming," requiring a "constant disavowal of one's own flesh" (155). Following this logic, it makes sense to then say that undergoing weight loss surgery is then an acquiescence to this dominant force, the opposite of an act of resistance. However, a sizeable portion of bariatric surgery patients express that they are not simply passive, self-hating subjects, but exercise power and resistance in subtle, nuanced ways.

To exist as both fat and a woman intensifies the "production of the docile body" (Throsby 2008, 124). Diet and exercise, in its modern incarnation, originate from and reproduce "normative feminine practices of our culture," practices that "train the female body in docility and obedience to cultural demands" while allowing for the ability to express power and control (Bordo 2013, 27). Bariatric surgery, as a more radical tool to train and discipline the female body, allows women who get the procedure to feel "in control," even if it does not reflect their actual social position. Foucault also emphasizes that "where there is power, there is also resistance," and this encapsulates the complexity inherent to the experiences of fat women who have had bariatric surgery (28). In some ways, the act of getting the surgery represents a relinquishing of bodily control, of becoming a transformed, thin, rehabilitated docile body. However, in other ways, choosing to commit to this life-changing medical procedure signifies a decisive act of agency and control over one's embodied life.

Patricia Drew, in her study of popular bariatric surgery discourses, stresses that while mainstream discourses regarding a phenomenon have substantial effects on the thoughts and actions of individuals, "they do not eliminate all individual innovation or subjective agency" (2011, 1232). Individuals use and negotiate discourses, "unravel[ing] or embroider[ing them] in order to understand their world better" (Collins 2003, 244). Karen Throsby, who has produced a large body of work about identity, power, gender, and bariatric surgery, deftly analyzes the microphysics patients find themselves navigating. In "Happy Re-Birthday" (2008) and "How Could Y let Yourself Get Like That?" (2007) she focuses on the construction, evolution, and maintenance of bodily identity in the face of weight loss surgery, in differing ways. Both gravitate toward themes that remain relevant to the literature over a decade later: the impact of media and the internet and how people who undergo bariatric surgery conceptualize their bodies. Her work engages with both men and women, but gender remains relevant to how people navigate the process of controlling and reconfiguring their relationship to food, exercise, and the body.

In "How Could You Let Yourself Get Like That?" Throsby aims to understand "what stories can be told … about the origins of fatness in order to negotiate and resist the discreditation of the fat self" (Throsby 2007, 1562). Furthermore, she highlights, and complicates the theoretical and social tension between the Size/Fat Positive movement's characteristic rejection of bariatric surgery as inherently fatphobic/discriminatory (see Braziel and LeBesco 2001; Cooper 1998), and the health and morality focused rhetoric of the "obesity epidemic."

Lynch's "When the Honeymoon Is Over, the Real Work Begins" (2016) focuses on the post-surgery experience, as opposed to the pre- and during-surgery perspectives of patients. Lynch concludes that firstly, "successful" weight loss is generally defined arbitrarily as a "as a percentage of excess weight lost or a percentage of weight lost kept off, as measured at a single point in time" (247). The static nature of these benchmarks appears to be an insufficient way to measure weight management and patient satisfaction post gastric bypass meaningfully. Furthermore, Lynch posits that "weight regain after gastric bypass surgery is not simply a matter of non-compliance, nor is weight maintenance simply occurring due to forced changes of the surgery," echoing Throsby's nuance on the topic of patient agency and the meaning of bariatric surgery (248).

Natvik, Gjengedal, and Råheim (2013), centering their work within the context of Norway, present three series of interviews with post-surgery patients. Their results show two main dynamics of "the altered body and bodily functions: between emancipation and control, and[…] a body among other bodies: rediscovering oneself" (Natvik, Gjengedal, and Råheim 2013, 73). This is an apt description not only of this piece, but of much of the post-surgery literature. Post-surgery patients frequently exhibit nuanced expressions of both resistance and compliance, pushing back against the idea that people who undergo bariatric surgery are either completely coerced or wholly averse to fat positive ideals. Instead, there seems to be a tension that comes with the experience of being "morbidly obese" in the eyes of the medical establishment, "fat" in the sociocultural sense, and, most directly, a person existing in a physical body, dealing with the complexities of health and social life as it is currently constructed. This tension is also present in Meleo-Erwin's "No One Is as Invested in Your Continued Good Health as You Should Be" (2019), as well as Trainer, Brewis, and Wutich's "Not 'taking the easy way out'" (2017). Though it is worth mentioning that Meleo-Erwin also highlights the lingering experiences of fat stigma experienced even by post-surgery patients, heightened by their "highly specialised medical needs" and their "surgically altered digestive systems and lack of sufficient post-operative follow-up care from their home bariatric clinics" (Meleo-Erwin 2019, 285).

Fatness and womanhood work together to create a doubly unruly, doubly undisciplined subject, physically imposing and incapable of self-control or rationality. In contrast, the ideal woman's body is "tight, contained, 'bolted down' … a body that is protected against eruption from within, whose internal processes are under control" (Bordo 2013, 190). By opting for bariatric surgery, fat women take a proactive stance by exercising power over their own bodies, but at the same time are still participating in an assimilatory process by pursuing thinness and dominant disciplines of diet and exercise. As mentioned above, weight loss surgery, for those who pursue it, is often an endeavor rife with various justifications, rationalizations, and interpretations.

Conclusion

If bariatric surgeries continue to increase at the same exponential rates seen over the last 20 years, it is safe to say that the procedure is not going anywhere.

Weight loss surgery continues to be a contentious phenomenon, producing strong opinions from various parties with differing connections to each other. From large scale discursive conflicts to individual social interactions in the doctor's office, the world of bariatric surgery is by no means simple. Furthermore, it is important to consider how gender shapes and defines the phenomenon, given the heavily skewed rates of weight loss surgery in the United States. Of course, this is an incomplete analysis, and the literature on weight loss surgery continues to diversify as the procedure grows in popularity. The "microphysics of power" Foucault described goes a long way to conceptualize the intricate network of relationships, power, and ideologies that affect a small, but significant, portion of the population. Even if the total populace of bariatric surgery patients is miniscule, it is important to keep in mind that fat people are, indeed, the majority of the U.S. population. The struggles for credibility, power, and resistance in the realm of obesity science hold consequences for all fat people, fat women in particular, and as such it is imperative that we continue to ask questions about how science, medicine, and technology shapes our lives, and our bodies.

Notes

1   Some sources claim that Hasdai's medicinal concoction was also known as Al-Faruk, and there is a chance they refer to the same thing, with "Al-Faruk" being a regional/linguistic variation (Rössner 2011, 995).
2   The links between obesity and comorbid conditions are often not as clear cut as mainstream public health discourse would imply. For example, consider the "obesity paradox" currently being studied (see De Schutter et al. 2013; Kittiskulnam and Johansen 2019; Tsur et al. 2017 for examples). For this analysis though, I defer to the general conventions put forth by the medical research community, whose normalized discourses are central to this analysis of bariatric surgery.
3   Specifically, I am referring to the body of research focusing on "Western" Anglophone countries such as the United States, Canada, Australia, and England. Of course, anti-fat attitudes can and have varied widely by location and time period.
4   By "implicitly causal," I am not referring to the actual clinical research conducted by scientists, but more so the broader socio-medical understanding of obesity of the "lay" person, communicated by public health officials and public-facing scientists; being obese will eventually, *naturally*, lead to (what I call in a colloquial sense) "fat people diseases," comorbidities such as heart disease, hypertension, or type 2 diabetes.
5   Again, this is generally anecdotal assertion and should be taken as such. I have attempted to find official data on the statistics of gender in fat activists circles, but given the amorphous and grassroots nature of these groups, it would appear not to be the subject of intense empirical scrutiny.
6   There is work within the literature focusing on both male and female bariatric patients, however, in this analysis, I focus on women. As mentioned above, most patients are women, and as such most of the work looks at the experiences of women. There is some research looking at men, bariatric surgery, and gender, but it is a substantially smaller body. There is also a dearth of research looking at bariatric surgery for trans, nonbinary, and gender nonconforming individuals, and hopefully work in the future will address this.

Bibliography

Ackerman, Norman B. 1999. *Fat No More: The Answer for the Dangerously Overweight.* Amherst, NY: Prometheus Books.

American Society for Metabolic and Bariatric Surgeons. 2021. "ASMBS 2020 Year End Review."

American Society for Metabolic and Bariatric Surgery. 2018. "Estimate of Bariatric Surgery Numbers, 2011–2018." American Society for Metabolic and Bariatric Surgery. June 26, 2018. https://asmbs.org/resources/estimate-of-bariatric-surgery-numbers

———. n.d. "About." American Society for Metabolic and Bariatric Surgery. Accessed May 16, 2021. https://asmbs.org/about

Anon. 2020. "Definition & Facts of Weight-Loss Surgery - NIDDK." National Institute of Diabetes and Digestive and Kidney Diseases. Accessed March 22, 2023. https://www.niddk.nih.gov/health-information/weight-management/bariatric-surgery/definition-facts

Association of American Medical Colleges. 2021. "Nation's Physician Workforce Evolves: More Women, a Bit Older, and toward Different Specialties." AAMC. February 2, 2021. www.aamc.org/news-insights/nation-s-physician-workforce-evolves-more-women-bit-older-and-toward-different-specialties

Bacon, Linda. 2010. *Health at Every Size: The Surprising Truth about Your Weight.* Rev. & Updated. Dallas, TX: BenBella Books.

Baltasar, Aniceto. 2004. "More than 1,000 Years Ago, Sancho the Fat Lost His Kingdom…" *Obesity Surgery* 14 (8): 1138. https://doi.org/10.1381/0960892041975514

Boero, Natalie. 2007. "All the News That's Fat to Print: The American 'Obesity Epidemic' and the Media." *Qualitative Sociology* 30 (1): 41–60. https://doi.org/10.1007/s11133-006-9010-4

Bombak, Andrea E., Deborah McPhail, and Pamela Ward. 2016. "Reproducing Stigma: Interpreting 'Overweight' and 'Obese' Women's Experiences of Weight-Based Discrimination in Reproductive Healthcare." *Social Science & Medicine* 166 (October): 94–101. https://doi.org/10.1016/j.socscimed.2016.08.015.

Bordo, Susan. 2013. *Unbearable Weight: Feminism, Western Culture, and the Body.* 10. anniversary ed., [Nachdr.]. Berkeley, CA.: University of California Press.

Braziel, Jana Evans, and Kathleen LeBesco, eds. 2001. *Bodies out of Bounds: Fatness and Transgression.* Berkeley, CA: University of California Press.

Brenton, Joslyn, and Sinikka Elliott. 2014. "Undoing Gender? The Case of Complementary and Alternative Medicine." *Sociology of Health & Illness* 36 (1): 91–107. https://doi.org/10.1111/1467-9566.12043

Buchwald, Henry. 2005. "Bariatric Surgery for Morbid Obesity: Health Implications for Patients, Health Professionals, and Third-Party Payers." *Journal of the American College of Surgeons* 200 (4): 593–604. https://doi.org/10.1016/j.jamcollsurg.2004.10.039

———. 2008. "Introduction and Current Status of Bariatric Procedures." *Surgery for Obesity and Related Diseases* 4 (3): S1–6. https://doi.org/10.1016/j.soard.2008.04.001

Cahnman, Werner J. 1968. "The Stigma of Obesity." *The Sociological Quarterly* 9 (3): 283–99. https://doi.org/10.1111/j.1533-8525.1968.tb01121.x

Collins, Peter. 2003. "Storying Self and Others: The Construction of Narrative Identity." *Journal of Language and Politics* 2 (2): 243–64. https://doi.org/10.1075/jlp.2.2.04col

Cooper, Charlotte. 1998. *Fat and Proud: The Politics of Size.* London: Women's Press.

Cooper, Charlotte. 2010. "Fat Studies: Mapping the Field." *Sociology Compass* 4 (12): 1020–34. doi: 10.1111/j.1751-9020.2010.00336.x

De Schutter, Alban, Carl J. Lavie, Dharmendrakumar A. Patel, and Richard V. Milani. 2013. "Obesity Paradox and the Heart: Which Indicator of Obesity Best Describes This Complex Relationship?" *Current Opinion in Clinical Nutrition & Metabolic Care* 16 (5): 517–24. https://doi.org/10.1097/MCO.0b013e328363bcca

Drew, Patricia. 2011. "'But Then I Learned…': Weight Loss Surgery Patients Negotiate Surgery Discourses." *Social Science & Medicine* 73 (8): 1230–37. https://doi.org/10.1016/j.socscimed.2011.07.023

Epstein, Steven. 1995. "The Construction of Lay Expertise: AIDS Activism and the Forging of Credibility in the Reform of Clinical Trials." *Science, Technology, & Human Values* 20 (4): 408–37.

———. 1996. *Impure Science: AIDS, Activism, and the Politics of Knowledge.* Reprint. Medicine and Society 7. Berkeley, CA: University of California Press.

Ertelt, Troy W., James E. Mitchell, Kathryn Lancaster, Ross D. Crosby, Kristine J. Steffen, and Joanna M. Marino. 2008. "Alcohol Abuse and Dependence before and after Bariatric Surgery: A Review of the Literature and Report of a New Data Set." *Surgery for Obesity and Related Diseases* 4 (5): 647–50. https://doi.org/10.1016/j.soard.2008.01.004

Faria, Gil R. 2017. "A Brief History of Bariatric Surgery." *Porto Biomedical Journal* 2 (3): 90–92. https://doi.org/10.1016/j.pbj.2017.01.008

Fee, Holly R., and Michael R. Nusbaumer. 2012. "Social Distance and the Formerly Obese: Does the Stigma of Obesity Linger?" *Sociological Inquiry* 82 (3): 356–77. https://doi.org/10.1111/j.1475-682X.2012.00420.x

Foucault, Michel. 1995. *Discipline and Punish: The Birth of the Prison.* 2nd Vintage Books ed. New York: Vintage Books.

Fryar, Cheryl D., Margaret D. Carroll, and Joseph Afful. 2020. "Prevalence of Overweight, Obesity, and Severe Obesity among Adults Aged 20 and over: United States, 1960–1962 through 2017–2018." *NCHS Health E-Stats.*

Fuchs, Hans F., Ryan C. Broderick, Cristina R. Harnsberger, David C. Chang, Bryan J. Sandler, Garth R. Jacobsen, and Santiago Horgan. 2015. "Benefits of Bariatric Surgery Do Not Reach Obese Men." *Journal of Laparoendoscopic & Advanced Surgical Techniques* 25 (3): 196–201. https://doi.org/10.1089/lap.2014.0639

Gard, Michael, and Jan Wright. 2005. *The Obesity Epidemic: Science, Morality and Ideology.* 1st ed. London: Routledge. https://doi.org/10.4324/9780203619308

Gargantilla Madera, Pedro, and Noelia Arroyo Pardo. 2016. "Hasday: Treatment of Obesity in 10th Century." *Endocrinología y Nutrición (English Edition)* 63 (2): 100–101. https://doi.org/10.1016/j.endoen.2016.02.002

Gieryn, Thomas F. 1983. "Boundary-Work and the Demarcation of Science from Non-Science: Strains and Interests in Professional Ideologies of Scientists." *American Sociological Review* 48 (6): 781–95. https://doi.org/10.2307/2095325.

Granero-Molina, José, María José Torrente-Sánchez, Manuel Ferrer-Márquez, José Manuel Hernández-Padilla, Alicia Ruiz-Muelle, Olga María López-Entrambasaguas, and Cayetano Fernández-Sola. 2020. "Sexuality amongst Heterosexual Men with Morbid Obesity in a Bariatric Surgery Programme: A Qualitative Study." *Journal of Clinical Nursing* 29 (21–22): 4258–69. https://doi.org/10.1111/jocn.15461

Groven, Karen Synne, Paul Galdas, and Kari Nyheim Solbrække. 2015. "Becoming a Normal Guy: Men Making Sense of Long-Term Bodily Changes Following Bariatric Surgery." *International Journal of Qualitative Studies on Health and Well-Being* 10 (1): 29923. https://doi.org/10.3402/qhw.v10.29923

Hansen, Barbara, and Meredith Huey Dye. 2018. "Damned If You Do, Damned If You Don't: The Stigma of Weight Loss Surgery." *Deviant Behavior* 39 (2): 137–47. https://doi.org/10.1080/01639625.2016.1263081

Hecht, Leah, Chazlyn Miller, Lisa R. Miller-Matero, Aaron Hamann, Arthur M. Carlin, and Kellie Martens. 2019. "A Review of Psychosocial Risk Factors among Transgender Patients Seeking Bariatric Surgery." *Obesity Surgery* 29 (10): 3365–70. https://doi.org/10.1007/s11695-019-04076-z

Henrikson, Viktor. 1994 [1952]. "Can Small Bowel Resection Be Defended as Therapy for Obesity?" *Obesity Surgery* 4 (1): 54–54. https://doi.org/10.1381/096089294765558926

Hopkins, Kathleen D., and Eldon David Lehmann. 1995. "Successful Medical Treatment of Obesity in 10th Century Spain." *The Lancet* 346 (8972): 452. https://doi.org/10.1016/S0140-6736(95)92830-8

Kalarchian, Melissa A., Marsha D. Marcus, Michele D. Levine, Anita P. Courcoulas, Paul A. Pilkonis, Rebecca M. Ringham, Julia N. Soulakova, Lisa A. Weissfeld, and Dana L. Rofey. 2007. "Psychiatric Disorders among Bariatric Surgery Candidates: Relationship to Obesity and Functional Health Status." *American Journal of Psychiatry* 164 (2): 328–34. https://doi.org/10.1176/ajp.2007.164.2.328

Kittiskulnam, Piyawan, and Kirsten L. Johansen. 2019. "The Obesity Paradox: A Further Consideration in Dialysis Patients." *Seminars in Dialysis* 32 (6): 485–89. https://doi.org/10.1111/sdi.12834

Kremen, Arnold J., John H. Linner, and Charles H. Nelson. 1954. "An Experimental Evaluation of the Nutritional Importance of Proximal and Distal Small Intestine." *Annals of Surgery* 140 (3): 439. https://doi.org/10.1097/00000658-195409000-00018

Kuczmarski, Robert J, and Katherine M Flegal. 2000. "Criteria for Definition of Overweight in Transition: Background and Recommendations for the United States." *The American Journal of Clinical Nutrition* 72 (5): 1074–81. https://doi.org/10.1093/ajcn/72.5.1074

Linner, John H. 2007. "Early History of Bariatric Surgery." *Surgery for Obesity and Related Diseases* 3 (5): 569–70. https://doi.org/10.1016/j.soard.2007.06.007

Lynch, Amanda. 2016. "'When the Honeymoon Is Over, the Real Work Begins:' Gastric Bypass Patients' Weight Loss Trajectories and Dietary Change Experiences." *Social Science & Medicine* 151 (February): 241–49. https://doi.org/10.1016/j.socscimed.2015.12.024

McCreary, Donald R., Deborah M. Saucier, and Will H. Courtenay. 2005. "The Drive for Muscularity and Masculinity: Testing the Associations Among Gender-Role Traits, Behaviors, Attitudes, and Conflict." *Psychology of Men & Masculinity* 6 (2): 83–94. https://doi.org/10.1037/1524-9220.6.2.83

Meleo-Erwin, Zoë C. 2019. "'No One Is as Invested in Your Continued Good Health as You Should Be:' An Exploration of the Post-Surgical Relationships between Weight-Loss Surgery Patients and Their Home Bariatric Clinics." *Sociology of Health & Illness* 41 (2): 285–302. https://doi.org/10.1111/1467-9566.12823

Monaghan, Lee F. 2007. "Body Mass Index, Masculinities and Moral Worth: Men's Critical Understandings of 'Appropriate' Weight-for-Height: Body Mass Index, Masculinities and Moral Worth." *Sociology of Health & Illness* 29 (4): 584–609. https://doi.org/10.1111/j.1467-9566.2007.01007.x

Murray, Samantha. 2005. "(Un/Be)Coming Out? Rethinking Fat Politics." *Social Semiotics* 15 (2): 153–63. https://doi.org/10.1080/10350330500154667

———. 2008. *The "Fat" Female Body.* Basingstoke [England]; New York: Palgrave Macmillan. https://search.ebscohost.com/login.aspx?direct=true&scope=site&db=nlebk&db=nlabk&AN=283355

National Association for the Advancement of Fat Acceptance. n.d. "Weight Loss Surgery." Accessed October 30, 2021. https://static1.squarespace.com/static/5e7be2c55ceb2 61b71eadde2/t/5e8013b51173962cc0bfd531/1585451958254/Weight_Loss_Surg ery-2015.pdf

National Institute of Diabetes and Digestive and Kidney Diseases. | NIDDK. n.d. "Definition & Facts for Bariatric Surgery." Accessed September 4, 2020. www.niddk. nih.gov/health-information/weight-management/bariatric-surgery/definition-facts

Natvik, Eli, Eva Gjengedal, Christian Moltu, and Målfrid Råheim. 2015. "Translating Weight Loss into Agency: Men's Experiences 5 Years after Bariatric Surgery." *International Journal of Qualitative Studies on Health and Well-Being* 10 (1): 27729. https:// doi.org/10.3402/qhw.v10.27729

Natvik, Eli, Eva Gjengedal, and Målfrid Råheim. 2013. "Totally Changed, Yet Still the Same: Patients' Lived Experiences 5 Years Beyond Bariatric Surgery." *Qualitative Health Research* 23 (9): 1202–14. https://doi.org/10.1177/1049732313501888

Newhook, Julia Temple, Deborah Gregory, and Laurie Twells. 2015. "'Fat Girls' and 'Big Guys': Gendered Meanings of Weight Loss Surgery." *Sociology of Health & Illness* 37 (5): 653–67. https://doi.org/10.1111/1467-9566.12219

New York Times, Richard D. Lyons. Special to The New York. 1977. "Easing of a Ban on Saccharin Fails to Halt Outcry; F.D.A. Asserts Cancer Test on Rats Was Valid." *The New York Times*, April 15, 1977, sec. Archives. https://www.nytimes.com/1977/04/15/ archives/easing-of-a-ban-on-saccharin-fails-to-halt-outcry-fda-asserts.html

Nuttall, Frank Q. 2015. "Body Mass Index: Obesity, BMI, and Health." *Nutrition Today* 50 (3): 117–28. https://doi.org/10.1097/NT.0000000000000092

Puhl, Rebecca M., Joerg Luedicke, and Carlos M. Grilo. 2014. "Obesity Bias in Training: Attitudes, Beliefs, and Observations among Advanced Trainees in Professional Health Disciplines: Obesity Bias in Training." *Obesity* 22 (4): 1008–15. https://doi.org/10.1002/oby.20637

Puhl, Rebecca M., Tatiana, Andreyeva, and Kelly. D. Brownell. 2008. "Perceptions of Weight Discrimination: Prevalence and Comparison to Race and Gender Discrimination in America." *International Journal of Obesity* 32 (6): 992–1000. https:// doi.org/10.1038/ijo.2008.22

Robertson, Steve, Kay Sheikh, and Andrew Moore. 2010. "Embodied Masculinities in the Context of Cardiac Rehabilitation: Embodied Masculinities and Cardiac Rehabilitation." *Sociology of Health & Illness* 32 (5): 695–710. https://doi.org/10.1111/ j.1467-9566.2010.01249.x

Rössner, Stephan. 2011. "Sancho the Fat: King of León, Spain." *Obesity Reviews* 12 (11): 995–995. https://doi.org/10.1111/j.1467-789X.2011.00934.x

Sabin, Janice A., Maddalena Marini, and Brian A. Nosek. 2012. "Implicit and Explicit Anti-Fat Bias among a Large Sample of Medical Doctors by BMI, Race/Ethnicity and Gender." Edited by Richard Fielding. *PLoS ONE* 7 (11): e48448. https://doi. org/10.1371/journal.pone.0048448

Salameh, J. R. 2006. "Bariatric Surgery: Past and Present." *The American Journal of the Medical Sciences* 331 (4): 194–200. https://doi.org/10.1097/00000441-200604000-00005

Schwartz, Marlene B., Heather O'Neal Chambliss, Kelly D. Brownell, Steven N. Blair, and Charles Billington. 2003. "Weight Bias among Health Professionals Specializing in Obesity." *Obesity Research* 11 (9): 1033–39. https://doi.org/10.1038/oby.2003.142

Serracino-Inglott, Imelda. 1986. "Theriac: A Selected Annotated Bibliography of the History of Theriac." *The Pharmacist*, no. 13 (May). www.um.edu.mt/library/oar/han dle/123456789/48213

Sluis, Wouter B. van der, Rick J. M. de Bruin, Thomas D. Steensma, and Mark-Bram Bouman. 2021. "Gender-Affirmation Surgery and Bariatric Surgery in Transgender Individuals in The Netherlands: Considerations, Surgical Techniques and Outcomes." *International Journal of Transgender Health* 23 (3): 1–7. https://doi.org/10.1080/26895 269.2021.1890302

The National Institutes of Health (NIH) Consensus Statement Online. 1985. "Health Implications of Obesity." February 11, 1985. https://consensus.nih.gov/1985/1985obe sity049html.htm

Throsby, Karen. 2007. "'How Could You Let Yourself Get like That?': Stories of the Origins of Obesity in Accounts of Weight Loss Surgery." *Social Science & Medicine* 65 (8): 1561–71. https://doi.org/10.1016/j.socscimed.2007.06.005

———. 2008. "Happy Re-Birthday: Weight Loss Surgery and the 'New Me'." *Body & Society* 14 (1): 117–33. https://doi.org/10.1177/1357034X07087534

———. 2012a. "Obesity Surgery and the Management of Excess: Exploring the Body Multiple: Obesity Surgery and the Management of Excess." *Sociology of Health & Illness* 34 (1): 1–15. https://doi.org/10.1111/j.1467-9566.2011.01358.x

———. 2012b. "'I'd Kill Anyone Who Tried to Take My Band Away': Obesity Surgery, Critical Fat Politics and the 'Problem' of Patient Demand." *Somatechnics* 2 (1): 107–26. https://doi.org/10.3366/soma.2012.0044

Trainer, Sarah, Alexandra Brewis, and Amber Wutich. 2017. "Not 'Taking the Easy Way Out': Reframing Bariatric Surgery from Low-Effort Weight Loss to Hard Work." *Anthropology & Medicine* 24 (1): 96–110. https://doi.org/10.1080/13648470.2016.1249339

Tsur, Abraham, John A. Mayo, Ronald J. Wong, George M. Shaw, David K. Stevenson, and Jeffrey B. Gould. 2017. "'The Obesity Paradox': A Reconsideration of Obesity and the Risk of Preterm Birth." *Journal of Perinatology* 37 (10): 1088–92. https://doi. org/10.1038/jp.2017.104

Vogel, Else. 2018. "Operating (on) the Self: Transforming Agency through Obesity Surgery and Treatment." *Sociology of Health & Illness* 40 (3): 508–22. https://doi. org/10.1111/1467-9566.12654

Wann, Marilyn. 1998. *Fat! So? Because You Don't Have to Apologize for Your Size!* Berkeley, CA: Ten Speed Press.

WHO Expert Committee on Physical Status: the Use and Interpretation of Anthropometry, ed. 1995. *Physical Status: The Use and Interpretation of Anthropometry: Report of a WHO Expert Committee.* WHO Technical Report Series 854. Geneva: World Health Organization.

Young, Monica T., Michael J. Phelan, and Ninh T. Nguyen. 2016. "A Decade Analysis of Trends and Outcomes of Male vs Female Patients Who Underwent Bariatric Surgery." *Journal of the American College of Surgeons* 222 (3): 226–31. https://doi.org/10.1016/j.jamc ollsurg.2015.11.033

15

GENDER, FAT, AND "REPRODUCTIVE" HEALTH CARE

Negotiating Fat Pregnancy in the Context of Eugenics

Emily R.M. Lind, Deborah McPhail, and Lindsey Mazur

It goes without saying that pregnancy is an intensely gendered process. In the conventional medical imagination, pregnancy is constructed as something that normal female bodies are able to achieve without clinical intervention. Not surprisingly, ideas about who is considered normal, who is considered female, and what a reproductive body looks like play out in the delivery of reproductive health care. Reproductive medicine circles around a physical process in which young to middle-aged women get progressively larger during pregnancy, a process that takes place in a social context in which that very same demographic of women are socially encouraged to pursue smaller body sizes. Antifat bias in reproductive health care sits at a critical intersection of institutional power and socially acceptable discrimination. Understanding the significance of this field is essential to the study of gender and fat, as antifat bias plays out in reproductive health care not only in how pregnancies are managed and treated clinically, but also in the provision of reproductive technologies designed to prevent pregnancy or to achieve pregnancy (Ward and McPhail 2019).

This chapter reviews the literature on weight stigma in reproductive health care, identifying the ways that antifat stigma in the field serves a disciplining function, reinforcing broader myths of race, ability, gender conformity, and social citizenship. We identify key patterns in the field, including the study of the impact weight stigma has on the self-identity of pregnant people and the ways in which they make sense of their bodies' capacities to reproduce human life. We end by spending some time with the words of fat people who have experienced care, as shared with us during our qualitative research project *Reproducing Stigma*. Through this, we demonstrate how a variety of practices that dissuade reproduction among fat people within reproductive care, running the gamut from refusal of care to a more diffuse stigmatization of the fat body, can be considered part of a logics

DOI: 10.4324/9781003140665-21

of eugenics. To conclude the chapter, we suggest ways to confront and disrupt eugenics-based health care and make recommendations for providing radically compassionate care for fat people in conception, pregnancy, and birthing care contexts.

A Word on Language

The field of weight stigma in reproductive health care sits at the intersection of critical health research and Fat Studies. The disciplinary conventions of critical health research are invested in bridge-building work between medical practitioners and critical social scientists. Consequently, "weight stigma" is typically found in research published in journals with a broader scope of research engagement. Fat Studies scholars, informed by activist movements and critical turns in research to reclaim and recentre patient experience, refer to antifat bias or antifat stigma. Further, we would like to outline our decisions around the use of gendered language when referring to "reproductive care" and pregnancy. First, we recognize that the term "reproductive care" is highly gendered in that it assumes first that body parts such as the uterus or ovaries and so on that can be used for human reproduction always *are* or *should be* used for reproduction. Of course, this idea continues to link heteronormative sex to reproduction. Since the participants involved in the study *Reproducing Stigma* were in fact involved in reproductive processes, we do use the term "reproductive care," however. Second, we recognize that not all pregnant people, or people attempting to conceive, are women-identified. Indeed, two participants in one of our research sites identified as trans masculine. At the same time, the majority of participants in our study identified as women. As such, we take our cue from Parker, Pausé, and Le Grice (2019) and alternate the terms "pregnant people" and "pregnant women" to recognize gender variation and diversity, while at the same time also paying critical attention to the gendered politics of reproduction, whereby it is primarily women's and trans bodies that are contained, restrained, and monitored within patriarchal structures and imaginaries of human reproduction.

Understanding Stigma in Reproductive Health Care

Before defining weight stigma in reproductive health care, it is imperative that we approach clinical contexts as sites of social reproduction. Dominant discourses of health, gender, race, class, and worthiness are embedded in the clinical environment and physician–patient encounters. Weight stigma in reproductive health care impacts how the medical industry determines which bodies are classified as good or bad candidates for fertility treatments, the kinds of birthing protocols made available and the particular people defined as high risk. As Fat Studies scholars have established, fat bodies are approached medically and socially as failed thin bodies, and the ways in which fat bodies are considered to have failed are enacted in discourses of gender, parenthood, health, respectability, and productivity. In the context of pregnancy, this dynamic is intensified, because pregnant bodies become sites of speculation about the fitness of that body to parent and raise a successful next generation. Reproductive health care has a history of enacting a surveiling function in the lives of women – advising them on when to reproduce, controlling their reproductive capacities, and pathologizing their choices or bodies when reproduction is not pursued.

Antifat stigma is an umbrella term for the ideas, stereotypes, myths, and acts of social exclusion that code fat bodies as unworthy. It is now well established in Fat Studies scholarship that stigmatizing ideas about fatness include the myth that fat bodies are consequences of poor personal choices, as opposed to being naturally occurring variants of the human condition. Fat patients routinely report being perceived in clinical environments as over-eaters, under-exercisers, and overall lacking in self-control or self-discipline. In other words, medicalized interactions between physicians and patients create a unique iteration of fat stigma, because stigmatizing stereotypes construct fat patients as irresponsible with regard to their health. Despite clear clinical evidence that fat bodies are not inherently unhealthy, and that fat stigma leads to poor health outcomes for fat patients (Bombak 2014; Farrell 2011), doctors and medical students are inadequately trained to recognize and mitigate fat stigma. Further, fat stigma impacts every facet of daily life. Consequently, service providers default to "common sense" understandings of body size and its implication for health outcomes, thereby reproducing fat stigma in clinical settings (Ward and McPhail 2019).

Examples of fat stigma in health care settings can include: patients' hesitation or unwillingness to seek medical care for fear of being stigmatized (including the inability to self-advocate in the face of fatphobic comments from providers); criticism, jokes, and/or stigmatizing comments from service providers about one's diet, body size, or physical appearance; a lack of accessible equipment, seating, beds, scales, and hospital garments that fit; the denial of care until a weight loss threshold is attained; speculation that all physical symptoms are directly and only connected to body weight; and misdiagnosis and malpractice (Chrisler and Barney 2016; McPhail and Orsini 2021; Thille 2019; Tomiyama et al. 2018). These examples point to the assumptions within the medical imagination that fat bodies are both unexpected and illegitimate phenotypes. The medical imagination is deeply invested in distinguishing normal from abnormal bodies using standardized measurements. Moreover, normal and abnormal bodies are similarly distinguished from each other through discourses of medicalization. Fat stigma is embedded within a logic of medicalization whereby fat bodies become medicalized as "overweight" or "obese" using standardized measurements (McPhail and Mazur 2019). To be obese, then, is to be labelled with a health condition based on body size alone. Bodies labelled obese become objectified within this stigmatizing process as problems to be solved through medical intervention. Within the medical imagination, there is no possibility that "obesity" could be attributed to a healthy and active lifestyle. An obese body, therefore, is virtually synonymous with moral ineptitude.

Importantly, the medicalization of body fat was established by the end of the twentieth century (McPhail 2017) just as a series of ideas about gender, race, sexuality, and citizenship were becoming retriangulated with each other as neoliberalism began to dominate the political economy in the West (Lee and Pausé 2016). Throughout the nineteenth and twentieth centuries, thin bodies became progressively more identifiable as socially normal, sexually ideal, and morally virtuous. In the nineteenth century, colonial racism and its taxonomies of physical distinction began to associate excessive body size with Blackness and therefore, undesirability (Strings 2019). As food security increased with industrialized food production, thinness was associated with wealth and self-control, particularly for bourgeois white women, who were active in social reform movements to civilize and "improve" immigrant populations in booming urban centres. Many have noted that throughout these shifts in cultural values, medical doctors generally avoided equating thinness with health. Research has shown that for generations, it was considered developmentally normal for people to gain weight progressively as they aged (cf. Mitchenson 2018; Rice 2014). Towards the end of the twentieth century, this medical attitude began to change. In the 1980s and 1990s in particular, the BMI scale was increasingly used as a diagnostic tool in health care (Ellison 2020), and it continues to be a mechanism by which some bodies are labelled normal, and others as problematic, or at risk in the provision of care.

The medicalization of fatness as obesity coincides with the antifeminist backlash of the 1980s and 1990s, which promoted fear-mongering myths about the physical, economic, and emotional dangers of delaying pregnancies and heterosexual marriage in favour of career development (Faludi 1991). Further, throughout the 1980s and early 1990s the AIDS epidemic was popularly attributed to immoral sexual behaviour, framed in the language of homophobia (Treichler 1999). The cultural context in which the obesity epidemic became established as social and institutional truth was thus a discursive terrain laden with the message that idealized womanhood was associated with reproduction; that problems with reproduction are likely result of a woman's poor life choices, and that illness is linked to immoral sexual practices. This is the cultural context in which we investigate the power of fat stigma on reproductive medical care provision.

The Role of Risk in Antifat Stigma

In reproductive care, fat bodies are highly medicalized through narratives about "maternal obesity," whereby discourses of risk emphasize the fat pregnant body as a dire threat to the health and well-being – and very life – of the foetus (Furber and McGowan 2011; Heslehurst et al. 2015; McPhail and Mazur 2019; Mulherin et al. 2013). Within the discourse of obesity, the responsibility for mitigating any potential health risk to the gestating patient or their foetus falls onto the patient in the form of exercise and dietary changes. Fat pregnant bodies are frequently held responsible for gestational diabetes, large-for-gestational age babies, increased risk of C-section delivery and post-operative complications, infectious morbidity, miscarriage, stillbirth, childhood obesity, and general birth defects (Bombak, McPhail, and Ward 2016). The logic of responsibilization is imposed upon fat bodies, thereby displacing part of the burden of risk from the clinician and clinical environment onto the perceived failure of the patient to have avoided becoming 'obese' in the first place. Consequently, fat patients report clinical encounters whereby service providers admonish them for being large-bodied, prescribe weight loss as a first course of treatment for a variety of ailments, and consistently fail to acknowledge how these comments echo the incessant messages from the broader culture about thinness as an aesthetic ideal. Further, fat patients frequently report being blamed for the insufficiencies of the clinical environment (gowns that cannot tie up, epidural needles that are not long enough, additional staff required to aid in a transfer, etc.) rather than being eligible for respectful and compassionate accommodation (ibid.). Therefore, fat patients describe medical encounters as reliably stigmatizing. The need for stigma-informed practitioner protocols is urgently needed. Without them, clinicians risk causing harm by reproducing weight stigma at best, and applying eugenicist ideas at worst.

Soft Eugenics

Previous research has focused on obesity stigma in the health care system generally and has linked fat stigma to serious health disparities such as misdiagnosis and the denial of care (Budd et al. 2009; Farrell 2011; Wray and Dreery 2008). A few researchers have also begun to explore the experiences and effects of obesity stigma on women in reproductive care (Smith and Lavender 2011), showing that the types of stigma fat people encounter are specific to their weight, and include humiliation, bullying, and the denial of certain tests and procedures that often preclude pregnancy (McPhail et al. 2016). The active curtailment of fat women's reproduction suggests that they may face a very specific and significant type of stigma based on body size that connects to a long history of eugenic population control in Canada (Jette and Rail 2013; McLaren 1990).

"Eugenics" includes a wide variety of discourses and techniques, from so-called hard practices like forced sterilization to "soft" ones such as ideologies of "good" and "bad" mothering, and from "positive" practices that encourage reproduction to "negative" ones that prevent it (Paul and Moore 2010). Developed initially by the cousin of Charles Darwin, Francis Galton, eugenics was integral to Western colonial projects, providing the ideological foundation for systems of governance whereby local Indigenous bodies as well as a variety of Othered white bodies were contained, constrained, and often killed (Rice 2014). Such violence was made condonable in part through eugenic constructions of racialization resting largely on the concept of the "family tree of man" (McClintock 1995), whereby white men were positioned as the pinnacle of "civil society," or at the top of the tree, and all Others were ranked on lower branches. Based on such ideology, and in order to "prune the tree" to encourage "optimal" human reproduction and "racial fitness," eugenics was practiced on the bodies of the working class and impoverished, people with disabilities, populations of colour, "ethnic" populations, those regarded as "feeble minded," and Indigenous peoples (Bashford and Levine 2010; Davin 1978; Dyck 2013; Grekul, Krahn, and Odynak 2004; McLaren 1990). While most imagine eugenics to be something of the distant past, scholars have argued that eugenic practices remain operant. Dikotter, for example, has shown how policies encouraging contraceptive use in African American women on government assistance – so-called welfare mothers – intend, on the face of it, not to curtail the reproduction of low-income Black women but to cut back on government spending (Bell 2010; Roberts 2014). Such programmes, though, could still be considered eugenic in that they prevent the reproduction of people of colour and, as Stern argues, it is not the stated *intent* of a practice but rather its *outcome* that best assesses whether it is eugenic (Stern 2005). Many supposedly well-intentioned programmes and practices may have the effect of reducing the numbers of unwanted populations. These types of diffuse practices with the overall, cumulative effect of curtailing certain types of people from reproducing have been labelled the "new eugenics" by some (see Cain 2013; Daar 2017).

It should be noted that scholars debate the notion of the "new eugenics." Rose, for instance, writes against articulating the term eugenics to describe current biopolitical approaches to reproduction, maintaining that they are seldom deployed to achieve national or geopolitical strength (Rose 2007; see also Rabinow and Rose 2006). Others, however, argue the opposite – particularly in relation to contemporary politics of reproduction (Bell 2010; Bitler and Schmidt 2006; Kindregan and McBrien 2006; Macintosh 2010; Taussig et al. 2003), and the disparities of access to quality reproductive care and conception technologies between white middle-/upper-class women and low-income women and/or people of colour (Inhorn and Fakih 2006; Jain 2006; Seifer et al. 2006). Here, it is not the state's intentional bodily enforcement policies such as sterilization that precludes the reproduction of Others, but rather the inadvertent, informal, and unorganized behaviours of state actors or, in our case, health care professionals operating within neoliberal and capitalist systems of governance. In other words, the decisions that health professionals make about who is fit to reproduce and who should have access to reproductive technology is itself a way of producing more "desired" populations (Daar 2017).

When fatness is factored into a eugenics lens, and given that eugenics is at its core about race and the building of whiteness, it becomes evident that current medical approaches to "maternal obesity" can be considered an inflection of soft eugenics, both in the discouragement of fat people's reproduction *and* through the encouragement of particular practices of diet, exercise, and weight loss that are typically associated with wealthy white normative bodies (Rice 2014). In maternal obesity, fatness becomes a focal point of pregnancy and, due to the fact that it is a medicalized and diagnostic category, a legitimate basis by which health care practitioners can discourage reproduction.

North American Fat Studies scholars have demonstrated that since Indigenous people and people of colour are understood to have the highest rates of obesity (McPhail 2017; Strings 2019), fatness is discursively coded as racialized. As such, for a white body to be or become fat elicits a racial panic within the context of white supremacist societies, whereby white bodies are imagined to take on a racialized biological and behavioural attribute associated with Indigenous bodies and bodies of colour. This does not mean that white fat bodies experience racism, because they certainly do not. Rather, scholars suggest that fatness on a body operates within a system of racist phenotypical distinction, much like Sander Gilman has famously argued other body parts such as large noses and buttocks have in previous colonialist and eugenic periods: as an abjected embodiment that white subjects must continuously expunge to obtain racial fitness (Gilman 1985, 1999). Concomitantly, fat pregnant Indigenous and bodies of colour become targets of state, medical, and public health hyper-surveillance and containment not for their race, supposedly, but due to their fatness. For example, in their qualitative study interviewing 11 Maori and Pasifika cisgender fat women, Parker, Pausé, and Le Grice (2019) describe the ways in which participants were constructed by health care professionals as risks and burdensome while pregnant, which "led participants to question the extent to which the problematizing of their fatness actually masked a racist … motivated interest in discouraging them from having babies" (ibid.). The authors thus conclude that "contemporary discourses of pregnancy and fatness work to perpetuate the harmful relations of colonization and reproductive legacies of reproductive injustice" as enacted by, specifically, eugenic practices and ideologies operationalized in ongoing processes of colonialism.

"Maternal obesity" operates, then, in a performative sense (Butler 1993) to materialize whiteness and white bodies through repeated fat phobic discourses and practices while, at the same time, to foreclosing bodies of colour and Indigenous bodies through the material and discursive (attempted) prevention of reproduction. But how, specifically, are these embodied materializations and foreclosures practiced and experienced in the lived realities of fat women? Our analysis of the research project *Reproducing Stigma* begins to answer this question which is, at its essence, a question about how fat people negotiate the discursive practices of new eugenics.

Patient Experiences

Research into the experiences of antifat stigma in health care describes weight stigma as dehumanizing. Patients describe weight stigma preventing their accessing of health care to be about choice and physical possibility, instead reinscribing shame. Many patients describe weight loss counselling being a key part of their experience of reproductive health care, and a lack of clarity about whether or not higher weight bodies are actually less fertile or actually more risky. Further, the clinical experience of being labelled a high-risk body results in a different experience of the hospital: high-risk areas, different protocols, gowns, and equipment that do not work. Patients describe being blamed for their bodies and for the limitations of the clinical environment itself.

Our own research in this area is illuminating in terms of fat patients' experiences of reproductive care. As such, we will use what remains of our paper describing our study's findings to demonstrate the ways that stigma and health eugenics have devastating impacts on care. *Reproducing Stigma* is a cross-national, qualitative study with a total of 59 participants who identified as fat or "obese" as determined through a screening process upon initial contact with researchers. Data in this chapter refer to interviews undertaken at one of our research sites – in Winnipeg, Canada – with 25 fat women who had accessed reproductive care at some point typically within the previous ten years. We recruited participants via the following methods: postering at key venues, social media ads and posts, word-of-mouth, and snowball sampling. We also developed a project website and placed ads in community newspapers, Kijiji, and Craigslist. All participants in Winnipeg identified as cisgender women. Thirteen identified as white, four as Indigenous, four as people of colour, two as Métis (of Indigenous and French heritage), and two as Jewish. Interviews were semi-structured and lasted approximately 50 minutes to 1 hour, and took place within venues in which participants felt most comfortable – at participants' homes, in coffee shops, or in the interviewer's office. Author B conducted all interviews. The interview guide was iterative, in that data gleaned from participants were incorporated into questions as the research moved forward. The code list was developed by the research team as a whole after interviews were completed, and after an initial review of the data. We then coded the data thematically, beginning with open coding and then revisiting the data to conduct axial coding, attuned in particular to intersectional themes, incorporating this lens in the coding to explore ways in which the fat body was lived differently given such vectors of identity like race and indigeneity.

Our interviews revealed that participants were discouraged from reproducing in both subtle and not so subtle ways. One of the primary mechanisms by which this was accomplished was through health moralism or healthism (Crawford 1980). In the healthism of obesity more generally, embodied largesse is attributed with "bad" citizenship, while "good" citizens are perceived as both maintaining slenderness and, importantly, avoiding the supposed skyrocketing health care costs associated with obesity (Norman, Rail, and Jette 2016). In the case of maternal obesity, as we have noted elsewhere (McPhail et al. 2016; McPhail and Mazur 2019), health moralities attached to fatness dovetail with the highly intense and eugenically infused moral edicts of "good mothering" levelled at pregnant women to protect the health, safety, and welfare of the foetus over and above that of their own selves (Blum 2007; Ladd-Taylor and Umansky 1998; Singh 2004). For participants in our study, health morality was communicated through intense and pervasive conversations about the ways in which their bodies posed a severe risk to the health and sometimes very life of the foetus.

Discouragement Through Risk Talk

Almost all of the women described receiving reproductive care with a stigma-based approach, meaning that health care professionals made almost all medical decisions within the discursive bubble of fat as not only unhealthy, but also, quite simply, wrong. This is in opposition to a stigma-informed approach, which in our view not only avoids perpetuating stigma in a health care practice, but also addresses it through serious reflection about weight bias and understanding how that bias can create health conditions and disparities. Participants in our study were told that, in becoming or being pregnant, they were exposing their (potential) foetus to a variety of medical ailments, including birth defects, gestational diabetes, and stillbirth. Our participants all reported their doctors' warnings about risk to include the implication that these risks would not exist if their BMI was lower. For example, Freddi (white, middle class, queer; all names are pseudonyms) related the story of seeing her OB/GYN for the first time while pregnant:

> He mentioned at one point that I <u>might</u> have difficulty because of how heavy I was to start with. Talked about gestational diabetes and the risks of that, being overweight to start and overweight through my whole pregnancy. Lots of <u>cautionary</u> things. He never actually said, "You know, you are too overweight to do this." But, he always tells me how much I should exercise, and you know, that how, where my weight <u>should</u> be, and if I've gained weight, between visits, he makes comment about that, so. ... I was anxious through the whole pregnancy. Like, would I get diabetes? You know, or would that affect, you know, the baby? <u>It's still something that I think about (emphases ours)</u>.

In Freddi's case, discouraging care was embedded into the ways in which her doctor communicated the clinical risks associated with her pregnancy. While Freddi did not develop gestational diabetes, the implications of her doctor's cautionary discourse were that gestational diabetes would be *caused by* – as opposed to correlated to – her pre-pregnancy body mass. By emphasizing the risks associated with an "overweight" body mass, Freddi's doctor encouraged her to anticipate a difficult pregnancy. Being encouraged to anticipate pregnancy distress clearly caused harm – it increased Freddi's anxiety, and continues to impact her mental health, as demonstrated by the fact she still thinks anxious thoughts about her body mass in relation to reproductive care. Her doctor's characterization of health risks did not empower Freddi to anticipate a clinical treatment plan that was prepared to mitigate risks and work towards the best possible outcome.

Instead, Freddi was advised to pursue weight loss while simultaneously gestating a foetus to term.

Importantly, Freddi's doctor did not emphasize the reality that weight gain in pregnancy is a sign of healthy pregnancy, nor did he disclose the health risks to pursuing weight loss during pregnancy. Therefore, the doctor's comments are clear examples of weight stigma, their comments stigmatizing because they were informed not by A1C levels or genetic history, but by body size alone. These comments, however, did not operate in a social vacuum. They reinforce fatphobic social myths about large-bodied people being inherently lazy, inactive, and disinvested in nutritional wellness. If "hard" or traditional eugenics deems some populations worthy of reproducing while others are forcibly sterilized, soft eugenics involves a gentler approach. Rather than forcibly rendering some bodies infertile, soft eugenics is reflected in the disciplinary messages patients receive to change their bodies – and therefore their phenotypic membership in undesirable populations.

When Freddi's doctor implied that future pregnancies would have better outcomes if she first laboured to change her body, he implied that the risks she faced as a large patient were directly caused by her behaviour. Of note, he did not ask her what that behaviour may have been. The doctor was not talking to Freddi in a way informed by the knowledge that a fat woman has likely tried to diet many times in her life. Nor did the doctor approach her body size as a potential consequence of yo-yo dieting. The doctor made many assumptions about Freddi's diet and exercise regime, but given the statistics could have far more accurately assumed Freddi faces weight stigma every day of her life. A stigma-informed approach would have recognized the negative impacts of clinician encouragement to lose weight and would have understood that advising weight loss has the power to shame a patient so severely that months later they will still be worried about whether or not their body could have harmed their baby.

Brooklyn's (white, working class) experience with risk discourse occurred whilst seeking conception advice from her family doctor. In addition to being told that "excess" weight could create ovarian cysts that could impede pregnancy, Brooklyn related the following conversation with her doctor:

> Being fat, being over obese is bad, in many ways, because you got blood clots. … So yeah, she told me a lot, like, to take better care of myself. I think she was more focused on, not getting pregnant, I think she was focused on getting me more healthier. Because first what they do, is they look at you, and they look at you, where you stand and where you're at, and what you're eating and how you're taking care of yourself; what you're living life like; how much stress can you handle; what's going on, like, you know? And those are honest questions, right? … Interviewer: It was sort of a general thing, like, "You need to get healthy first." B: Just, just, yeah. "You need to get healthy first. You need to love yourself." And then you can get pregnant.

In this case, risk discourse was articulated more generally, as the doctor encouraged Brooklyn to "get healthy" prior to pregnancy, equated in large part with losing body fat. Brooklyn's recounting of her interactions with her doctor demonstrates the ubiquity of the association of thinness with good health. When she refers to "being obese is bad" she signals the ways in which her body was constructed as always already in need of repair. Discursively, her doctor did not recommend weight loss explicitly but rather euphemistically through the catch-all of "getting healthy." Brooklyn did not report any cautions against the health risks of deliberate weight loss, nor an acknowledgement that she has tried pursuing weight loss in the past. Weight loss was framed as a prerequisite to receiving reproductive health care. What was communicated most strongly was who is considered to be a worthy patient, and that the labour towards worthiness was labour the patient needed to undertake. In this sense, the doctor's recommendations served a disciplinary function to only pursue pregnancy in particular conditions, as opposed to outlining how the physician would assist Brooklyn through medical care.

Brianne (Indigenous, middle class) connected the risk discourse communicated by her doctors directly to the affective frameworks of "good" mothering, noting:

I mean, if you have a baby, you shouldn't do it for strictly selfish reasons. You should be caring about the baby, and so, I wanted to get pregnant, but I realized that I could be harming my baby if I tried. I mean, the doctor had made that really clear. The blood pressure and the diabetes, and you know, I don't know, like, I was too big.

Brianne's body was constructed as evidence of her lack of care – an aesthetic read that is linked to colonial ideas about the inadequacy of Indigenous family systems. Brianne was told that pursuing pregnancy would lead to harm. It is unclear whether or not weight loss leads to significant reduction in blood glucose levels or blood pressure (Ward and McPhail 2019). Brianne's experience of reproductive health care was not to outline treatments that would be available or strategies to mitigate risks. Instead, her doctor prescribed physiological changes as a prerequisite to accessing care. Because of this, Brianne consented to have gastric bypass surgery. Heartbreakingly, the ensuing health effects of this surgery prevented her from becoming pregnant for the foreseeable future.

For some participants, risk discourse had consequences in the form of spatial edicts and restrictions within medical settings. At the time that fieldwork was conducted, participants related that the classification of their bodies at a certain category of obesity could land them on the "high risk" section of a birth and delivery ward, which was extremely worrisome for some. Victoria (white, middle class) related:

Automatically, even though I had a healthy pregnancy, even before knowing he was breech, I was considered a high risk pregnancy, and would have to be in a high risk area of the hospital. It's BMI based. So, even though I had no health concerns with my pregnancy, that was, you know, always a factor, which meant different protocol for delivery, which was very stressful for me, because I really wanted to have a natural birth.

Victoria's story is particularly disturbing, as the anaesthesiologist first assigned to her could not insert an IV, which was blamed on the fact that she was a "poor candidate" for an epidural due to her weight. She noted: "Again I was referred to as a 'poor candidate' … I kept hearing those words." Eventually, Victoria gave birth in such pain that she developed, in her words: "post traumatic stress disorder from my birth … experience." She told the interviewer: "that's why I will never have any more children." In Victoria's case, then, the stress, anxiety, and pain that flowed directly and indirectly from the label "high risk" as well as "poor candidate" prevented her from considering future pregnancies. Importantly, the discursive construction of pregnant patients as "high risk" and "poor candidate" locates the burden of responsibility onto the patient's body, rather than clinician skill or institutional environment. A stigma-informed approach would invite terms such as "limited operating room equipment" or "poor needle placement" to be ways of making sense of the need to accommodate the diversity of patients in the reproductive care ward. Constructing the patient's body as incompatible with the provision of reproductive health care encourages a gatekeeping relationship between clinician and patient with regard to human reproduction, echoing eugenicist logics.

Discouragement Through "Care"

In addition to healthism and risk talk, fat pregnancies were discouraged in our study through the denial and deferral of care. In the case of conception care, certain tests, referrals, drugs, or sometimes even fulsome consultations were denied or delayed. Patricia's gynaecologist, for example, refused to give Patricia a referral for further conception care by literally walking out of the appointment. Patricia had first approached the gynaecologist with the symptom of cramping, wondering if this could be impeding conception. Patricia believed her symptoms were not taken seriously, and brought them up at a subsequent appointment:

So, in three weeks, I went back, and I was upset. It's like, "Okay, I want this cramping to stop. I want you to take care of this. Like, you're not doing anything." … All she was concerned about was me losing weight. And I told her "If you don't want to deal with this, send me to the [fertility clinic]" because I had, under my husband's benefit at the time, I had full coverage. I said, "Send me, let me deal with them, if you don't want to take care of this." And that's when she started yelling at me, and told me I can get out of her office, and if I wanted to get pregnant, that I could do it on my own. And she said "I'll send you a referral – " and I don't think she ever sent it. … And then she walked out of the appointment.

Patricia eventually became pregnant without any medical intervention. Patricia's account is an important reminder of the gatekeeping role physicians can play in denying access to specialized reproductive health care. Weight stigma, in this case, contributed to a negative relationship with the clinician, and the suspected denial of a referral. A stigma-informed approach would not have included a strong emphasis on weight loss, but instead fully informing the patient of risk-informed protocols they would be eligible for.

Mirroring the experiences of participants in other studies (McPhail 2016; McPhail and Ward 2019), some participants were often deferred care by specialists until they achieved weight loss. Chantelle (white, middle class), for example, was told to lose 10% of her body weight before fertility treatment:

> I don't mind a doctor being truthful and to the point, but when they're coming out and saying "Oh, you're obese. You need to lose ten percent of your body weight in three months"? And okay, maybe there's some people who can do it. But for some reason, I'm not one of them. It's just, you just want to shake them. Like, like thinking, I'm thinking to myself, like, to this doctor, like I'm thinking "Well, do you have fertility issues? Do you know what I'm going through?" Are other people coming in here in our shoes? Like, unless you've been in the shoes of an obese woman trying to have a family, then you don't really know what they're feeling.

Chantelle's comments highlight how counselling from physicians on weight loss does not take the patient's lived experience into account. Research shows that despite clear clinical data demonstrating weight loss to be impossible 95% of the time (Bobak, 2014), that health care practitioners continue to recommend it. In Chantelle's case, the physician's insistence that she pursue an unattainable goal prior to beginning fertility treatment effectively bars her from accessing medically assisted conception. The refusal of care based on BMI in reproductive health settings begs further scrutiny as it reflects eugenicist values and power relations.

Not all participants shared Chantelle's experience, and a small handful related positive or neutral experiences with reproductive health care professionals. Cara (white, middle class), in anticipation for an upcoming appointment with a specialist, was delaying care until weight loss on her *own volition*, though this was due to a previous experience with her family doctor who focused solely on her weight when advising her about conception:

> I: Do you have, like, a goal in terms of like, you want to lose a specific amount of weight before you go see the gynaecologist, for example or? C: That's what I'm hoping. I don't think I'll be able to lose fifty pounds before I see her. But

I do want to shape up a little bit, just because I dread her reaction, like if it's the same reaction as with my GP, then like I would not like that at all.

Cara's approach to seeking care reflects the systemic nature of weight stigma in reproductive health care. The pursuit of weight loss has become part of an unquestioned and anticipated dynamic fat patients internalize in order to prove their worthiness as reproductive subjects. A stigma-informed approach is needed to mitigate the spoken and unspoken pressures patients encounter in order to ensure their reproductive agency is not compromised by weight stigma.

Begrudging Care

The final type of discouragement participants experienced was through what we call "begrudging care." In these instances, health care was provided – it was neither denied nor deferred – but only reticently and with a high degree of obvious judgement about participants' weight. Saanvi's (South Asian, middle class) story encapsulates this particular type of care. Saanvi had been referred to a gynaecologist when attempting to conceive. The gynaecologist immediately prescribed fertility drugs:

> She started with Clomid. Her bedside manners weren't good. Out front, she was like, "Oh, you're too obese." And at that time, I wasn't what I am right now. Like, I was way less than what I am now. So she's like, "Well, I can give you medicine, but it's not really going to do anything to you, if you don't lose weight." And it's the way she said, she said, um, if she would have just explained to me, "You know what, for each pound you lose, blah, blah, blah, this is how it's going to help you." No, it was more like, "You're fat. Lose it. Or you're not going to conceive." That's what it was. So I went there for about three months, and I just felt that the Clomid wasn't doing anything … So I asked my doctor if I can go and see somebody else.

Thus, Saanvi was not denied care outright, but the care she received was reticent and tempered with judgement, so much so that Saanvi decided to remove herself from the care relationship. It is important to note that as body mass changes, these clinical encounters later determine patients' perceptions of their bodies. As Saanvi mentioned, she was told she was too large when she was at a much smaller size than she is now. The long-term impacts of these comments are multifold and inform how patients can assess their own body's set weight range, their own perceptions of health and wellness, as well as their confidence in seeking clinical care. Stigmatizing comments constitute examples of soft eugenics because they ultimately encourage patients to consider themselves unworthy or unable of pursuing pregnancy.

Samantha (Jewish, middle class) had a similar experience of a high degree of judgement in prenatal care:

> It was just the worst experience of my entire life. He looked at me and just saw fat. Like, that's what he saw. Like, I walked into his office. He was "Okay, we're putting you on insulin." blah, blah, blah, blah, blah, blah. "You have to have a c-section." blah, blah, blah. I said "What are you talking about?" I said, "I'm having a birth. I'm having a vaginal birth. I don't need to go on insulin. Have you looked at my sugar numbers? I don't need to go on insulin. I'm doing this diet. I don't need to go on pills, nothing, nothing." "No, you have to go on insulin." blah, blah, blah. "You're having a c-section. This is what I say. You're getting induced early, because the baby's going to die." blah, blah, blah.

In Samantha's case, as in Saanvi's, there was not a denial or deferral of care – indeed, one may argue that there was an *excess* of it. In the provision of care, however, Samantha's OB/GYN failed to adequately inform Samantha of the options available to her, limiting her ability to provide informed consent to the recommended treatment plan. Further, her doctor phrased the treatment recommendations as directly related to body mass, as opposed to A1C levels (regarding insulin) or foetal placement and size (regarding the recommended C-section). Regardless of whether the doctor's recommendations were informed by diagnostic data in addition to body size, Samantha's experience of the encounter was that body mass was the only metric used to explain why the doctor was insisting on interventions. Samantha is signalling the dehumanizing nature of weight stigma, that "he looked at me and just saw fat," an experience that she remembers as "the worst experience of my entire life." Insulin injections during pregnancy, as well as C-sections, are routine in pregnancy care. Patients of all sizes are prescribed insulin during pregnancy and are induced with planned C-sections. There is no reason that advising a patient of these protocols should be so damaging. It is clear from Samantha's interview that her body was framed as a problem based on size, rather than common risks in pregnancy. A stigma-informed approach would have prioritized compassionate communication to a socially marginalized patient, and ensured all options were explained using evidence-based protocols so that she would be able to make an informed choice. Stigma-informed protocols must be informed by the fact that their absence in clinical encounters has the potential to encourage eugenicist practices.

Conclusion: Recommendations for Change

In pregnancy, fatness is most certainly a liability. In a convergence of gendered and racist histories of eugenics as contemporaneously embodied and imagined, fatness is positioned as always-already risky and dangerous to both the potential foetus and the parent. To conclude this chapter, we would like to contemplate how to move forward, quite practically, in terms of interrupting the types of eugenics-based fat phobia that was faced and then negotiated by our participants. Throughout this chapter, we have called for the adoption of a stigma-informed approach in reproductive health care service provision that has the potential to interrupt eugenicist logics. As such, we close with some recommendations for moving forward towards radically compassionate, anti-oppressive care based in the lessening of the stigma described almost unanimously by our participants.

We recommend robust training for clinicians on antifat stigma, particularly how it is reinforced in clinical encounters. We recommend a discursive audit of language used to describe the limitations of the treatment environment and treatment protocols to ensure patients' bodies are not implicitly blamed for the need for accommodation or risk management. Finally, we recommend that health care providers communicate the risks of weight loss during pregnancy along with statistics about the long-term health impacts of dieting. These recommendations are informed by the weight stigma participants reported in our study, and we argue that the reduction of stigma can ultimately increase access to reproductive health care, rather than discouraging it through eugenicist logics.

References

Bashford, A., & Levine, P. (Eds.). *The Oxford Handbook of the History of Eugenics*. Oxford: Oxford University Press, 2010.

Bell, V. "Beyond (Financial) Accessibility: Inequalities Within the Medicalisation of Infertility." *Sociology of Health & Illness*. 32:4. (2010): 631–646.

Bitler, M., & Lucie, S. "Health Disparities and Infertility: Impacts of State-level Insurance Mandates." *Fertility and Sterility*. 85:4. (2006): 858–865.

Blum, L. "Mother-blame in the Prozac Nation: Raising Kids with Invisible Disabilities." *Gender & Society*. 21:2. (2007): 202–226.

Bombak, A. "Obeisty, Health at Every Size, and Public Health Policy." *American Journal of Public Health*. 104. (2014): e60–e67.

Bombak, A. E., McPhail, D., & Ward, P. "Reproducing Stigma: Interpreting 'Overweight' and 'Obese' Women's Experiences of Weight-based Discrimination in Reproductive Healthcare." *Social Science & Medicine*. 166. 2016: 94–101.

Budd, G., Mariotti, M., Graff, D., & Falkenstein, K. "Health Care Professionals' Attitudes About Obesity: An Integrative Review." *Applied Nursing Research*. 24:3. (2009): 127–137.

Butler, J. *Bodies that Matter: On the Discursive Limits of Sex*. New York: Routledge, 1993.

Cain, R. "'This Growing Genetic Disaster': Obesogenic Mothers, the Obesity 'Epidemic' and the Persistence of Eugenics." *Studies in the Maternal*. 5:2. (2013).

Chrisler, J. C., & Barney, A. "Sizeism Is a Health Hazard." *Fat Studies*. 6:1. (2016): 38–53.

Crawford, R. "Healthism and the Medicalization of Everyday Life." *International Journal of Health Services*. 10:3. (1980): 365–388.

Daar, J. *The New Eugenics: Selective Breeding in an Era of Reproductive Technologies*. New Haven & London: Yale, 2017.

Davin, A. "Imperialism and Motherhood." *History Workshop*. 5. (1978): 9–55.

Dyck, E. *Facing Eugenics: Reproduction, Sterilization, and the Politics of Choice*. Toronto: University of Toronto Press, 2013.

Ellison, J. *Being Fat: Women, Weight, and Feminist Activism in Canada*. Toronto: University of Toronto Press, 2020.

Faludi, S. *Backlash: The Undeclared War Against Women*. New York: Crown Publishing Group, 1991.

Farrell, A. E. *Fat Shame: Stigma and the Fat Body in American Culture*. New York: New York University Press, 2011.

Furber, C. M., & McGowan, L. "A Qualitative Study of the Experiences of Women Who Are Obese and Pregnant in the UK." *Midwifery*. 27:4. (2011): 437–444.

Gilman, S. *Difference and Pathology: Stereotypes of Sexuality, Race, and Madness*. New York: Cornell University Press, 1985.

Gilman, S. *Making the Body Beautiful: A Cultural History of Aesthetic Surgery*. Princeton: Princeton University Press, 1999.

Grekul, J., Krahn, A., & Odynak, D. "Sterilizing the 'Feeble-minded': Eugenics in Alberta, Canada, 1929–1972." *Journal of Historical Sociology*. 17:4. (2004): 358–384.

Heslehurst, N., Russell, S., Brandon, H., Johnston, C., Summerbell, C., & Rankin, J. "Women's Perspectives are Required to Inform the Development of Maternal Obesity Services: A Qualitative Study of Obese Pregnant Women's Experiences. *Health Expectations*. 18:5. (2015): 969–981.

Inhorn, M. C., & Michael, H. F. "Arab Americans, African Americans, and Infertility: Barriers to Reproduction and Medical Care." *Fertility and Sterility*. 85:4. (2006): 844–852.

Jain, T. "Socioeconomic and Racial Disparities Among Infertility Patients Seeking Care." *Fertility and Sterility*. 85:4. (2006): 876–881.

Jette, S., & Rail, G. (2013). "Ills from the Womb? A Critical Examination of Clinical Guidelines for Obesity in Pregnancy." *Health*. 17:4. (2013): 407–421.

Kindregan, C. P., & McBrien, M. "Assisted Reproductive Technology: A Lawyer's Guide to Emerging Law and Science." American Bar Association, 2006.

Ladd-Taylor, M., & Umansky, L. (Eds.). *"Bad" Mothers: The Politics of Blame in Twentieth-century America*. New York: NYU Press, 1998.

Lee, J. A. & Pausé, C. J. "Stigma in Practice: Barriers to Health for Fat Women." *Frontiers in Psychology*. 7. (2016): 2063. 10.3389/fpsyg.2016.02063

Macintosh, K. L. "Brave New Eugenics: Regulating Assisted Reproductive Technologies in the Name of Better Babies." *University of Illinois Journal of Law, Technology & Policy* (2010): 257.

McClintock, A. *Imperial Leather: Race, Gender, and Sexuality in the Colonial Context*. New York: Routledge, 1995.

McLaren, A. *Our Own Master Race: Eugenics in Canada, 1885–1945*. Toronto: M&S, 1990.

McPhail, D. *Contours of the Nation: Making 'Obesity' and Imagining Canada, 1945–1970*. Toronto: University of Toronto Press, 2017.

McPhail, D., Bombak, A., Ward, P., & Allison, J. "Wombs at Risk, Wombs as Risk: Fat Women's Experiences of Reproductive Care." *Fat Studies*. 5:2. (2016): 98–115.

McPhail, D, & Mazur, L. "Medicalization, Maternity, and the Materiality of Resistance: 'Maternal Obesity' and Experiences of Reproductive Care." In M. Friedman, C. Rice, & J. Rinaldi (Eds.), *Thickening Fat: Fat Bodies, Intersectionality, and Social Justice* (pp. 122–136). New York: Routledge, 2019.

McPhail, D., & Orsini, M. "Fat Acceptance as Social Justice." *Canadian Medical Association Journal*. 193:35. (2021): E1398–E1399.

Mitchenson, W. *Fighting Fat: Canada 1920–1980*. Toronto: University of Toronto Press, 2018.

Mulherin, K., Miller, Y. D., Barlow, F. K., Diedrichs, P. C., & Thompson, R. "Weight Stigma in Maternity Care: Women's Experiences and Care Providers' Attitudes." *BMC Pregnancy and Childbirth*. 13. (2013). doi:10.1186/1471-2393-13-19.

Norman, M. E., Rail, G., & Jette, S. "Screening the Un-Scene: De-Constructing the (Bio) Politics of Storytelling in a Reality Makeover Weight Loss Series." In J. Ellison, D. McPhail, & W. Michison (Eds.), *Obesity in Canada: Historical and Critical Perspectives* (pp. 342–372). Toronto: University of Toronto Press, 2016.

Parker, G., Pausé, C., & Le Grice, J. "You're Just Another Friggin' Number to Add to the Problem." In M. Friedman, C. Rice, and J. Rinaldi (Eds.), *Thickening Fat: Fat Bodies, Intersectionality, and Social Justice* (pp. 97–109). New York: Routledge, 2019.

Paul, D., & Moore, J. "The Darwinian Context: Evolution and Inheritance." In A. Bashford and P. Levine (Eds.), *The Oxford Handbook of the History of Eugenics* (pp. 27–42). Oxford: Oxford University Press, 2010.

Rabinow, P., & Nikolas, R. "Biopower Today." *BioSocieties*. 1:2. (2006). 195–217.

Rice, C. *Becoming Women: The Embodied Self in Image Culture*. Toronto: University of Toronto Press, 2014.

Roberts, D. *Killing the Black Body: Race, Reproduction, and the Meaning of Liberty*. New York: Vintage, 2014.

Rose, N. "Molecular Biopolitics, Somatic Ethics and the Spirit of Biocapital." *Social Theory & Health*. 5 (2007): 3–29.

Seifer, D. B., Rosey, Z., David, A. G., & Society for Assisted Reproductive Technology Writing Group Report. "Trends of Racial Disparities in Assisted Reproductive Technology Outcomes in Black Women Compared with White Women: Society for Assisted Reproductive Technology 1999 and 2000 vs. 2004–2006." *Fertility and Sterility*. 93:2. (2010): 626–635.

Singh, I. "Doing Their Jobs: Mothering with Ritalin in a Culture of Mother-Blame." *Social Science & Medicine*. 59:6. (2004): 1193–1205.

Smith, D., & Lavender, T. "The Maternity Experience for Women with a Body Mass Index: A Meta-Synthesis. *BJOG*. 118:7. (2011): 779–789.

Stern, A. *Eugenic Nation: Faults and Frontiers of Better Breeding in Modern America*. Berkeley: University of California Press, 2005.

Strings, S. *Fearing the Black Body: The Racial Origins of Fat Phobia*. New York: New York University Press, 2019.

Thille, P. "Managing Anti-Fat Stigma in Primary Care: An Observational Study." *Health Communication*. 34:8. (2019): 892–903.

Taussig, K-S., Rayna, R., & Deborah, H. "Flexible Eugenics." In *Genetic nature/culture*, pp. 58–76. Chicago: University of California Press, 2003.

Tomiyama, A. J., Carr, D., Granberg, E. M., Major, B., Robinson, E., Sutin, A. R., & Brewis, A. R. "How and Why Weight Stigma Drives the Obesity 'Epidemic' and Harms Health." *BMC Medicine*. 16. (2018): 123. https://doi.org/10.1186/s12916-018-1116-5

Treichler, P. A. *How to Have Theory in an Epidemic: Cultural Chronicles of AIDS* Durham: Duke University Press, 1999.

Ward, P., & McPhail, D. "A Shared Vision for Reducing Fat Shame and Blame in Reproductive Care." *Women's Reproductive Health*. 6:4. (2019): 265–270.

Wray, S., & Dreery, R. (2008). "The Medicalization of Body Size and Women's Healthcare." *Healthcare for Women International*. 29:3. (2008): 227–243.

PART VII

Gender and Fat in Popular Culture and Media

Mass media and popular culture are major sources for the stories we consume about gender and fatness. The authors in this section take us into three different arenas, from the world of plus-size modeling to the cultures of big-gay men's subcultures to the media representations of fat Black women. In each, we see how these stories shift over time and how they possibly continue to constrain us, even when they purport to be emancipatory.

DOI: 10.4324/9781003140665-22

16

SEXY, DOCILE BODIES

The Objectification and Paternalistic Management of Plus-Size Models

Amanda M. Czerniawski

Try this little experiment: Google the term "plus-size model." Most likely, the algorithm will present you with images of popular plus-size models, such as Ashley Graham, Denise Bidot, Hunter McGrady, Iskra Lawrence, Precious Lee, Tess Holiday, and Yumi Nu. In many of the images, these models will be wearing very little, either swimsuits or lingerie. Now, Google the term "model." Notice anything different from the previous assortment of images? Most of these images are headshots, and most of these models are fully clothed. Finally, look at what Google spits out when asked to search for "fashion model": fully clothed, straight-size[1] models. There may be a male model or two but not one plus-size model on the first page.

Think back to that first Google search. Why are many of those images featuring nearly nude plus-size models? Why, when we examine the media landscape, are they often naked?

Over the past few years, plus-size models have become, literally, more visible. In September 2009, an image of plus-size model Lizzie Miller appeared tucked near the back of an issue of *Glamour* magazine. The photograph showed her smiling and casually sitting in her underwear. The image itself was only a three-inch square but made quite the impression on readers because it exposed Miller's "normal" belly and stretch marks. In response to a boost in sales and a flood of encouraging emails where readers clamored to see more women with "normal" bodies within the pages of the magazine, the editors of *Glamour* followed up with a photo spread featuring several naked plus-size models in their November issue. *PLUS Model Magazine* also featured plus-size models in the nude in its October 2012 issue, which was aimed at confronting the topic of body shaming. Over the years, more body positive campaigns, featuring naked plus-size modes, have appeared, all in the name of promoting body confidence.

DOI: 10.4324/9781003140665-23

While sexuality is implicit for a thin, straight-size model, a plus-size model must work to overcome the stigma of fat that erases her sexuality and desirability. These intentionally provocative images are meant to counter the stigma of fat. These images expose the flesh and show plus-size models proudly flaunting their bodies amid a fat-phobic society that seeks to cover them up in shame. These models are not hiding behind clothes or shapewear that "perfects" their silhouettes; instead, they strip down and arch their backs to emphasize their curves.

In this chapter, I discuss the role of stigma, discipline, and objectification in plus-size modeling. The rise of plus-size models expands the fashion landscape and challenges cultural conceptions of beauty. Yet, as they achieve increased media visibility, plus-size models are subject to the same paternalistic management practices within agencies that plague fashion models of all sizes and genders and ultimately transform these women into docile bodies that are sexually objectified. Stigmatized fat bodies become manipulated sex objects.

Maybe She's Born with It. Maybe It's …

Feminist philosopher Susan Bordo (1993, 212) argues, "No body can escape either the imprint of culture or its gendered meanings." Today, in the United States, the dominant narrative regarding fat is negative. The culture, via media, medicine, and state actions, legitimizes ideologies that privilege the thin body and shed an unflattering spotlight on fat. For example, the 2008 Pixar film, *Wall-E*, serves as a cautionary tale about the dangers of overconsumption that lead not only to the destruction of the planet but our very bodies. In the film, the future humans feed on fast food and hover around on chaise lounges to the detriment of their muscles that have atrophied to the point of immobility. Lecturing through imagery, the film clearly equates fat with laziness and physical decay. More vocal about the dangers of fat, medical researchers continue to identify a high body mass index (BMI) as a risk factor for several diseases and health conditions, including severe COVID-19, despite growing evidence that this anthropometric measure is an unreliable indicator of general health (Dhurandhar 2016). Putting warnings into action, the government took a stand against fat in 2015 when the Food and Drug Administration (FDA) banned food manufacturers from adding partially hydrogenated oils to foods.

The United States' fat-phobia emerged during the nineteenth century, as dietary reformers, such as William Banting and Sylvester Graham, demonized excess flesh as an undesirable physical state that speaks to an individual's personal failings.[2] Since then, weight bias has proliferated, as empirical studies by psychologists show we equate fatness with a lack of self-discipline, laziness, and even stupidity (Puhl and Brownell 2003).

In *Body of Truth: How Science, History, and Culture Drive Our Obsession with Weight—and What We Can Do about It*, writer and journalist Harriet Brown recounts the time a therapist asked her a seemingly peculiar question, "What if you were OK with your body the way it is right now?" Brown was, at first, surprised and angered by the question. She writes:

> Of course I've never considered the possibility of being OK with this body. This unacceptable body. And I'm not going to consider it. That would be letting myself go … I will never let myself go. I will never, ever, ever be the sloppy, lazy, dull, fat friend or mother or relative people like my grandmother shake their heads about.
>
> *(2015, xvi)*

For Brown to accept her body—her fat—she would have to admit her failure to keep up with contemporary standards of beauty that value thinness and malign fat.

Western consumer culture places a high premium on the look and shape of bodies. As feminist philosopher Sandra Bartky (1988) argues, the female body is constructed as an object to be watched. Because of this intense focus on appearance, women experience their bodies as not solely for their pleasure and amusement but as under the constant gaze of others. As a result, women discipline themselves to achieve modern-day aesthetics. As feminist author Naomi Wolf (1992) argued in *The Beauty Myth*, women become trapped in a never-ending cycle of cosmetics, beauty aids, diets, and exercise fanaticism—all in the name of beauty.

Her therapist's question, nonetheless, continued to haunt Brown and forced her to evaluate not only her personal obsession with weight but a society-wide obsession that, she adamantly argues, has become "epidemic, endemic, and pandemic" (2015, xxiv). Brown does her research to uncover that many of the medical "truths" we hold dear, i.e., obesity is strongly linked with mortality and obesity causes serious illnesses such as heart disease and diabetes, are misleading and contribute to a growing cultural fear of fat. More accurately, the relationship between body weight, disease, and mortality is far more complex and nuanced than these kinds of blanket statements would have you believe.

Like Brown, contemporary scholars in the field of Fat Studies, such as Pattie Thomas (2005) in her sociological memoir *Taking Up Space: How Eating Well and Exercising Regularly Changed My Life*, confront the many myths about fat. Some of these include the belief that those who are fat are unhealthy, androgynous, asexual, incompetent, jolly, lazy, and ugly. These controlling images of fat are rife with moralistic innuendos that place blame on the individual and ignore the role cultural institutions play in manipulating bodily ideals.

So, if the dominant culture teaches women to scorn fat and do whatever they can to reduce and ultimately eliminate it, where do these plus-size models with super-sized self-esteems and body confidence come from? How do they navigate through the slender runways of fashion? How do they craft a provocative image of the plus-size woman?

While sociologist Erving Goffman's (1963) view of stigma suggests that plus-size women should be more inclined to cover up their curves and excess flesh, these models chose to enter a field where they publicly parade their fat bodies for an opinionated public. Essentially, it is this very courage to flaunt their bodies that sets plus–size models apart from traditional, straight-size models.

During my ethnographic research for *Fashioning Fat: Inside Plus-Size Modeling* (Czerniawski 2015), I encountered women who thought modeling to be an unattainable career prospect. Many never imagined that they could work as models because of their fat bodies. For example, Stephanie was approached by a makeup artist while she was shopping for clothes:

> I was in the checkout line, just chatting, when she suggested I try plus[-size] modeling. I hadn't thought about it before, but she made me think. If an established professional in the biz says I should do it, why not?

Recruited by another plus-size model, Mary was shocked by the suggestion, admitting, "I thought only anorexic girls modeled … I spent so many years hating my body that the idea of selling it was foreign to me." Given the normative expectation of fashion models as young, tall, and thin,[3] it is no wonder that women like Stephanie and Mary had trouble envisioning a place for themselves in fashion.

Many of these women had grown up struggling with their bodies, spending years in shame, and trying to cover up their self-perceived flaws; yet, when they discovered plus-size modeling, the way they saw themselves was transformed. Like Mary, Joelle began modeling after attending an open modeling call with her friend who worked as a plus-size model:

> At first, I didn't want to go because of my body issues. She basically dragged me to the casting. But it was the best thing I could've done for myself … After the casting, I saw myself differently. I looked around the room and saw a group of plus beauties. I belonged. "I could do that," I thought to myself. I really did believe it … Finally, I appreciated my body instead of hiding from it.

Once working as plus-size models, both Mary and Joelle realized that the bodies that they had hated for so many years could offer them work opportunities.

By working as models, these women started to appreciate their bodies and began a journey of personal growth where they overcame their body issues. They shed a penetrating layer of shame and guilt built up over the years to reveal a new, confident self that was no longer afraid to enjoy their size and shape. Now as models, these women broke with conventional interpretations of their gender identity by flaunting their fat bodies in hopes of changing the cultural discourse. Many of them developed more positive self-images through modeling and embraced the mantle of spokesmodel for body acceptance. This did not mean, however, that these women have perfect body images. In fact, Angellika, the first plus-size model inducted into the Modeling Hall of Fame, admitted that she did not like her stomach, so she played up her other assets (Amador 2006).

Ultimately, these plus-size models aim to change the cultural ideals of beauty to include their kinds of bodies—larger, more diverse bodies—but they cannot do it alone. Once within the agency system, these women work under oppressive heterosexist constraints.[4] Plus-size models may liberate themselves from the stigma of fat but soon find themselves ensnarled in a web of paternalistic management practices.

Just Do It (with Your Agent's Permission)

The modeling industry is structured in such a way that models (of all types, straight or plus-size, and genders) are independent contractors who depend on modeling agencies to find them work. Agents, the gatekeepers of this cultural industry, network with fashion clients on behalf of their models, just like agents do for actors. In Deborah Dean's (2013) study of stage and screen actors from an industrial relations perspective, agents influence the casting process by offering their choice in performers and negotiating with casting behind the scenes. In modeling, agents (also referred to as "bookers") similarly seek and proceed to "talk up" their models to clients. They also handle all the financial aspects of the job, i.e., negotiating modeling rates with clients, processing work vouchers, scheduling a model's bookings and castings, and navigating through a fluctuating market demand for modeling talent. Agents—assuming the role as talent scout, mentor, and job hunter—are responsible for finding and producing marketable models.

As in other body performance-centric fields such as boxing and dance (Crossley 2001), modeling requires models to develop their bodies according to fashion's tastes. Models work with agents to develop marketable bodies. Throughout this process, agents develop a paternalistic management style with their models, often affectionately referring to their models as "my girls." Sociologist Ashley Mears (2008), while working as a model in New York City, received explicit instruction from her booker to lie about her age to clients, a practice common among straight-size models because they typically age-out of the business at 25. Mears (2008, 444) recalls being called a "little girl" by a client. As she explains, the expectation for models to embody youthful femininity functions to discipline them into being weak and deferential. During interviews with agents at plus-size agencies, I, too, heard agents and bookers refer to their models as "girls," even though the average age of plus-size models is older than straight-size models since many are hired to represent mature brands.

Highlighting the personal and possessive dimensions of the job, one agent cheerfully described her plus-size division to me as "a family-oriented board. We are constantly advising our models and discuss among ourselves [the other agents] what direction to take each of them." Agents meet with their models in the agency office or email them, provide details on bookings and castings, discuss career options, or check-in on the condition of their bodies. They advise models on how to dress for a particular client and what to say to land the job. For models new to the industry, an agent will take the time to coach them on walking the runway and posing for the camera. Agents send models for test shoots, organize their portfolios, and put together their composite cards. For established models, little direction is needed. As an agent confessed to me, "If a product works, why change it?" This candid revelation, where the agent equates the model with a product, speaks of the commodification of the model's body and the role the agent plays in preparing it for "production." Models are products that clients fix up and dress up to present a desirable package. Agents sell these manufactured packages to clients, who in turn resell them to consumers. Overall, the agent's role is to develop and market the strengths of "their girls," which is evidenced by the care taken by agencies to cultivate their "boards."

At the heart of any modeling agency is the booking board. Once comprised of sleek shelving that held rows of composite cards[5] centrally located in the agency office but now more often digitally contained in the agency website, the booking board is a pictorial roster of the agency's signed models, a catalog of the agency's collective body capital. This instrument is continually referred to by the agents as they pick and choose which models to send out to castings. Agents take great pride in their boards and continually work to improve their overall image by manipulating the images themselves as well as the models depicted in them.

Agents exude great pride when speaking of their boards. After an interview with an agent for a plus–size division at a top New York City agency, I was asked with great enthusiasm, "You want to see my board?" This pride also translates into how these agents perceive and work on their boards. As another agent described, she continually tweaks the board, focusing on the color palate and the angles used in the photographs, because "it all speaks to my division. It is about the energy of the board, which clients read." The agent personally picks the photographers used to shoot the models. The board represents the agency and the kind of models it produces. Agents take ownership of not only the individual models but the collection of bodies they represent.

Ultimately, models are at the mercy of their agents, who are in control of their schedules and their earnings. Models do not have any say in the matter and must follow their agent's direction. The organizational structure of the agency system is such that models need agents and agents need models; yet it is the model who is more easily replaceable as countless more bodies await their turn for a shot at a modeling career.

As sociologists Joanne Entwistle and Elizabeth Wissinger argue in their case study of fashion modeling in New York and London, aesthetic labor is more than just a display and performance at work but is "part of the reproduction of the worker for employment ... and involves longer-term commitments to bodily projects" (2006, 777). The fashion industry commodifies the bodies of models as goods for market exchange, and these models must quickly learn how to develop their bodies to meet fashion's faddish demands. This aesthetic labor process, in which models strive to harness their interpersonal energy, rein in emotions, and actively monitor and sculpt their bodies, is an ongoing production of the body and self that extends beyond the confines of modeling work into models' everyday lives. This continuous work of manipulating the body extends beyond the physical structure to direct aesthetic practices involving hair, make-up, clothing, and movements of the body as it poses and walks the runway.

Models spend significant time and attention preparing their bodies for the performance of modeling. They engage in round-the-clock self-discipline and surveillance, which Bartky (1988) argues is evidence of women's obedience to the patriarchy and, here, the plus-size model's obedience to fashion's gaze. They tone and shape their bodies through diet and exercise or, as normalized in the case of plus-size models, resort to artificial enhancements like shapewear and strategically placed padding. While plus-size models do have curves and fat, they must control and smooth it out with a pair of Spanx or similar shapewear. Similarly, sociologist Ariane Prohaska (2021), in her study of plus-size pageant participants, details how several women used duct tape to "control the jiggle." All this physical labor of "disciplining corpulence" is aimed at preparing models' bodies for clients (Czerniawski 2012).

As freelance workers, models continue to modify their physical capital amid fluctuating conditions in the fashion market, as their agents guide and approve their actions. Individual body projects are no longer private but, rather, group efforts. Agents may recommend various forms of body modification, such as a weight change or cosmetic surgery, and demand compliance for continued representation. Models' bodies must fit within specific look and size specifications dictated by their agency; unauthorized body modifications may result in loss of job opportunities and/or agency representation. For example, in her ethnographic study of modeling industries in Europe, sociologist Sylvia Holla (2016) interviewed an editorial model named Mirthe who was given a free membership to a gym by her agency as an incentive to work on maintaining her thin, straight-size physique. Another model was chastised by her agent for eating crisps in their presence. In another case, agents demanded commercial model Nancy come to the agency once a week to be measured because they deemed her "too fat" (Holla 2016, 494). Holla concludes that agents and bookers "expect absolute devotion of their models in attaining beauty standards" (2016, 488) and hold them accountable to that standard. For plus-size models, these agent-directed body projects may involve a weight loss or gain to achieve the most marketable body of the moment. Models experience an overt, constant pressure to maintain their figures, since there is always someone, whether an agent or client, present with a tape measure— the industry's technology of control that legitimizes and normalizes constant surveillance of the body. A model's body is always under coercive surveillance.

Models and agents engage in an intimate working relationship, where private matters of the body are subject to public scrutiny. Individual body projects, such as a simple haircut or something more permanent like a piercing or tattoo, become subject to public debate. Models need to present any desired body modification to their agent, who, in turn, evaluates the proposed change based on fashion trends and employment potential. Any physical changes that affect a model's appearance need to be approved by the agency. She surrenders herself to a collective of aesthetic professionals—agents and bookers, designers, and stylists—who makes decisions about her body. The model plays a passive role in determining her appearance, i.e., modeling "look." Entwistle and Mears (2012) observed a booker at a New York agency recommend their models stop by for an "outfit check" before an important casting. Mears (2013) explains this level of surveillance creates an alienating experience for the model, who becomes a passive object on display who is always in constant anticipation of being judged. In London and New York, Entwistle and Mears (2012) observed models during castings in various stages of undress in semi-public spaces being measured, touched, and generally treated like mannequins.

The bodies of fashion models (whether straight or plus) are subject to the gaze of modeling agents and potential clients. Due to working within this kind of Foucauldian web of power relations with floating norms and constant surveillance, models become "docile" bodies disciplined to survey and continually improve upon their bodies. Agents evaluate and critique their models. In exchange for offering their models access to castings and clients, agents expect full disclosure and compliance from them. For example, Entwistle and Wissinger (2006, 783–84) interviewed a model who wanted to improve her marketability, so she asked her booker about "what *we* [emphasis added] need to do," i.e., change hairstyle or reshoot images for her portfolio. Agents determine the final look of their models. Agents, not the models themselves, have the final say.

During my time in the industry as a participant observer, I quickly learned that, as a model, I lost agency over my own body during my first meeting with an agent offering me representation. He advised me to "keep clean" Sunday night through the workweek till Friday. He warned, "I don't care what you do on your weekends but be sober and not bloated for Monday morning. You will not know too much in advance when you will have a casting, so be prepared." With this admonishment without provocation, he set the control parameters on my behaviors. Even on my personal time, I was subject to the agent's gaze.

Got Sexiness?

As subjects to fashion's and, more directly, an agent's gaze, models become objects in their own projects of becoming models. Susan Bordo (1993), in Foucauldian fashion, acknowledges that these pursuits ultimately lead women to become "docile" bodies duped into adhering to idealized constructions of feminine embodiment. Fashion, serving as a cosmetic panopticon, dictates the desirable parameters of physical appearance and keeps the body under its watchful eye. Amid this constant state of surveillance and judgment, sociologist Marcia

Millman argues women are prone to disembodiment because "they are taught to regard their bodies as passive objects others should admire" (1980, 202). This disembodiment intensifies in the fat body, where the fat woman resorts to only "living from the neck up."

Scholars in the field of Fat Studies, in response to this alienation and objectification, call for a change to the narrative, i.e., removal of stigma, and the reclamation of embodiment for the fat body. As seen in studies of burlesque and theatrical performers (Asbill 2009; McAllister 2009; Jester 2009; Kuppers 2001), fat women may achieve liberation from the stigma by revealing and redefining fatness through performance. For example, a burlesque performer uses the stage to reclaim her agency; her performance "supports a new, positive vision of fat sexual embodiment" (Asbill 2009, 300). To have a lasting effect, however, this performance must sexualize and beautify the fat body without relying on thin aesthetics, according to fat activist and communications scholar Kathleen LeBesco (2001). This is problematic because, as cultural theorist Samantha Murray argues, fat women continue to affirm the dictates of the cosmetic panopticon. According to Murray, "fat politics still privileges the thin body and attempts to imitate it. As fat girls, we still want to know what it is to be thin, even if we do not want to alter our fat" (2005, 161). With fat pool parties and lingerie parties, "we simply reverse the kind of response that fat bodies elicit within a dominant heteronormative framework" and "reproduce the obsession with the visible and the power of aesthetic ideals" (2005, 161). Therefore, even with the increase of plus-size models on the catwalk and within the pages of fashion magazines and catalogues, we still judge these models based on looks, not content. We still sexualize and objectify their bodies, reducing them to breasts and other assets.

In recent years, *Sports Illustrated*, for example, has taken steps to diversify the models included in its annual swimsuit issue. Robyn Lawley made headlines in 2015 when she became the first plus-size model featured in the swimsuit issue. The following year, the magazine chose plus-size model Ashley Graham for one of its covers. Then, Hunter McGrady became the "curviest model" to be featured by the magazine in 2017. In 2021, Yumi Nu became the issue's first Asian plus-size model.

These models, by way of posing to expose their sensual curves and directing their own gaze through the camera lens to the viewer, evoke a sultry 1950s pin-up vibe. In the online galleries, we see these models crawling through the sand, caressing their breasts, kneeling in the water with their chests pushed forward, pulling at their bikini bottoms, and even straddling a rowboat (Lawley in the 2015 issue). In the 2020 issue, Hunter McGrady appears styled with a retro updo accessorized with a bandana, a hairstyle associated with the pin-up era. Their flesh is exposed; plus-size models have appeared topless (e.g., Ashley Graham in the 2018 issue), in only body paint (e.g., Hunter McGrady in the 2017 issue), or completely naked (e.g., Tara Lynn in the 2019 issue). These stylized poses demand a rejection of bodily shame. In the 2021 issue, Yumi Nu arches her back as she lies on a surfboard in one image and wraps herself in a fishing net in another, daring the viewer to "catch me if you can." Ashley Graham, in 2016, flirtatiously uses only a large straw sun hat with "wish you were here" embroidered on the brim to cover her naked body. These women are confident and curvy, sensual, and seductive.

These sexy images may combat narrow definitions of beauty, but they do nothing to resist our culture's obsession with objectification. While this performance of fat appears to support a form of sexual liberation for plus-size women, it is really an act of reproducing heteronormative bodily ideals and what Samantha Murray calls "an obsession with the visible" (2005, 161). These plus-size models imitate the sexual displays of their straight-size counterparts of today and throughout the twentieth century. While the cover of the 2021 issue reads, "Opening Eyes, Speaking Truths, Changing Minds," the viewer sees an abundance of flesh and hears the images cry out, "desire me!" The truth is that women, including plus-size ones, are sexualized objects subject to the male gaze. The only progress made around the conversation over beauty and body positivity is that of inclusivity—more types of bodies are now worthy of objectification.

Notes

1 Straight-size models typically wear a US size 0–4 while plus-size models wear size 10–18.
2 See Banner 1983; Gilman 2008; Schwartz 1986; Stearns 1997 for more on the history of the fat body.
3 For more on the nature of size in fashion modeling, see Czerniawski (2021).
4 While research by Entwistle and Wissinger (2006) and Holla (2016) discus the bodily management practices of straight-size male models, research is needed to understand the case of plus-size male models.
5 Known as a "comp card," this 5x7-inch card is a model's business card. It includes the model's headshot on the front and a series of body display shots on the back. It also lists some personal statistics (i.e., height, dress size, bust, waist, and hip measurements, shoe size, hair color, and eye color) and the contact information for the model's agency.

References

Amador, Valery. 2006. "Plus Model Magazine Launches 2nd Issue with Curvy Cover Model Angellika." *PLUS Model Magazine*, September 1, 2006,.plus-model-mag.com/2006/09/plus-model-magazine-launches-2nd-issue-with-curvy-cover-model-angellika/. Accessed February 12, 2013.

Asbill, D. Lacy. 2009. "'I'm Allowed to Be a Sexual Being': The Distinctive Social Conditions of the Fat Burlesque Stage." In *The Fat Studies Reader*, edited by Esther Rothblum and Sondra Solovay, 299–304. New York: New York University Press.

Banner, Lois W. 1983. *American Beauty*. New York: Knopf, Distributed by Random House.

Bartky, Sandra. 1988. "Foucault, Femininity and the Modernization of Patriarchal Power." In *Feminism and Foucault: Paths of Resistance*, edited by Lee Quinby and Irene Diamond, 61–86. Boston: Northeastern University Press.

Bordo, Susan. 1993. *Unbearable Weight: Feminism, Western Culture, and the Body*. Berkeley, CA: University of California Press.

Brown, Harriet. 2015. *Body of Truth: How Science, History, and Culture Drive Our Obsession with Weight—and What We Can Do about It*. Boston, MA: Da Capo Press.

Crossley, Nick. 2001. *The Social Body: Habit, Identity and Desire*. London: Sage.

Czerniawski, Amanda M. 2012. "Disciplining Corpulence: The Case of Plus-Size Fashion Models." *Journal of Contemporary Ethnography* 41, 2, 3–29.

Czerniawski, Amanda M. 2015. *Fashioning Fat: Inside Plus-Size Modeling*, New York City: New York University Press.

Czerniawski, Amanda M. 2021. "Size Matters (in Modeling)." In *The Routledge Companion to Beauty Politics*, edited by Maxine Leeds Craig, 297–305. London: Routledge.

Dean, Deborah. 2013. *Performing Ourselves: Actors, Social Stratification and Work*. Basingstoke: Palgrave Macmillan.

Dhurandhar, Emily. 2016. "The Downfalls of BMI-focused Policies." *International Journal of Obesity* 40, 729–30.

Entwistle, Joanne and Ashley Mears. 2012. "Gender on Display: Performativity in Fashion Modelling." *Cultural Sociology* 7, 3, 320–35.

Entwistle, Joanne and Elizabeth Wissinger. 2006. "Keeping Up Appearances: Aesthetic Labour in the Fashion Modelling Industries of London and New York." *The Sociological Review* 54, 4, 774–94.

Gilman, Sander L. 2008. *Fat: A Cultural History of Obesity*. Cambridge, UK; Malden, MA: Polity.

Goffman, Erving. 1963. *Stigma: Notes on the Management of Spoiled Identity*. Englewood Cliffs, NJ: Prentice-Hall.

Holla, Sylvia. 2016. "Justifying Aesthetic Labor: How Fashion Models Enact Coherent Selves." *Journal of Contemporary Ethnography* 45, 4, 474–500.

Jester, Julia Grace. 2009. "Placing Fat Women on Center Stage." In *The Fat Studies Reader*, edited by Esther Rothblum and Sondra Solovay, 249–55. New York: New York University Press.

Kuppers, Petra. 2001. "Fatties on Stage: Feminist Performances." In *Bodies Out of Bounds: Fatness and Transgression*, edited by Jana Evans Braziel and Kathleen LeBesco, 277–91. Berkeley and Los Angeles: University of California Press.

LeBesco, Kathleen. 2001. "Queering Fat Bodies/Politics." In *Bodies Out of Bounds: Fatness and Transgression*, edited by Jana Evans Braziel and Kathleen LeBesco, 74–87. Berkeley and Los Angeles: University of California Press.

McAllister, Heather. 2009. "Embodying Fat Liberation." In *The Fat Studies Reader*, edited by Esther Rothblum and Sondra Solovay, 305–11. New York: New York University Press.

Mears, Ashley. 2008. "Discipline of the Catwalk: Gender, Power and Uncertainty in Fashion Modeling." *Ethnography* 9, 4, 429–56.

Mears, Ashley. 2013. "Made in Japan: Fashion Modeling in Tokyo." In *Fashioning Models: Image, Text and Industry*, edited by Joanne Entwistle and Elizabeth Wissinger, 134–56. London: Berg.

Millman, Marcia. 1980. *Such a Pretty Face: Being Fat in America*. New York: Norton.

Murray, Samantha. 2005. "(Un/Be)Coming Out? Rethinking Fat Politics." *Social Semiotics* 15, 2, 153–63.

Prohaska, Ariane. 2022. "'Nothing Should Jiggle While You're Moving'": Preparing the Fat Body for an American 'Plus-Size' Pageant." *Fat Studies* 11, 3, 258–72.

Puhl, Rebecca M. and Kelly D. Brownell. 2003. "Psychosocial Origins of Obesity Stigma: Toward Changing a Powerful and Pervasive Bias." *Obesity Reviews* 4, 213–27.

Schwartz, Hillel. 1986. *Never Satisfied: A Cultural History of Diets, Fantasies, and Fat.* New York: Free Press.

Stearns, Peter N. 1997. *Fat History: Bodies and Beauty in the Modern West.* New York: New York University Press.

Thomas, Pattie and Carl Wilkerson. 2005. *Taking Up Space: How Eating Well and Exercising Regularly Changed My Life.* Nashville, TN: Pearlsong Press.

Wolf, Naomi. 1992. *The Beauty Myth: How Images of Beauty Are Used against Women.* New York: Anchor Books.

17

BIG-GAY MEN ENTERING THE TWENTY-FIRST CENTURY

Global Perspectives on Fat-Affirming Subcultures and Imagery

Jason Whitesel

Reflecting on his 14-year-old self, a gay author writes: "I was fat, fem, and a fag. Too much? Maybe?" (Antebi 2015, 214). This author is burdened by embodying three identities that go against and exceed what is socially "desirable" for a man (Hillman 2021). Only recently is scholarship beginning to explore the multiple "marginalities that fat-and-femme queers must navigate" (Conte 2018, 25). For example, the dating app, Grindr, is called out for users deeming "fatness … as gross and unattractive," for devaluing and degrading a gay man's femininity, and for relegating fat/femme/racialized queer people to the "queer unwanted" (Conte 2018, 25–26). On homonormative dating apps and websites, fat-queer bodies, gendered and racialized, become targets for unbelonging (Volp 2017).

Reduced to a state of abjection, the undesirable "Otherness" of the queer unwanted amounts to people cast out as unfit candidates for *sexual citizenship* (Volp 2017). This term denotes a struggle for fundamental human and civil rights that everyone pursuing happiness in a democratic society expects: freedom of association and intimate companionship; authority over one's body; liberty to make bodily determinations; and protection from violence, abuse, and oppression. It includes equal access to intimacy, privacy, and safe spaces to explore pleasure. *Sexual citizenship* identifies the sexual encounter as a site of potential oppression. It expands sociological discourse around belonging to include entrenched hierarchies of sexual inclusion/exclusion. Synonyms for this term abound: *sexual personhood* to avoid trivializing legal status denial of migrants as rightless subjects through coopting the word "citizenship"; *partial citizenship*, meaning nonnormative bodies as sexual subjects are only okay if they keep it to themselves; *affective-* or *intimate citizenship*, referring to how people *ought to* handle their body and connect erotically with others as gendered beings; and the *sexual stranger* who crosses the line, maybe tolerated, but more likely invalidated as a "pervert" (Robson and

DOI: 10.4324/9781003140665-24

Kessler 2008). As sexual citizens, we're not all equal to love whom we want to love. Those who control their own bodies and body-image, or "self-regulate," are cast as liberated, while those who "fail" to do so are marked as the queer unwanted or "deviant." Preconditions for sexual recognition and inclusion serve a disciplinary function, yet some resist with their unruliness, live life differently, and reconfigure community boundaries of belonging through reactionary social movements and transgressive media and art worlds.

This chapter reviews visual culture, media, and scholarship on fat-gay men. It considers mainstream gay tastes; addresses fat shame in the gay world; discusses big-gay-men's fat-affirming subcultures and their responses to the body as an object of stigmatization. Unlike traditional approaches to body shape, size, and weight, it takes a Fat-Studies approach and asks: Why do we oppress people of size, and Who benefits from that oppression (Rothblum 2012, 3)? As Black/fat/ femme Jonathan Higgins (2019) puts it, "Why does the world hate me simply because I am larger than others?" (70).

As a relatively recent research subject, "fat-gay men" have not been firmly situated in the Fat Studies paradigm. I therefore go farther afield and incorporate allied perspectives that remain somewhat in the spirit of Fat Studies, though not calling itself such. For example, a quick Google Scholar search for "gay male body image" yields studies in clinical psychology, social work, health communications, public health, men's health, sexuality studies, and sociology. Research in these areas consistently reports anti-fat bias among gay men and heightened body-image concerns.

Coined within the fat-acceptance movement, *looksism* refers to a rigid set of standards for physical beauty pressures. Those who "fail" to measure up are deemed physically unattractive and sexually undesirable. In (sub)cultures in which the physical body is held in high esteem and given such power, those who cannot or do not conform to the ideal body type are dehumanized. According to psychological item surveys, most gay men are unhappy with their own bodies and they readily fat shame one another (Foster-Gimbel and Engeln 2016). Likewise, according to cyber-ethnographers, gay men compare and quantify bodies on social networking, dating, and hookup sites and they brazenly dole out sizeism (Robinson 2018). Such anti-fat bias makes it particularly difficult for big-gay men on dating apps. In all, one can surmise a domino effect of promoting a gay male *beauty myth*, promoting an *appearance stereotype*, and inculcating a sense of *body shame* in those striving to live up to the myth and stereotype.

To drive home the fact that visible fat-queer bodies have become a battleground, consider this example: people with fat gender-crossed identities living in a poor section of Manila, Philippines. There, a plus-size beauty pageant is held annually for gay, bi, and trans contestants who are fat in an urban-poor neighborhood (David and Cruz 2018). Thus, big/brown/queer bodies campily renegotiate global beauty ideals onstage. Generally, among the urban poor in Manila, fatness registers as a sign of wealth—that is, overconsumption. It represents big bodies being accused of "taking up too many resources" without regard to those suffering economically. However, in this pageant, fat occurs in bodies of sexual and gender minorities. Thus, the pageant enables researchers to study a complex intersection between size-acceptance of economically marginalized "third-gender" performers known as the effeminate *bakla* (David and Cruz 2018). Meanwhile, burly gay Bear men who party in Makati's posh Dasmariñas Village or charter a bus to the luxury seaside resort of Pico de Lorro distance themselves from economic inequity in the Global South while they trivialize the flamboyant *bakla* as an affront to middle-class respectability (Ardivilla 2017).

Scholarship on gay men has expanded to include subcultures that operate in defiance of the myth of body "perfection," proposing, instead, a different set of aesthetic ideals for the gay-male body. These subcultures include Girth & Mirthers who are big-gay men, or "chubs," and "chasers" (who are admirers of chubs and can be of any body type); Bears who celebrate and eroticize larger, furry, *masculinized* male bodies; and "Gainers & Encourages" who seek to intentionally "bulk up" and loosen the restrictions on their waistlines, and those who support them (Adams and Berry 2013; Textor 1999). Sociologist Lee Monaghan (2005) referred to these particular groups of gay men in the United Kingdom as "big handsome men" who reconfigure the politics of fat male embodiment. A couple of older studies provide an overview of organized subgroups and clubs for fat-gay men and their admirers. Among them is Alex Textor's (1999) taxonomic history of the community-organizing features of various subgroups that fall under the umbrella of big-gay-men and the media they produced. In addition, Lee Monaghan's (2005) *Body and Society* article is based on his ten-month ethnographic observation of websites, chat rooms, and e-mail exchanges with primarily gay informants involved in the eroticization of expansive male bodies online. Other researchers have studied specific groups for big-gay men, including Girth & Mirth, Bears, and Gainers & Encouragers. I will discuss these subcultures in turn, as well as examine the visual culture, media representations, and burgeoning scholarship on big-gay men.

The Girth-&-Mirth Subculture

"Feminine stigma" is attached to fat-gay men (Durgadas 1998, 370). Obviously, "not all fats are fems and vice versa" (Chow 2021, 13). Rather, the discriminatory phrase on gay dating apps, "No Fats, No Fems," co-constructs the two categories as "undesirable modes of gay being" (ibid.). Gay men who seek to build their masculine capital distance themselves from this "implicit identity conflation: Fats *are* Fems, Fems *are* Fats … leaving no space for shades of grey in gender performance" (Chow 2021, 13–14). Members of a subculture such as Girth & Mirth, however, do not *necessarily* seek to disavow effeminacy. Some seem open to embracing femininity as an integral component of an active fat-and-gay sexuality (Whitesel 2019). One fat-gay man commented that the group, Girth & Mirth, fosters a space where members do not have to put on the "butch" act (Whitesel 2014, 135).

Collectivities such as Girth & Mirth developed in reaction to gay fatphobia and to being ostracized. The subculture evolved into an organized network of social groups with international reach for big-gay men and their admirers to assuage their social injuries (Pyle and Loewy 2009; Whitesel 2014). Girth & Mirth promotes size acceptance and is suspicious of weight-loss surgery or other body modifications to cope with the gay-thinness imperative or the compulsion for muscularity (Whitesel and Shuman 2016). Not much scholarship has been published on Girth & Mirthers, notwithstanding *Fat Gay Men: Girth, Mirth, and the Politics of Stigma*, now almost a decade old, and its spinoff publications. Girth & Mirthers trouble and interrogate the thin-and-muscular body ideal in the gay male community through their performative play. They redefine themselves as embodied and sexual beings, motivated by the desire for, and of, other men.

Girth & Mirth started in the United States as a social-movement organization in the mid-1970s. It began in reaction to weight discrimination and big men's need for acceptance in the gay community (Whitesel 2014; Pyle and Loewy 2009; Textor 1999). Local clubs of Girth & Mirth provide a safe haven for men who are doubly stigmatized, both by body size and by sexual orientation. Such groups allow members to stake a claim to be ordinary in a society that sometimes regards them as "misfits." Worldwide, the organization offers a friendship circle to bring big-gay men out of social isolation. Members help one another deal with their "wounded attachment" to the gay community (Brown 1993). The activities the group sponsors have to do with the ordinary: ordinary people attending ordinary events, like a potluck supper with friends (Whitesel 2014). However, the COVID-19 pandemic has taken a toll on these local social and dining clubs, with even their online presence going silent or club websites down, as they have no activity calendars to post, of late.

Members of local chapters of Girth & Mirth also attend annual weekend reunions. One of these is the Super Weekend held every July within the premises of a gay-operated motel. It has taken place for over 25 years in America's heartland, Oklahoma City. This event features salacious pool parties, delicious cuisine, and fun-filled festivities, including a chub-and-chaser beauty pageant. Most guests are from the United States, but registrants have come from over 10 different countries. This venue provides a fat-affirming sanctuary for the big men and their admirers where they can express their sexuality without fear of ridicule or rejection. In July 2020, the 26th annual event was canceled due to COVID-19; in July 2021, barely 20 people attended the gathering; and for July 2022, the president responsible to organize the event posted to Facebook that the Super Weekend, "as it once was, has been killed by COVID … maybe we will find a new place to start over in 2023."

Another annual chub-and-chaser event is Convergence. For the last 30-plus years, it has been coordinated around Labor Day Weekend in the United States by the Big Gay Men's Organization. In American society, size often intersects with a class-based debasement; the assumption is that fat equals being "lazy" and "poor."

Therefore, some of the big-gay men in Girth & Mirth take a class-elevating route toward reducing fat stigma. They become middle-class consumers. Converging at a mainstream luxury hotel, they attend seminars, themed dances, and sightseeing excursions, all of which are about gay big men's seeking class validation (Whitesel 2014; Pyle and Loewy 2009). Those who attend Convergence differ somewhat from the "uncouth" Super Weekenders, who mostly make a mockery of status-seeking behavior. The 37th annual Convergence, slated to be held in San Diego in 2019 was canceled, reportedly due to high employee turnover rates at the host hotel. A spinoff event called BiggerVegas took off in 2009, described as "an annual international conference and social gathering of gay men of size and their admirers [which] serves the Chubs and Chasers community; a vibrant sub-culture of the gay community at large." At the time of this writing, over 1,600 people from more than 30 countries had signed up to attend the summer 2022 event (biggervegas.com n.d.).

Today versus immediately post-Stonewall, Girth & Mirth does not appear all that political. As explained in "Double stigma: Fat men and their male admirers" (2009), the group does not have an activist agenda, except as it pertains to identity politics. Although club members may not think of getting together for a pitch-in dinner as a political statement, group organizers understand the Girth-&-Mirth movement in identity-based terms (Whitesel 2014). As the board of directors for the 1996 anniversary of the San Francisco chapter wrote, "gay and bisexual bigmen, and those who prefer bigmen, have cast off the [restrictions] of hiding and insecurity and now revel in their proudly accepted identity" (Textor 1999, 219). Yet others find Girth & Mirth to be a "queer [segregated space] too small" and cramped (Giles 1998, 356), even identifying bigotry in some of the chubby-chasers' sexual exploits (Blotcher 1998). Nevertheless, "gay pioneers' initial work with Girth & Mirth was not simply to socialize; it was part of a whole culture of liberationist activity. Girth & Mirth was active before any mainstream fat-acceptance groups" (Suresha 2002b, 63–64). Therefore, Girth & Mirth is not just a manifestation of the gay scene divided, but also about political self-expression in a minor key, a softer, less perceptible fat activism. This politic coexists alongside the well-established big men's erotic media, another collective communication outlet that has "provided the backbone of the big men's movement's social networks" (ibid.).

Thus, the fat-gay male body is both a site of shame and stigma resistance (Whitesel 2019; McGrady 2016) and an "embodied contestation" (Pyle and Klein 2011). Through queer "fat performative protest," gay big men attempt to reclaim their "sexual citizenship" (Whitesel 2019). *Fat performative protest* involves embodied, sexual beings expressing disapproval of, or objection to, weight-based discrimination. Rather than accept body shaming, some joyfully disregard it, acting out imaginative responses to sizeism. This embodied protest playfully transforms stigmatized subjectivity and transgresses rules of corporeal conduct, in order to experience the same pleasures that others of normative size take for granted. Girth-&-Mirthers' activities range from the everyday to the carnivalesque, as they negotiate both invisible and visible forms of body-based discrimination. They provide an opportunity to examine how a stigmatized group of gay big men campily reconfigure their sullied identities (Whitesel 2014; *see also* Whitesel and Shuman 2013).

The Bear Subculture

The largest literature on groups for fat-gay men, whose weight plays a significant role in their self-identification, is devoted to big-and-hairy gay men: The Bear community, originally a splinter group from Girth & Mirth, "in the late 1970s and early 1980s" (McGrady 2016, 1699), which successfully branded itself to become a gay household name. The vibrant subculture of hirsute big-gay men, the Bears, is debatably kinder to not only those who are full-figured, but also perhaps getting on in years (Hennen 2008; McGrady 2016; Pyle and Klein 2011). Bears celebrate and eroticize larger, furry, masculinized male bodies. A wider discourse depicts fat as "feminizing filth": in response, Bears parlay their bigger build into masculine capital as having bodies like burly lumberjacks or football players (Edmonds and Zieff 2015, 419). It was estimated that in 2007, 1.4 million gay Bears lived in the United States (Mann 2010). Later, two large-scale surveys in 2013 reported that the Bears comprise 14–22 percent of the gay and bi-men's community (Moskowitz et al. 2013). The Bear community buffers against those pushing a sizeist, heteronormative agenda. It fosters resilience in the face of weight- and sexual-minority stigma (Mijas et al. 2020), and it promotes a healthy skepticism of fatphobic health messages, though sometimes uneven.

Having synthesized emerging health-research literature on Bears, Quidley-Rodriguez and De Santis (2017, 2016) discuss the clinical implications for healthcare providers working with Bears and the impact of weight-related stigma on Bears' self-esteem. Gough and Flanders (2009) discuss how Bears manage their subjectivities in a healthist and sizeist culture. Based on interviews with self-identified white British Bears in northern England, they report anti-fat abuse and negative stereotyping in childhood, medical settings, and the wider gay community. They find supportive and sexualized acceptance of bodily attributes, large bellies and body hair, within the Bear community (Gough and Flanders 2009). Bear talk emasculates young, slim "twinks," shaming and othering them as "shallow." It frames this thin-ideal of gay beauty as "prissy"—the oppositional anchor to the Bears' "regular-guy" masculinity (Hennen 2005). This rhetorical move expressing femmephobia further reifies the structures that perpetuate gay body shaming. Nevertheless, Bears counter dominant assumptions that pathologize ample size. They equate "fatter" with "healthier and happier," and, as relevant, they express discomfort with their thinner selves as looking unhealthy, especially with reference to HIV/AIDS-related stigma. They project self-confidence through the Bear ideal, and draw on "My body, my choice" to defy and rebel against social and media pressures to look like a Greek Adonis (Gough and Flanders 2009).

Similar themes appear in Patrick McGrady's (2016) content analysis of the magazine, *A Bear's Life,* and life-history interviews with Bears. McGrady traces a stage model of gay men "feeling weight stigma," "finding bears," "embracing the bear body," and "emulating the bear body." Bear-body emulation now includes anxieties around the "muscle bear phenomenon" (McGrady 2016, 1719). A flock of gym Bears obsessed with turning their bulk into muscle revives other Bears' feelings of being self-conscious about their weight and body type.

Edmonds and Zieff (2015) conduct interviews with Bear men and participant observation among San Francisco's Bear community. In the spirit of Fat Studies, they discuss "obesity" and "Body Mass Index" as oppressive terms and measures and promote "politically resistive … terminology that reintegrates the fleshy corporeality of lived experience" (417). Overall, they find evidence of the Bears' biopolitical resistance to body ideals, fat stigma, and mainstream gay values. But Bears find themselves in a double bind. Their community aims to be a safe space to build resilience and process the effect of fat stigma on their beliefs and actions, yet Bear life itself sometimes reproduces sizeist and healthist norms.

Edmonds and Zieff (2015) find that Bears suffer from compounded stigma. One respondent conflates his budding sexual orientation with body-image issues. He hates his fat body, covets other men's slim-and-muscular builds, and explains away his own developing sexual orientation as body envy versus same-sex romantic interest. Another respondent, attuned to "living fat in a thin-centric world" (Owen 2012, 290), describes his shortage of erotic capital in college as "a Bear trapped in a Twink's experience" (Edmonds and Zieff 2015, 423). Others report feeling physically incompatible with the trendy gay scene as their own bodies become ampler. Edmonds and Zieff (2015) also observe Bears *avoid fat stigma.* They bypass mainstream gay spaces that lack fat-friendly furniture and accommodations (*see also* McGlynn 2021) or where their intellectual and social contributions become diminished. One respondent enjoys the intense physicality of dancing with his shirt off, but only at Bear dance events where he feels safer from being judged. Other Bears say they avoid the gym, despite finding physical activity pleasurable, due to fat shame. Yet another enjoys surfboarding at the beach but goes less often than he desires because he feels self-conscious around most surfers due to his belly not befitting the traditional image of a surfer's body. Bears also suffer from *internalizing sizeism,* i.e., having been inculcated with the belief that their weight impinges on their quality of life; others accept the dominant position that their fat comes from their lack of physical discipline and bemoan falling short of the ideal muscle-Bear masculinity (McGrady 2016). Entering Bear spaces increases erotic capital for those who share an embodied likeness and eases them through the stigma of being fat and gay. Overall, like Girth & Mirthers, Bears contribute to greater public awareness of the need to diversify gay-male body images that allow for more democratic participation in the queer community.

In the late 1990s, on into the early 2000s, attempts were made to document Bear groups around the globe, mostly Euro-Bears (McCann 1997) or Bear group formation in Oceanic countries like Australia (Hay 1997; Hyslop 2001) and New Zealand (Webster 1997). One scholar assembles voices of different Bears from around the world (Suresha 2002a). He published a focus-group transcript that includes voices from three Bears in the Global South (Mexico, Argentina, and South Africa) and one from Turkey. More recently, a research team quantitatively examined predictors of self-esteem among members of The Bears of Poland Association (Mijas et al. 2020).

In interviews in one study, fat-gay- and bi-men in Delhi, India, affirm having internalized dominant discourses about fat as unhealthy, unsightly, and conveying social stigma (Patnaik 2014). Some Delhiite men seeking men are partial to reconfiguring their identities through the "Bear" label; others find the term too Western; still others dislike the unclean-animal association. *Bhallu*, Hindi for "Bear," also signifies "dumb," so Western gay terminology often does not universally translate. One older fat-gay Indian man laments that fatness makes him feel physically emasculated and devalued as a "fatty uncle" type on gay dating sites even as his social-class comforts appeal to younger gay men desiring an expensive date. One fat-gay Sikh man says his potential partners get turned off more by his turban and long flowing hair, which feminize him, than his body shape and size and furriness. Some of the fat-bodied interviewees say they feel they are sought out to cuddle or play with, but not taken seriously as sexual beings. On a Delhi gay dating site on the internet, popular cliques form around traditionally ideal male bodies.

A few studies on fat-gay men focus on gay Bears in East- and Southeast Asia (Lin 2014; Tan 2016, 2017). Gay Bear men in mainland China, Hong-Kong, Taiwan, and Malaysia pursue an "idealized gay bear appearance" (heavier, hairier, and masculine) to achieve higher status (Lin 2014, 188), wanting to become popular within Chinese gay Bear circuits. They report having higher self-esteem than do non-Bear-identified gay men. On the flipside, they also report being teased because of their appearance and feeling isolated in mainstream gay male communities. They do not create diverse "personal styles" like Western gay Bears supposedly do, but live up to the collectivist, "stereotypical Chinese gay Bear look," according to respondents (Lin 2014, 189–190). In the 1980s, U.S. gay Bears' popularity was diffused first to Japan, represented in fantasy drawings of *gatchiri* men or "G-men" eroticizing strongly built blue-collar bodies, and next to the rest of Northeast Asia, blossoming in Taiwan (Tan 2016, 2017).

In the United States, many gay Bears might blend into the suburbs as "regular guys"; but in Taipei, Bears stand out based on the inordinate time they spend in the gym, or by the tank tops with Bear emblems that they regularly wear. This speaks to the Bear changing global gay masculinity. While the early gay Bear subculture in the United States set out to celebrate bodily diversity, it is rendered quite the opposite in contemporary Taipei (Tan 2016, 2017).

In Taiwan, like in the United States, fat-gay men and Bears were once one and the same; by the late 1990s/early 2000s in Taiwan, *xiong* (meaning "bear" in Mandarin) differentiated themselves from the *zhu* (meaning "pig"), a pejorative term for a fat person, as in English. The muscle-bear body became the look to emulate, compelled, in part, by competition to differentiate oneself from the Bear pack by being bulky and muscular versus fat. Nevertheless, fat-gay men continue to try to self-identify as Bear, capitalizing on the label's fuzzy definition as to whether one registers as "Bear" or "Pig," which mostly depends on one's popularity in the gay circuit and vice versa (Tan 2016, 2017). Gay Bear men in Taipei report using their bodies and clothes to increase their erotic capital; their homogenized Taiwanese Bear look is due to their interpersonal competition (Tan 2016, 2017). Taiwanese gay Bears reject the Orientalizing label of "Panda" used in the United States to describe Asian gay Bear men. Instead, they use the label *xiong*. As it is evident, there is room for far more research on Bears outside the United States.

The Gaining Subculture

The subculture of Gainers and Encouragers reinforces both "the desire to look and feel like a 'real' man" among gainers overall and an interactive "attempt to work against the stereotype of the youthful, thin-and-fit gay male … 'twinks'" being the center of attention (Adams and Berry 2013, 318). The gaining community cites strict or cruel beauty norms to support what gainers are doing (Berlant 2011). They are committed to bodily transformation formed within a queer counterpublic (Warner 2005). They introduce flexibility into the rigid social system, experimenting with an alternate reality: *fat by choice, not by chance*; not unlike, and related to, unapologetically claiming one is "queer by choice, not by chance" (King-Miller 2011). Gainers reclaim "agency in their fatness" (Grimm 2021, 259), with one stating "the size of my body isn't an accident. I am in control of this. Being fat is what I want" (ibid., 260).

The gaining subculture includes those who encourage one another to expand physically and engage in gay-fat kink and "queer" bodily practices such as belly rubs and pro-weight-gain fantasies and behaviors. It also includes online forums and special events where big bellies are celebrated and flaunted. Gaining can be intensely pleasurable for some gay men; it often involves gay men seeking someone to mentally (and sometimes physically) nurture them to build a bigger body of fat (Campbell 2004, 137). This gaining subculture "disrupt[s] culturally prevalent ideas about size and sexual attractiveness" (Boylorn and Adams 2016, 93). Gainer-Encourager communities give participants permission to explore socially "deviant" bodily and sexual desires for gay men. For them, the taboo of their body being out-of-bounds adds to pleasurable gaining (Textor 1999). They discursively reconfigure what constitutes "sexy" (Campbell 2004, 136). Their online communication can involve physical exploration or may solely exist in the realm of mythmaking and fantasy, as imagined body transformation, which itself can be fulfilling (Oliverio 2016, 232).

Following the age of gay "Castro clones" who cruised one another and showed off their identical gym-toned bodies in snug jeans and tight T-shirts, the HIV-AIDS era brought oppositional pairings: big men with those of smaller build, chub with chaser, or gainer with encourager. Gainers often are concerned with "a particular kind of weight gain" (Textor 1999, 228). Some strive for an "*ex*-jock" body; that is, a "non-muscular weight gain" (ibid.). These men celebrate a beer belly loaded as a masculine signifier. HIV/AIDS also contributed to gay- and bi-men celebrating generously fleshed bodies, making ample size a counterpoint to the gradual wasting of the body from sickness (Textor 1999, 230; *see* also Kruger 1998).

Some gay men purposefully "stuff" or bloat themselves (Richardson 2010). Some entertain male pregnancy fantasies; but then again, such a "pregnancy" is masculinized, with the men often *pushing* the limits of how much their stomach can hold as it expands (Kyrölä 2011). Bloaters rarely desire to gain weight, but get pleasure on their own, or through the adoration of others, from abdominal distention (Adams and Berry 2013, 308). They move less against gendered norms as they become creators of their own growth, whereby size signals masculinity. They find pleasure in queering gender dynamics by looking like they are about to give birth. They are turned on by getting attention from others for their big belly; or they find "sensual pleasure" in "abandon[ing] restraint" on the abdominal muscles so that "a butch enough gay man" may like letting his belly "stick out" versus "sucking it in" (Stoltenberg 1998, 406).

Gainers' behavior is "counterintuitive," because desiring to inhabit a fatter body counters the assumption by those who sit in judgment that one becomes fat through self-neglect, having "let oneself go" (Adams and Berry 2013, 140). It troubles the dominant narrative that people must manage their weight for health reasons; that bodies should be small versus large; and should they expand, it should *not* be the result of enthusiastic, unapologetic choices. "Bodies out of bounds," meaning fatness as transgression, are understood as illogical and engender social disapproval from "good gays" (Adams and Berry 2013; Braziel and LeBesco 2001). Therefore, gainers worry that non-gainers may find out that they enjoy their fat body or will negatively react to them "coming out as a gainer" (Grimm, Morales, and Ferentini 2021, 15).

In the 1980s and 90s, gaining and encouraging newsletters were launched, followed by a 1-900 phoneline for men to record gaining fantasy ads (Textor 1999). In 1992, an erotically charged weight-gain convention started, called "EncourageCon." By 1996, the internet site GainRWeb was founded where men could meet online, and the print and phone media moved to this and other internet sites. The contemporary website, Grommr, chronicles this unfolding history on its webpage for the "Abridged Gainer History Project."

Online, pro-weight-gain communities shower big bellies achieved through trying to put on weight with messages of encouraging adoration. "FatClub.com," a pseudonym for an online gay-gainer community, started in 2003 and continued until 2011, with approximately 1,500 (mostly white) gay or occasionally bi-men members who were into weight gain. This community embodied its unique naming practices: "Gainers" (who want to get bigger), "Encouragers" (who motivate/feed gainers), and "Bloaters" (who expand with excessive fluid intake) (Adams and Berry 2013, 308). Among events that disrupt the thin-and-fit gay-male aesthetic is the "Belly Rub Weekend" over Labor Day Weekend in Chicago started in 2010/2011. This event "espouses queer sensibilities ... that ... disrupt ... norms of body size, desire, and sexuality ... celebrating bigger, expanding bodies" (Boylorn and Adams 2016, 95).

Big-Gay Men's Visual Culture: Art, Performance, Digital Media, Fashion, and Pornography

Art

Fat-gay men strive to democratize and diversify gay desire; in their visual and virtual culture they trend toward the "art of sexual transgression, and in particular the sexualized art of the body" (McNair 2002, 13). For example, Bear Art "opens up wider fields of erotic possibility beyond that of the conventionally hard phallic body" (Beattie 2014, 115). It represents diverse forms of intimate relations between big-gay men; tactile expressions like Bear hugs at a play party or nuzzling another man's ample furry chest at a bar or campground. Such imagery has been censored from gay representation in the main and first emerged in homoerotic Bear magazines and zine culture.

Bear and Chubby Art makes room for a rounder aesthetic than representations of the iconic chiseled gay physique. It offers images of gay men that depart from the Grecian ideal of the sculpted hard body in classical art and favors images of men with squeezable curves and fat accumulated along the chin and neck or around the chest, abdomen, flanks, buttocks, and thighs (Whitesel 2017a). Art depicting Bear and chubby men's bodies may cause a paradigmatic shift in the viewer's own aesthetic and erotic politics (Beattie 2014). Haptic Bear art involves a sense of touch. It invites one to imagine fondling flabby, round, dimpled parts of the body, which are generally off limits to touch or admire. Such art turns big men into sites of whole-body sensuality versus phallic pleasures as the be-all and end-all of gay sex (Whitesel 2017a; Beattie 2014; Hennen 2005).

Bear Art can be seen by insider academics as a form of queer-fat activism (Beattie 2014). Its viewers may be ample-bodied or not. Such art allows admirers, thick or thin, to not feel socially deviant, but to feel okay for having such desires. One Bear artist has said, elevating fat-gay men to the level of art "reflects how I see my own position in a world that tells me I should find skinny women attractive, and I happen to find fat men attractive" (Whitesel 2017a, 5). Likewise, Jerome Stueart (2021), a creative writer who makes watercolor paintings of Bear fairies in gardens or fat-queer Bearish superheroes, writes about having used his own body as the subject of artistic exploration to teach him who he was, love his body, and be able to see his fat hairy body as sensual, especially having grown up being taught he was supposed to be a good Baptist boy attracted to girls.

Bear and Chubby Art reaches beyond big men's subcultures alone and has found its way into galleries. A recent art exhibition, "Girth and Mirth," by UK artist James Unsworth, represented scantily clad fat-gay men once featured in the erotic magazine, *Bulk Male* (Nagle 2020; Whitesel 2017a). Likewise, James Gobel, a Californian artist, uses felt, yarn, and fabric—materials associated with feminine handicrafts—to celebrate big-gay men's unsung sensuality in art (Blake 2000; *see also* Watson 2016). New York City artist Nayland Blake—a bearish, bi-racial, nonbinary artist—probes changing relationships with one's fat body, depicting ample weight and fat as erotic signifiers, otherwise known as symbolic inversion of norms. Blake's performance piece, *Starting Over* (2000), is a video of the artist struggling to dance with taps on in an oversized bunny suit stuffed with 140 pounds of dried beans. That weight is equal to the weight of Blake's partner of 12 years. Or the same artist's 1998 video installation, "Gorge," features the artist sitting shirtless, being handfed copious amounts of food for an hour by a shirtless Black man (Russeth 2019). Later staged live, the audience was invited to feed Blake. Similarly, Campbell (2004) analyzes pictures of Gainer Art he found circulating in his online study of the embodied sensual experiences of gay men; similar images appear in a documentary, *Hard Fat* (2002) by Frédéric Moffet.

Performance

Another reaction to the stigma of gay effeminacy is drag. Ami Pomerantz (2017) studies the representation of fat drag-queens on the reality-TV contest, *RuPaul's Drag Race*. This show sends conflicting messages to contestants of size. Sometimes, it supports fat pride; at others, it fails to embrace "big girls," rarely allowing fat contestants to win the crown. It simultaneously supports bodily diversity but is also quick to discriminate against larger queens. The show typecasts fat performers as comedy queens, consistently the butt of fat/eating jokes, even as it exploits contestants' storylines about body image and weight struggles to tug at viewers' heartstrings. The show feigns size acceptance, even as it condemns fatness. After 14 years of the show on television, fat queens get more airtime as the seasons progress and the franchise expands, yet they continue to struggle over compliance with, and resistance to, fat oppression.

Digital Media

Conventional and mainstream gay media is dissatisfying for those who possess or desire a body that does not conform to the gay male beauty myth. In response, some construct and consume imagery of men's bodies that transcend, yet do not fully reject, the "pretty-boy" aesthetic that has dominated gay representation. A 2010 study explores "fatvertisements" that recreate commercial images by recasting fat bodies for the original models or by photoshopping existing images to give the male model a paunch. Media hype around male celebrities—whose photographs undergo retouching to hide their "spare tire" around the middle—serve as inspiration for these morphed images (Whitesel 2010). Online fatvertisements appear to be a mixed mode of resistance, as they still rely on the worship of other idealized male qualities such as facial attractiveness or "babyfaces" that signal youthful appearance.

Other virtual worlds include BiggerCity, the largest online community for gay chubby men and their admiring chasers to form a "collective identity" (Pyle and Klein 2011, 82) or smartphone apps like Scruff that originally were "targeted primarily at bears and their admirers … generally [an] older, larger-bodied… demographic" (Roth 2014, 2113, 2124), though recent studies find the app is trending toward prioritization of muscled bodies (Chow 2021). They also include Grommr, a hybrid word melded from the "gro" in "growth" plus the "mm" in "community," and a social network and dating site for gay and bisexual men self-described as being "into fat and fatter bellies, chubby men, beer guts, big muscle and chunky muscle, bears and non-bears, and so much more" (Grommr n.d.). Photos, videos, artwork, and original stories about fat-gay men circulate on a variety of platforms, including Twitter, Instagram, Tumblr, and YouTube, while varieties of relatively inexpensive gainer/encourager erotic fiction abound on the e-commerce site, Amazon.

Fashion

Hegemonic masculinity, or the ideal, dominant conception of what it means to be a man, comes down to anti-femininity (Barry 2019). In the contemporary West, fashion equates with women, plus self-care and bodily flaunting makes one vulnerable, marked as feminine. Still, recent shifts in menswear include sensual slim-fit clothes and designs celebrating gender play and androgyny. Yet, these changes did not destabilize hegemonic masculinity, but rather added a new ideal, the boyish or gender-neutral waif, in addition to the masculine, muscular ideal. The addition of the skinny male ideal further marginalizes fat men, and most clothing for people of size (if available at all) is concealing as a normalizing mechanism to cover up fat people (Barry 2019).

Self-couture (versus *haute couture*) relies on crafting one's own outfits to be fabulous, developing a style politic to displace and expose norms of fashion and claim visibility. Fabulousness exceeds the archetypical looks of men being cowboys who wear jean jackets, or ivy leaguers who wear varsity jackets over a button-down shirt tucked into khakis. Fabulousness subverts the connection between sex-and-gender-dressed bodies (Barry 2019).

Ben Barry (2019), who studies social transformation through fashion, assembled case studies of queer, working-class fat people's engagement with fashion. A fat-queer trans man who had top surgery to be flat-chested cut off the bottom of a *Hooter's* shirt to make a crop top, challenging gender norms and thin-body ideals by exposing his fat, hairy stomach in a shirt meant for a Florida beach girl to show off her toned stomach and breasts. This fashion choice disrupts gender norms while it signals fat acceptance. This same person wears a "Nothing tastes as good as skinny feels" shirt, a quote by supermodel Kate Moss touting the size-zero aesthetic. In so doing, the fat-queer man disrupts the notion that only a thin body feels good because he goes about his daily activities, including dining out, wearing this shirt. Note that as a man-identified wearer, he can feel somewhat confident in breaking these norms due to relative gender privilege.

Likewise, Barry (2019) reported on a fat Black gay performer who wears bedazzled, exaggerated silhouettes to take up space when he walks into a room or dons revealing lace tops and leopard-print attire. This flies in the face of the Black and big body inciting fear, with his flamboyant dress rebelling against the devaluation of the fat, Black body. He posts pictures on social media of himself dancing, defying the stereotype of the fat, Black body as lazy, expanding beyond white women's fat activism. He also wears a sequin deep-V-neck top to expose his lush chest hair, which unsettles clothing along a gender binary where women wear such shirts showing their cleavage or gay men would only do so if they manscaped their chests. In sum, style can offer the possibility to dream up another world that embraces gender nonconforming fat bodies (Barry 2019).

Websites have formed in response to lack of fashion for queer men of size. For example, a blog on Tumblr, "Chubby Guy Swag," supports those feeling defeated by the fashion industry, looking to get their groove back. This site serves as a confidence booster with style references from which fat-queer people could borrow. It can assist not only fat-gay men, but also fat-trans men, fat gender-queer people, and people labeled with "Down syndrome" who may have a short, stocky body. It is clear that the democratization of fashion starts from do-it-yourself looks. It forges creative style inspiration from a lack of extended size options, and then shares it with others (Whitesel 2015). Chubby Guy Swag was co-founded in 2010 by Cara Eser and Abigail Spooner as a "safe space for plus-size men ... to include them in the conversation on ... fat acceptance" and "to promote body diversity ... amongst men" (Eser and Spooner n.d.). This community has international reach, providing a forum for big men and others who do not fit the mass media's image of the "ideal" body type, but aspire toward becoming fashionable. They therefore appreciate the information and wisdom users share on this site. In fact, several users submit selfies in their favorite outfits. The site features posts and photos by men of size who are queer, disabled, people of color, and/or "flat broke." They are mostly young adults who are underrepresented in both mainstream and queer media (Whitesel 2015).

Pornography

Chubby-gay porn offers a venue where gay men with ample builds have their body type taken seriously, thereby rendering them sexual citizens (Highberg 2011). Porn, like being gay, fat, or both, is often treated as shameful and moves one to cover up and hide one's fat body, yet chubby-gay porn is a visible performance, albeit one that constitutes itself outside of "official" public opinion, a "queer counterpublic," as it were (Berlant and Warner 1998, 558).

Chubby-gay porn online includes both user-generated photos and videos (open access, some paywalled) and longer films produced by small suppliers accessed for a fee (Highberg 2011). In these videos and films, men engage intimately, erotically, and sexually with themselves and other men of various shapes and sizes. Frequently "real-life" porn, they often begin with interviews and confessionals of amateur performers accompanied by occasional dialogue throughout. This self-authored style allows big-gay men's archive of personal, private, embodied expressions to become social, cultural, and public histories of sexuality. In these erotic films, fat-gay pornographic "performers" are sometimes shown as intimate partners in fulfilling, loving relationships. This depiction makes the films not just about fat sex to titillate the viewers, but also about "real" relationships and mutually pleasurable activities, including eating, as an embodied practice, wherein real-life "actors" in the films highlight the ways in which a fleshy body and fat distribution across one's various body parts can be evoked in all aspects of sensuality. Fat-gay men have a place within other pornographic genres like sadomasochistic and fetish porn as well (Highberg 2011). In all, fat-gay porn provides a much-needed venue for viewers to see desires and to vicariously feel pleasures that might otherwise be denied to them in a thin and straight world. In films and television shows, big-gay men are often portrayed as shoulders to cry on or as the comic relief; rarely, if ever, do they play the love interest, get showered with attention, or get treated seriously as adult sexual beings.

Some researchers have questioned whether chubby-gay porn makes a progressive statement for fat-and-queer people (Bunzl 2005). While porn desires to be seen, fat is supposed to be hidden, yet fat-queer porn wants gay-chubby sexuality to be known (Kipnis 1996). Chubby-gay porn films like Maximum Density Productions' infamous *Bustin' Apart at the Seams* from 1998 or *Bulk Male* magazine, the fat/gay equivalent to *Playboy*, feature big-gay men who weigh 200–300 pounds. They cater to the tastes of chasers, those defined by their desire for bigger men. Although such media may be sexually liberating, it is far from providing sexual equality; superchubs, who weigh significantly more than chubs, are often absent from the imagery or appear as bedbound objects of handsy chasers. Moreover, little racial/ethnic diversity or gender nonconformity exists in fat-gay pornographic media (Bunzl 2005; Nagle 2020). In response to older pornography on Bears that tended to feature only white men of size, two San Francisco film producers created and directed an erotic series called "Real Bears of Color." They themselves were queer- and fat-identified gay men with Bear bodies in a romantic relationship (Ingraham 2015).

Future Research Directions

Outside U.S. Borders

Little-to-no effort has been made to establish research into social networks for fat-gay men in Latin America, Africa, and the Middle East. Seldom having gone beyond U.S. borders for its material, Fat Studies of gay men should consider how body shape and size affects people across nations, races, ethnicities, and religions. Future researchers studying fat-gay men should engage in greater cross-national, comparative research. For example, an autoethnography by Spyridon Chairetis (2019) draws on the author's personal experience "of what it means to be queer, Greek, fat, and male in Greece and the UK" and acknowledges the ambiguity of fat/queer/binational embodied experience (184).

Same-Gender-Loving Big Men of Color

Prior work on fat-gay men has rarely been critically examined for allowing white-male privilege to dominate the narratives. Future Fat Studies researchers must better articulate the intersectionalities of size, sexual orientation, and gender identity with race, class, age, ability, and nationality. They must consider how big men's racial or ethnic identity co-construct their fat gayness, such as how it positions them differently within any of the subcultures chronicled in this chapter.

Same-gender-loving big men of color remain overlooked in the event advertisements and erotic imagery of various big men's groups. Gay prides and circuit parties across America also leave out big men of color. They reinforce the mainstream gay media's focus on young, hairless, thin, or muscular *white* men. In reaction to being excluded by various big men's communities in the United States, big men of color have created their own weekend events that place men of size and color at the fore. These include Heetizm Myami, Big Boy Pride Orlando, and Heavy Hitters Pride Houston. For example, the 2017 theme for Heavy Hitters' weekend was "My Presence Matters." The group describes itself as "a place where EVERY pound has a story" and where attendees come to "celebrate the urban man of size, his admirers and allies." If it weren't for imagery like that put out by Heetizm, Big Boy Pride, and Heavy Hitters, same-gender-loving big men of color might have difficulty recognizing themselves in existing white-dominant big-gay-men's imagery (Hennen 2005), and thus might internalize the message, "You are not welcome" (Whitesel 2017b, 2019).

Fat/Femme/Brown and Feeling Down

Caleb Luna (2014) writes, "Under colonial constructions of beauty and desire, being fat and brown and queer and femme means being ugly [and] feeling unlovable" (para. 4). To be fat, "in queer male communities, seems to only be desired in hairy, bear bodies, as the beard provides confirmation of masculinity to offset the feminization of fatness" (Luna 2014, para. 10). Luna, a birth-assigned male who is gender apathetic, traces their smooth brown body with very little facial-hair to "indigenous roots," bristling when two of the three Bs of Bearness rattled off, "beard, belly, body hair" (ibid.), leaves them feeling "too brown, too femme, [and] too queer for the bears" (para. 11). Like women, Luna (2021) faces public harassment for feminized brown-skin fatness. Men observe Luna's "breasts" and "big, soft belly" with the view that onlookers are entitled to make gender attributions based on "subtle intricacies of a body beyond genitals" (73, 75). Luna will not be pressured to gender-identify, but concedes "my gender *is* fat" (ibid., 77); "my fatness produces my gender" (ibid., 73). Conversations about gender complexity must reckon with the multidimensional forms of appearance-based discrimination and sexual harassment that fat-queer Black, Indigenous, and people of color experience.

Jonathan Lyndon Chase presents a case study of an artist who grapples with the race-gender inequality Luna brings up in their critique of the Bears. Chase (born 1989) inhabits a Black, genderfluid, neuro-divergent body, using it to deliver messages about empowerment in the midst of a toxic sociopolitical climate in America. They create paintings of Black-and-queer joy, of intimately engaged fat and gender-nonconforming bodies. Chase has commented that in the era of gay marriage, as a fat, queer, Black, nonbinary person, this marriage right will not stop gendered, racist violence or execution by a police officer. Thus, Chase's artwork depicts policed bodies—exploring race, gender, sexuality, and body type on the artist's own terms rather than those imposed by white, cisgender, straight, slender powerbrokers or those of "respectable" Black people who might wish to distance themselves from a fat-and-queer Black body. Chase wants to create imagery depicting Black people, who were assigned male at birth, as desired for being round, soft, and having breasts. They believe we need new images to blast people out of standards of respectability and dominant beauty norms. Critics have described Chase's art as "Picasso-meets-Paris is Burning" (Tilley 2018, para. 2) and have chronicled them at the vanguard of exposing racist, fatphobic, and femme-hating sectors of the LGBTQ+ community.

Chase, as a rising mixed-media artist based in Philadelphia, combines traditional and digital collage, and further expresses themselves through art journaling, poetry, storytelling, social fiction writing, sci-fi fantasy, and embodied arts-based research. They draw, paint, and photograph half-naked or nude contorted figures with large full lips, tight fade haircuts, and perfectly trimmed facial hair. They depict Black queer bodies in affectionate, sexually suggestive poses of performing a sexual act. The bodies in the artwork come in all shapes and sizes, but tend toward fleshy chests, protruding stomachs, round buttocks, and fat rolls. Some figures exhibit a clearly defined penis through their athletic shorts while others tug at their erect organ or insert it in their partner's anus; still others take the "prone position, anus in the air" (Puar 2007, 85), indicative of the "role in queer theory played by the anus, an orifice all genders have in common" (Paul 2015,

241). Models in the artwork don backwards-turned baseball caps, du-rags, or streetwear juxtaposed near lipstick shown with the lid removed (Chase 2018); or in a self-portrait photo they wear a casual wavy wig and lingerie, revealing black-line tattoos on their arms and, in another photo, on their *décolletage* (Chase 2020). Chase's artistic imagery draws from their day-to-day experiences as a Black, fat, nonbinary, queer, and bipolar artist to complicate racial meanings, ideal bodies, gender ideologies, sexual stereotypes, and neurotypicality.

With Chase's artwork currently in my thoughts, I concur with Luna's (2014) desire to better "work … through what it means to be ugly and be beautiful, and [to] better understand … investments in beauty" (14). In " 'Moving Toward the Ugly: A Politic Beyond Desirability,' Mia Mingus pushes [readers] to transcend the beauty binary and move toward what she calls magnificence, and embracement of the ugly and the diversity of the body—of *every* body. Mingus frames beauty as an inherently exclusionary construct that erases people of color, trans and gender non-conforming folks, and disabled folks" (ibid.). Thus, for many of the groups chronicled herein, "is reclaiming beauty radical or assimilationist" and "does it mean something different for … fat, brown, queer femme" bodies (ibid.)? Future research must go beyond the Western context, expand its focus to same-gender-loving big men of color, and deeply consider fat … queer, nonbinary or femme … Black, Brown, Indigenous, or biracial people assigned male at birth. The wealth of creative writing published as of late by Latinx and Black fat-gay/queer men is encouraging. For example, Miguel Morales's (2019) "Does this poem make me look fat?" and other creative writing found in *The (Other) F Word* and *Fat and Queer.*

In *Belly of the Beast* (2021), Da'Shaun L. Harrison calls for a paradigm shift in the world order of anti-fatness rooted in antiblackness that became a one-two punch for fat-Black people, making the world inhospitable to their bodies. A fat, Black, disabled, queer and trans-nonbinary writer and community organizer who was assigned male at birth, Harrison indicts the popular body-positivity movement urging "good fatties" to love their bodies and flaunt health ideals. As a continuation of the racist history of "benevolent anti-fatness" (4), the movement reinforces ableism. However, Harrison (2021) argues, no amount of self-love will liberate fat-Black people from being refused or fired from a job due to weight and race bias; neither from being sexually assaulted at higher rates yet deemed undesirable, all the while eliciting less empathy; nor from being misdiagnosed or underdiagnosed, enduring untimely deaths due to medical negligence; nor from being executed by the police.

"Desire Capital" represents Harrison's (2021, 12) take on sexual citizenship. Based on appearance capital, the politics of "pretty privilege" (11) and ugly subjugation grants or restricts access: it ensures resources to flow toward "highly desirable" people and leaves "ugly Others" uncared for. Thus, Black people, gender nonconformists, and the fat and disabled are barred from equal access to status, love, and security to navigate the world with confidence. The imbrication between antiblackness and the persecution of ugliness renders Black-fat people undesirable and "deserving" structural violence for being too dark and too big— an arrangement that benefits those with desire capital. No safety net exists for those considered too fat, too gay, and too Black; as Harrison (2021) points out, even "the closet can't offer safety" (43). Erasure of fat-Black queer people occurs in-house too. Harrison (2021) found that fat-Black trans people who identified as male, transmasculine, or nonbinary did not fit comfortably into existing social arrangements. In a world invested in preserving white cis-heteronormative comfort, their only option is to "commit themselves to repressing or doing away with their queerness and their fatness" (ibid.).

Harrison (2021) echoes Luna's take on gender: "fatness functions as a gender of its own. Fatness fails, and therefore disrupts, the foundation on which gender is built" (102). This explains why doctors expect fat-trans men to lose weight before approving gender-affirming procedures or why some fat-Black boys experience a racialized un-gendering of their body by down-low men, such as those who sexually assaulted young Harrison whose ample thighs and undulating buttocks read like a Black girl's, rather than an athletic boy's, body. Harrison (2021) thereby argues that "gender is birthed from violence, and therefore fatness operating as its own gender is not liberatory so much as it is forced. [F]at bodies ... are already positioned outside of the designated or assigned 'look' of gender" (103). Thinness for women and muscularity for men define binary gender. Either way, if one seeks gender affirmation, one "must always be pushing away from fatness" (ibid.) in order to fit comfortably within the parameters of "ideal" gender.

Conclusion: Encouraging Fatness as a Form of Protest

As sociologists of the body and embodiment, or as Fat Studies scholars, we need to continue asking ourselves: Who gets represented in fat-affirming queer communities? Who gets left behind? Fat Studies highlights historical and cross-cultural variations in attitudes toward ample weight; counters dominant beliefs about how people of size ought to act; affords alternative reconfigurations of talk surrounding those who are targets of bias and stigma; promotes self-acceptance and "health at every size" as an alternative to "healthy-weight" fanaticism upon which much current public-health policy rests; and calls for social change in the sizeist (American) society.

Future research should embrace Crawford's (2017) clarion call to continue to explore how people creatively occupy fatness as a form of protest in their desires to imagine a fat presence and fat futures, despite fatphobes who work from the controlling image that fat people are "lazy" and not able to do much and therefore fatness is not able to signify much, which speaks to the "visual injustices" at hand (Przybylo and Rodrigues 2018). Yet fat bodies defy thin-normative expectations, queer in the sense that they interrupt and unsettle what we think we always-already knew, and I look forward not only to optimistic organizing (e.g., Girth &

Mirthers) against fatphobic cruelty, but also to reactions that understand fat more ambiguously, even muddling gender norms with fatness, refusing to facilely settle, but rather embracing fat in protestation of any bodily normative future.

References

Adams, T., & Berry, K. (2013). Size matters: Performing (il)logical male bodies on fatclub. com. *Text and Performance Quarterly*, 4, 308–325.

Antebi, N. (2015). On being different and loving it. In R. Chastain (Ed.), *The politics of size: Perspectives from the fat acceptance movement* (pp. 207–216). Santa Barbara, CA: Praeger.

Ardivilla, J. (2017). From the one growling from a corner in the dark: Metro Manilla bear culture and the pandering to patriarchy. *The Reflective Practitioner*, 2, 28–42.

Barry, B. (2019). Fabulous masculinities: Refashioning the fat and disabled male body. *Fashion Theory: The Journal of Dress, Body and Culture*, 23(2), 275–307.

Beattie, S. (2014). Bear arts naked: Queer activism and the fat male body. In C. Pausé, J. Wykes, & S. Murray (Eds.), *Queering fat embodiment* (pp. 115–129). New York, NY: Routledge.

Berlant, L. (2011). *Cruel optimism*. Durham, NC: Duke University Press.

Berlant, L., & Warner, M. (1998). Sex in public. *Critical Inquiry*, 24(2), 547–566.

BiggerVegas. (n.d.). What is BiggerVegas. Retrieved from www.biggervegas.com/help/faq

Blake, N. (2000). James Gobel [Exhibition essay]. Los Angeles, CA: Hammer Museum. Retrieved from hammer.ucla.edu/exhibitions/2000/hammer-projects-james-gobel/

Blotcher, J. (1998). Justify my love handles: How the queer community trims the fat. In D. Atkins (Ed.), *Looking queer: Body image and identity in lesbian, bisexual, gay, and transgender communities* (pp. 359–366). New York, NY: Harrington Park Press.

Boylorn, R., & Adams, T. (2016). Queer and quare autoethnography. In N. Denzin & M. Giardina (Eds.), *Qualitative inquiry through a critical lens* (pp. 8–98). New York, NY: Routledge.

Braziel, J., & LeBesco, K. (2001). *Bodies out of bounds: Fatness and transgression*. Berkeley, CA: University of California Press.

Brown, W. (1993). Wounded attachments. *Political Theory*, 21(3), 390–410.

Bunzl, M. (2005). Chaser. In D. Kulick & A. Meneley (Eds.), *Fat: The anthropology of obsession* (pp. 199–210). New York, NY: Penguin.

Campbell, J. (2004). *Getting it on online: Cyberspace, gay male sexuality, and embodied identity*. New York, NY: Harrington Park Press.

Chairetis, S. (2019). Ambivalence in encounters with my big fat Greek closet. *Whatever. A Transdisciplinary Journal of Queer Theories and Studies*, 2, 179–198.

Chase, J. (2018). *Quiet storm*. New York, NY: Capricious.

Chase, J. (2020). *Wild, wild, wild west & haunting of the seahorse*. New York, NY: Capricious.

Chow, J. (2021). No fats, no fems, no problems? Working out and the gay muscled body. *Sexualities*. Advance online publication. doi: 10.1177/13634607211018331

Conte, M. (2018). More fats, more femmes: A critical examination of fatphobia and femmephobia on grindr. *Feral Feminisms: Queer Feminine Affinities*, 7, 25–32.

Crawford, L. (2017). Slender trouble: From Berlant's cruel figuring of figure to Sedgwick's fat presence. *GLQ: A Journal of Lesbian and Gay Studies*, 23(4), 447–472.

David, E., & Cruz, J. (2018). Big, bakla, and beautiful: Transformations on a Manila pageant stage. *Women's Studies Quarterly* 46, 1–2, 29–45.

Durgadas, G. (1998). Fatness and the feminized man. In D. Atkins (Ed.), *Looking queer: Body image and identity in lesbian, bisexual, gay, and transgender communities* (pp. 367–371). New York, NY: Harrington Park Press.

Edmonds, S., & Zieff, S. (2015). Bearing bodies: Physical activity, obesity stigma, and sexuality in the bear community. *Sociology of Sport Journal*, 32(4), 415–435.

Eser, C., & Spooner, A. (n.d.). Chubby Guy Swag was founded by bodyposi activist and dj/producer, zacheser, in 2010. Retrieved from chubbyguyswag.tumblr.com

Foster-Gimbel, O., & R. Engeln. (2016). Fat chance! Experiences and expectations of antifat bias in the gay male community. *Psychology of Sexual Orientation and Gender Diversity*, 3(1), 63–70.

Giles, P. (1998). A matter of size. In D. Atkins (Ed.), *Looking queer: Body image and identity in lesbian, bisexual, gay, and transgender communities* (pp. 355–358). New York, NY: Harrington Park Press.

Gough, B., & Flanders, G. (2009). Celebrating "obese" bodies: Gay "bears" talk about weight, body image and health. *International Journal of Men's Health*, 8(3), 235–253.

Grimm, B. (2021). Dropping fictions and gaining visibility. In B. Grimm, M. Morales, & T. Ferentini (Eds.), *Fat and queer: An anthology of queer and trans bodies and lives* (pp. 251–260). London, UK: Jessica Kingsley Publishers.

Grimm, B., Morales, M., & Ferentini, T. (2021). *Fat and queer: An anthology of queer and trans bodies and lives*. London, UK: Jessica Kingsley Publishers.

Grommr. (n.d.). Abridged gainer history project. Retrieved from www.grommr.com/Home/Community

Harrison, D. (2021). *Belly of the beast: The politics of anti-fatness as anti-blackness*. Berkeley, CA: North Atlantic Books.

Hay, B. (1997). Bears in the land down under. In L. Wright (Ed.), *The bear book: Readings in the history and evolution of a gay male subculture* (pp. 225–238). New York, NY: Haworth Press.

Heavy Hitters Pride. (2017). My presence matters empowerment summit. Retrieved from www.facebook.com/events/1809292522725796

Hennen, P. (2005). Bear bodies, bear masculinity: Recuperation, resistance, or retreat? *Gender and Society*, 19(1), 25–43.

Hennen, P. (2008). *Faeries, bears, and leathermen: Men in community queering the masculine*. Chicago, IL: University of Chicago Press.

Higgins, J. (2019). Black, fat, fem: The weight of a queen. In A. Manfredi (Ed.), *The (other) F word: A celebration of the fat and fierce* (pp. 67–71). New York, NY: Amulet Books.

Highberg, N. (2011). More than a comic sidekick: Fat men in gay porn. *Performing Ethos: International Journal of Ethics in Theatre & Performance*, 2(2), 109–120.

Hillman, J. (2021). F-words. In B. Grimm, M. Morales, & T. Ferentini (Eds.), *Fat and queer: An anthology of queer and trans bodies and lives* (pp. 123–125). London, UK: Jessica Kingsley Publishers.

Hyslop, S. (2001). The rise of the Australian bear community since 1995. In L. Wright (Ed.), *The bear book II: Further readings in the history and evolution of a gay male subculture* (pp. 269–283). New York, NY: Harrington Park Press.

Ingraham, N. (2015). Queering porn: Gender and size diversity within SF Bay area queer pornography. In H. Hester & C. Walters (Eds.), *Fat sex: New directions in theory and activism* (pp. 115–132). Farnham, UK: Ashgate.

King-Miller, L. (2011, September 12). Queer by choice, not by chance: Against being "born this way." *The Atlantic*. Retrieved from www.theatlantic.com/health/archive/2011/09/queer-by-choice-not-by-chance-against-being-born-this-way/244898/

Kipnis, L. (1996). Life in the fat lane. In L. Kipnis, *Bound and gagged: Pornography and the politics of fantasy in America* (pp. 93–121). Durham, N.C.: Duke University Press.

Kruger, S. (1998). "Get fat, don't die!": Eating and AIDS in gay men's culture. In R. Scapp & B. Seitz (Eds.), *Eating culture* (pp. 36–59). Albany, NY: SUNY Press.

Kyrölä, K. (2011). Adults growing sideways: Feederist pornography and fantasies of infantilism. *Lambda Nordica*, 16(2–3), 128–158.

Lin, C. (2014). Chinese gay bear men. *Culture, Society & Masculinities*, 6(2), 183–193.

Luna, C. (2014, July 21). On being fat, brown, femme, ugly, and unloveable. *Black Girl Dangerous*. Retrieved www.bgdblog.org/2014/07/fat-brown-femme-ugly-unloveable/

Luna, C. (2021). The gender nonconformity of my fatness. In B. Grimm, M. Morales, & T. Ferentini (Eds.), *Fat and queer: An anthology of queer and trans bodies and lives* (pp. 72–77). London, UK: Jessica Kingsley Publishers.

Mann, J. (2010). Bear culture 101 (no prerequisite). *The Gay & Lesbian Review Worldwide*, 17(5), 22–24.

McCann, T. (1997). Atlantic crossing: The development of the eurobear. In L. Wright (Ed.), *The bear book: Readings in the history and evolution of a gay male subculture* (pp. 251–259). New York, NY: Haworth Press.

McGlynn, N. (2021). Bears in space: Geographies of a global community of big and hairy gay/bi/queer men. *Geography Compass*, 15(2), 1–13.

McGrady, P. (2016). "Grow the beard, wear the costume": Resisting weight and sexual orientation stigmas in the bear subculture. *Journal of Homosexuality*, 63(12), 1698–1725.

McNair, B. (2002). *Striptease culture: Sex, media and the democratization of desire.* New York, NY: Routledge.

Mijas, M., Koziara, K., Galbarczyk, A., & Jasienska, G. (2020). Chubby, hairy and fearless: Subcultural identities and predictors of self-esteem in a sample of Polish members of bear community. *International Journal of Environmental Research and Public Health*, 17(2), 1–12.

Moffet, F. (Producer). (2002). *Hard Fat* [Documentary film]. Montréal, QC: Vidéographe.

Monaghan, L. (2005). Big handsome men, bears and others: Virtual constructions of "fat male embodiment." *Body & Society*, 11(2), 81–111.

Morales, M. (2019). Does this poem make me look fat? In A. Manfredi (Ed.), *The (other) F word: A celebration of the fat and fierce* (pp. 162–163). New York, NY: Amulet Books.

Moskowitz, D., Turrubiates, J., Lozano, H., & Hajek, C. (2013). Physical, behavioral, and psychological traits of gay men identifying as bears. *Archives of Sexual Behavior*, 42(5), 775–784.

Nagle, J. (2020). Affective touch in the archive of *Bulk Male* magazine. *Sightlines*, 70–81. Retrieved from static1.squarespace.com/static/5d546015fb293c0001f7ae73/t/5f7ff511 e2129337fe575309/1602221330944/VCS_Sightlines_KH_Nagel_Justin.pdf

Oliverio, D. (2016). *The round world: Life at the intersection of love, sex, and fat.* West Hollywood, CA: The Antrobus Group.

Owen, L. (2012). Living fat in a thin-centric world: Effects of spatial discrimination on fat bodies and selves. *Feminism & Psychology* 2(3), 290–306.

Patnaik, P. (2014). Bearly Indian: "Fat" gay men's negotiation of embodiment, culture, and masculinity. In R. Dasgupta & K. Gokulsing (Eds.), *Masculinity and its challenges in India: Essays on changing perceptions* (pp. 93–105). Jefferson, NC: McFarland.

Paul, B. (2015). Between "bodies without bodies" and body landscapes: Queer artistic negotiations. In Erharter et al. (Eds.), *Pink labor on golden streets: Queer art practices* (pp. 238–250). Berlin, Germany: Sternberg Press.

Pomerantz, A. (2017). Big-girls don't cry: Portrayals of the fat body in RuPaul's Drag Race. In N. Brennan and D. Gudelunas (Eds.), *RuPaul's Drag Race and the shifting visibility of drag culture: The boundaries of reality TV* (pp. 103–120). Cham, Switzerland: Palgrave Macmillan.

Przybylo, E., & Rodrigues, S. (2018). Introduction: On the politics of ugliness. In S. Rodrigues and E. Przybylo (Eds.), *On the politics of ugliness* (pp. 1–30). Cham, Switzerland: Palgrave Macmillan.

Puar, J. (2007). *Terrorist assemblages: Homonationalism in queer times.* Durham, NC: Duke University Press.

Pyle, N., & Klein, N. (2011). Fat. hairy. sexy: Contesting standards of beauty and sexuality in the gay community. In C. Bobel & S. Kwan (Eds.), *Embodied resistance: Challenging the norms, breaking the rules* (pp. 78–87). Nashville, TN: Vanderbilt University Press.

Pyle, N., & Loewy, M. (2009). Double stigma: Fat men and their male admirers. In E. Rothblum & S. Solovay (Eds.), *The fat studies reader* (pp. 143–150). New York, NY: NYU Press.

Quidley-Rodriquez, N., & De Santis, J. (2016). Physical, psychosocial, and social health of men who identify as bears: A systematic review. *Journal of Clinical Nursing*, 25(23–24), 3484–3496.

Quidley-Rodriquez, N., & De Santis, J. (2017). A literature review of health risks in the bear community, a gay subculture. *American Journal of Men's Health*, 11(6), 1673–1679.

Richardson, N. (2010). *Transgressive bodies: Representation in film and popular culture.* Farnham, UK: Ashgate.

Robinson, B. (2018). The quantifiable-body discourse: "Height-weight proportionality" and gay men's bodies in cyberspace. *Social Currents*, 3(2), 172–185.

Robson, R., & Kessler, T. (2008). Unsettling sexual citizenship. *McGill Law Journal*, 53(3), 535–571.

Roth, Y. (2014). Locating the "scruff guy": Theorizing body and space in gay geosocial media. *International Journal of Communication*, 8, 2113–2133.

Rothblum, E. (2012). Why a journal on fat studies? *Fat Studies*, 1(1), 3–5.

Russeth, A. (2019). Serious play: Nayland Blake's gifts from the department of transformation. *ARTnews*, 118(1), 80. Retrieved from www.artnews.com/2019/04/09/nayland-blake/

Stoltenberg, J. (1998). Learning the F words. In D. Atkins (Ed.), *Looking queer: Body image and identity in lesbian, bisexual, gay, and transgender communities* (pp. 393–411). New York, NY: Harrington Park Press.

Stueart, J. 2021. A fat lot of good that did: How an art studio transformed my eyes. In B. Grimm, M. Morales, & T. Ferentini (Eds.), *Fat and queer: An anthology of queer and trans bodies and lives* (pp. 93–104). London, UK: Jessica Kingsley Publishers.

Suresha, R. (2002a). *Bears on bears: Interviews and discussions.* Los Angeles, CA: Alyson Books.

Suresha, R. (2002b). The birth of Girth & Mirth: An interview with Reed Wilgoren. In R. Suresha (Ed.), *Bears on bears: Interviews and discussions* (pp. 63–76). Los Angeles, CA: Alyson Books.

Tan, C. (2016). Gaydar: Using skilled vision to spot gay "bears" in Taipei. *Anthropological Quarterly*, 89(3), 841–864.

Tan, C. (2017). Taipei gay "bear" culture as a sexual field, or, why did Nanbu bear fail? *Journal of Contemporary Ethnography*, 48(4), 563–585.

Textor, A. (1999). Organization, specialization, and desires in the big men's movement: Preliminary research in the study of subculture-formation. *International Journal of Sexuality and Gender Studies*, 4(3), 217–239.

Tilley, J. (2018, May 30). Gender blender. *Office Magazine*. Retrieved from officemagazine. net/gender-blender

Volp, L. (2017). Feminist, sexual, and queer citizenship. In A. Shachar, R. Bauböck, I. Bloemraad, & M Vink (Eds.), *The Oxford Handbook of Citizenship* [Online] (pp. 1–30). Oxford, UK: Oxford University Press.

Warner, M. (2005). *Publics and counterpublics.* New York, NY: Zone Books.

Watson, X. (2016, June 29). Fat threads: James Gobel's queer portraiture [Online Presentation]. Retrieved from webcast.massey.ac.nz/Mediasite/Play/9870005cbc4b43 a1be411d00c2c9d9921d

Webster, J. (1997). Kiwi bears. In L. Wright (Ed.), *The bear book: Readings in the history and evolution of a gay male subculture* (pp. 239–250). New York, NY: Haworth Press:

Whitesel, J. (2010). Gay men's use of online pictures in fat-affirming groups. In C. Pullen & M. Cooper (Eds.), *LGBT identity and online new media* (pp. 215–229). New York, NY: Routledge.

Whitesel, J. (2014). *Fat gay men: Girth, mirth, and the politics of stigma.* New York, NY: NYU Press

Whitesel, J. (2015, September 15). Chubby guy swag [Blog post]. Retrieved from www. fromthesquare.org/chubby-guy-swag

Whitesel, J. (2017a). *James Unsworth: Girth and Mirth* [Exhibition catalogue]. Tel Aviv, Israel: Raw Art Gallery. Retrieved from rawartmedia.s3-eu-west-2.amazonaws.com/ exhibitions_catalogues/2017-12-04/James_Unsworth_catalog_girth_and_mirth-_final. pdf

Whitesel, J. (2017b, June 30). Same-gender-loving big men of color [Blog post]. Retrieved from www.fromthesquare.org/same-gender-loving-big-men-color

Whitesel, J. (2019). Big gay men's performative protest against body shaming: The case of Girth and Mirth. In C. Bobel & S. Kwan (Eds.), *Body battlegrounds: Transgressions, tensions, and transformations* (pp. 129–143). Nashville, TN: Vanderbilt University Press.

Whitesel, J., & Shuman, A. (2013). Normalizing desire: Stigma and the carnivalesque in gay bigmen's cultural practices. *Men and Masculinities*, 16(4), 478–496.

Whitesel, J., & Shuman, A. (2016). Discursive entanglements, diffractive readings: Weight-loss-surgery narratives of girth & mirthers. *Fat Studies*, 5(1), 32–56.

18

FROM HATTIE MCDANIEL TO QUEEN LATIFAH

Examining a New Mammy and Other Fat Black Women Representations in Contemporary Media

Roshaunda L. Breeden and Terah J. Stewart

Notable Black actresses, Hattie McDaniel from *Gone with the Wind* (1939) and Louise Beavers from *Imitation of Life* (1934), portrayed roles that had a significant impact on and implications for American media and film (Meares 2021). From the 1930s well into the 1960s, McDaniel and Beavers appeared in more than 200 Hollywood films, often depicted as the "Mammy" figure—a docile, fat, Black woman, whose primary responsibilities included taking care of white children (Collins 2000; Harris-Perry 2011; West 1995). McDaniel once shared, "I would rather play a maid for 700 dollars a week th[an] be a maid for seven dollars a week" (Eckels 2019, par. 11). While both McDaniel and Beavers were artists and trailblazers in real life, their characterizations as Mammy within the media served to maintain systems of domination. Often depicted as "beloved friends of the family" on screen, the Mammy character offered harmful, flawed, and simplistic depictions about the role of Black women in the US context.

McDaniel and Beavers shared similar identities as fat, Black, and dark-skinned women. On a spectrum of desirability, whiteness and thinness are praised as pure and feminine, while Blackness and fatness exist at the opposite end of the spectrum (Strings 2019). Under this antiblack context, McDaniel and Beavers represented an extreme departure from western Eurocentric beauty standards in film. Juxtaposed to their whiter and thinner counterparts, the creation of these characters was rooted in antiblackness. For example, characters like McDaniel and Beavers were placed in proximity to white women to highlight who served in domestic roles and make white women feel beautiful. While films featuring McDaniel and Beavers are considered "old Hollywood," we argue that for fat Black women, tropes and stereotypes like that of the Mammy archetype still animate our understanding of who fat Black women are in film and, by extension, social life. While some may believe that mass media, film, and television are

DOI: 10.4324/9781003140665-25

politically neutral, we lean into bell hooks' (2008) assertion that media helps shape reality, particularly for fat Black women. Like hooks' work in the text *Reel to Real: Race, Sex, and Class at the Movies,* in this chapter, we highlight the ways in which popular culture can function subversively to maintain the status quo (2008). Furthermore, we emphasize the critical need for scholars and writers to focus their thinking, researching, and theorizing on fat Black women.

In this chapter, we extend hooks' (2008) argument that contemporary media simply recreates Black women stereotypes by highlighting how perceptions of Blackness and fatness create unique axes of problematic representation. Using the deep intersectionality of Black women's identity around race, gender, and body size as analytical frames, we position this work within three main and archaic stereotypes about Black women, including the Mammy, Sapphire, and Jezebel archetypes (Collins 2000; Harris-Perry 2011; West 1995). While literature related to these harmful depictions usually includes systems of oppression, such as racism, sexism, and patriarchy, our goal was to extend the conversation by adding in the presence of anti-fatness. This is to say, we are interested in what fatness imports on these stereotypes by examining the multiplicative nature of fatphobia.

Centering Black women as agents of knowledge (Collins 2000), one author crowdsourced among a group of Black women and femmes their suggestions of notable examples of fat Black women in media and film. Using the most popular responses, in this chapter we examine fat Black women in popular culture and their relation to three central Black women archetypes (e.g., Mammy, Sapphire, and Jezebel). We then discuss how fat Black women in popular culture come to be exaggerations of how fat Black women are perceived. We conclude with a discussion of the ways in which harmful rhetoric on-screen can translate to actual harm in real life.

Why Fat Black Women?

As scholars committed to the liberation of all Black women, we focused on the experiences of fat Black women for many reasons. First, we know that few scholars have addressed the role of fatness, race, and racism in their analysis (Taylor 2018), explicitly highlighting how racial and religious ideologies worked to shame Black women. Specifically, Strings (2019) suggests that anti-fatness began during the Transatlantic Slave Trade, with the intent to disgrace, belittle, and distance fat Black women from beauty. By positioning fat Black women as immoral during enslavement, Protestant ideologies attributed larger bodies to gluttonous behavior and lack of self-control. Seeing and naming themselves as a superior race, Europeans believed and idolized the white and thin aesthetic as the standard (Strings 2019). Based on historical evidence, race and body size became ways to determine who was deserving of freedom.

Today, underlying racist and fatphobic beliefs about body size and fatness still exist. Strings (2019) asserts that "the image of fat Black women as 'savage' and 'barbarous' in art, philosophy, and science ... has been used to both degrade Black women and discipline white women" (211). These attitudes inform the medical industry, diet culture, and popular culture, which centers on thinness and equates whiteness and slenderness to health and moral virtue (Strings 2019; Taylor 2018). Therefore, specifically for Black women,

> the origins of fatphobia were grounded in seeking the highest form of beauty, which is intrinsically connected to the experience and perceived worth of women broadly; therefore, [fat] Black women have specifically become the antithesis of what beauty, "health," or "wellness" is or can be, especially as it relates to the body."
>
> *(Stewart and Breeden 2021, 223)*

Thus, our work helps further situate the harm Black women experience at the intersections of fatphobia, racism, and sexism.

Depictions of Black Women in Popular Culture

Historically in the US context, Black women in media and culture have been showcased as one or some combination of three images: (1) as the Mammy, (2) as the Sapphire, and/or (3) as the Jezebel character (Collins 2000; Sims-Wood 1988; Weitz and Gordon 1993). To help explain these images, Melissa Harris-Perry's text, *Sister Citizen* (2011), uses the "crooked room" metaphor to show the ways in which Black women are often seen as distorted images by white people, people of color, and Black men. These images illustrate the systems of oppression (e.g., racism, sexism, patriarchy, sizeism) Black women must navigate. To help frame the conversation in contemporary popular culture, we provide a brief description of each stereotype or controlling image (Collins 2000)—"images designed to make racism, sexism, poverty, and other forms of social injustice appear to be natural, normal, and inevitable parts of everyday life" (69).

Mammy Archetype—The Self-Sacrificer

The Mammy archetype portrays Black women as desexualized, docile, and often fat-bodied, with primary caretaking responsibilities, specifically for white children (Harris-Perry 2011). This stereotype functions in present-day society as expecting Black women to be the "maternal" figure who puts everyone's needs and desires above her own (Collins 2000; West 1995). Examples of the Mammy in media and film have included Nell Harper in *Gimme a Break* (1981–1987), Celie Harris in *The Color Purple* (1985), and Aibileen Clark in *The Help* (2011).

Sapphire Archetype—The Hypercritical One

Sapphire, or the angry Black woman archetype, functions to see Black women as malicious, domineering, and loud (Harris-Perry 2011). While historically, Black women have a lot to be mad about (Cooper 2018), this Sapphire image allows for one emotion—rage. Contemporary media might showcase this Sapphire trope as one who is always argumentative, hypercritical, verbally abusive, bitter, and sometimes overbearing. Examples of the Sapphire in media and film have included Aunt Esther in *Sanford and Son* (1972–1977), Pamela James in *Martin* (1992–1997), and Angela Williams in *Why Did I Get Married* (2007).

Jezebel Archetype—The Seductive Succubus

The Jezebel archetype showcases Black women as loose, promiscuous women or seductive temptresses (Collins 2000; Harris-Perry 2011). The roots of the Jezebel construction can be traced to chattel slavery, where Black women were perceived to be unrapable because they were first and foremost property (McGuire 2010). This framing allowed white slaveowners to abuse and assault Black women with impunity, and often they would suggest Black women asked, invited, or desired the rape. Even after the abolition of slavery, this frame persisted, for example, white police officers, lawyers, and judges often resorted to this stereotype as a strategy to undermine legal cases involving white men raping Black women (McGuire 2010). In this way, framing Black women as loose, jezebels, and prostitutes resulted in logic that they were hypersexual and, therefore, it was unlikely they were raped (McGuire 2010). This controlling image relegates Black women only to their excessive and insatiable sexual appetites. Examples of the Jezebel in media and film have included Shug Avery in *The Color Purple* (1985), Leticia Musgrove in *Monster's Ball* (2001), and Gail Best in *Baggage Claim* (2013).

Ask Black Women on Instagram

Grounded in Black women's ways of knowing (Collins 2000; Dillard 2006), which honors the collective nature of Black women's knowledge as legitimate, we asked Black women and femmes on social media to share examples of fat Black women in media and film. We solicited Black women's feedback on social media because we understand that Black women use digital spaces as counterspaces and sites of resistance—places that they can engage about their issues and concerns that center their lived experiences (Glenn 2015; Stewart 2019; Williams 2015; Yang 2016). Further, social media is a place and space for Black women to share information, build community, and advocate for their needs, particularly in a world that often ignores them (Stewart 2019; Williams 2015).

Using Instagram's poll feature, one author posted the following message: "*Share an example of a fat Black woman in media and film.*" At the conclusion of the poll, she received 65 responses and the top three included: Dana Owens, an actress who starred in *Living Single, Secret Life of Bees, Beauty Shop,* and *Just Wright*, Mo'Nique Hicks, an actress who played in *The Parkers, Soul Plane*, and *Two Can Play That Game*, and Natasha Rothwell, an actress who appeared in the HBO show, *Insecure*.

While followers named Black women such as Gabourey Sidibe, Jill Scott, Amber Riley, Nicole Byer, and Danielle Brooks, the aforementioned Black women had the most mentions. Based on the feedback of Black women and femmes, we examined three fat Black women in popular culture, highlighting how their characters fit within three central Black women archetypes.

At the Intersection of Fatness, Blackness, and Womanhood

In their text, *The Rising Song of African American Women*, Barbara Omolade (1994) asserts that while the historical context of archetypes like the Mammy has changed over the years, these stereotypes have not disappeared. Instead, they have assumed a new shape. According to Collins (2000), as Black feminist scholars, our work lies in figuring out these new images, their changes, and extending conversations across generations and identities. Thus, this chapter illustrates the contemporary connections between fatness, Blackness, and womanhood, using three fat Black women in media and film. For this analysis, we made connections between each fat Black woman and one of the controlling images or archetypes. As a caveat, these archetypes and stereotypes are not explicitly discrete, which is to say there may be qualities of a particular representation that surfaces in another. Our intent is not to argue for clear and clean delineations of each representation but rather to engage the spirit of the most obvious stereotypical framings within any given characterization.

Meet Dana Owens

Professionally known as Queen Latifah, Dana Owens is a fat Black woman and powerhouse in the entertainment industry as a rapper, singer, songwriter, producer, actress, and talk show host. In the late 1980s and early 1990s, Owens reigned supreme as a Black woman hip hop artist with singles like "Ladies First" and "U.N.I.T.Y." Based on her representations of Black womanhood, independence, and power, Owens starred in movies like *House Party 2* (1991), *Jungle Fever* (1991), and the notable television series, *Living Single* (1993). Owens is further known for pivotal roles in movies like *Set It Off* (1996) and *Chicago* (2002), along with the talk show, *The Queen Latifah Show* (2013). While simultaneously making music and performing, Owens appeared in films like *Bringing Down the House* (2003), *Last Holiday* (2006), *Hairspray* (2007), and *Girls Trip* (2017). For over three decades, Owens has garnered a bevy of awards, including a Grammy and several Emmys, Golden Globes, BET, and NAACP Awards.

Living Single

When asked on social media, Black women shared that Owens' role in *Living Single* was a notable example of a fat Black woman on television. *Living Single*

(1993–1998) was a groundbreaking sitcom that explored the lives of young Black women in the 1990s (Zook 1999). As one of the first prime-time series created by a Black woman, for Black women, *Living Single* was supposed to be a comedy about girlfriends called *My Girls* (67). Instead, network executives at Fox named the show *Living Single* focusing on pursuing intimate relationships or the "Fight for Mr. Right" (Zook 1999, 67). Exploring the life of four liberated Black women (Khadijah James, Regine Hunter, Synclaire James, and Maxine Shaw) who shared a New York Brownstone, *Living Single* was pivotal in challenging normative standards ideas around sexuality and gender (Smallwood and Weekley 2018). Specifically, the Black women on *Living Single* moved confidently in their sexuality, talked publicly about sex, worked in historically male-dominated careers, and unapologetically shared their opinions.

Khadijah James: A Recreation of the Mammy Trope

In the show, Dana Owens played Khadijah James, a 20-something, fat-bodied, Black woman and outspoken journalist dedicated to her magazine, *Flavor* (Smith-Shomade 2002). Harris-Perry (2011) identifies the Mammy figure as fat, usually desexualized, and whose primary role within any given context is to take care of those around her. If contemporary representations of the Mammy used historical tropes, however, showing her in an apron, with her hair wrapped, and only engaged in domestic kinds of labor, it would be obvious and not nearly as elusive as what the contemporary Mammy imports. Contemporary representations of the Mammy might situate her in ways that Khadijah was portrayed. While some Black women, in media and real life, can achieve jobs outside of domestic servitude (Collins 2000), the idea of "mammy work" has morphed into the fat Black women owning a large share of emotional nurturing and "cleaning up after" others, at home and work. For example, in *Living Single*, Khadijah devotes most of her time and energy to keeping her urban magazine afloat. While she is a successful entrepreneur with a relatively large staff, Khadijah is wholly committed to her job, works long hours, comes to work sick, and expects the same type of diehard devotion from her team—perhaps in line with "new mammy" behavior. Throughout the show's five seasons, most of Khadijah's storyline involves labor with very few leisure opportunities. Viewers seldomly find Khadijah resting or pursuing passions outside of work or taking care of others. She is always chasing a story for her magazine or fixing a malfunctioning piece of office equipment; she's working twice as hard as everyone else.

Similarly, in her personal life, Khadijah serves as a stable anchor, leader, and protector in the home—the "family matriarch." When roommates move out, Khadijah is the one who stays and keeps the family together. For example, in Season 4, Episode 2, Maxine named Khadijah, the mother of their group. During an argument with Maxine, Khajidah endorses another candidate for a local elected position, and Maxine responds by sharing:

Well, see, up until now, you've been the self-appointed leader of our little foursome. The great provider. Synclaire needs a job, work for Khadijah. Regine needs a place to live, live with Khadijah. Suddenly I'm on the verge of winning this election without any help from you, and *mother* cannot stand to share the spotlight, can you?

(Living Single, -10:36–10:00)

The day after this encounter, Khadijah responds to Maxine, mentioning: "*Mother* hasn't thought about you all day." The essence of this exchange is rooted in many traits related to the Mammy character, who, by societal expectations for fat Black women, has to be the warm and nurturing maternal figure. At the same time, the three other thinner Black women who could be considered to represent different stereotypes (Regine—the gold digger, Maxine—the maneater, and Synclaire—the simpleton) strive to live full lives at home, at work, and in their intimate relationships. Viewers see that Khadijah, the fat Black woman, generally has to balance the needs of others before her own. Not until the show's finale, Season 5, Episode 13, after everyone has moved on to new life adventures, do viewers and onlookers see Khadijah choosing to run away with her love interest.

Throughout the five seasons of *Living Single*, no one in the show questions why her character, the fat Black woman, performs in this way. Despite the upgrades to this Mammy figure, including being a career woman working for herself, the prevalence of the archetype marches on as she was still beholden to caretaking for the others around her. While she was an entrepreneur, her magazine became another entity she must care for, sacrificing herself in the process. This reality is noteworthy because Maxine Shaw was an attorney and worked considerably less to the point of it being a running joke in the series; the contemporary Mammy needed to be represented as the workaholic. In this way, our analysis underscores how important it is to add fat to our analyses of race and gender in new readings of media.

Meet Mo'Nique Hicks

Grammy-nominated Mo'Nique Hicks, professionally known as Mo'Nique, is a Black American comedian, actress, and talk-show host. She began her career in stand-up in 1989 with a dare by her brother to take the stage at a comedy club in Baltimore, Maryland (Haynes 2006). After much success from her incredible impromptu performance, Hicks decided to pursue a career in entertainment by night while working full-time by day. Establishing herself for a decade within the comedy club scene as a stand-up comedian, Hicks later found herself on syndicated television shows such as *Moesha* (1999–2000) and *The Parkers* (1999–2004). Her success on television earned Hicks a starring role in the *Queens of Comedy* (2001), a spin-off comedy film from the *Kings of Comedy* (Haynes 2006). From her debut with *Queens of Comedy*, Hicks introduced herself as a fat, beautiful, and relatable diva. From her success, she starred in movies like *Two Can Play That Game* (2001), *Hair Show* (2004), and *Phat Girlz* (2006), embracing her identity as a fat Black woman. In keeping with her initial embrace of her size, in 2006, Hicks joined the New York Times best-seller list for her book, *Skinny Women Are Evil: Notes of a Big Girl in a Small-Minded World*, and hosted *Mo'Nique's Fat Chance*, a beauty pageant for the "Fabulous and Thick" (Haynes 2006, par. 9). Later in the 2000s, after much success in television and film, Hicks won an Academy Award for her role in *Precious* (2009).

Precious: Based on the Novel "Push" by Sapphire

In the film *Precious* based on the novel "Push" by Sapphire (1996), Mo'Nique plays the character of Mary Jones, an unemployed fat Black woman in Harlem, New York, in the late 1980s. In the film, Mary is the mother to Claireece "Precious" Jones, a fat Black adolescent girl navigating sexual, physical, and verbal abuse at the hands of her parents. Pregnant by her father Carl, Precious transfers to an alternative school and receives support from a teacher and a social worker, both thinner and lighter-skinned Black women, who help change Precious's life.

Mary Jones: A Recreation of the Sapphire Trope

For this essay, we focus on analyzing Mary Jones, Precious's mother. Throughout the film, Mary Jones is the opposite of a supportive parental figure; she is hateful and cruel, the epitome of the Sapphire stereotype. As a reminder, the Sapphire is animated by hypercritical, argumentative, and domineering qualities. In the movie, viewers see Mary as irrationally angry and vicious, constantly talking down to Precious and her granddaughter, Mongo. In one scene, after Precious' school principal visits the home to discuss attending an alternative school, Mary becomes enraged, hurling insults at Precious to make her feel inferior. She yells:

> School ain't gonna help none. Take your ass down to the welfare! Who the fuck she thinks she is?! So I guess you think you cute now, right?! Ol' uppity bitch! You should've kept yo fuckin' mouth shut! Just because he gon' give you more children than he gave me, you think you're something fuckin' special?! Fuck you and fuck him!
>
> *(Fletcher 2007, 15a–16)*

In the scene, Mary takes pride in lashing out at Precious. She calls her names, talks down to her, and situates Precious (who is also a fat Black woman) as a fat Jezebel when she alludes to the father's rape of Precious. She blames Precious for the rape and goes as far as to suggest that the act was not rape, and instead, Precious "stole" her father from her mother. Even though another Black woman leverages the logic, it is rooted in historical conceptions that Black women are always already jezebels and therefore unrapable. Mary broadly situates herself in competition with her daughter by framing rape as something special he gave Precious mentioning: "Just because he gon' give you more children than he gave me" (Fletcher 2007, 15a). Clearly, difficult and toxic relationships abound. Only at the end of the film do viewers begin to learn about Mary's trauma and pain. At a social workers' office, Mary shares (edited for length and clarity):

> I had a man and I have a child. And I had to take care of both of them. Okay? And Carl would be laying on the other side and then we would start doing it and he reached over and he touched my baby and I asked him, I said, Carl what are you doing? And he told me to shut, to shut my fat ass up and it was good for her … I shut my fat ass up. I did not want him to abuse my daughter. I did not want him to hurt her. I did not want him to do nothing to her. I wanted him to make love to me. That was my man. That was my fuckin' man. That was my man and he wanted my daughter. And that's why I hated her because it was my man who was supposed to be loving me, who was supposed to be making love to me, he was fucking my baby and she made him leave, she made him go away.
>
> *(Fletcher 2007, 111)*

From this dialogue, one might assume that Mary's anger is rooted in previous trauma related to love and self-worth; however, as viewers and onlookers, all we gather through the entirety of the film is Mary, attempting to harm Precious— hitting her with pots, throwing a television at her, and verbally abusing her without intentional explanation. Seeking to humanize Mary as a character is difficult because her trauma and pain, while important, do not excuse her behavior toward another Black woman who also happens to be her daughter. To better understand Mary's representation as a contemporary fat Sapphire, we turn to another film representation, the adaptation of the book *The Color Purple* (1985).

In the film, Oprah Winfrey portrays Sofia, a no-nonsense character who refuses to shrink herself as a Black person or a woman. This reality is evidenced by her verbal and physical encounters with both Black men, white men, and white women. While both characters fulfill the Sapphire role, Mary's differs in that she abandons her care and love for her children—angry and bitter—at the life she wished she had. Alternatively, Sofia was committed to protecting and loving her children—evidenced by a scene where she becomes surrounded by a white mob after she physically defended herself from a white man who struck her. Sofia yells over and over, "Take my children home, get my children out of here" (Spielberg 1985, 1:25:27–1:25:30). Despite the care Sofia conveys, it could be argued that both characters ultimately choose anger over their children; Sofia fought back when she could have chosen differently, Mary resented and abused Precious when she could have found ways to heal and love her.

However, it becomes hard to ignore Sofia's anger as more humanized than Mary's. Sofia reminds us that "all [her] life she had to fight" (Spielberg 1985,

43:56), referencing abuse by men including her father, her brothers, her uncles, and at that time, her partner; justifying why she is so angry, and viewers might find understanding of Sofia in this context. Mary's portrayal, however, lay exclusively in her being an angry, bitter mother as a result of a life bereft of love. Her Sapphire qualities are further complicated given that Precious exists alongside her in the film as a fat Black woman. In this way, Mary's lack of love, care, and desire for companionship is not necessarily framed as a cause worthy of her corresponding anger and ultimate virulent abuse.

All of this taken together Mary's portrayal somewhat obscures context and almost renders fatness as an irrational evil along with the evils Mary enacts, making the fat Sapphire holistically and exponentially irrational and dangerous. While viewers are offered some of the complexity of her life, audiences do not get to see more of the nuance of this character, one who has her own trauma, a human being who has been impacted by systems of oppression in her own life, a person whose anger is justified. It is as if her fatness renders her unexplainable. Again, it is essential to analyze fatness to understand a complete picture of the representation of Black women.

Meet Natasha Rothwell on HBO's *Insecure*

Newcomer to Hollywood, Natasha Rothwell is a writer, actor, producer, and comedian. She garnered much success as a writer for *Saturday Night Live* (2014–2015) and *The Characters* (2016) comedy sketch show. Later in 2016, joining the writing and production team for the HBO television show *Insecure* (2016–2021), Rothwell showcases the awkward everyday experiences of Black women in Los Angeles, California. Aside from her role on the writing team, Rothwell also stars as Kelli Prenny, the funny, no-nonsense, fat girl in the dynamic foursome, including Issa Dee—awkward Black girl, Molly Carter—the insufferable workaholic, and Tiffany DuBose—the pretentious one.

Kelli Prenny: A Recreation of the Jezebel Trope

For this analysis, we frame Kelli as a recreation of the Jezebel archetype. As a reminder, the Jezebel trope is a sex-crazed and loose woman whose life revolves solely around her sexual exploits. We are introduced to Kelli's character in Season 1, Episode 3, of *Insecure*, when the four women are at a party. In retelling a story, Kelli recaps a first date, mentioning: "He took me apple picking ... we fucked in the orchard" (*Insecure* 2016, 10:16–10:22). At first, onlookers might assume that Kelli is a sexually free character, who happens to be fat, and since viewers hardly see larger bodies like hers exploring sexuality in media and film, the audience is at first delighted. However, after a closer examination, viewers realize that aside from her sexual appetite, this character is one-dimensional, often used as comic relief in any given scenario.

Four seasons of *Insecure*, with the fifth one in production, demonstrate that Kelli's character lacks depth (Barlow 2016). While Kelli works as a certified personal accountant, the show hardly ever shows her at work or discussing work in any meaningful way, which is an interesting comparison to her counterparts, Issa, Molly, and Tiffany, who are frequently at work and whose work occupies significant storylines within the series. Across 32 episodes, there are only two occasions that Kelli mentions anything related to her career.

Furthermore, everything about Kelli is either connected to her sexual appetite (e.g., hooking up with strangers) or nonexistent. In scene after scene, Kelli makes remarks about her sexual exploits. Still, viewers never see these exploits on camera, suggesting that writers recognize the history of fat Black women as undesirable (Strings 2019). Audiences watch very intimate and detailed sex scenes featuring Issa and Molly, but for the fat Black woman character, who exudes sex and flirtatious banter—audiences seldom see her in the act. The only time Kelli is represented as engaging in sexual behavior is in Season 2, Episode 4, is when the scene suggests that another character is actively stimulating her genitals with his hand and fingers under the table while having breakfast at a restaurant.

Aside from those encounters, *Insecure* fans know very little about Kelli Prenny. While she is a secondary character, she rarely has a storyline, unlike other secondary characters. For example, Tiffany, who is thinner, has a more detailed story. Audiences know about Tiffany's sorority membership, pregnancy woes, details about her relationship, and viewers are even introduced to her family and friends. The only time the fat Black character, Kelli, is centered is when she speaks about her sexual prowess or in a drunken stupor. Similarly, the only time she addresses anything nonsexual is in Season 2, when she, a fatter Black woman, ran a marathon and her friends came to support her. Aside from Season 2, fans hardly see Kelli as a character with depth. Whether intentionally or unintentionally, showrunners seem to position Kelli to serve as comedic relief—a fat-specific trope—and support for her thinner costars, which also hints at mammy work.

For some, Kelli may be a fat Black woman who is free to explore her sexuality and, as such, a holistically positive representation. For others, these sexual stories, rooted in the Jezebel archetype, may fall short because onlookers never get to see other intimate details of her life. *Insecure* fans know Kelli has a sexual appetite. Still, without any nuance or additional storylines, we echo cultural critiques who argue that Kelli is "an oversexed, boy-crazy, exaggerated trope of a plus-size woman" (Barlow 2016, par. 3). Kelli's representation perhaps underscores the way fatness and sex obscure any other real analysis on the lives and experiences of fat Black women.

Art Created by Black Women for Black Audiences

While writing this chapter, we noticed our examples (e.g., Khadijah James, Mary Jones, Sofia, and Kelli Prenny) were characters created by Black creators for majority Black audiences. We pondered the central question: *What does it mean that these images show up in Black media by Black writers, directors, and producers, including those identifying as Black women?* While meditations on this question potentially lead to numerous directions, there are two considerations that we seek to raise. First, to make sense of this phenomenon, we revisit Harris–Perry's (2011) concept of a crooked room. In her text, Harris–Perry mentions that due to the proverbial room being "crooked," stereotypes about Black women influence how Black women—and perhaps Black people broadly—see *themselves*. Harris–Perry asserts these stereotypes "influence how [Black women understand themselves as citizens, what they believe ... and what they expect...]" (2011, 35). Said differently, it is possible that Black writers recirculate harmful archetypes rooted in historical conceptions of Blackness both intentionally and unintentionally. Further, shared experience of one minoritized identity does not necessarily mean empathy, understanding, or desire for liberation of another. Which is to say, one being Black does not inherently means one embraces or models a radical politic around fatness.

Further, our analysis/critique must be assumed to bear with it an understanding of gaze in relation to these representations. As Black authors, if we were writing to only Black audiences, we might not need to take up—in the same ways— the complexities of how race informs/ed issues pertaining to fatness. The reality, however, requires us to hold the complexity of this constellation; thereby, we must consider what Blackness adds to fatness or vice versa and what it all means in relation to a white gaze, which is a gaze mediated by whiteness (of which white people are not needed for that gaze to function). Specifically, we assert, as other scholars have the co-constitutive nature of antiblackness and anti-fatness (Harrison 2021; Strings 2019) this is to say contemporary manifestations of anti-fat bias are directly connected to whiteness and white supremacy; therefore, those contemporary manifestations should be brought to bear on our understandings of how and why they show up in Black representations. Yet by reestablishing these problematic messages, Black writers, particularly Black women, continue to use harmful messaging to shape reality and maintain the status quo.

Finally, we lean on hooks' (1997) articulation of what it means to be "enlightened witness" to media representations. The term enlightened witness was established by psychoanalyst Alice Miller (hooks, 2003), who introduced the term within the context of how neglect or abuse informs how and why certain people choose violence or other behavioral choices that may be undesirable and cause harm. Within the context of media representations, hooks operationalized the term to portray how consumers of media engage their consumption with a conscious awareness of the representation even when they are imperfect or problematic. hooks shares:

> the issue is not freeing ourselves from representation. It's really about being enlightened witnesses when we watch representations, which means we are

able to be critically vigilant about both what is being told to us and how we respond to what is being told. Because I think that the answer is not the kind of censoring absolutism of a right-wing political correctness but in fact a proactive sense of agency that requires all of us a greater level of literacy.

(hooks 1997)

In this way, we aim to be clear that our offering in this chapter is not a desire for picture-perfect representations of fatness or Blackness, in fact, a perfect representation likely does not exist and could be argued to be a relatively anti-black desire, as Blackness is inherently imperfect in reality and within media imaginary. Instead, what we raise is that we must be enlightened witnesses to the marrying of fatness and Blackness in media representations and how it informs how we think about both. As we can both admit, we enjoyed all of the media and representations we critique, and our ability to enjoy is rooted in the praxis of enlightened witnessing where we are, as hooks names critically vigilant about the representations and how we respond to them.

Conclusion: Fat Black Women Matter on Television and in Real Life

Almost 100 years ago, Hattie McDaniel and Louise Beavers sought to render visible fat Black women in media, film, and society. Facing discrimination at the intersection of their identities, McDaniel and Beavers fought to take up space in Hollywood, making way for generations to come. Based on our examination, we argue that fat Black women are *still* fighting for the right to be seen in their fullness, complexity, and humanity—in a world that often chooses to acknowledge them only through harmful, racist, sexist, and sizeist prisms. Our analysis suggests that problematic representations of fat Black women are present in popular movies and television. Popular representations of fat Black women are not accidental or simple mistakes as the media play an intentional and deliberate role in shaping reality and maintaining the status quo (hooks 2008). Thus, these fat Mammy, Sapphire, and Jezebel images in the media come to be how people make sense of fat Black women in real life. We ask the reader to consider if television/media audiences come to know fat Black women in these ways, what are the implications?

While we focus our analysis and offering on the ways the Mammy, Jezebel, and Sapphire take on new meaning when they become fat, we want to be clear that our argument is not that the thin versions of these stereotypes are better. Instead, our analysis underscores a reality that the politics of the body, and specifically body size, offer new analytics, new challenges, and new opportunities for understanding power at the nexus of race, gender, and size. Which is to say, scholars must trouble research, writing, and analysis that does not invite a reading of the body even in the absence of fatness. When Black women entered in any given work are thin, it is important that we understand how that corresponding thinness animates the particularities of what is offered. Black feminist scholars rightly urged us to understand intersectionality as an analysis of power (Crenshaw 1991); thus, we argue that body size, fatness, and thinness must be incorporated accordingly.

Overall, perceptions of Blackness and fatness create unique axes of problematic representation in contemporary film and media that may extend to social and political life. Messages rooted in racism, sexism, and anti-fatness have not disappeared yet have simply transformed. For those taking up work with and about Black women, it is essential to be concerned with the fullness of what a fat analysis might import. As scholars, researchers, and writers, we understand the importance of nuance in identity-related power-conscious work; thus, we argue that it is imperative that being Black and woman are always in conversation with size.

Bibliography

Barlow, L. 2016. "Insecure Gets Wrong Plus-sized Sidekick" *Wear Your Voice Magazine*, December 9. www.wearyourvoicemag.com/insecure-gets-wrong-plus-sized-sidekick/

Collins, P. H. 2000. *Black Feminist Thought: Knowledge, Consciousness, and the Politics of Empowerment. Perspectives on Gender.* 2nd ed. New York: Routledge. https://uniteyout hdu blin.files.wordpress.com/2015/01/black-feminist-though-by-patricia-hill-collins. pdf

Cooper, B. C. 2018. *Eloquent Rage: A Black Feminist Discovers Her Superpower.* New York, NY: St. Martin's Press.

Crenshaw, K. 1991. "Mapping the Margins: Intersectionality, Identity Politics, and Violence Against Women of Color." *Stanford Law Review* 43 (1): 1241–1299.

Dillard, C. B. 2006. *On Spiritual Strivings: Transforming an African American Woman's Academic Life.* SUNY Series in Women in Education. Albany: State University of New York Press.

Eckels, C. 2019. "First Black Oscar Winner Hattie McDaniel Lacks Recognition in Her Hometown of Wichita." *KMUW*, September 12. www.kmuw.org/arts/2019-09-12/ first-black-oscar-winner-hattie-mcdaniel-lacks-recognition-in-her-hometown-of-wichita

Fletcher, G. 2007. *Precious* www.scriptslug.com/assets/scripts/precious-2009.pdf

Glenn, C. L. 2015. "Activism or 'Slacktivism?': Digital Media and Organizing for Social Change." *Communication Teacher*, 29 (2): 81–85. https://doi.org/10.1080/17404 622.2014.1003310

Harris-Perry, M. V. 2011. *Sister Citizen: Shame, Stereotypes, and Black women in America.* New Haven, CT: Yale University Press.

Harrison, D. L. 2021. *Belly of the Beast: The Politics of Anti-Fatness as Anti-Blackness.* Berkeley, CA: North Atlantic Books.

Haynes, M. 2006. "Mo'Nique Capitalizes on Her Plus Size Confidence." *Pittsburgh Post-Gazette*, April 10. www.post-gazette.com/life/lifestyle/2006/04/10/Mo-Nique-capi talizes-on-her-plus-size-confidence/stories/200604100103

hooks, b. 1997. *bell hooks: Cultural Criticism and Transformation.* [DVD] Media Education Foundation. London.

hooks, b. 2003. *Teaching Community: A Pedagogy of Hope.* New York, NY: Routledge.

hooks, b. 2008. *Reel to Real: Race, Sex, and Class at the Movies.* New York: Routledge.

McGuire, D. L. 2010. *At the Dark End of the Street: Black Women, Rape, and Resistance – A New History of the Civil Rights Movement from Rosa Parks to the Rise of Black power.* New York: Alfred A. Knopf.

Meares, H. H. 2021. "The Icon and the Outcast: Hattie McDaniel's Epic Double Life." *VanityFair,* April 21. www.vanityfair.com/hollywood/2021/04/hattie-mcdaniel-gone-with-the-wind-oscars-autobiography

Omolade, B. 1994. *The Rising Song of African American Women.* New York: Routledge.

Sims-Wood, J. 1988. The Black female: Mammy, Jemima, Sapphire, and other images. *In* J. C. Smith (Ed.), *Images of Blacks in American Culture: A Reference Guide to Information Sources.* Westport, CT: Greenwood, 235–265.

Smallwood, A. J. and Weekley, A. 2018. "A Black Feminist Content Analysis of Gender and Sexuality in Living Single." *Student Summer Scholars Manuscripts* 200 (1): 1–19. https://scholarworks.gvsu.edu/sss/200

Smith-Shomade, B. E. 2002. *Shaded Lives: African American Women and Television.* New Brunswick, NJ: Rutgers University Press.

Spielberg, Steven. 1985. *The Color Purple.* Lilesville, NC: Warner Bros.

Stewart, T. J. 2019. "'Where We Are, Resistance Lives': Black Women, Social Media, and Everyday Resistance in Higher Education." *Journal Committed to Social Change on Race and Ethnicity* 5 (2): 3–32.

Stewart, T. J. and Breeden, R. L. 2021. "'Feeling Good as Hell': Black Women and the Nuances of Fat Resistance." *Fat Studies* 10 (3): 221–236, DOI: 10.1080/21604851.2021.1907964

Strings, S. 2019. *Fearing the Black Body: The Racial Origins of Fat Phobia.* New York: University Press.

Taylor, S. R. 2018. *The Body Is Not an Apology: The Power of Radical Self-Love.* Oakland, CA: Berrett-Koehler Publishers.

Weitz, R. and Gordon, L. 1993. "Images of Black Women Among Anglo College Students." *Sex Roles* 28 (1/2): 19–34. https://link.springer.com/article/10.1007/BF00289745

West, C. M. 1995. "Mammy, Sapphire, and Jezebel: Historical Images of Black Women and Their Implications for Psychotherapy." *Psychotherapy* 32 (3): 458–466.

Williams, S. 2015. "Digital Defense: Black Feminists Resist Violence with Hashtag Activism." *Feminist Media Studies* 15 (2): 341–344.

Yang, G. 2016. "Narrative Agency in Hashtag Activism: The Case of #BlackLivesMatter." *Media & Communication* 4 (4): 13–17. https://doi.org/10.17645/mac.v4i4.692

Zook, K. B. 1999. *Color by Fox: The Fox Network and the Revolution in Black Television.* Cary: Oxford University Press, Incorporated.

PART VIII
Gender, Fat, and Resistance

Misogyny, homophobia, and anti-fatness have constructed a circle of oppression difficult to challenge. Yet people always have. These chapters give us just a taste of that resistance, of that decision to "come out as fat," from the 1970s in the world that Judith Stein describes, to the online activism that Mibelli and Meloni chart in contemporary Italy, to the ways that Rabbi Bromberg digs deep into the roots of Judaism to locate resistance. What resistance can you imagine? How can you "show up in joy," as Joy Cox asks?

DOI: 10.4324/9781003140665-26

19

COMING OUT AS FAT

Rachele Salvatelli

In the traditional meaning of the expression, "coming out" means to publicly declare someone's sexual orientation or gender identity (Appleby 2001; Oswald 1999; Guittar 2013). Coming out implies that there is an aspect of one's identity waiting to be disclosed and shared, and that the individual who decides to reveal this once-hidden trait, no longer wants it to be kept a secret and therefore they want to "come out of the closet" (Guittar 2013; Plummer 1995). Defined as such, the concept of "coming out" does not seem *prima facie* to be applicable to fat individuals. How could fatness ever be concealed when it is already and necessarily visible?

Being closeted as a fat person does not refer to the act of hiding one's body size but rather, it is about attempting to mitigate societal judgement about one's fat body. As some LGBTQIA+ literature has already discussed, remaining in the closet protects stigmatised individuals from harm and discrimination as well as allowing people to conform to the cultural values of their society (Corrigan et al. 2009). In this sense, remaining in the closet about one's fat embodiment might protect fat individuals – and fat women, in particular – from receiving further harm and discrimination. It is well documented in the literature that fat women have been historically been the target of much stigmatisation because of their size (Farrell 2011; Puhl, Peterson, and Luedicke 2013; Saguy and Ward 2011) and how weight-based stigmatisation has disproportionately been affecting women more than men (Boero 2012; Tischner 2013; Harjunen 2009; Gailey 2014). For this reason, remaining closeted about one's fat embodiment can function as a stigma management strategy aimed at mitigating society's harsh reaction to a woman's "unruly" body.

Staying in the closet about one's fat embodiment is a gendered practice. In her study about teenage girls and diet talks, Nichter (2000) found that participating

DOI: 10.4324/9781003140665-27

in what she termed "fat talk" – i.e., exchanges involving sentences such as "I'm so fat" – was one of the ways in which non-fat teenage girls performed their gender identity, achieved group solidarity and negotiated personal identity. Predictably, fat teenagers would not partake in "fat talk", as that would have "call[ed] attention to their problem" (2000, 52). This reveals how "fat talk" was not about disclosing one's fatness a much as receiving confirmation of the opposite, i.e., that these girls were, in fact, *not* fat. Nichter (2000)'s findings are useful to understand how if gender can be performed through "fat talk", by coming out of the closet, fat women are challenging dominant ways of constructing gender performance. In other words, by stripping away negative connotations to the sentence "I'm so fat", fat women are unveiling the intricate web of meanings that has been attached to fatness all the while questioning gender performances.

So far in this chapter I have explained the gendered nature of being in the closet, but what does it actually mean to come out of the closet as fat? All coming out stories seem to have in common three elements: having a stigmatised identity; the possibility of disclosing one's stigmatised identity and therefore "coming out of the closet"; and having a community of like-minded individuals to join after the "coming out" process. In this chapter, I illustrate how coming out as fat stories meet these three requirements and therefore the concept of "coming out" can soundly be applied to fatness. In other words, fat people have a stigmatised identity, they can use the metaphor of the closet, and they can join a community of like-minded individuals after coming out as fat.

The first section explains how fatness constitutes a stigmatised identity. Using the work of both fat activists and scholars, I list a series of examples of the pervasive and impactful ways in which fat individuals experience weight-based discrimination (Shackelford 2018; Puhl, Peterson, and Luedicke 2013; Boero 2007). I discuss Goffman's (1963) understanding of stigmatisation to explain the link between coming out and stigma management. In particular, I build on the literature on stigma – including Charlton (1998), Oliver (1992) and Link and Phelan (2001) – to explain how coming out can be interpreted as a type of stigma management.

In the second section, I explore the meaning of the metaphor of the closet in the case of fat identity. Aided by the findings of my latest research project (Salvatelli 2019, 2022), I discuss how in coming out as fat stories, the closet is represented by the fear of seeing one's stigma cues being revealed to the public. In other words, although fatness cannot be concealed, fat individuals put in place a series of stigma management strategies aimed at minimising their stigma cues when they are in front of other non-fat individuals. This understanding of the closet means that instead of reclaiming visibility, a fat person coming out as fat is reaffirming their desire to rediscuss their identity, instead of revealing something that was previously hidden. This allows for a broader understanding of coming out, one that does not preclude the possibility of having to come out more than once, even to the same individuals.

The third and final section of this chapter revolves around the concept of a community of like-minded individuals to join after the coming out as fat process. I argue that the formation of a collective identity is based on the perception of a shared knowledge of what fatness entails. The participants of my study manifested a sense of belonging and mutual understanding with other fat individuals. However, this experience is only shared with those fat individuals who have a positive relationship with one's fatness, which reinforces the idea of a fat community that generates after coming out.

Fat Stigma

In order to successfully apply the concept of "coming out" to fatness, it is necessary to discuss whether fatness constitutes a stigmatising trait. A long list of both fat scholars and fat activists have been working to explain the extent and pervasive nature of fatphobia and weight-based discrimination. For example, in 2017, the body liberation organisation *Free Figure Revolution* collected the answers of 6320 participants and published the *2017 Fat Census*, a report created to investigate the intersectional nature of fat discrimination. In particular, they wanted to evaluate "the current state of fat folks in the context of interlocking systems of antifat oppression" (Shackelford 2018, 3). The report revealed a series of widespread weight-based discriminations. For example, 64% of the respondents reported having been misdiagnosed by a healthcare provider because of their weight. In terms of employment discrimination, 40% of participants reported that they had been denied jobs or promotional opportunities because of their size. Weight-based discrimination also impacted respondents' access to facilities – for example, 62% reported being unable to fit in a facility, including restaurants, schools, airlines, and bathroom stalls. The vast majority of the respondents – almost 80% – did not exceed a US size 24, which suggests that larger individuals might be facing even higher discrimination. Nevertheless, this report was able to collect the responses of an ample sample of participants and the scenario that it depicted was one where fat individuals experienced numerous forms of weight-based discriminations disseminated across different aspects of their lives.

The findings of the *2017 Fat Census* are corroborated by wider academic literature. In fact, research overwhelmingly has shown that fat individuals are subjected to various forms of stigmatisation and weight-based discrimination, particularly in the realms of employment, healthcare, education, and representation in the media (Puhl, Peterson, and Luedicke 2013). In relation to employment discrimination, Giel et al. (2012) conducted a study on HR professionals and their hiring strategies. They found that fat candidates are often overlooked and are less likely to be hired compared to their thinner, less qualified competitors. Fatness not only affects the likelihood of being employed, it impacts the wages that fat individuals receive, with some research showing that with every unit increase in body mass index (BMI), women's salary drops by 1.83% in hourly wages (Han, Norton, and Powell 2011).

Weight discrimination also has a detrimental effect on the quality of healthcare that fat people receive. Numerous studies have documented the fat bias that medical providers hold against fat people and how these stigmatising attitudes are enacted by healthcare providers (Brown and Flint 2013; Malterud and Ulriksen 2011). Sabin, Marini, and Nosek (2012) sampled 2284 medical doctors and they found strong implicit and explicit anti-fat bias in their approach to fat patients. Similarly, a study conducted by Gudzune et al. (2013) reported that GPs tend to spend on average less time with their heavier patients.

In terms of education, fat students experience forms of discrimination and weight bias from both their peers and educators alike. Fat students are considered to be less cooperative, intellectually incapable, and having poor social skills (Neumark-Sztainer et al. 1999; Greenleaf and Weiller 2005). These beliefs have lasting impacts on fat students' academic career, as they are less likely than their thinner peers to be offered a place at university (Burmeister et al. 2013).

These forms of weight bias also reflect on the ways in which fatness is constructed in the public discourse (Campo and Mastin 2007; Yoo and Kim 2012). News media create stories of personal responsibility around fatness, significantly overlooking other significant factors outside of a person's control – such as genetic, socio-economic and environmental factors that, it has been argued, play a more important role in determining a person's weight (Kim and Willis 2007). Instead, fatness is mainly presented as a personal responsibility. Boero (2007) conducted a study on articles published in the *New York Times* between 1990 and 2001 and found that these stories portrayed "obesity" as a personal responsibility and fat individuals were described using words such as "stupid", "irresponsible", "lazy", and "repugnant" (Boero 2007).

In the discussion on weight-based discrimination, gender does play a role in the level of stigmatisation that fat people experience. A number of scholars have argued that women are disproportionately affected by weight discrimination compared to their male counterparts (see Mason 2012; Fikkan and Rothblum 2012; Gailey 2014). However, gender is not the only criterion that adds to the level of stigmatisation that fat individuals can encounter in their everyday lives. In fact, weight-based discrimination perfectly captures the intersectionality at play when dealing with issues concerning fatness, i.e., fat discrimination becomes more salient when it intersects with a number of marginalised identities. Gender, race, sexual orientation, disability status – all add layers to the level of stigmatisation that fat individuals face (see Jones 2012; White 2014; Nash and Warin 2017; Fikkan and Rothblum 2012).

The aforementioned examples are not intended to be exhaustive of the many, multifaceted and pervasive forms of discrimination that fat people are forced to endure on a daily basis. However, they do provide necessary context for our understanding of what is like to go through the world in a fat body. As we have established that fat people are subjected to various forms of stigmatisation, what is left to discuss in this section are the stigma management strategies that these individuals put in place in order to mitigate the impact of fat stigma and ultimately, to find a way to live in society with other non-fat people.

Tyler (2020) argues that stigma is a socially determined concept with its own history. Our 21st century understanding of stigmatisation is modelled around 20th century North American sociology and social psychology, which in turn is highly influenced by the work of Erving Goffman (Tyler and Slater 2018). Goffman defines stigma as "the situation of the individual who is disqualified from full social acceptance" (Goffman 1963, 1). He argues that a stigma is an "attribute that is deeply discrediting" (1963, 10), but he also makes the important clarification that rather than seeing stigma as an attribute, we should consider it as a "language of relationships" (1963, 10). This constitutes one of the most original and significant aspects of his contribution: social relationships transform a simple characteristic into a stigmatising trait. Therefore, stigma is not a fixed trait to read on someone else's body, but a contingent entity that moves beyond the individuals and it is socially constructed. In doing so, Goffman opens the doors to the reinterpretation of stigma as a dialectically constructed concept. If stigma is not an attribute, individuals can attach new meanings to it.

As the subtitle of Goffman's book implies, *Stigma* is about the management of spoiled identities, i.e., strategies that stigmatised individuals put in place in order to negotiate their identities and survive in the hostile environment generated by the "normals" (Pausé 2012). According to Goffman, individuals with a stigmatising trait engage in three types of identity management: passing, covering, and withdrawing (Goffman 1963). Passing is the ability of the stigmatised individual to blend in with "normal" society, to pass as a member of the dominant group. Covering is the act of reducing the tension between a stigmatised identity and a disapproving society. Unlike passing – which is necessarily impossible for fat individuals to achieve – covering can be attempted in the case of fatness: "Fat women who are openly shameful and apologetic for their size are covering. Fat individuals who openly share with others that they are dieting, that they are trying to become less than who they are, are covering" (Pausé 2012, 47). The last technique of identity management proposed by Goffman is withdrawal. When stigmatised individuals remove themselves from social activities with other non-stigmatised individuals, they are withdrawing. With the display of these three forms of stigma management, fat people who partake in these performances are at once recreating stigma around fatness – because they actively engage in the creation of negative meanings of it – and are showing signs of the influence that a fatphobic culture has on them, or they would not feel compelled to enact these strategies.

Goffman's theorising of stigma management strategies reveals an element of modernity, particularly for what concerns the act of passing. In the following passage, Goffman – without explicitly mentioning transgender individuals – seem to describe the moment when a transgender person publicly declares their identity:

It may be noted that when relatively complete passing is essayed, the individual sometimes consciously arranges his own *rite de passage*, going to another city, holing up in a room for a few days with preselected clothing and cosmetics he has brought with him, and then, like a butterfly, emerging to try the brand new wings.

(Goffman 1963, 79)

Despite having been written almost 60 years ago, this quote resonates with transgender coming out stories and anticipates the work of a number of transgender studies scholars (see Cooley and Harrison 2012; Fuller, Chang, and Rubin 2009; Zimman 2009; Brumbaugh-Johnson and Hull 2019). However, it is within the same LGBTQIA+ community that Goffman's notion of "passing" shows its limits, as some consider this concept to be outdated and inapplicable (Billard 2019). For many in the trans community, "passing" seems to imply that trans individuals are trying to deceive others: "The ultimate implication is that trans women are not real women but are playing dress-up—and our femininity is merely a costume or disguise" (Daniari 2017). Moreover, for all those individuals who do not identify as female or male – e.g., gender nonconforming, gender queer, non-binary individuals, agender – the concept of "passing" is ultimately meaningless and to some extents counterproductive: "Existing in a society that has been conditioned to believe there are only two genders can present a confusing and painful dilemma" (Daniari 2017).

In Goffman's theorising, these strategies of stigma management are presented as unavoidable, i.e., the stigmatised individual has no other option than passing, covering, or withdrawing if they want to have a positive relationship with the "normals". Goffman's account of stigmatisation has been criticised on multiple fronts, not least because his theorising on the management of spoiled identities only prospects bleak alternatives for stigmatised individuals. In fact, discredited individuals can merely focus their attention on tension management in the social interactions with "normals" and discreditable ones can only hope to hide their "yet-unrevealed" stigma convincingly enough in order to not get discovered. The scenario Goffman creates is one of terror, either of being rejected or being discovered. Passing is, in his words, "inevitable, whether desired or not" (Goffman 1963, 75). Many scholars of stigma – particularly, from a disability studies perspective – have found this approach limited and have built on Goffman's work in order to develop a broader understanding of stigma management (Link and Phelan 2001; Oliver 1992; Charlton 1998; Taylor 2018).

Link and Phelan (2001) suggest that the knowledge on stigmatisation should be created from the standpoint of an individual who experiences stigmatisation or should, at least, be informed by the lived experiences of the people under study. In other words, the knowledge generated by scholars who do not have a stigmatising trait should be informed by the lived experiences of stigmatised individuals. Similarly, Tyler (2018) notes that much work produced on stigmatisation does not perceive stigmatised individuals as knowledgeable subjects: "Stigma draws on the writing of people who understood themselves in various ways as stigmatised [...] but it fails to engage with the authors of this stigma data as 'knowers' or understand these confessional literatures as knowledge" (Tyler 2018, 755). In relation to fatness, a similar argument has been put forward by Cooper (2016) and Pausè (2012, 2019), who argue that fat people should be the central knowledge-creators around fatness and academics as well as policymakers should support fat people in the creation of knowledge around fatness.

The work of disability scholars such as Charlton (1998) and Oliver (1992) as well as Link and Phelan (2001) and Tyler (2018, 2020) are useful in order to develop a broader understanding of stigma management. Disability scholars have argued that it is possible to come out as disabled as a way to express dissatisfaction with the tragic stereotypes attached to disabled identity. For example, McRuer (2006) encourages disabled people to start using the word "crip" to define themselves as an act of rebellious self-affirmation. He exhorts them to come out as "crip". Oliver (1992), on the contrary, prefers the expression "disabled people" as a form of defiant self-labelling. The words "crip", "disabled people", but also "queer" and "fat" are examples of the semantic turn that transformed offences into badges of pride (Shakespeare 1993): "When a despised minority becomes strong enough to bend language to its own uses, some of the stigma formerly attached to it falls away" (Cruikshank 1992, 3). These accounts open up the discussion to a further possibility for stigmatised individuals, one that does not intend to cover their stigmatised identity but rather one that wants to celebrate it. The practice that provides an alternative to the management of spoiled identity – that both incorporates first-hand knowledge of stigmatised individuals and revolves around the notion of a collective identity – is coming out. This line of argument is similar to what fat scholars and activists have been developing around the usage of the word "fat" and the stigma attached to fat identity (Wann 1998; Saguy and Ward 2011; Cooper 1998). In the next section, I will discuss their accounts of coming out as fat and whether the metaphor of the closet can soundly apply to fat identity.

Is There a Closet for Fat People?

In the previous section, I have explained how fatness can soundly be considered a stigmatising trait and the stigma management strategies that fat individuals put in place in order to mitigate the consequences of having a stigmatised identity. The second element necessary in order to claim that it is possible to come out as fat is the existence of a closet, i.e., fat individuals need to be able to conceal their stigmatising identity. Goffman (1963) argued that stigma can be categorised according to its visible or invisible form in discreditable (unknown) and discredited (known/obvious). In this case, fatness is a discredited type of stigma because fat is always already visible and fat individuals cannot hide their fatness. But if fat individuals can never hide their fatness, how could the metaphor of the closet soundly be applied to fat identity?

In the discussion around stigmatised identities, it is useful to distinguish between enacted and felt stigma (Scambler and Hopkins 1986; Goffman 1963). When stigma is enacted, the group of individuals who have a stigmatising trait experience forms of discriminations motivated by a supposed state of inferiority attributed to them. On the contrary, in the case of felt stigma, the individual has internalised the fear of enacted stigma and starts associating feelings of shame with their condition (Salvatelli 2019). In their study on epilepsy, Scrambler and Hopkins (1986) have found that not only felt stigma is not the result of enacted stigma, but rather, that felt stigma precedes enacted stigma. In their research, they found that even when epileptic individuals had disclosed to their employers their condition, they still were "committed to a policy of covering" (1986, 36). This means that individuals whose stigmatised identity is not kept "in the closet" are committed to partaking in stigma management strategies aimed at covering their stigmatising identity: "even once a stigmatized identity is 'out', the fear of being exposed though stigmata or stigmata cues remains untouched" (Salvatelli 2019, 47). By "stigmata cues" I refer to all those signifiers of fatness that although do not render a stigmatised identity visible – because it already necessarily is in the case of fatness – they do function as social reminders of such stigmatised identity. In the case of fatness, there are a number of stigmata or stigma cues that come to mind, such as being out of breath while walking or spilling over someone's seat. In both examples, the fatness is already always visible but being out of breath and spilling over someone's seat function as social reminders of what fatness entails.

I have recently conducted a study on the narratives of fat body positive individuals (Salvatelli 2019, 2022). This study collected the stories of 11 individuals, of whom 7 identified as women, 2 as men and 2 as non-binary. Gender identity and sexual orientation were not used as criteria to sample participants. However, it is important in the context of this discussion to mention that most participants (7 out of 11) self-identified as members of the LGBTQIA+ community. Although I investigated during my fieldwork whether being a member of the LGBTQIA+ community had an influence on the respondents' understanding of coming out as fat, I couldn't identify any meaningful similarities between their coming out as fat stories and their coming out as LGBTQIA+ stories. Most importantly, the coming out as fat stories of LGBTQIA+ participants did not differ in any meaningful way from the ones told by non-LGBTQIA+ participants. This suggests that coming out is a genre in itself and it is not necessarily linked to LGBTQIA+ narratives.

If sexual orientation did not play a role in understanding my participants' coming out stories, gender identity on the contrary constituted an important element of my analysis. When I asked my participants to describe what it was like to be fat, most women and non-binary participants described their fatness as a state of constant alert and defence. Sophie used the example of walking up a flight of stairs and having to reserve a few minutes before joining her friends in order to catch her breath:

> [Being fat] It's just lots of day-to-day things that you aren't aware of, that go through our heads because we're trying to sort of keep up. Not appearances, because I'm not trying to pretend I'm skinny but … pretend I'm just like a normal human and obviously, like I said, if I'm out of breath, they're gonna be like 'Jesus! She should go for a run!'
>
> *(Sophie)*

Much like all the other participants in the study, Sophie would self-identify as fat and expressed a positive attitude in relation to her fatness ("I am happy to genuinely call myself fat"). Nevertheless, she also manifested covering strategies aimed at mitigating the extent of her stigmatised identity. In reserving a few minutes to catch her breath before meeting up with her friends, Sophie was not trying to hide her stigmatised identity, but she was trying to conceal the stigma cues of fatness. In another part of the interview, Sophie described that she enjoyed going for long walks and that they were at times challenging. She expressed a familiarity with the feeling of being out of breath. Nevertheless, this stigma cue becomes relevant only when she is situated in a public space with other non-fat individuals.

Unlike Sophie and most of the other women and non-binary participants, the men who took part in my study emphasised how unconcerned they were with other people looking at their fat bodies:

> They [people] can look at me however they want. They can see me as an Indian guy for goodness sake, I don't care! It's not affecting me. I know who I am. The way somebody else looks at me is not gonna change me. I'm me. They could look at me like I'm a … Navarro Indian or something. It's not gonna make me a Navarro Indian. I'm me.
>
> *(John)*

Throughout the interviews, my male participants dismissed any concern in relation to other people evaluating their bodies. Their accounts echo Monaghan and Malson (2013)'s research on embodied masculinity and weight-related talk. In their study, they argue that men – unlike women – felt indifferent to the possibility of felt or enacted stigma:

> Ah. With guys, well, I get grief for it. And all my mates get grief. I give grief for it. But it generally washes over us, whereas a woman will take it a lot more to heart. I know from my ex-girlfriend, that when she did start to put weight on, and if she heard something, that would be it [i.e. she would be very upset]. Whereas guys would be like [shrugs his shoulders].
>
> *(Noel, 29 in Monaghan and Mason 2013, 310)*

In other words, the men who took part in their study manifested indifference towards other people commenting on their fat bodies as they consider it a "womanly" thing to get bothered by it: "such indifference is suggestive of masculine emotional resilience or toughness, differentiating 'appropriately' masculine narrators from 'sensitive women' and perhaps 'weaker men'" (2013, 310). Similarly, in her study about the experiences of fat college students, Stevens (2018) found that the male participants of her study reported feelings of discomfort with the idea of people evaluating their bodies as they were unaccustomed to this experience, while for the women in her study that gaze seemed to be a part of daily life. This connects with what Gailey (2014) termed "hyper(in)visibility", i.e., women are at one time visible and under public scrutiny, and yet it is also marginalised and erased. As already discussed in the introduction, women have historically been the target of much stigmatisation in relation to their bodies, in general, and fat bodies, in particular (Farrell 2011; Puhl, Peterson, and Luedicke 2013; Saguy and Ward 2011). For this reason, it is possible to understand why the experience of being fat differs in terms of gender: while men appear to be unbothered by how others perceive their fat bodies, women and non-binary individuals are more conscious of how they are perceived by others because this has historically led to them being harmed and discriminated in a way that men have not. The discrepancies of these gendered approaches to fat embodiments suggest that women and non-binary individuals might be more involved than men in stigma management strategies, which include the act of coming out.

The important thing to remember when discussing stigmatised identity is that both stigmatised individuals and "the normals", to use again Goffman's (1963) terminology, share the same sense of normality: "the stigmata are also recognised by the stigmatised" (Riddell and Watson 2003, 37). The findings of my study align with those of Scrambler and Hopkins (1986), i.e., even when a stigmatised identity is already disclosed, stigmatised individuals might partake in stigma management strategies like passing, covering, and withdrawing. In the case of fat identity, the closet does not represent a possibility to hide one's identity. Instead, it refers to the fear of seeing one's stigma cues being exposed. In this sense, every time a fat person publicly discussed their fat identity, they are stripping away their felt stigma (Salvatelli 2019).

A number of fat scholars have argued that it is possible to soundly apply the concept of "coming out" to fat individuals. Rather than reclaiming visibility, a fat person "coming out as fat" reaffirms her desire to rediscuss her identity:

> In proudly coming out as fat, one rejects cultural attitudes that fatness is unhealthy, immoral, ugly, or otherwise undesirable. One claims the right to define the meaning of one's own body and to stake out new cultural meanings and practices around body size.
>
> *(Saguy and Ward 2011, 14)*

When a fat person uses the word "fat" to describe oneself, they stop perceiving their body as a project and start considering it a factuality: "The act of declaring *to be* a fat body, in opposition *to have* a fat body, signifies that the fat person has stopped considering herself as a "not-thin-yet" body, and in doing so she rejects the compulsory thin-bodiedness" (Salvatelli 2019, 48). Much like the word "gay", "queer", and "crip", in using the word "fat" to describe oneself, a fat individual is expressing the desire to initiate a conversation about the meanings attached to fatness and therefore they are also expressing a desire to question common assumptions and stereotypes linked to such stigmatised identity. Pausé (2012) perfectly captures what these stereotypes might be: "Anti-fat attitudes are shaped around the belief that fat people are ugly, sloppy, lazy, asexual, socially unattractive, sexually inactive, undisciplined, dishonest, less productive, and most of all, out of control" (Pausé 2012, 45).

Despite the fact that some fat scholars – including the already mentioned Saguy and Ward (2011) and Pausé (2012) – have positively associated coming out with fatness, it is important to notice that not all fat scholars agree with this position. For example, Sedwick (1990) does not believe in the possibility of a closet for a fat person to come out from and similarly, Murray (2008) has argued that fat women live their embodiment in "multiple, contradictory and eminently ambiguous" ways (Murray 2008, 90) and this prevents them from the act of "coming out", which requires in Murray's view, the capability of declaring an unambiguous identity. Unlike Murray (2008), I do not believe that coming out as fat requires an unambiguous identity. In fact, the very idea of an unambiguous identity – whatever the identity might be – seems an impossibility as every identity is always necessarily ambiguous due to the fact that human existence is complex and multifaceted and therefore can only be characterised by ambiguity. Instead, I understand coming out as fat as a declaration of intent: it is the public affirmation of one's stigmatised identity and the desire to (re)discuss the meanings attached to fatness.

Scholars who have worked with the concept of "coming out" have theorised it as a one-time occurrence (Sedwick 1990; Zimman 2009). Samules (2003) uses the distinction between coming out and coming out *to* someone in order to describe the specific moment in which a person either comes to term with their stigmatised identity or articulates their so-called "coming out story". In both scenarios, coming out only occurs one time. Similarly, Liang (1994) understands coming out as "the last straw" (141), i.e., the clearly identifiable moment in a person's life where they can no longer keep their stigmatised identity "in the closet" and therefore decide to publicly let it all out. Even Plummer (1995), whose account of coming out extends beyond its traditional LGBTQIA+ meaning, only theorises coming out as a one-time occurrence, i.e., the first time someone comes out to their parents, friends, colleagues, etc. None of these scholars has ever questioned the possibility to have to come out *again*. But as I understand coming out – and coming out as fat, in particular – as a public affirmation of the desire to rediscuss one's stigmatised identity, then it would be possible to come out more than once. Every time a fat person uses the word "fat" to describe themselves, they are coming out as fat. This means that coming out as fat is not a one-time occurrence, but instead it is an act that can be repeated overtime. A fat person can come out for the first time to their family members, their friends, colleagues etc. but also, they might come out a second time, a third, and so on.

Although coming out as fat exemplifies how it is possible for someone with a stigmatised identity to come out repeatedly, even to the same person, this revelatory act is not exclusive of fat bodies. In fact, I would argue that this new understanding of coming out – i.e., coming out as a declaration of intents and desires to challenge common assumptions about a certain stigmatised identity – can soundly be applied to a variety of stigmatised identities, including LGBTQIA+ identities. Within LGBTQIA+ literature, coming out as already been framed as an act that can be repeated overtime. For example, Brumbaugh-Johnson and Hull (2019) argue that coming out as transgender is as an ongoing and socially embedded practice and Guittar and Rayburn (2016) define LGBQ coming out as a "career", i.e., "a perpetually managed social endeavour which requires concurrent internal and external identity management" (352–353). Despite leaving room for the act of coming out to be repeated over time, these accounts still frame coming out as an event whose purpose is to disclose something about one's identity that was previously hidden. Instead, I propose a more inclusive understanding of coming out, one that does not consider coming out as a "crossing the bridge" scenario and instead allows for the possibility to come out more than once, even to the same individuals. Defined as such, coming out serves the purpose of initiating a conversation about stigmatised identities, including, but not limited to, fat identity, transgender identity, gay identity, lesbian identity, and so on. "Because our understanding of coming out is not bound to the revelatory act of revealing something that was previously hidden, we can imagine a series of scenarios in which coming out is repeated through time" (Salvatelli 2019, 49). Every time a fat person decides to use the word "fat" to describe themselves in public with the intent of discussing the meanings attached to their stigmatised identity, they are coming out.

Collective Fat Identity

In the previous two sections, I have discussed how fatness can be considered a stigmatising trait and have explored the possibility of applying the metaphor of the closet to fat individuals. The third and final element left to discuss in order to successfully apply the concept of "coming out" to fatness is the possibility of having a community of like-minded individuals to join after the coming out process. The findings of my research project on the narratives of fat body positive individuals provide again some useful insight on this matter (Salvatelli 2022). After having started to use the word "fat" to describe themselves and having attributed positive connotations to their fat identity, most participants reported a sense of belonging and shared experiences in relation to other fat individuals:

I just feel a bit more comfortable around people who have been through the same stuff that I've been through. Insults … the same struggles. […] Coming to these events [fat friendly, body positive events] I can dance. At other places I wouldn't really dance. Just because I feel a bit self-conscious. But there, I'm just on the dancefloor boogieing.

(Leor)

Yeah, I guess people with a similar body type, I'm probably more inclined to initially get along with and I know that sounds terrible, I think it's because you know there is going to be a mutual understanding there. Even if you don't have a conversation, you know there's gonna be like mutual, similar experiences … about the daily little thoughts. The changes you have to make. So I think it changed that because I'm immediately more, "oh that person is like me, we're gonna have a similar understanding on a big part of my life".

(Sophie)

This sense of belonging that fat body positive individuals experience after having developed a positive relationship with one's fat embodiment is the result of their coming out as fat, i.e., after they have started to publicly affirm the desire to rediscuss their stigmatised identity and question common assumptions around fatness, they have found a community of like-minded individuals. It is important to mention in this context, that this sense of collective fat identity was found in the stories of all participants, regardless of their gender identity. That is to say that women, as well as men and non-binary individuals felt a connection with other fat individuals based on their shared understanding of fatness. It is not clear whether this fat community actually exists, but it is perceived by them as real. As Polletta and Jasper (2001) have argued, collective identity does not have to be experienced directly, but it can also be imagined:

Collective identity describes imagined as well as concrete communities, involves an act of perception and construction as well as the discovery of preexisting bonds, interests, and boundaries. It is fluid and relational, emerging out of interactions with a number of different audiences […] rather than fixed. It channels words and actions, enabling some claims and deeds but delegitimizing others. It provides categories by which individuals divide up and make sense of the social world.

(Polletta and Jasper 2001, 298)

This fat collective identity is not the results of individuals sharing a stigmatising trait. In fact, as Young (1990) has argued, having similar attributes does not constitute per se a collective identity. What is required in the formation of a collective identity is the perception of a shared knowledge of what fatness entails (Salvatelli 2019). Sophie's words perfectly capture this when she says, "you know there is going to be like mutual, similar experiences". This sense of collective fat identity is not always experienced by all fat individuals, but only with those who are fat *and* positive about their fatness, which reinforces the idea of a fat community that generates after "coming out":

> If I'm on a train and I'm gonna sit down, there is a look that I've noticed and I'm probably just speculating a bit, I'm wearing something flamboyant or that is like close-cut, I do notice a look that I get from other plus size people. Why are you wearing that? You shouldn't be wearing that. Sometimes I'll find it, I'm very intimidated by the other plus size people because I've lived in a plus size body without a body positive mind and I know that is very easy to be like ... I used to go into a room and think, "am I the fattest person in this room?" And I see somebody that is bigger than me, I'll be like, "I'm fine then". But I will also be a bit judgemental, "oh well ... As long as I'm not as fat as them, then I'm fine". You know what I mean? But then if I see another fat person and they're like really cool or smiley, have a cool backpack or shoes then I'm like, oh hey brother, what's happening?
>
> *(Nancy)*

This sense of collective fat identity is not shared indiscriminately with all fat people, but only with those who are perceived to be positive about their fatness. However, this community is far less homogenous than one might think. Some of my participants were what in the "fatosphere" – an online fat-acceptance community (Dickins et al. 2011) – would be considered "small fats" (UK dress size 18), while others were significantly larger (UK dress size 26 and above). In their narratives, participants tended to narrate stories in which their experiences were directly set against other "less fat" or "fatter" individuals. So even within the same small group of people, we see how divided this community can be. In discussing the implications of identity claims, Fraser (2000) exhorts us to be caution about the risks of reification, i.e., by forcing individuals to display an "authentic, self-affirming and self-generated collective identity" there is a risk that individuals might feel pressured into conforming to a given group identity (2000, 111). This means that even though participants might feel a sense of collective identity with other fat body positive individuals, this should not lead us to believe that this community is unambiguous or cohesive. The community that develops after the coming out process is not a homogenous one and in fact, given the variety of experiences that these individuals face, a great deal of ambiguity is present within the data. In other words, we should be mindful of the complexities of human experience when discussing collective identities. Nevertheless, despite its diversity, it is possible to identify a community that generates after the coming out as fat process. This reinforces the idea that – much like other individuals who have used coming out stories as a mean to positively evaluate one's stigmatised identity – fat individuals who are positive about their fatness can join a community of like-minded individuals after coming out as fat.

Conclusion

In this chapter, I have discussed how the concept of coming out can soundly be applied to fatness as coming out as fat fulfils the three requirements of every coming out story, i.e., fatness constitutes a stigmatised identity; the metaphor of "the closet" can be applied to fatness, and it is possible to join a community of like-minded individuals after coming out as fat. The women and non-binary participants who took part in my study about the narratives of fat body positive individuals have shared with me a series of coming out stories, including the first time they realised they were fat, the first time they decided to use to word "fat" to describe themselves, the first time they had a conversation with their loved ones about their fat identity. They also told me stories of "second times", like the repeated discussions they had with family members about their fat positive and body positive identity and the many times when they had to keep reaffirming their desire to challenge fat stereotypes both with friends, family members, and medical professionals. The fact that women and non-binary participants – unlike men – participated in the creation of coming out stories sheds a light on the gendered nature of these practices. In all of these stories, they were coming out as fat, i.e., they were expressing a desire to publicly rediscuss the meaning of their stigmatised identity. As I have argued in this chapter, not only the concept of "coming out" can soundly apply to fatness but we should also entertain the possibility that coming out might not be a "crossing-the-bridge" scenario, but an act that can be repeated overtime. Every time a fat person decides to publicly affirm one's stigmatised identity, they are coming out. The desire of publicly discussing the meanings attached to one's stigmatised identity that results from coming out as fat generated a community of other fat individuals who wanted to rediscuss the meanings of fatness. The participants of my study on the narratives of fat body positive individuals experienced a sense of collective fat identity with other fat individuals who – much like them – had come out as fat and therefore had started expressing positive feelings about their fatness. This reinforces the idea that it is possible to join a community of like-minded individuals after having come out as fat.

Bibliography

Appleby, George Alan. 2001. "Ethnographic study of gay and bisexual working-class men in the United States." *Journal of Gay & Lesbian Social Services.* 12 (3–4): 51–62.

Billard, Thomas J. 2019. "'Passing' and the politics of deception: Transgender bodies, cisgender aesthetics, and the policing of inconspicuous marginal identities." In Docan-Morgan T. (ed) *The Palgrave Handbook of Deceptive Communication*, pp. 463–477. London: Palgrave Macmillan.

Boero, Natalie. 2007. "All the news that's fat to print: The American 'obesity epidemic' and the media." *Qualitative Sociology*. 30 (1): 41–60.

Boero, Natalie. 2012 *Killer Fat*. New Brunswick: Rutgers University Press.

Brown, Ian, and Stuart W. Flint. 2013. "Weight bias and the training of health professionals to better manage obesity: What do we know and what should we do?" *Current Obesity Reports*. 2 (4): 333–340.

Brumbaugh-Johnson, Stacey M., and Kathleen E. Hull. 2019. "Coming out as transgender: Navigating the social implications of a transgender identity." *Journal of Homosexuality*. 66 (8): 1148–1177.

Burmeister, Jacob M., Allison E. Kiefner, Robert A. Carels, and Dara R. Musher-Eizenman. 2013. "Weight bias in graduate school admissions." *Obesity*. 21 (5): 918–920.

Campo, Shelly, and Teresa Mastin. 2007. "Placing the burden on the individual: Overweight and obesity in African American and mainstream women's magazines." *Health Communication*. 22 (3): 229–240.

Charlton, James. 1998. *Nothing About Us Without Us. Disability Oppression and Empowerment*. Berkeley, CA: University of California Press.

Cooley, Dennis R., and Kelby Harrison. 2012 *Passing/Out: Sexual Identity Veiled and Revealed*. London: Routledge.

Cooper, Charlotte. 1998. *Fat and Proud*. London: The Women's Press.

Cooper, Charlotte. 2016. *Fat Activism. A Radical Social Movement*. Bristol: HammerOn Press.

Corrigan, Patrick W., Jonathon E. Larson, Julie Hautamaki, Alicia Matthews, Sachi Kuwabara, Jennifer Rafacz, Jessica Walton, Abigail Wassel, and John O'Shaughnessy. 2009. "What lessons do coming out as gay men or lesbians have for people stigmatized by mental illness?" *Community Mental Health Journal*. 45 (5): 366–374.

Cruikshank, Margaret. 1992. *The Gay and Lesbian Liberation Movement*. London: Routledge.

Daniari, Serena. 2017. *Walking While Trans. An Immersive Look into the Transgender Experience*. [Online]. Available at: https://mic.com/articles/186998/walking-while-trans#.lo8w9FiOE [Accessed 08 January 2022].

Dickins, Marissa, Samantha L. Thomas, Bri King, Sophie Lewis, and Kate Holland. 2011. "The role of the fatosphere in fat adults' responses to obesity stigma: A model of empowerment without a focus on weight loss." *Qualitative Health Research*. 21 (12): 1679–1691.

Farrell, Amy Erdman. 2011. *Fat Shame: Stigma and the Fat Body in American Culture*. New York: NYU Press.

Fikkan, Janna L., and Esther D. Rothblum. 2012. "Is fat a feminist issue? Exploring the gendered nature of weight bias." *Sex Roles*. 66 (9): 575–592.

Fraser, Nancy. 2000. "Rethinking recognition." *New Left Review*. 3: 107.

Fuller, Craig B., Doris F. Chang, and Lisa R. Rubin. 2009. "Sliding under the radar: Passing and power among sexual minorities." *Journal of LGBT Issues in Counseling*. 3 (2): 128–151.

Gailey, Jeannine. 2014. *The Hyper (In) visible Fat Woman: Weight and Gender Discourse in Contemporary Society*. London: Springer.

Giel, Katrin E., Stephan Zipfel, Manuela Alizadeh, Norbert Schäffeler, Carmen Zahn, Daniel Wessel, Friedrich W. Hesse, Syra Thiel, and Ansgar Thiel. 2012. "Stigmatization of obese individuals by human resource professionals: An experimental study." *BMC Public Health*. 12 (1): 1–9.

Goffman, Ervin. 1963. *Stigma. Notes on the Management of Spoiled Identity*. Englewood Cliffs, NJ: Prentice Hall.

Greenleaf, Christy, and Karen Weiller. 2005. "Perceptions of youth obesity among physical educators." *Social Psychology of Education*. 8 (4): 407–423.

Gudzune, Kimberly A., Mary Catherine Beach, Debra L. Roter, and Lisa A. Cooper. 2013. "Physicians build less rapport with obese patients." *Obesity*. 21 (10): 2146–2152.

Guittar, Nicholas A. 2013. "The meaning of coming out: From self-affirmation to full disclosure." *Qualitative Sociology Review*. 9 (3): 168–187.

Guittar, Nicholas A., and Rachel L. Rayburn. 2016 "Coming out: The career management of one's sexuality." *Sexuality & Culture*. 20 (2): 336–357.

Han, Euna, Edward C. Norton, and Lisa M. Powell. 2011. "Direct and indirect effects of body weight on adult wages." *Economics & Human Biology*. 9 (4): 381–392.

Harjunen, Hannele. 2009. *Women and Fat: Approaches to the Social Study of Fatness*. PhD Thesis. Jyväskylä: University of Jyväskylä.

Jones, Lauren E. 2012. "The framing of fat: Narratives of health and disability in fat discrimination litigation." *New York University Law Review*. 87 (6): 1996–2039.

Kim, Sei-Hill, and L. Anne Willis. 2007. "Talking about obesity: News framing of who is responsible for causing and fixing the problem." *Journal of Health Communication*. 12 (4): 359–376.

Liang, A. C. 1994. "Coming out as transition and transcendence of the public/private dichotomy." In *Cultural Performances: Proceedings of the Third Berkeley Women and Language Conference*, pp. 409–420. Berkeley, CA: University of California Press.

Link, Bruce G., and Jo C. Phelan. 2001. "Conceptualizing stigma." *Annual Review of Sociology*. 27 (1): 363–385.

Malterud, Kirsti, and Kjersti Ulriksen. 2011. "Obesity, stigma, and responsibility in health care: A synthesis of qualitative studies." *International Journal of Qualitative Studies on Health and Well-being*. 6 (4): 8404.

Mason, Katherine. 2012. "The unequal weight of discrimination: Gender, body size, and income inequality." *Social Problems*. 59 (3): 411–435.

McRuer, Robert. 2006. *Crip Theory: Cultural Signs of Queerness and Disability*. New York: New York University Press.

Monaghan, Lee F., and Helen Malson. 2013. "'It's worse for women and girls': Negotiating embodied masculinities through weight-related talk." *Critical Public Health*. 23 (3): 304–319.

Murray, Samantha. 2008. *The "Fat" Female Body*. London: Palgrave Macmillan.

Nash, Meredith, and Megan Warin. 2017. "Squeezed between identity politics and intersectionality: A critique of 'thin privilege' in Fat Studies." *Feminist Theory*. 18 (1): 69–87.

Neumark-Sztainer, Dianne, Mary Story, Cheryl Perry, and Mary Anne Casey. 1999. "Factors influencing food choices of adolescents: Findings from focus-group discussions with adolescents." *Journal of the American Dietetic Association*. 99 (8): 929–937.

Nichter, Mimi. 2000. *Fat Talk*. Cambridge, MA: Harvard University Press.

Oliver, Michael. 1992. *Understanding Disability: From Theory to Practice*. New York: St Martin's Press.

Oswald, Ramona Faith. 1999. "Family and friendship relationships after young women come out as bisexual or lesbian." *Journal of Homosexuality*. 38, no. 3: 65–83.

Pausé, Cat. 2020. Ray of Light: Standpoint Theory, Fat Studies, and a New Fat Ethics, *Fat Studies*. 9 (2): 175–187. DOI: 10.1080/21604851.2019.1630203

Pausè, Cat. 2012. "Live to tell: Coming out as fat". *Somatechnics*. 2 (1): 42–56.

Pausé, Cat, and Sonya Renee Taylor, eds. 2021. *The Routledge International Handbook of Fat Studies*. New York: Taylor & Francis.

Plummer, Kenneth. 1995. *Telling Sexual Stories: Power, Change and Social Worlds*. London: Routledge.

Polletta, Francesca, and James M. Jasper. 2001. "Collective identity and social movements." *Annual Review of Sociology.* 27 (1): 283–305.

Puhl, Rebecca, Jamie Lee Peterson, and Joerg Luedicke. 2013. "Fighting obesity or obese persons? Public perceptions of obesity-related health messages." *International Journal of Obesity.* 37 (6): 774–782.

Riddell, Sheila, and Nick Watson. 2003. *Disability, Culture and Identity.* London: Routledge.

Sabin, Janice A., Maddalena Marini, and Brian A. Nosek. 2012. "Implicit and explicit anti-fat bias among a large sample of medical doctors by BMI, race/ethnicity and gender." *PloS One.* 7 (11): e48448.

Saguy, Abigail C., and Anna Ward. 2011 "Coming out as fat: Rethinking stigma." *Social Psychology Quarterly.* 74 (1): 53–75.

Salvatelli, Rachele. 2019. "On fat female embodiment: Narratives of 'coming out as fat'". *International Journal of Social Sciences and Interdisciplinary Studies.* 4 (1): 43–52.

Salvatelli, Rachele. 2022. *A Study on the Body Positive Movement: Narratives of Fat Body Positive Individuals.* PhD Thesis. York: University of York.

Samuels, Ellen. 2003. "My body, my closet." *GLQ: Journal of Lesbian and Gay Studies.* 9 (1): 233–255.

Scambler, Graham, and Anthony Hopkins. 1986. "Being epileptic: Coming to terms with stigma." *Sociology of Health & Illness.* 8 (1): 26–43.

Sedgwick, Eve. 1990. *Epistemology of the Closet.* Berkeley, CA: University of California Press.

Shackelford, Ashleigh. 2018. *The Executive Summary of the 2017 Fat Census.* Atlanta, GA: Free Figure Revolution.

Shakespeare, Tom. 1993. "Disabled people's self-organisation: A new social movement?" *Disability, Handicap & Society.* 8 (3): 249–264.

Stevens, Corey. 2018. "Fat on campus: Fat college students and hyper (in) visible stigma." *Sociological Focus.* 51 (2): 130–149.

Taylor, Allison. 2018 "'Flabulously' femme: Queer fat femme women's identities and experiences." *Journal of Lesbian Studies.* 22 (4): 459–481.

Tischner, Irmgard. 2013. *Fat lives: A Feminist Psychological Exploration.* London: Routledge.

Tyler, Imogen. 2018. "Resituating Erving Goffman: From stigma power to black power." *The Sociological Review.* 66 (4): 744–765.

Tyler, Imogen. 2020. *Stigma. The Machinery of Inequality.* London: ZED.

Tyler, Imogen, and Tom Slater. 2018. "Rethinking the sociology of stigma." *The Sociological Review Monographs.* 66 (4): 721–743.

Wann, Marilyn. 1998. *Fat! So?: Because You Don't Have to Apologize for Your Size!.* Berkeley: Ten Speed Press.

White, Francis Ray. 2014. "Fat/trans: Queering the activist body." *Fat Studies* 3 (2): 86–100.

Yoo, Jina H., and Junghyun Kim. 2012. "Obesity in the new media: A content analysis of obesity videos on YouTube." *Health Communication.* 27 (1): 86–97.

Young, Iris Marion. 1990. *Justice and the Politics of Difference.* Princeton, NJ: Princeton University Press.

Zimman, Lal. 2009. "'The other kind of coming out': Transgender people and the coming out narrative genre." *Gender & Language.* 3 (1): 53–80.

20

FAT AIR

Judith Stein with Meridith Lawrence and Susan Stinson

Judith Stein: In early 1995, for reasons that no one remembers, three friends, all fat activists in Massachusetts, sat down to tape an interview. The interviewer was writer Susan Stinson. The interviewed activists were me – Judith Stein – and Meridith Lawrence. We were a lesbian couple who had been together for 12 years at that time. The final interview was called "Fat Air." Now, 26 years later, we are publishing the interview, which gives a picture of a moment in the history of the East Coast Fat Liberation movement, in this volume, the *Reader in Gender and Fat Studies*.

In the 15 years or so before the time of the interview, there was an active fat lesbian community in Boston. We organized social activities, clothing swaps, fat swims, going to dances together – all ways to challenge the existing mentality of the time, that fat women were deeply flawed and should really hate ourselves and certainly should be dieting. We definitely should not go out into the world. And most especially, we should not go out into the world together.

Fat Liberation in Boston sponsored a number of activities to spread our message. We believed that being fat was fine; that the medical community misrepresented their own research about the supposed dangers of being fat; that it was possible *and* desirable to have a wonderful life in the body you had. We held workshops at women's music festivals; we organized a benefit fashion show that included fat models. We went out to eat together, ordered everything we wanted to eat and ate it with relish. We shared ideas about how to choose to ignore or respond to the hostility and stares we incurred. We wrote articles for local gay and feminist newspapers, commenting on fat oppression where we saw it. We distributed the groundbreaking materials from the Fat Underground.[1] We did everything we could to spread the word and support fat women learning to love themselves.

DOI: 10.4324/9781003140665-28

Most of us in the movement as I knew it at that time were white lesbians. We were very aware of how fat-hatred, misogyny and homophobia merged into one large weapon used to oppress us. (We knew there were fat men who experienced fat oppression. But in those years, that was not something we wanted to take on.) Unfortunately, we were not as aware of the intersections of fat hatred with other oppressions – white supremacy or classism – or at least I wasn't. Although our lens was flawed it was definitely political. Every kind of organizing we did was political, even if it was something as simple as going out for ice cream together.

By the late 1980s, I had stepped away from most Fat Liberation organizing. Meridith stepped up to run fat women's discussion groups and other activities promoting Fat Liberation.

Reading this interview again in 2021 makes me feel wistful and tender. I miss believing that we were changing the world in fundamental ways. I am comforted now by the newer modes of Fat Liberation organizing and the care the movement is taking to attend to the connections between fat oppression and white supremacy. I still believe that radical change is needed, and I am encouraged by the presence of so many younger activists.

What follows is our 1995 interview. (Judith Stein is "J." Meridith Lawrence is "M." And Susan Stinson is "S.")

★★★

J: When I first heard about the Fat Dyke anthology,[2] I thought it was a great idea. I started thinking about what I could write, and I drew a total blank. That floored me – I felt like I had nothing I needed to say about being fat. What a change from when I started doing fat liberation work. Then I began to wonder how is it that being fat gets to be not an issue? I mean, fat oppression is still raw and happens to me really often and still hurts me. But a lot of the time, it's like "Who cares?"

S: I want to ask if part of how you got that feeling is that you are together, two fat lesbians. Were you consciously looking for fat lovers?

M: I was. Right before Judith and I got together, I said to a friend, "my next girlfriend is going to be fat and Jewish." I had already met Judith in 1979 and this was in early 1982. Judith and I got together in September '82. I had been thinking about her and when I moved back to Boston in '81. I thought "Oh I gotta get in touch with the fat community here." At the time, I knew Judith Stein and one other fat dyke.

S: How did you know them?

M: I had met them at the Michigan Womyn's Music Festival in 1979. And I had also seen Judith at the Michigan Womyn's Music Festival in 81 ….

S: (interrupting) And what was she wearing? I want details … (laughs)

M: She was wearing dyed balloon pants from Making It Big and that's it!

S: Ooooohhh …

M: There were all these women behind her. And I thought. "oh, Here comes the queen with her entourage." She said hi. I said hi. And that was it. I felt like just one of the girls following her, although I didn't really follow her around. But I knew I wanted someone fat because I had started thinking about fat liberation in '77 or '78. I was living in Michigan in a collective household and a dyke I lived with brought back the Fat Underground information with her from Los Angeles. I read this stuff and it was like, Oh! Major Click. Immediately it was "OK, I am going to stop dieting." I was 23 at the time. When I went to Michigan in '79, it was like. "Oh wow, fat liberation is here." so my way of thinking changed.

S: How about you Judith, were you looking for a fat lover??

J: My last lover was a fat woman and that was deliberate. I wasn't looking to get into a relationship when Meridith and I got together because I had just broken up with my last lover three weeks before and I was kind of a ragged mess. But I did want to have sex with Meridith, and it just worked out to be bigger than … (laughs).

I started organizing Fat Lesbians in early 1978 in Boston, that was the first group. I did that because *I* needed it. I had gotten the Fat Underground literature, maybe I sent to California, I don't even know where I got it. It came in the mail, and I was ready to kick ass. So, we had this group in Cambridge and we did some organizing in the lesbian and feminist communities.

I went to Michigan in 1979 and a couple of the other Boston fat dykes went also. When I saw the program from Michigan and there was no fat liberation stuff, I thought, "Oh, I'm gonna organize some fat lesbian stuff, support groups, something." So, I did, and we met, you know, I just put up signs. R. was there and she had a tipi, so we started meeting at her tipi because it was a real easy landmark to find. That was in 1979. She and I got involved and she moved to Boston, I think somewhere earlyish in 1980.

I wanted a lover who understood my life and my body. The fact that she was fat and was into being fat was mandatory for me. So, I knew when R. and I broke up that I wasn't going to have a thin lover again, it was just too foreign, It wasn't affirming to me. It *was* affirming to have a fat lover.

M: You know, on our first date Judith and I slept together, and I remember thinking at some point in that night that any other time I had sex for the first time, I was scared to take off my clothes. I had some trepidation. Because they were going to see my body for the first time and would they run screaming from the room, or would they not? I just knew that when Judith and I got undressed that there wasn't going to be any of that and it was just a whole different mindset, right from the get-go for me.

S: How long ago was that?

M: Twelve years.

S: That's a long time!

J: (Laughing) It's shocking that it's been such a long time.

S: So now I want to talk to you about where you live, what your home is like.

M: We moved in together after we had been together for seven years.

Anything we've bought since we moved in together, a priority has always been "Is this going to be comfortable?" There's nowhere in the house where we really have to squeeze by anything to get anywhere. We set it up so that you can walk freely throughout, and you don't bump into furniture. And then a lot of the decorations are fat images. There are pictures, tiles, artwork, little Venus of Willendorf statues ...

J: Everywhere you look.

M: There are a lot of Venus of Willendorfs!

J: The last time I lived with a lover before Meridith was the first woman I was lovers with. In our apartment we had furniture that I couldn't sit on. She had furniture, antiques from her family, that I was not allowed to sit on in case I broke them. I tolerated a lot in that relationship that I would never tolerate again. Certainly, I was never again going to live with furniture that I couldn't sit on.

S: I've been to your house. When I walk in there I get this blast of, you know, it's such a beautiful house and there are *so* many fat, positive, beautiful things anywhere you look, in the bathroom, in the living room. Do you still notice it or is it just normal to you now to be surrounded by gorgeous fat images?

M: It's new and it's old all at once for me. The other day I was sitting in the living room and I was looking at this clay sculpture we have of a fat woman and I thought "That is so beautiful."

J: There are a few images I have that I am always aware of. I have this little wall sculpture in my bedroom of a fat woman whose legs surround a mirror. I bought it about ten or eleven years ago when I was shopping with my parents. My mother couldn't understand why I would buy it. She said, "See, you buy that sculpture. That's why you can't buy a car!"

Well, that was a typical kind of twisted logic for her – that a $12 purchase made the difference between owning a car or not. I think the sculpture probably made her very uncomfortable, because it was a naked woman, and a naked fat woman to boot! But buying that sculpture was the first time I flew in the face of very overt disapproval and censure. I knew this sculpture was special, these images don't exist everywhere. I knew that if I didn't buy this fat image, I was never going to see it again. It's this fat woman playing a flute with fish around her. It's really wonderful. So sometimes I notice things, because buying them was a deliberate act of affirmation. Other times all these fat images are just like the air we breathe. The air in the house is fat air, nice, you know, you walk in and it's like there is nothing in there that is not fat or fat positive.

S: Do you have rules? Like do you talk about fat oppression in your house? Or do you constantly keep it positive?

M: I don't think we talk about fat oppression per se, in our house, but we do talk about what it means to be a fat woman in the world. I'm not without my own self-doubts and so I don't feel like I'm Wonder Woman every day that I wake up. Then, of course, once you step out of our wonderful house there is the rest of the world. I have diabetes, so there have been discussions in the past about diet products coming into the house because sometimes I want something that has NutraSweet in it. There have been discussions like that. I don't know, did we ever set up, ever have a conscious conversation like "Oh, let's put up fat images?" I mean we see fat images, we buy them. They look like us, we love them.!

J: I think we need all these real images. The one thing about having the Venus of Willendorf all around our house is that she's not exactly a true-to-life image. We do have some pictures that are real women with whole bodies. I mean we're real women and we have lumps and bumps and varicose veins and scars and hanging breasts. I just think that the more you can see real fat women, the better.

There are some other things about living with a fat woman that are nice. We'll be watching a sitcom and it gets fat oppressive. I mean, I know that hardly ever happens. (giggle), but you don't even have to ask, you just flip off of it. Diet commercials, you flip off. You don't even have to ask.

M: We've had conversations about language, but not so much about our surroundings.

S: What about language?

M: Well, once Judith said to me, "Oh, my ankles aren't so shapely." I might either make a joke like. "Well, they are shaped like the Venus of Willendorf now." or I might just say "You're full of shit!" (hearty laugh). "Where is that coming from?"

I remember when we first got together we were cooking dinner and someone started eating a snack. This happened once from me and once from her. We both kind of said to the other one "You'll ruin your dinner." We were kind of shocked that we even said something like that, so we talked and agreed that we don't say that stuff anymore. From time to time we say things and realize that they come from the old tapes that we want to get out of our heads. So, I think these conversations just foster this atmosphere of loving ourselves even more than we already do.

J: I was thinking about food because we are really committed to abundance. Because we are both working at good jobs we buy a lot of groceries, we have good food in the house, and we have a lot of food in the house. That's another thing we do. We make sure there is plenty so you never have to worry about there not being enough, or you can eat as much as you want to eat. You can eat seventeen bagels until all the bagels are gone. There is enough of everything and there is more where that came from. There is never any scarcity around food in our house.

M: The other thing is when I was in school and I got diagnosed with diabetes, we had a lot of conversations about living together. Neither of us had lived with lovers in a long time and the last time we both did, it didn't turn out so well. We had many conversations about where we were going to live, what it was going to look like and even down to what was going to be in the refrigerator. I remember saying to Judith, "OK, when we move in together and I'm making good salary, I want at least three kinds of cheese in the cheese drawer at all times." Partly from having been deprived of food as a kid, and partly from having diabetes, I want a lot of good stuff to eat that doesn't involve sugar.

S: I have another question. I don't know if you want to do this for the record. If you would talk about sex at all and sex with fat women, specifically each other ...

M: I love sex with fat women.

S: Would you like to have more sex with fat women?

M: Well, in general, although time gets to be a problem. And monogamy kind of gets in the way.

S: You are monogamous?

M: Yeah, yeah well yeah. (laughing) in my mind I'm not.

S: Well, you do openly admire other fat women.

M: We have a clause – you can look, you can talk, you can flirt, you can have crushes, but you cannot touch.

J: I mean I lust after other women a lot, but I am not going to do anything about it, it's not that serious. I don't want to deal with what it would mean.

M: And we don't get enough time alone. I mean we get time alone, but part of aging for me is that I need more time to rest and relax. But the desire is definitely there. That's the other thing, the last relationship I was in was a three- and one–half-year relationship and we stopped having sex after six months. I think part of that was because I was fat. So, after all this time we are still having sex, probably not as much as when we first got together, but there is still lust, there is still desire, there is still grabbing at each other. Every day we tell each other how cute we are, and if someone doesn't say "Oh, you're cute" then one of us will say "Aren't I just adorable!" (hearty laughter). Or it might be, "I'm just irresistible, I don't know how you resist me." That's my big line, and she goes "Yeah, who's resisting?" (giggles)

J: One thing I like with fat women, a fat lover, is that you don't have to worry if you're going to smash her if you roll over on her. There are not too many sharp edges. There are some things that I think are a little harder physically to do, like that concept of rubbing cunts together. That has been gone since I was about 11 when I got a stomach; I've never quite figured that one out. But there are more things that make up for it, I mean, a fat stomach and a big fat tushie are the most glorious things on the planet. So, sex is really swell.

The fat women that I became lovers with were loving themselves or working to love themselves. So that is a whole different thing. I don't know what it would be like to be lovers with a fat woman who is dieting or is really just hating herself, because I don't know how any woman in that state could have really jolly sex anyway. For me, one of the things that is nice about being long-term is that we've gotten to know a lot about what each other likes. And you just don't have to worry about the things that are embarrassing when you have sex with someone for the first time.

M: There really isn't anything that has not happened in twelve years, so nothing is embarrassing. Sometimes Judith will get embarrassed and I will say, "It's me, me! There is no one, no one else here. OK, the cat's here, but he's covering his eyes."

J: One of the things about being together so long is that I am twelve years older so on a Sunday night the thought of staying up all night to have sex as opposed to sleeping before I go to work is a little less appealing. Other things get in the way of sex more. I don't think that's because we're fat. When Meri got diabetes, that was a big issue; my job changed a lot, and I was under a lot of stress – these things come up in front of sexual desire more than they did when we were newly in love and younger.

M: When we were newly in love, our sexual desire was in front of us all the time. I wasn't particularly happy at my job. But then there you were, so I could put the job aside and just have sex. "Let's call in sick and just have sex all day." There was a point where it became really clear to me that the whole relationship moved into this really, really safe place. I don't think that's a function of us being fat, I think it's a function of long term, that we just sort of moved into this place where everything became really nice and comfortable. I don't mean that in a negative way, I mean very stable, very secure, very just ... I know I'm loved. A lot of times I describe the way I feel loved is that I am in this warm bath of Judith's love and everywhere I turn. I know it's around me, it's a sphere around my body.

S: How do you know?

M: I feel it because it's affirmed every day. It's affirmed through sex, because we are still having sex after twelve years, and she just tells me all the time. In the car on the way here she told me "I'm just crazy about you."

J: I also said I wish that you could do something that we can't do while we're driving down the highway. (laughter)

S: Older and wiser, that's good ...

M: We used to do that when we were young. We would, yeah. (laughter)

J: I don't know how you could be a lesbian of any size and not be damaged by the society we live in. I think we bring our damages into our relationships and part of why I wanted to have a fat lover and a Jewish lover was I was hoping that I could avoid some of the surprise hurts that happen when people who don't share an identity do something hurtful and they don't know they've done it. That is part of the safety, and for me I don't think I could feel that way with a thin lover no matter how long we had been together or how wonderful she was. No matter how much you are understood, there are certain things that thin woman just wouldn't know. I love that there are certain things that Meri and I know about each other because we come from similar backgrounds and have had some similar experiences moving through the world as fat women. I don't ever have to worry about being surprised by a remark that hurts me about my size or a remark that hurts me about being Jewish. That's lovely!

I know women in mixed-size relationships, and it works for them. For me it is a pleasure not to have to work with all those particular issues. We've had to work through all the standard stuff, you know, trust, monogamy, separate personalities, friends, money, all that sort of regular relationship stuff. So, I love not having to work through fat issues as well.

M: Although when we got together, you didn't know that I was self-loving. You didn't know if I was Ms. Self-Loving or Ms. Self-Hating. Actually, I was sort of Ms. Just-had-started-loving-herself.

J: But I knew you were committed to being self-loving …

S: When did you know that?

J: Well, for one thing, Meri and I met through fat liberation activities, so that told me something. But even before Meri and I got involved she did something that showed me that she did love herself. A fat dyke from the Midwest came to visit, so we had a potluck for her to meet other fat dykes. And we also had a clothing swap at the potluck. The visitor, my lover and I walked up the stairs to the apartment where we were going to have this potluck dinner. Some of the other dykes were there, looking through the clothes at the clothing swap. At the very moment we walked into the apartment, Meri turned around, bare-breasted, and gave us a big hello. It was clear the timing was deliberate – to show off her chest! That's how I knew you were already into self-loving. You already thought you were hot stuff.

S: (laughing) I can picture it!

J: In those days, fat dykes socialized together, went to dances and out to eat. Sometimes it was more than other lesbians could deal with because we were rowdy and sitting on each other's laps and running around and not behaving properly. It was a complete reaction to the kind of constraint we usually felt, and it was great.

S: Do you still have that kind of fat network? Do you see fat women regularly in your lives?

J: Well, that may have been the golden era in some ways, you know, before the first couple broke up and got involved with somebody else in the same circle. Now, that could blow things out of the water!

S: I've heard of that, yeah. (laughter)

J: So, we don't have the same community, not in the same way. And I need more from the women in my life now. It isn't enough for me anymore to connect with someone just because she's fat. That was a period in my life where I would overlook all the other difficulties or differences in order to have that fat connection with someone. I have less ability to tolerate the things that are difficult – class differences, other political difference – just to make a fat connection.

S: I wanted to ask about differences in size because you're not exactly the same size. Has there been any work or anything that you've done around your size differences in your relationship?

M: Well, right now I weigh about 315, and I am five-foot six and a half. I am shaped as a classic pear, I guess, I'm bigger in the hips ….

J: I weigh about 250 and I'm about five foot five and I'm a pickle.

S: I've never heard of that!

J: Pickle means I go straight up and down, you know, I don't have any waist.

M: We wear very different size pants, but if we are shopping for a shirt or a jacket, a lot of times we will wear the same size. If we both see something that we like Judith will usually say, "Well, if you want it, you get first dibs."

J: We talked about that actually, way back in the beginning. If there was something that fit us both and you wanted it, you got it. There are two reasons: it's easier for me to find clothes, and I've also been working longer so I had a bigger wardrobe. Especially once Meri got out of school and started working, when we went shopping she usually needed clothes more than me. Actually, you say I've ruined you, Meri. When I met her, she wore overalls and flannel shirts. I'm kind of a clothes horse and I like to go shopping and I like to buy clothes. So, I guess from hanging around me so long, Meri got into shopping and now she's into clothes.

M: And now I have a wardrobe for work, which looks vastly different than my wardrobe not at work.

J: With furniture or new restaurants, it's been a new process for me that when I sit someplace, I try to figure out whether Meri can fit or not. I can sit in almost any chair because of the way I'm shaped, but there are lots of places Meri can't sit in, so we just cross them off our list.

M: Like movie theaters or restaurants where the seating isn't comfortable and they can't bring an armless chair. We don't patronize places that aren't comfortable. I used to go to one movie theater that was sort of an art house and got movies that weren't anywhere else. For years I went and I sat on my side, and finally I said to Judith "It isn't worth it for me to go for two or three hours and be so uncomfortable." I just stopped doing it. At the time it was distressing, but I can't not be comfortable anymore. It's not OK. I just won't do that to myself.

J: One of the ideas that I learned in the early days of fat liberation was the understanding that I'm not too big – the world is too small. You don't really deal with that everyday vocabulary. So, when we don't go to this movie theater, it's because the seats are too small and the theater is inaccessible. It's important to take the blame off of us and put it where it belongs.

S: So now it seems like we are kind of out and in the world. Welcome to the world. Fat lesbians together. And I know you get reactions walking down the street. What is it like?

M: When we first got together and I was starting to learn to love myself, I was very aware of people around me and comments they were making. We would go somewhere, and I would say, "My God, what was he just muttering?" or "Did you see that asshole doing that?" and Judith would be like "Huh, what?" I wondered why I noticed so much more. For a while I thought it was because I'm bigger and I get more shit on the street. But I realized a couple of weeks ago that since we've been living together, or maybe the last three or four years, that I just don't notice the harassment so much. If the comments are really overt, if someone is standing there and saying something, usually we will say something back. But mostly I just don't notice the muttering and the looks anymore. I don't think the world changed, so it must be me.

J: I don't think there's a time that we go out of the house that we don't get stared at. I just don't notice it very often. I can't sort out if we're being stared at because we're big fat women or we have short hair and we look dykey, or we are wearing jeans and T shirts and we don't look like proper girls. We don't ask people why if they're staring at us or making remarks, but sometimes if people are really staring, we just walk up and say, "Do you have a problem?"

S: You do?

J&M: Oh yeah.

J: Because it disempowers me not to say something. But this other thing happens, and I know it also happens with other fat lesbian couples. People on the street are always telling us that we must be sisters or even twins. I think people sometimes say sisters because they see the energy, the connection between us, but mostly I think these comments are really about fat oppression. Meri's face is totally different structure than mine, her coloring, eye color and hair color are different, her build is different. We don't look alike, any more than any two other white girls with brown hair look alike.

But we get told that we're sisters a lot. And people are really insistent, as if we wouldn't know. Some years ago we made a decision that unless we were in some physical jeopardy, if someone asked, "Are you sisters?" we would say "No, we're lovers." Sometimes I don't have the nerve to say that, so I say

"No, we're not sisters but we are kin." And that shuts people up and also doesn't deny the relationship. But it's obnoxious.

The other thing that has happened to us is that we have been mistaken for another fat lesbian couple that we know. Neither of us look anything like either of them except we all have short brown or black hair. Two different times we went into two different stores, and the clerk said, "Weren't you just here yesterday?" and they were quite insistent that we had been there, which we had not. Because we know the other couple and knew that they had been to that store, we knew what was happening. It was totally obnoxious!

M: Since we made the decision to out ourselves, it's a lot easier. We get the sisters or twins routine and when we say "No, we're lesbians." There's a lot of stammering, and I have to say it three or four times before it gets into their brains. It just takes the bullshit totally off of us. Let them go deal with their homophobia or whatever.

S: Is it different if one of you goes out by yourself then what you notice if you are together?

M: Oh yeah.

S: What's the difference?

J: A lot more hostility …

S: When you're together?

M: Oh yeah. When I go out by myself I am a lot more timid. I'm your typical fat girl, I mean, as much as I love myself, if I want to go to a restaurant or a sub shop by myself I always scan it to see if I'm going to get any shit. A lot of times that's the basis how I decide where I'm going to go in the world when I'm by myself. Can I go in there and feeyl relatively safe? A lot of times I don't give a shit, but I have days where I really don't want to deal with anything.

S: Is there something else that you want to talk about? I want to be sure we get to the stuff that you think is important.

J: I want to try to understand how I moved from fat being just the most tender and most militant place to something that just is ordinary about me.

S: You were talking about your own transition with fat.

J: How does that happen, that being fat becomes so normal? It's not supposed to be ordinary, it's never supposed to be OK to be fat.

M: I would say it's something about loving yourself so much and for so long that it just becomes commonplace. When I'm at home it is totally normal. Once I'm at work, since I'm a pharmacist I'm confronted with health stuff all the time. I'm also aware that I'm the biggest person at my job. But then there are times, like yesterday when we had taken the cat to the vet. I was leaning against the wall and I thought, "Wow, I feel so small to myself, I'm just in this body."

I think it's about loving yourself, I also think it's about having clothes that fit you well, and that you don't feel squeezed into. It's having a comfort with food and making peace with whatever issues you've had around eating and having foods in your house that are delicious. Having a partner who is all those things, that to me is one of the biggest parts of it, having this constant ally in my life.

For a long time I didn't understand what support I gave Judith, because she had been this big organizer for years, but she needs the support as much as any other fat woman. I know that the support that she has given me has helped me to be able to go into the world and do what I have done in my life.

J: I feel that the world hates us so much. I don't think we can say I love you enough, you're beautiful, you are cute, I want to suck your nipples. There is never too much of that, so we say it a lot and we smooch goodbye on the phone and all these things that are kind of nauseating. But there is a way in which they are not just nauseating, they are counteracting all this hatred in the universe. We are both so many things that we're not supposed to be, you know, we are unladylike Jewish fat lesbians, and so we're basically not supposed to exist. And if we must exist, we really shouldn't leave the house.

Part of that support is not intellectual at all, it's just that I like to have the lovey-dovey stuff really out there because it does create an energy barrier between us and the world that hates us. I just want to create this little cocoon of knowing that I am extraordinarily loved and that whatever else happens that is going to be true. I want that with me all the time and I want it with Meri all the time.

S: And I know that you do that, I can see the cocoon and you both talked about it and that is incredibly powerful thing. But I also know you both organized in the larger sense, not just within, but you are political about this. You met because Judith was an organizer and she was organizing Fat Liberation. So that is how you could find each other.

Are there other things that you would say about how your political work has affected your lives as fat lesbians?

M: We're both feminists, we're both still identified as feminist, we both do little things.

J: There was a period for me where I was doing a lot more active organizing in fat liberation. I was writing about fat liberation and I'm not doing that now. But in some ways I think I'm just more of who I am in the world. I think about this at work. I'm out at work and I've gotten more involved in university life, committees and such, so here I am this very fat out lesbian doing my life. I talk about my partner, others talk about their hubbies or wives or whatever.

But that is not political organizing. I just feel that I'm less cut off from different parts of myself than I used to be. I am in the world as a confident, attractive, sexually active, married, fat woman with a fat lover. There is a way that I hope this just creates a little space for passage.

And when people say dieting stuff, about food, like "This is bad," or "Oh, I'm bad," I have a stock response that I can use most of the time, even when I don't want confrontation. I say "I don't know about you, but I've only got one life and I am not going to waste it worrying about what I eat. I'm going to enjoy myself." That's not heavy-duty fat organizing, but it is a way to disrupt the constant ideology about being bad, food is bad. The ability to interrupt that kind of fat-oppressive conversation comes from the relationship.

M: When we first got together, Judith was doing a lot of organizing and a lot of speaking engagements. And I would go with her. That was very liberating for me, because even as someone who's been fat all my life and as someone who was getting into fat liberation, it was very powerful to hear that information, over and over and over again.

But now what I want is a gathering of fat women who have been Fat Liberationists for a long time. I want to do everything with fat women, I want to do physical activity with fat women. I want to go on trips with fat women. And if I could, I would only have fat women who love themselves as my friends. I know all the fat liberation ideology and now I just want to go beyond that, it's yet to be seen how that can be done.

S: I want to list the things that you've done just so it's on the tape when you are editing it, because you've definitely had been a political force in my life, both of you.

The first thing that pops into my head is that fashion show that Judith organized. It was a benefit for lesbian sex magazines and it wasn't all fat women, but you were very deliberate about including fat models. You did the music for it, Meri. It was all different kinds of women, including gorgeous fat women. It changed my life: Hey, I could be a model for a room full of screaming lesbians! (laughter) ... The fat group that you cofacilitated, Meri, was my first exposure to fat liberation. It was organized so there were meetings and also social times. I could see that there was fat culture, and that there were other fat lesbians.

Sometimes I think that your power and the changes that follow in your wake are not visible to you, but they really do happen. You just have a habit, you have created this habit for each other of being visible, vocal, affirming, fat, political lesbians. And that has affected other women around you, it really has.

Notes

1   Sara Golda Bracha Fishman,

> The Fat Underground was active in Los Angeles throughout the decade of the 1970s. Feminist in perspective, it asserted that American culture fears fat because it fears powerful women, particularly their sensuality and their sexuality. The Fat Underground employed slashing rhetoric: Doctors are the enemy. Weight loss is genocide. Friends in the mainstream – sympathetic academics and others in the

early fat rights movement – urged them to tone it down, but ultimately came to adopt much of the Fat Underground's underlying logic as their own.

(*Life In The Fat Underground*, Radiance Online, Winter 1998)

2 Stein, Judith. 1983. "On Getting Strong: Notes from a Fat Woman, in Two Parts." In *Shadow on a Tightrope: Writings by Women on Fat Oppression*, edited by Lisa Schoenfielder and Barb Wieser, 106–113. Iowa City: Aunt Lute Book Company.

21

BELLE DI FACCIA

Fat Activism in Italy

Mara Mibelli and Chiara Meloni

Sardinia is the second-largest island in the Mediterranean sea and is a globally renowned tourist destination, especially its North-Eastern coast: more specifically, Porto Cervo is the favourite luxury seaside resort of personalities like Jeff Bezos, Bill Gates, Beyonce and Jay Z. The images of the bays lit up at night by the play of lights of immense yachts put Costa Smeralda on luxury bucket travel lists around the world. We grew up a few kilometres from this "enchanted" place, for which millions of tourists every year get beach-body ready, investing the savings of years to be able, for a few seconds, to breathe the same air of the "people who matter." Our city, Olbia is the gateway to this hotspot for the rich. A municipality of just over 60,000 people, Olbia is not famous for its political ferment, feminist associations or radical political scene. On the contrary, it is infamous as the municipality that has awarded the sadly known Silvio Berlusconi as an honorary citizen. Nevertheless, to the amazement of communication experts, it is from here that we created what has become a case study for its impact on social and mainstream media: Belle di Faccia, known in English as Pretty Face. We're not bragging, as we are still very shocked too!

After years spent trying to change ourselves to conform to what we believed to be the standard par excellence, not even in our wildest dreams would we have imagined finding ourselves one day discussing fatness, talking about our experience as fat women, claiming it with pride and creating a fat liberation project – the first in Italy to create awareness about fatphobia and Fat Studies outreach. It started with the microaggression that has accompanied us throughout our lives and that more than any other has influenced our character and personality: the phrase "you have such a pretty face". We had never thought about this particular fact before: our project, Belle di Faccia (Pretty Faces), was born in the beach-body ready wonderland. Being a fat woman is not easy regardless of where one lives,

DOI: 10.4324/9781003140665-29

but it becomes even trickier when living on the sea where the pressure of having a flawless body is even stronger and makes it necessary to find alibis for not living one's life to the fullest, because living in shame is not enough; one also has to pretend that it is not like that: making plausible excuses for not going to the beach even when it is 40 Celsius (over 90 degrees Fahrenheit) degrees outside, answering all the questions about why one is fully covered or so pale even when everybody can easily assume why. We are two cisgender women who grew up during the 1990s and 2000s, the years of heroin chic, ultra-low-waisted jeans and supermodels like Kate Moss. Nevertheless, when talking about Italian beauty standards concerning the female body, the first image that will come to mind will be Sofia Loren's hourglass figure or Monica Bellucci. Or perhaps, one might imagine a Dolce & Gabbana advertisement set in a rural, old-fashioned Sicily where moustachioed men wearing Borsalino hats surround women with shapely thighs and bursting breasts. For many years, for us, the soft figures of the 1960s were a kind of reference: they were probably the closest images of our bodies we had ever seen in the most formative years of our lives. It is no coincidence that, during our twenties, being a fat woman meant having access to two styles of clothing – the only available, by the way: shapeless dark dresses or the Betty Page's cosplay. The only way to make up for the fat was to place ourselves outside of time, in an era where we could be forgiven for having a more curvaceous figure. The keyword in all this is, in fact: curvaceous. In this chapter, we will examine the development of fat consciousness in Italy, how it moved from a pop media phenomenon to something that we might now call a social movement, something bigger than one might have expected considering its tepid beginnings.

The So-called "Curvy Revolution"

In our country, before the body positivity' self-love and self-confidence claims, people were talking about the representation of bodies that for the first time did not resemble those of the models on Milano Fashion Week's catwalks with terms like "curvy revolution". The dictionary entry for revolution reads: an organized and violent movement by which a new social order is established and, again, an upheaval of customs and habits. This fledgling movement was not very revolutionary compared to what had happened in other countries such as England and the United States; in fact, it was during the writing of this chapter that we realized that this term was used only in the Italian scenario. However, it must be acknowledged that like it or not, it certainly prepared the ground for what will be the dialogue around mainstream body positivity and a timid beginning of fat acceptance in Italy. The curvy revolution was not, predictably, a revolution: while in other countries, women were questioning the beauty standards in political spaces, in Italy, the overthrow started precisely in the temple of the ideal body, the fashion system. The body positivity movement was not involved in this first step, nor was fat acceptance. The curvy revolution gave the illusion that the standards that annihilated the so-called natural female beauty were finally dismissed. It is essential to underline that femininity, in the context of the Italian fashion system, is binary, masculine and patriarchal: a body that is feminine is the one that has "curves in the right places", the parts of the body most objectified by the male gaze: the breasts, the hips, the butt. In fact, the curvy revolution seemed more like a scramble to claim one's place in the hierarchy of women considered worthy of attention by the male gaze. There were no tools at the time to contextualize politically the power of what was happening: it could have been an opportunity to rebel against beauty standards, to question them, but instead, it was simply interpreted as a way to reclaim one's place at the table and not to overthrow it. The influence of the phenomenon was, however, powerful. In 2011 *Vogue Italia* dedicated a cover to "true beauty" and, for the first time in the history of the magazine's Italian edition, the cover story, shot by Steven Meisel, featured the curvy models Candice Huffington, Tara Lynn and Robyn Lawley (women who could not even be defined as small fat to use the lexicon of the fat activist movement) (*Vogue Italia* June 3rd 2011). This catwalk revolution soon became a trend on the Internet where blogs dedicated to curvy fashion flourished, and a fundamental debate opened up. Who has the right to call themselves curvy? Who is a Rubenesque triumph of beauty, and who is a boiler who should cover up and stop wearing leggings and offending others with the vastness of their butt? The media seemed determined to set boundaries and distance from actual fat people, finding a definition that could oust them and draw a clear line of separation between curvy beauties and regular fat people. The nascent curvy movement was keen to question the stereotypes of female beauty but took care to put some stakes that distanced it from the so-called "obese", "overweight", "fat" people and made it clear that the curvy revolution was not meant to be a manifesto to promote obesity.

By then, however, despite the attempts to police the boundaries of who was "too fat", it was too late. It was clear that it was possible to go beyond the imposed canon of beauty, mainly thanks to the new medium that guaranteed an immense space to express oneself without compromise: the Internet. If in the traditionalist media it was not possible to see oneself, to feel represented, to find something relatable with one's own experience of women out of proportion for the societal canons, the Internet was an untouched territory in which to dare, perhaps far from one's small town, to talk about oneself and about that body considered taboo. Plus-size fashion blogging becomes relevant, but the main topics mainly were fashion-related: advice on outfits, colours and patterns combinations, methods for enhancing the body shape by highlighting the best body features and remedies for the chub rub. They were, however, valuable pieces of advice, especially for those who, like us, lived in the provinces and had even less access to brands that carried our sizes. With the arrival of Instagram in our lives, we were able to go beyond the national scene, and that is how we started to understand that there was so much more than we thought, that we had to go further, that it was not enough to find the courage to wear a swimsuit or a short skirt, that it was more complex than that. So we came across the work of activists like Virgie Tovar and Your Fat Friend. As we became familiar with terms like fatphobia and stigma, we tried to google these words in our language, hoping to find someone, a safe place, a community to belong to.

In our search for signs of the presence of the fat acceptance movement in Italy, through Charlotte Cooper's blog "Obesity Timebomb" we found Elisa Manici's work, a fat queer activist, journalist and librarian based in Bologna. Manici's experience is unique, and in using this word, we do not mean "one of a kind": we mean it literally! Manici was the only person talking about fat acceptance in Italy until 2018. Manici's journey represents the only attempt to open a discourse on fat body stigma in Italy with political and militant connotations, free from pietism, health discourses and the fat body's medicalization. One question suddenly arose: Why was the Italian feminist movement not interested in fat acceptance? Manici replied to us: the issue regarding the body, in lesbian and feminist collectives, was basically addressed as an escape from the male gaze, but without any elaboration of fat identity and its intersections with other marginalized identities. Manici also stressed how fundamental it is to remember how in Italy in those years, the feminist movement was engaged in other urgent matters. For example, until February 1996, rape was considered a crime against public morals and not against the person. So there were objectively other social needs: protesting in public squares had been abandoned after the political ferment of the 1960s because of terrorism, so most of the activists kept doing their work in academic circles. The public discourse on women's bodies was almost entirely focused on body autonomy and reproductive rights, and for many years, the topic of the body was not addressed until the mainstream media adopted the body positivity's language to reinvent themselves.

Fat Acceptance: How the Movement Has Been Communicated in Italy

The lack of activists, publications and studies on fatphobia in Italy has made it so challenging to develop a political discourse around the fat body; thus, ironically, it was body positivity that introduced us to these topics, albeit in their sweetened and watered-down version that focused mainly on beauty and self-esteem. In the United States, this was the other way around: militant activism turned into tepid commercial body positivism, but in Italy the body positivism opened up a space for activism. In particular, our curiosity about fat acceptance was born out of a sense of dissatisfaction and incompleteness given by body positivity, which seemed to embrace all bodies while making distinctions based on health status and rejecting bodies that challenged the standard too much. This dichotomy between good intentions, inclusivity and acceptance on the one hand and fatphobia, concern trolling and healthism on the other, was not limited to the mainstream but proliferated in progressive circles as well.

An unpleasant discussion in a feminist Facebook group triggered our anger which eventually led to our project's creation. The discussion stemmed from an infamous article published in 2017 in the online magazine *The Vision* titled "Curvy pride cannot turn obesity into a value to be glorified". The author, Alice Olivieri, spoke in these terms about fat acceptance:

> However, when one's choices affect the functioning of society negatively, then an individual's weight, both metaphorical and physical, becomes a problem. Obese people are objectively a cost to a country's health system, and being fat, although everyone should be able to decide what to do with their lives and their bodies, is a problem both for those who are and those who have to cope with this condition. Moreover, rather than being offended by a stereotype in a cartoon, it would be wiser, perhaps, not to deny the existence of a problem.

We read incredulously the comments of those who were supposed to be our allies: these feminist activists associated fat with laziness, gluttony, junk food, food waste, world hunger and disease, and even those who were against the article still argued that there should be a limit to the liberation of bodies, that health was the most important thing and that we could not validate and normalize the existence of fat and therefore unhealthy body. Being curvy or small fat could be acceptable, but they continued to reiterate the legitimacy of the "fight against obesity" at any cost, even justifying offending someone for the sake of their good. Furthermore, they endorsed the idea that a fat person expressing themselves unapologetically inherently promotes obesity and unhealthy lifestyles by urging people to accept themselves as they are. Our way of discussing the fat body was interpreted as an exaggeration, a distortion of genuine body positivity, the healthy and balanced one that should have pushed people to love themselves while trying to be their best version, a thinner one. We were, even according to many self-proclaimed feminist and body positive activists and influencers, extremists. They argued that even the acceptance and liberation of bodies had a limit and that we had crossed it: rejecting diet culture was possible, but only women with a normalized body had the right to do it as part of their revolt against the male gaze and the white cishet standards of beauty. It was OK to reject the idea of an unrealistic flawless body and instead embrace its natural changes over time, with post–pregnancy and older bodies, such as stretch marks, hair and wrinkles. Fatness is a different story: it is an error, deviance, something not to be encouraged but to be corrected. It is symptomatic, for example, that in the work of Lorella Zanardo, author of the book and documentary *Il corpo delle Donne* (*Women's Body*), which had much relevance in the first decade of the 2000s, fat women were completely absent. Zanardo documented how Italian television portrayed women in the 1990s–2000s, speaking of the objectification and hypersexualization of the female body, of the push and search for perfection, of plastic surgery, of the erasure of older women. But Zarnardo never spoke of fatness.

As Elisa Manici told us, speeches against diet culture and a specific claim of freedom to contravene the rules of beauty and the male gaze were well accepted in feminism and LGBTQIA+ circles, but only if fatness was not thematized: Manici, instinctively, defined herself as fat even before knowing fat activism tout court, and even in progressive circles the word "fat" created tremendous discomfort, resulting in awkward conversations such as " you are not fat, you are beautiful". However, her real awakening as a fat person who reclaimed their fatness arrived thanks to a chance encounter with the artist and fat queer activist Allison Mitchell, whom Manici invited to "Soggettive", a lesbian festival she organized. The result was a discussion about bodies and fatphobia with a queer perspective (Manici's fat body was featured on the poster, which caused a sensation), resulting in a series of speeches that took place in various Italian LGBTQIA+ collectives between 2010 and 2011 and which culminated in her graduation thesis in 2016. It seemed there was fertile ground for the foundation of a collective or a movement for fat liberation in Italy; however, unfortunately, it did not happen. On the contrary, as Manici recalls, fat people among the audience often were uncomfortable and rejected the discussion of fatness, left the debate annoyed (conversely, Manici found a particular empathy in some women who had suffered from anorexia, probably because they were already accustomed to discussing body issues), a sign that their reflections were too far ahead even for progressive circles not yet ready to accept that fatphobia was another form of discrimination to be eradicated.

Except in sporadic cases, feminist spaces had accepted the distorted media narrative about fat acceptance in Italy: that it was a funny and bizarre American fashion, a colourful oddity of custom coming from the land of fast food and the "obesity epidemic", where jolly fat people organize absurd extra-large beauty contests and demand the right to be considered beautiful and to stuff themselves all together with junk food (considered, according to stereotypes, the only cause for their fatness). Fat people were represented in articles and news reports as mythological beings living on distant continents, giant viruses trying to infect the Italian healthy Mediterranean lifestyle. Usually, those kinds of news came along with inevitable shots and videos of headless fat people, captured while walking in the streets, edited to make them graceless and ridiculous. To acknowledge the existence of fat bodies in our country and even imagine that they were individuals with their bodily autonomy, political agenda and rights to claim was, and in some ways still is, inconceivable. In the Italian press and media, there is no trace of fat acceptance before 2009–2010. It was never described as a social and political movement. Headlines such as "Fat Pride", "The revenge of the obese" and "Fat is beautiful" appeared in the press and online magazines without ever touching on issues such as systemic discrimination, medical fat bias and accessibility. In the best scenario, fat acceptance was portrayed as the distortion of a righteous cause claiming that the right of everyone to be respected regardless of how they look was an excuse used by obese people to get rid of their responsibility to change their bodies. The fat body was described as the result of trauma and suffering using a pietistic and healthist language, while fat people were depicted as needy of help to care for themselves. In the worst cases, the tone was sarcastic and derisive. What both the patronizing and the accusatory narrative shared, however, was a perspective that ignored the history of fat activism. Some rare articles erroneously cited Paul Campos as the leader of fat acceptance along with Marylin Wann, whose height and weight was even indicated as a piece of relevant information, a fun fact that was meant to reinforce the ironic nature of the article. (See, for instance, Rampini 2018). The result was that the media reported fat acceptance as a joke to make fun of, an invention made by two fatties with way too much time to waste, and, obviously, a feminine matter of beauty and self-esteem instead of actual discrimination.

Our Experience as Activists: Belle di Faccia

Our project "Belle di Faccia" was born out of our annoyance with mainstream body positivity, which flattens the experience of fat people and puts on the same level the stigma and body shaming that every person in a capitalist society suffers. Born as an Instagram page in December 2018, Belle di Faccia became the first association in Italy to raise awareness on fatphobia and claim fat bodies' instances. In 2019 we self-published a colouring book, a fanzine, with representations of fat bodies and texts that talked about fatness; our idea was to introduce the topic in Italy by using the colouring book as a tool to start a conversation in schools engaging young audiences. The arrival of the pandemic a few months later hampered us (we were only able to talk to students virtually on a few occasions), but we hope to be able to do so in the future. The project's name was undoubtedly the luckiest choice: Belle di Faccia is indeed the compliment that every fat woman receives most often, and the message came through loud and clear to those who recognized themselves in those words. We are two cis, white, mid-fat women, and we wanted to avoid a mistake we had already identified in other contexts, which was putting our bodies at the centre of our message. Our experience, although the basis from which we start for our reflections in most of the posts we have published on Instagram, is not universal and does not pretend to describe the experience of super fat or infinifat, Black, disabled, non-binary or trans fat people. For this reason, Chiara's contribution as an illustrator has been central to making our message as inclusive – as much as we do not like this word, we cannot find a more suitable terminology – as possible. The project has been welcomed with unexpected warmth and has seen very rapid growth, and at the moment, with two full years of life, it counts 68,800 followers; a surprising result for us since the tenor of our content is unquestionably not considered palatable within mainstream media and feminist activism. We have entered a media landscape which primarily comforts "good fatties" who are able to do twenty planks in a row or the right amount of jumps rope, who post pictures of healthy food, who share trauma to justify being fat. We argue these perspectives do not shelter us from fatphobia, and neither does kindly asking permission for our existence. Early in our activism, we thought that the fight against fatphobia was about unhinging the stereotypes linked to the health status of fat people .... We changed our opinion, however, both by engaging with the literature on Fat Studies, and with encountering the invaluable work of Sofia Righetti, a disabled feminist activist, one of the most authoritative voices in the fight against ableism in Italy. Her work illuminated for us how important it was to sever the tie between ableism and health and the right to exist in a full way, free of discrimination.

When we launched our project, we faced resistance in the feminist milieu – too often extremely white and neoliberal – and we faced hate online. We knew that discussing fat acceptance online would expose us to an immense amount of hate speech, but we had not considered how our visibility would increase the hate, almost overwhelming us. As long as we had a small following, we enjoyed the benefit of a safe bubble, a sort of community that made us feel welcomed, heard and seen, in which we have found even allies. Nevertheless, once we reached a greater audience, and our work started to be vaguely relevant, also finding space in the mainstream press, we were intercepted by Men's Rights Activists and incels. We have learned how to protect ourselves and recognize sealioning tactics even when disguised as a desire to seek dialogue or to play "devil's advocate". Unfortunately, it was not only openly fatphobic people or haters who pointed out the alleged danger of fat acceptance, but also those who claimed to believe in body positivity. Despite these obstacles, our project almost immediately had a great media resonance, probably since we were the first activists to talk about fatness on Italian social networks in a political and militant way. The relationship with the press has not always been easy, however, and we have had to push for them to use the correct language. Many journalists, for instance, insist on using euphemisms to avoid the word "fat" or describe our activism as a matter of self-esteem and beauty. Nevertheless, something is changing at last. In recent years, the way fat acceptance is communicated in Italy has improved: words like fatphobia, fat liberation, fat stigma and diet culture have appeared in magazines, newspapers and even on TV. We are thrilled that something is changing in Italy, that fatness is becoming a topic to talk about, and that fatphobia is perceived as an actual discrimination to fight. We have finally seen the translation and publication of many texts on fatphobia and diet culture in Italian in the last few years, including our book published in February 2021 and Elisa Manici's one released in July of the same year, making the discussion about fat stigma accessible to those who do not read complex texts in English. This is a fundamental step to start giving people the tools to dismantle everything they have always believed about bodies. Now we are no longer alone in addressing these issues on social media, we are no longer the only fat women in the room, and near us, we have fat disabled, BIPOC activists and allies who have stopped ignoring the existence of fatness in the context of systemic discrimination.

One of the signs of this openness of public opinion towards these issues was deputy Filippo Sensi's speech in an agenda presented in Parliament on January 30, 2020: discussing a bill on bullying, Sensi spoke in-depth about fatphobia, starting from his personal experience (a courageous act in a country where cishet men rarely share their insecurities related to their bodies). Although in our opinion, the speech was bland, pietistic and healthist, it did make many people aware of antifat issues and had a great media resonance. We are finally starting to hear the voices of many professionals (physicians, psychologists, nutritionists) applying a more inclusive, weight-neutral and Health At Every Size-inspired approach. For the first time, we had the chance to meet physicians (and physicians to be) who not only listened to us but asked for our input and opinion as fat women and activists, and we were also able to talk to them about stigma, language, medical fat bias and our hopes for how medical institutions should treat fat people. Ours was, in short, a small and unexpected revolution that opened up a broader conversation about fat bodies, and we hope will evolve and mature more and more.

Conclusion

Even though diet culture and fatphobia are extremely deep-rooted in our country and hatred and discrimination against fat bodies is evident, in Italy, the discussion on fatness is still very young has had a different evolution than in the United Kingdom and the United States. Curvy fashion and body positivity have been the forerunners of fat activism in Italy. In recent years, a dialogue has started on the systemic consequences of hatred for fatness. Even Italian feminism has not paid much attention to fatness and has only recently has shown interest in the historical origins of fatphobia and fat acceptance movements. The body positive approach continues to monopolize the mainstream discourse on bodies, but finally, we are also witnessing a willingness to address a more profound and more articulated discourse that we hope will continue to develop and grow. The sore point is the lack in Italy of Fat Studies, of specific studies on fatness and fatphobia, but the number of scholars interested in these topics for their theses makes us hope that something is moving in this direction even in academic spaces.

Bibliography

Body Positivity di Belle di faccia - Anche questo è femminismo - 6 ottobre 2021 - Edizioni Tlon.

Daniela Condorelli, Daniela. "Il mio grosso grasso orgoglio." *Espresso* - 23 giugno 2019. https://espresso.repubblica.it/visioni/societa/2009/06/23/news/il-mio-grosso-grasso-orgoglio-1.14285/

Farrell, Amy Erdman. *Fat shame. Lo stigma del corpo grasso* 2020 – Edizioni Tlon.

Forth, Christopher E. *Grassi. Una storia culturale della materia della vita* Copertina flessibile, 2020. Espress Edizioni.

Linkpop. Basta parlare di "fat pride": non c'è niente di buono nell'essere grassi - Linkiesta - 11 aprile 2018. www.linkiesta.it/2018/04/basta-parlare-di-fat-pride-non-ce-niente-di-buono-nell'essere-grassi/

Manici, Elisa. *Grass*. Strategie e pensieri per corpi liberi dalla grassofobia* Copertina flessibile. 2021. Eris edizioni.

Manici, Elisa. "Secondo Te Sono Grassa?" La falla - 7 gennaio 2016. https://lafalla.cassero.it/secondo-te-sono-grassa/

Manici, Elisa. *Such a Pretty Face—Ovvero: Cosa Ce'entrano Le Grasse Con Froci E Lesbiche* La Falla - 14 ottobre 2016. https://lafalla.cassero.it/such-a-pretty-face-ovvero-cosa-centrano-le-grasse-con-froci-e-lesbiche/

Meloni, Chiara and Mara Mibelli. *Belle di faccia.* Tecniche per ribellarsi a un mondo grassofobico – 16 febbraio 2021 - Mondadori.

Olivieri, Alice. "L'orgoglio curvy non può trasformare l'obesità in un valore da glorificare – *The Vision* - 25 settembre 2017. https://thevision.com/cultura/orgoglio-curvy-obesita-glorificare/

Rampini, Federico. Usa, la rivolta degli obesi "Siamo grassi, e allora?" - La Repubblica 10 marzo 2018. www.repubblica.it/esteri/2010/03/10/news/la_rivolta_degli_obesi_siamo_grassi_e_allora_-2574563/

Righetti, Sofia and Marina Cuollo. La lotta all'abilismo passa dal linguaggio: termini da non usare quando si parla di disabilità - Bossy.it - 3 dicembre 2020. www.bossy.it/abilismo-linguaggio-termini-disabilita.html

Zanardo, Lorella. *Il corpo delle donne* - 1 marzo 2018 - Feltrinelli editore 3.

22

"YOUR BELLY IS A HEAP OF WHEAT"

A Torah of Fat Liberation

Rabbi Minna Bromberg

I am in synagogue, holding the Torah[1] in my arms like a sleepy toddler. I am singing ancient words of God's Oneness. My ear presses into the velvet of the scroll's cover and through its musty fuzz I can nearly hear Torah whisper to me, "Your *pupik*[2] is a wine goblet…Your belly is a heap of wheat…." (Song of Songs 7:3). These words in praise of the rounded belly sing out from my people's ancient source of wisdom and resonate in my own bones. In this moment, I am exactly where I want to be: joining my community in prayer, cuddling with Torah, her rolls against my rolls, her animal skin so close to mine.

We are promised in biblical words that Torah is "a tree of life for all who grasp her" (Proverbs 3:18). And in this moment, my roots in Jewish tradition, my roots in feminism, and my roots in fat liberation intertwine tightly and as I hold on to Torah with my own two arms, I feel myself held. I feel a deep sense of belonging, a deep sense that I can bring my whole self—body and mind, fatness, womanhood, and all—into relationship with my religious tradition. In this moment, I know that my birthright is to grab hold of Torah and, in this loving embrace, find a source of both personal spiritual support as well as sustenance for the ongoing work of creating a world of justice and joy.

What's more, I believe that every body is deserving of this kind of loving embrace. Everyone who wishes to[3] is worthy of forging a deep connection with their own religious and spiritual tradition(s) and drawing on the wisdom of their people for their own growth and healing and for the healing of the world. When put in these terms, the idea seems self-evident: fat people who feel drawn to do so, as well as our allies, should simply embrace and be embraced by our religious traditions for the sake of the liberation of all bodies.

Unfortunately, fatphobia—along with sexism, racism, ableism, homophobia, transphobia, and other oppressive systems—too often acts as a barrier to full

DOI: 10.4324/9781003140665-30

belonging in religious life. Our path to the richness of our traditions is blocked and we are left feeling less-than and undeserving of our own portion. In what follows we will explore how anti-fatness undermines our ability to fully embrace and be embraced by our traditions. I will then propose an antidote: a Torah of fat feminist liberation—an overflowing spring of changemaking in a wounded world.

In order to bring my whole self to this work and to this chapter, it is important to note how my body, like any body, carries its own particular mix of identities, roles, marginalizations, and privileges. I am a fat white female rabbi. Unlike many women I know who are Jewish leaders, I grew up in a time and a specific Jewish religious context in which I did not experience myself as a path-breaker—the rabbi at my own bat mitzvah was a woman. As a child I attended a Reform synagogue and the Reform Movement began ordaining women as rabbis in 1972, the year before I was born. As an adult, I have certainly been in many Jewish contexts where being a woman and a rabbi has been at best anomalous and at worst rejected or even scorned. However, it was important to my own development to have this foundational childhood experience of a Judaism that was as available to me as it was to my brothers.

As a white, cis, Ashkenazi[4] woman who has children and is married to a man, I carry privilege and am given access to participation and acceptance in Jewish[5] life that is not always offered in the same way to Black Jews and other Jews of color, to non-Ashkenazi Jews, to queer and trans Jews, and to Jewish women who are single or do not have children. My reflections on Jewish life in this chapter are very much coming from my own perspective, as it is shaped both by my marginalization as a fat woman and by the various forms of privilege I have. Nevertheless, I do intend this work to be available to be used by all to whom it speaks. While the stories I bring here come largely from Jewish communal life and the texts I draw on come from the Jewish tradition, I aspire to make Torah accessible to seekers of all faiths or no faith at all.

I feel deeply blessed that in my own life, Jewish tradition has bolstered my fat feminist journey for as long as I can remember. We are commanded, as Jews, to tell the story of *yetziat mitzrayim* (the exodus from Egypt) as if we ourselves had experienced this epic shift from slavery to freedom. There is also a tradition of creatively translating the word *mitzrayim* not as "Egypt" but as "The Narrow Place." Once I stopped dieting as a 16-year-old—after having been at it since age seven—I quickly began to feel that moving away from diet culture was my own experience of *yetziat mitzrayim*: freedom from Narrowness, from narrow ideas about what bodies should look like, and from a cultural ideal that erroneously valued thinness (physical narrowness) above all else—especially in those of us who are female-identified. Linking my own journey with the story my people have been telling for thousands of years lends it a deeply comforting weight, a sense that my own liberation from body hatred is tied up with the liberation of millions of others from all kinds of places of stuckness.

However—and this is and should be a deep source of sadness and anger—many of us too often experience the opposite: fatphobia interferes with our connection with our spiritual or religious traditions. This was driven home to me when I first started blogging about Torah as a source of fat liberation. I was not expecting much to come of it, but I put a little "donate" button at the bottom of each blog post. One day I received a sizable donation from someone I had never heard of before. Up until then, any contributions I received had been from my own friends and family. I was curious about what moved this person to make such a generous gift. When I reached out, the donor shared that—even though she was not Jewish—she was supporting our work because she had not been able to participate in her own spiritual community for some years. The weight stigma she experienced there was simply too triggering to the eating disorder she was desperately trying to recover from.

As my work has continued, I have learned just how common it is for anti-fatness to be a barrier to equal access to our own religious and spiritual traditions. Failure to provide a space that is physically accessible to the largest among us is the least metaphorical of these barriers. As someone who enjoys visiting many different congregations, I often find myself spending some portion of services standing up in the back of the worship space because the seating available is too narrow to accommodate my size or too flimsy to allow me to relax in my seat without fear that it will break. And having the right equipment is also not enough: one congregation I have worshiped with frequently actually has excellent sturdy chairs, some with arms (which are too narrow for me) and some without. However, it is not uncommon for all the armless chairs to be occupied or for the unoccupied ones to be in the middle of a row that I cannot access without imposing upon numerous people to get up in the middle of their prayers and make room for me. The number of times someone has noticed my need and offered me a chair that would fit me is exactly zero.

I feel that my size is obvious and that the difference between the size of my body and the width of the chair would be equally obvious. In other words, I feel extremely visible, exposed even. But the lack of a welcoming space makes me feel invisible. This collision of hyper-visibility and invisibility creates an almost Kafkaesque sense of unsettledness. And how can we feel settled when we cannot sit? Every moment of standing while others sit or shifting around painfully in a too-small seat sends the message that only certain kinds of bodies are truly welcome.

While the largest among us experience these physical barriers in ways that smaller people do not, weight stigma—especially in the form of speaking negatively of fatness and fat people—can impact people of all sizes.[6] Since the beginning of my work on fatphobia and fat liberation in a Jewish context, I have been honored to be entrusted with many stories (too many, really) of many experiences of feeling unwelcome in religious community. A number of people have shared with me how harmful it is when their clergy share their own "weight loss journey" from the pulpit, often in ways that deeply stigmatize fatness and fat bodies. Others—both clergy and lay people—have reported being bombarded with unwanted weight loss and "health" advice, including being "invited" by people in their communities to join (i.e., buy into) their multilevel marketing dieting schemes.

While people of all genders diet and are prone to speaking too much about their aspirations for and experiences with intentional weight loss, this kind of harm does impact women disproportionately. Casual conversation is a large part of the informal aspect of gatherings in religious communities and women's "schmoozing" is much more likely to be rife with anti-fatness—often in the form of women judging their own bodies and their own eating—than men's. The aspired-for intimacy of religious communities is itself an unfortunate culprit here, as too many female-identified people are taught that communal body-shaming is a way of bonding with one another.

It is a blessing that my own fat liberation journey has always felt entwined with my Judaism, yet I am certainly not immune to fatphobia in religious communal contexts. Just in the course of writing this piece, I have received unwelcome (and unwelcoming) comments about my fat body and how it does or does not move. Much of my time in Jewish communal spaces these days is spent running around after a toddler. This prompted a member of my community to say goodbye to me recently with the words, "Shabbat Shalom.[7] You just keep running after him...." His words trailed off into a smile that may as well have been a wink, leaving me to wonder what the end of that sentence could possibly be. This is a case of the micro-aggression "Mad Libs" that those of us in marginalized bodies are forced to play. What *was* he trying to say about me and my fat female body? "You just keep running after him because it will make you lose weight?" or "You just keep running after him and you'll eventually get 'in shape?'" I found both his comment and its incompleteness enraging: Why am I not allowed to be in community without people giving their opinion about my body?!?

One form of fatphobia in religious and spiritual contexts is especially damaging: the use of religious teachings themselves in the service of stigmatizing fatness and fat people. It is no wonder then that religion has largely been seen as oppressive in the worlds of fat activism and Fat Studies. Much of the previous work on religion in Fat Studies has looked at the denigration of fatness and fat people in religious contexts and how fatphobia is expressed in religious terms. When the editors of the special issue of *Fat Studies* (2015) on fat and religion issued their call for submissions, nearly every article they ended up including looked at how religion—mostly Protestant and evangelical Christianity—is deployed in the service of fat oppression.[8] When being fat is seen as sinful, there is no shortage of powerful imagery, doctrine, and religious coercion that can be called upon in the "service" of "helping" lost souls find their way.

From off-handed comments to rows of chairs placed too closely together, and from fatphobic sermons to "well-meaning" input about the "fattening" foods at *kiddush*,[9] religious communal life can feel like a hazardous maze that we are too often left to navigate alone. It does not have to be this way. We can take hold of our religious and spiritual traditions while rejecting and refusing to replicate the oppressive ways in which those traditions have too often been deployed against both fatness and femaleness. Spiritual and religious communities have plenty of work to do to make both structural and cultural shifts if they wish to be more welcoming to people of all sizes. One integral piece of the change that needs to happen is to begin recognizing the potential for our traditions themselves to be sources of body justice and fat liberation. To this end, I propose a Torah of fat liberation.

To begin, let's take a step back: What is "Torah?" To fully embrace and be embraced by this "Tree of Life," we need to begin with a sense of what it is. The word itself is often (mis)translated as "law," and while it does contain *mitzvot*[10] (commandments) and other instruction about how to live one's life, this interpretation leaves out too much of Torah's richness for our purposes. Additionally, translating Torah as "law" has too often been used as a tool of Christian supersessionism: framing Torah (and by extension, Jews) as outdated and devoid of relevance. A better translation of the word itself is "teaching." But even that does not help us fully grasp what Torah *is*, nor what it can be in our lives. How could it? As one ancient rabbi said of Torah: "Turn it over and over again for it contains everything."[11] We could even imagine Torah itself as fat: richly marbled with multiple significances, spreading out across boundaries of meaning. Torah's multivalence is a source of delight, but it can also be confusing. So before we get to the delight, let's unpack more of what we mean when we say "Torah."

As we saw in this chapter's opening image, a Torah is a scroll that is handwritten on parchment, kept on two wooden rollers, and "dressed" in a covering that is often beautifully decorated. One or more scrolls of Torah are kept in a special cabinet (the ark) in every synagogue. Each scroll of Torah contains exactly the same words: the first five books of the Hebrew Bible (Genesis, Exodus, Leviticus, Numbers, and Deuteronomy), sometimes called the Pentateuch or the Five Books of Moses. In the context of Jewish prayer services, we read selections from this Torah scroll (or *sefer Torah* in Hebrew) on the Sabbath, on festival days, on the New Moon and on Mondays and Thursdays. "Torah" can also refer to the contents of these first five books of the Hebrew Bible in any other form: printed in books, sung in songs, or scrolled through in an app.

From this most-focused of its meanings, the significance of "Torah" grows and grows, spreading out in concentric circles. Sometimes people use the word to refer to the entirety of the Hebrew Bible or *tanakh*.[12] "Torah" can also mean both the Written Torah (i.e., *tanakh*) as well as the Oral Torah. "Oral Torah" refers primarily, but not exclusively, to the Talmud, a set of rabbinic writings compiled from the 3rd through the 5th centuries CE.[13]

Beyond these sacred texts themselves, the meaning of "Torah" then leaps up from the printed or calligraphed page to refer to all of Jewish wisdom as it has been handed down through the generations. This can include biblical texts, the teachings of highly regarded commentators, Jewish legal works, as well as mystical texts. We can also speak—sometimes with a tongue in a cheek and sometimes less so—of finding "Torah" in all kinds of other "texts:" the works of contemporary poets and songwriters, the surprising verbal constructions of young children, a particularly moving work of art, the way the wind moves the leaves of a tree, the lines on the face of a beloved elder.

When a rabbi—or anyone else—offers a sermon in synagogue, the Hebrew term for it is *d'var Torah* ("a word of Torah"). And the expectation is that a *d'var Torah* will be that particular person's attempt to make Jewish tradition relevant to the lived experience of the community.

In addition to communal relevance, each of us can have our own individual relationship with Torah. One of my favorite moments at many bar or bat mitzvah ceremonies[14] is when the generations of the bar or bat mitzvah line up—parents, grandparents, and any other elders—and physically pass a scroll of Torah from the oldest relative to the youngest, symbolizing that the entire tradition of the Jewish people is now being offered to and received by the young adult. When I am officiating, I usually say something about how this tradition is being passed to this young person and it is now up to them to make it their own, to find their own way in it, knowing that their way of embracing tradition may be different from those of the generations from whom they are receiving Torah.

Becoming a bar or bat mitzvah symbolizes the beginning of the journey of relationship with Torah, of grabbing on to the tradition in our own way. From this expectation that each of us has our own relationship with Torah, it flows that we may also speak of "a person's Torah" meaning the particular wisdom that is uniquely yours to offer the world. For example, when we give eulogies for those who have died, we are often trying to share the Torah of the deceased with all those who have gathered to remember them.

Finally, "Torah" refers not only to sacred texts themselves, nor to the entire body of Jewish wisdom as it has been passed down to us, but to the process of engaging with this tradition. The blessing we say before studying Torah describes this process as *la'asok b'divrei torah* that means to be occupied or to make ourselves busy with words of Torah. Learning Torah is meant to be more than memorizing or even gleaning wisdom from written texts—though these can also be wondrous activities. Rather it is a process of continually coming into relationship with the tradition: asking what of my own passions, identities, experiences, strengths, weaknesses, and quirks is relevant to this tradition and how the connection I am forging with the text can shed light both on my own life and on the tradition itself.

My confidence in proposing a fat liberatory approach to Torah stems in part from knowing that I am following in the footsteps of those who bring other marginalized bodies into relationship with the tradition. Since the 1970s and 1980s, and especially since the publication in 1990 of *Standing Again at Sinai* (Plaskow

1990)—Judith Plaskow's groundbreaking feminist approach to Judaism—Jewish feminist activists and scholars have worked to amplify women's voices in Torah. In the wake of this ongoing feminist project, we have seen the wondrous rise of disability justice approaches to Jewish tradition, queer Torah, and those working to center the voices of Black Jews and other Jews of color. Our "fattening" project is thus part of a larger wave of marginalized voices in Judaism laying claim to Torah, grabbing on to it as our own. I say this both to acknowledge my gratitude for those who have gone before and also because it helps to remember that we are not alone (even though these other movements are not necessarily inherently free of fatphobia).

The rereading of Torah in liberatory ways can itself be seen as an ancient practice. In the book of Numbers, there is a case of a group of daughters who protest that the inheritance laws as Moses has laid them out are unjust. Their father, Tzelophachad, has died and he did not have a son. The law, as Moses has presented it, makes it clear that Tzelophachad's other more distant male relatives should inherit from him. His daughters claim that they should be allowed to inherit his portion instead. Moses takes their claim to God Godself. God responds, "The daughters of Tzelophachad speak right" (Numbers 27:7). One ancient commentary[15] teaches that God's response indicates not only that God agrees with the daughters about the inheritance law, but that God actually says that the way these daughters "read" the Torah is, in fact, the way it is written in God's version of the book. The Torah that Moses and the rest of the people (and especially, one assumes, the men) had been reading until that moment was in need of correction.

It would be foolish to claim that Torah could be read as simply one declaration of fat feminist liberation after another. There are definitely parts of the Bible that have been and are still used to stigmatize fatness in ways that are hard to simply "reread."[16] For example, it seems clear that King Eglon (Judges 3:12–30) is being made fun of for his fatness. And there is no doubt that the text is using fatness as part of its critique when it says that "Jeshurun grew fat and kicked" (Deuteronomy 32:15).[17] But when we understand Torah as a process of engagement with the text, and when I bring my own fat, female body into contact with the text, I find the dance of body and text to be richly rewarded.

I can take it upon myself to grab on to the text and dance and wrestle with it and dive into it and hold on tight and say to Torah as Jacob says to God/the angel with whom he wrestles, "I will not let you go until you bless me" (Genesis 32:26). And Torah's fat liberatory blessings are abundant: from its opening chapters, in which we learn that all human beings, all human bodies, of all sizes, races, and genders, are created in the Divine image, to Exodus' cries for freedom from Narrowness, to the clear knowing that fat itself can be a blessing as when Isaac blesses his sons with the blessings of "the fat of the earth" (Genesis 27:28).

But where to begin our wrestling? Torah's vastness should prompt both humility and audacity. None of us can know or learn or teach all of Torah. But each of us can bring to Torah our own particularity and find those teachings, those verses, those letters that are most our own in any moment. One of the great joys of gathering with other fat women has always been learning how individual our bodies are: the particular rolls on my body do not actually match yours exactly; each of us on the outside, and how much more so on the inside, has our own unique geography. In a society that seeks to dehumanize us and treat us as a mass of undifferentiated "headless fatties,"[18] grabbing onto Torah each in our own way necessitates claiming our own uniqueness even in the smallest of ways.

I am often asked what Torah has to say about fatness. If I claim to be teaching a Torah of fat liberation, what verses, stories, or commandments actually deal with fatness? The stories and verses I mentioned above (e.g., the story of King Eglon and the blessing of the "fat of the land") are absolutely worthy of further exploration. I have a growing list of just such places to visit in Torah. My list includes my curiosity about how and when "*bari,*" the word used to refer to a fat person or animal in *tanakh*, stopped meaning "fat and healthy" and started meaning merely "healthy" as it does in Modern Hebrew. And I certainly hope I or my students will one day give the fat (male) rabbis of the Talmud a proper Fat Torah analysis.[19]

However, this approach of scouring Torah for verses that deal in their most *p'shat*[20] (simple) way with fatness and fat people is far too shallow for our purposes of learning and teaching a Torah of fat liberation. When we begin instead by surfacing our own needs and desires, and most of all our own questions,[21] we can approach Torah's vast expanses with a fat liberatory lens. I can be reading the book of Psalms and suddenly a verse jumps out at me as being "all about" fat liberation in ways I had never seen before. Let me offer three brief examples of fat liberation Torah that have emerged from my own process: creating sacred space through welcoming guests; the creative and destructive power of speech; and loving the body as it is.[22]

A Torah of welcoming can serve as an antidote to the physical barriers to accessing religious and spiritual community faced by the largest among us. *Hakhnasat orkhim* (welcoming guests) is an obligation established by our founding matriarch and patriarch, Sarah and Abraham, as they rush to attend to the needs of the strangers who appear at their tent one day (Genesis 18:1–15).[23] One teaching in the Talmud even suggests that being welcoming to guests is more important than welcoming God Godself.[24] Following in Abraham and Sarah's footsteps, we too can aim to welcome all bodies into our sacred spaces by properly assessing and caring for the needs of all. When we do this we fulfill the prophetic vision "My house will be a house of prayer for all people" (Isaiah 56:7).

Teachings on the powerful creative and destructive power of speech can be used to address the ways that bodies and eating are talked about in religious communal life. The book of Proverbs (18:21) teaches that "Death and life are in the hand of the tongue." The Talmud strengthens this teaching, stating that not only can the tongue deliver a deadly blow as easily as a hand, but that the nature of speech is such that, while our hands can only kill through direct contact, our speech—like a sharpened arrow—can cause harm even at a great distance.[25] If we want our religious communities to be spaces of belonging we would do well to take this Torah to heart when thinking about speech that denigrates fatness, praises thinness, and polices how we eat.

Finally, let's come back to the verse with which we opened: "Your *pupik* is a wine goblet…Your belly is a heap of wheat…." (Song of Songs 7:3). One important way to confront the fatphobia we encounter in religious and spiritual spaces is to learn and teach a Torah of appreciating our bodies exactly as they are. The Song of Songs is an excellent place to start. A sensual love poem in which the voices of two lovers sing words of praise and longing, its verses contain one image after another in the search for language to adequately describe the wondrousness of one's beloved. Her lover's eyes are "like doves…bathing in milk" (Song of Songs 5:12). Or she imagines her love as a gazelle bounding over hills of spices (Song of Songs 8:14). He imagines his lover as a palm tree; its clusters are her breasts (Song of Songs 7:8).

It is a text that is so earthy and juicy that the ancient rabbis express some trepidation about including it in *tanakh* at all. Concerned that it would cause Torah to fall into the gutter, Rabbi Akiva, the great defender and lover of Song of Songs, warned that "Whoever warbles his voice with the Song of Songs at taverns, making it some sort of [profane] song, has no portion in the World to Come."[26] At the same time, Rabbi Akiva was clear about the Song's place in the tradition, making it known that "the whole world is not as worthy as the day on which the Song of Songs was given to Israel; for all the writings are holy but the Song of Songs is the Holy of Holies."[27]

While often imagined as an allegory of the loving relationship between God and the people, the Song of Songs' meaning is richest when we allow it to span all manner of relationships, including our relationships with our own bodies. In a society that pathologizes fat bodies—especially the bodies of fat women—and wishes we would disappear, it is wondrously uplifting to find these ancient words in praise of a round female belly! The richness and variety of the Song's body imagery invites us to find ways of appreciating the uniqueness of each body. It calls us to truly look at ourselves and at one another with a gaze that is attentive and loving.

And how important this can be especially for those of us who are most vulnerable to others wishing that we did not exist in our fat bodies, wishing us away. That man who told me to keep running after my son failed to finish his sentence of what exactly he was hoping for me, but it was clearly some kind of change in my body. There he was in synagogue rejecting the body that he was seeing in front of him, attempting to render invisible and nonexistent that which simply is.

Thousands of years ago, the Psalmist sang "Were not your Torah my delight, I would have perished in my affliction" (Psalms 119:92). As fat people, we never know where the next micro- or not-so-micro-aggression might come from. This sad fact renders even sweeter and more live-giving our encounter with a verse singing of the simple goodness and beauty of a woman's belly that is like a heap of wheat: golden, sun-warmed, sustaining.

Fat people deserve access to our religious and spiritual traditions just as much as we deserve competent healthcare, equal pay for our work, and fair treatment in educational settings. Learning and teaching Torah in liberatory ways is one important piece of making this possible. Continually deepening our connections with our own sacred texts and traditions creates change on two different levels: within our own hearts and in the world. In Jewish tradition, these two modes of healing are referred to as *tikkun halev* (repairing or healing the heart) and *tikkun olam* (repairing the world).

As I hope I have demonstrated from my own relationship with Torah, it can and ought to be a source of personal support and spiritual enrichment. Rooting myself deeply in a feminist, fat-liberatory approach to Torah gives me something to hold onto in the turbulent work of fat activism. My hope for us all is that grabbing hold of Torah for ourselves can be a fulfillment of the teaching of Proverbs (3:18) that "She is a tree of life to those who grasp her, And whoever holds on to her is happy."

At the same time, Torah can be the medium through which we create a better world. One rabbinic text from the 5th century begins by describing Torah as preexisting the rest of reality.[28] In this imagining, God looks into the scroll of Torah in order to create the world. The Torah is the blueprint for existence itself. Jewish tradition also understands human beings as having the capacity to be God's partners in the ongoing work of creating the world. Thus, engaging with Torah can also be the process by which we understand what we want our reality—our selves, our communities, our society—to become and uncover the wisdom we need to guide us in the work of changemaking. May we look into a Torah of fat liberation and create communities where all bodies belong.

Notes

1 "Torah" means many things, as this chapter aims to flesh out. In this opening image, I am using the word to refer to the hand-scribed scrolls of parchment that contain the first five books of the Hebrew Bible.

2 *Pupik* is Yiddish for belly button; often used affectionately. Many translations of this Biblical verse use the English "navel."

3 Genuine desire is key here. Religious coercion has no place in the kind of relationship I am describing.

4 Roughly, "Ashkenazi" refers to Jews from much of Europe and Russia, whose ancestors primarily spoke Yiddish.

5 I am referring here mainly to Jewish communal life in the United States. Some of these dynamics play out differently in Jewish communities in other parts of the world.

6 The statement that weight stigma in some form can impact people of all sizes is not meant to minimize the fact that not all people are subject to the same kind or amount of weight stigma.

7 "A Peaceful Sabbath."

8　The notable exception was Mycroft Masada Holmes' call to religious communities to join in the struggle for fat liberation, using Torah itself to urge this change. There have been some efforts in recent years to imagine what a fat liberatory Christianity would look like. See Morgan (2018) and Beck (2018).

9　*Kiddush* is a blessing made on Shabbat and other holy days to sanctify the day. But it also refers to the communal snack or meal that often follows prayer services on those days.

10　Jewish tradition holds that Torah, in fact, contains 613 *mitzvot*; these are rarely enumerated in full.

11　Pirkei Avot 5:21.

12　"Hebrew Bible" is the term that Christian scholars began using when it became too obvious that "Old Testament" was inherently anti-Jewish. The Jewish term, *tanakh*, is an acrostic of Torah (the Five Books of Moses), *nevi'im* (Prophets), and *k'tuvim* (Writings).

13　The date of the completion of the Talmud in its current form is a topic of some debate with most contemporary scholars believing that it was still being redacted and edited into the 7th century CE.

14　A bar or bat mitzvah is a coming of age ceremony in the Jewish tradition. At the age of 12 or 13, a Jewish child is considered to become responsible for keeping *mitzvot* (commandments). The bar or bat mitzvah ceremony usually takes place in the context of a prayer service. Bar mitzvah is the masculine form and bat mitzvah is the feminine; good work is currently underway in various Jewish communities to find less gendered ways of referring to this milestone.

15　Sifrei Bamidbar 134:1.

16　I would claim that, on the whole, the Hebrew Bible provides much less blatant ammunition for fatphobia than it does for misogyny, racism, homophobia, and transphobia. A fuller analysis of this claim is beyond our scope here.

17　Here fatness seems to be a stand-in for complacency.

18　A term coined by fat activist Charlotte Cooper.

19　I'm looking at you, dear fat rabbis of the Talmud whose bellies were so big that, if they stood tummy to tummy, a team of oxen could drive under the arch their bellies formed (apparently they were also either very tall or had very short-legged oxen). These stories are very gendered and the men's fatness is highly sexualized. See Baba Metzia 84a.

20　Jewish tradition asserts that there are four levels at which verses of Torah can be understood. *P'shat* refers to the literal meaning of the words themselves and is seen as the lowest of these four levels of understanding.

21　Some would argue that this approach detracts from the idea that we should study Torah "for its own sake," as if it were possible to approach the text without our own agenda. I find it more useful and more honest to acknowledge that we have our own desires and our own interests. Learning broadly in Torah and not narrowing our focus prematurely or too often can still be a goal, but we need not exclude the kind of learning that focuses on our own questions.

22　These three themes are not meant to be exclusive of other themes or in any way comprehensive. They are an invitation to each of us on our own journey with Torah.

23　Spoiler alert: The people turn out to be angels of God and/or God Godself depending on how you read the text.

24　Shabbat 127a.

25　BT Arakhin 15b.

26　Tosefta on Sanhedrin (12:10).

27　Mishna Yedayim 3:5.

28　Bereishit Rabbah 1:1.

References

Beck, Amanda Martinez. 2018. *Lovely: How I Learned to Embrace the Body God Gave Me.* Huntington Indiana: Our Sunday Visitor. *Fat Studies.* 2015. Volume 4, Issue 2, pages 81–233.

Morgan, J. Nicole. 2018. *Fat and Faithful: Learning to Love Our Bodies, Our Neighbors, and Ourselves.* Minneapolis MN: Fortress Press.

Plaskow, Judith. 1990. *Standing Again at Sinai: Judaism From a Feminist Perspective.* San Francisco: Harper & Row.

23

DON'T FORGET TO BE YOURSELF

Joy Cox

In a world that constantly demands you change, don't forget to be yourself. Take your time and soak in the joy that is often denied you due to the inaccessible and often deliberate fatphobic withdrawal of things like clothing, adventure, and meaningful relationships. Wear all the things! Take all the trips! Build friendships. Make love. Take naps. Get drunk with the fullness of you. I promise you, the world will deal.

Trust me when I tell you they will deal. They will deal and you will thrive. Past the hurt, shame, and fear, there will arise an identity that is worth more than *anything* society has to offer. YOU. It may not seem like it now, but you are fierce and a force to be reckoned with. You are beauty. Poetry in motion. Unrelentless. And may I say, even divine.

Being yourself only allows your qualities to shine their brightest. It allows you to be illuminated and light the path on life's journey. It shines so your people can find you and you them. Being yourself connects you to community. And this is not the community that you passively ingest. No, this is the community that reminds you as you scroll social media sites that broadcast the downsides of being unique, betting on you is *always* the best choice.

Community as we know it in this form, aides in your growth and development. They will call you in before calling you out. They will show empathy and compassion when the weight of the world is hard to bear. Community like this will not tell you what you want to hear but rather, what your true self needs to embrace. If the goal is to be yourself, true community is less about creating replicas and more about making space for what is and is yet evolving. They are family. Lean in.

I want to be frank and share that you can live a life of joy without having to change the size of your jeans. As someone who has lived in a fat Black body for

DOI: 10.4324/9781003140665-31

as long as I can remember, reminding myself that continuous joy is accessible to me has become routine. To that point, this brown skin having, kinky hair curling, and wide hips hipping woman has sashayed through different countries, celebrated friends and family without reservation, and achieved four degrees all in the body society says is undeserving. I have felt seen and heard. Often by family and at times more so by those I have never met. Throughout the years, I have learned to embrace the parts of me that I used to shun. In the beginning years of my journey in fat liberation, fact finding and uprooting lies about my body was my joy. Knowing these things no longer had a hold on who I was becoming, was my peace. Joy has become the gift that I continue to give myself. Unapologetically I get lost in the qualities of me.

Through community, I have imagined a world for us that centers our freedom much more than our oppression. We are more than the narratives often circulated that lend themselves to fodder for baseless debates. And though relevant to our lives, we are more than our negative fatphobic experiences. Seeing ourselves beyond one dimension is vital. Having balance is important.

If you listen closely, you'll hear the muffled sounds of celebration and jubilation expressed every time you decide to choose yourself. After some time, those sounds only get louder. The best is when they come from the inside out. Trusting the process, your process, is knowing that the sun is forever shining even in the rain. Acceptance is not an event as much as it is a perpetual choice.

Accept and bet on yourself in good days and bad. These include the days you cannot stand to look in the mirror, and the ones when you can't stop being mesmerized by what you see. Finding joy in your double chin, dimply thighs, full fupa, and back fat is possible, though not required. There is no requirement that our stretch marks transform to tiger stripes. No requirement that we have to love our bodies for them to count. To be yourself is to understand that you are not always going to be strong, resilient, or unbothered. You will cry. You will be frustrated. It's ok.

If you are reading this and have not considered what the value of being the genuine you could be, today is a good time to start. Baby steps are accepted. Remember, being you is about *you*. You hold the key to your inner liberation. If you're ready, it's time to unlock all the doors and be free.

PART IX

In Memoriam

Cat Pausé was a leading scholar and activist whose work bridged the fields of Gender Studies and Fat Studies in profound and nuanced ways. In this final section, the artist/activist Substantia Jones remembers their deep friendship and Pausé's jubilant participation in Jones' Adipositivity Project.

DOI: 10.4324/9781003140665-32

24

FRIEND OF CAT

Substantia Jones

Living on opposite sides of the planet (me in New York, Cat in New Zealand), Cat and I had regular video chats, entered in my schedule as "Cat Calls," where we would share what was going on in our personal lives, make merciless fun of sizeist bigots we'd encountered, and discuss the ins and outs (mostly outs) of the fat activism community. We'd laugh until we ached. Once we cried together. These Cat Calls were therapeutic and cleansing.

While Cat and I were co-writing an article ("The Adipositivity Project: the First Fifteen Years" for *Fat Studies: An Interdisciplinary Journal of Body Weight and Society*), we would work on it a few times a week, also via video chat, though with a far less jovial tone than our long-established personal hangs. Since the subject of our chapter was the first 15 years of my Fat Liberation photo-activism campaign, The Adipositivity Project, I'd draft aloud and she'd type, Chicago-ize, and remind me that made-up words and cursing were unwelcome in academic writing. Likewise made-up curse words. We'd set aside time to disagree about editing. Cat was a masterful plate-spinner of tasks, and during our writing sessions, she'd often be multitasking, or as I liked to call it, showing off how much more efficiently her brain worked than mine. She was a skilled and prolific contributor to academic publications, but I'm not designed for this sort of writing, and I found it to be wildly difficult. To lighten the mood, she'd sometimes type my raunchy fake recitations into the piece, forcing me to remind her it was not outside the realm of possibility that we'd both forget to remove it, and it would make it past the editors *and* the peer reviewers, ending up in a respected academic journal with both of our names on it.

But more often than not, her multitasking took the form of checking her email, much of it from her students. She would sometimes read to me the particularly enlightening or entertaining messages. One such email read, "Dr. Pausé! Have

DOI: 10.4324/9781003140665-33

FIGURE 24.1 Photo of Cat Pausé, courtesy Substantia Jones of The Adipositivity Project

you hidden Madonna song titles throughout all the articles you've written for academic journals!?" I said, "What an odd question. Why would they ask that?" Cat answered, "Because I've hidden Madonna song titles throughout all the articles I've written for academic journals."

Cat's New Zealand memorials were organized by her friend and co-officeholder, Sandra Grey, National Secretary for New Zealand's Tertiary Education Union. After telling the above story at the private memorial, I lamented to Sandra that I'd immediately afterward remembered a far better example of Cat Magic, a story Cat would surely have enjoyed being shared. *And* it involved a Broadway musical. I told her I wished I had a do-over. "Oh, you've got a do-over at Cat's public service next week," Sandra replied. "But the Madonna story stays in."

Good call, Sandra.

The best example of Cat Magic that I remember began on the day I first met Cat. She was one of my "Adiposers," the people who serve as the models for the Adipositivity Project, my fat liberation photographic series. She recreated a powerful pose she'd been striking for photographs since childhood, but this time she was naked on a Brooklyn rooftop, looking toward the Manhattan skyline across the river. After the shoot, we sped back to Manhattan to meet our mutual friend Leah for dinner in Hell's Kitchen, then on to see *Cabaret* on Broadway at the famed Studio 54. We had a great table on the aisle near the stage, and I mentioned that I'd seen the last Broadway production of Cabaret in the late '90s, also at Studio 54. I then recalled that the actor who plays the emcee, this night being the impishly divine Alan Cumming, would at one point come down into the audience and pull someone up onto the stage for a little dance and serenade. Cat's face lit up, revealing the calculations already happening in her head. She expressed … let's call it an enthusiastic interest in being the chosen one. I suggested we switch seats so she'd be on the aisle, because with an aisle seat and that thousand-watt smile, she was a shoo-in.

Soon the time came when Alan Cumming was in the aisle shopping for a dance partner. As he passes our table, Cat gazes up at him adoringly. I'm behind her, pointing at the top of her head, believing I'm helping the cause. Cumming glares at me and says sternly, "I don't take requests," then continues up the aisle. Cat was crestfallen and confused. I was mortified. After the show I was going to have to confess to my new friend (who's just hours earlier allowed me to drag her bare body onto a freezing Brooklyn rooftop in the name of Art and Fat Liberation), that in my effort to give her a great New York experience, I'd instead just ruined her chance to dance with Alan Cumming. By this time, Cumming is trying to convince a guy a few rows back, but that dude's absolutely refusing to budge.

Then! Cumming gives up on the guy behind us, spins around, grabs Cat's hand, and suddenly she's on a Broadway stage, in the middle of the hottest musical of the time, in her Jandals ('cause once a Kiwi, always a Kiwi, transplanted or not). I want you to envision this. She and Alan Cumming are sharing a slow dance. The spotlight's on them. He's singing a German song from the show. Suddenly Cat Pausé, possessor of the true spirit of Broadway musicals, and close enough to Cumming's mic to change the course of history a wee bit, sang the next verse of the song back to him. Beautifully, of course. In perfect German! The audience went wild. They loved it. Absolutely ate it up. Poor Alan looked scared for a beat or two, but then the dimples returned, and he appeared to appreciate the moment as much as the audience did.

Now that's a perfectly serviceable story, yes? The New York City Chamber of Commerce would be more than happy to use it to promote tourism. But in the immortal words of 1980s' late night TV commercials, "But wait! There's more!"

The next day her parents flew in to New York to join Cat for a few days, and the three of them were having lunch in an uptown restaurant, far from the Broadway district. A woman excitedly approached them and right there in front of the parents who were already awfully proud of their daughter, she breathlessly said to Cat, "I saw you in *Cabaret* last night! You were great!"

That, dear readers, is Cat Magic.

All this happened in just the first 24 hours of our friendship, including the *Cabaret* story, parts one and two, which Cat's father later told me was one of his favorites.

Many of my favorite—even life changing—experiences came at the hands of Cat Pausé. Cat was a devoted supporter of The Adipositivity Project. The *most* devoted supporter. Not only was she an enthusiastic Adiposer herself, she owned more of my photographs than anyone who is not a museum, as the walls of her living room and office attested. In 2016, she and Massey University brought me to New Zealand for a five-week lecture tour, and she worked with Te Manawa Museum to put on a solo exhibition of my work. (What she didn't tell me, though, which I learned only after she passed in a letter sent to me by Andy Lowe, then-CEO of Te Manawa, was that one particular educator covered all 44 images in their huge museum gallery with "scalpel-cut acid-free paper and delicate Mylar corners … to protect the children or whoever else could be 'negatively affected.'" Cat would have laughed at that!) We often talked about what would happen to the Adipositivity Project if I weren't around. Being much older than Cat, I was so happy when she agreed that she would lead a group of fellow Adiposers to take over the project after I would be gone, shepherding my images to perpetuity. That was a really big deal to me. But that's not what will happen now.

During the first of Cat's memorials—a beautiful celebration of her life—the live stream halted, mid-sentence. A mutual friend in New Zealand messaged me, "Are you still getting the stream?" I wrote back, "No. It was meant to last an hour and a half, and I guess that was firm. Not cool, but apropos, yes? Something wonderful ending abruptly? And way too soon."

Epilogue

As I write this, five months have come and gone since the memorial. Since her passing, I've had the oddest feeling she moved through life as if she knew she didn't have much time. Her work, her relationships, her generosity, all as if intentionally establishing a legacy. But I know that was in fact *not* the purpose of her deeds. She did what she did because it was the most helpful way to use her talents. The sparkling legacy was just a bonus, as is the lesson for us all.

Fraser Greig, the GM of Manawatu People's Radio, where Cat's podcast/show Friend of Marilyn (FOM) made its home for 11 years, asked me to co-host a memorial episode of FOM, saying, "That way it's not Tall Skinny White Dude Presents …" I told him Cat had taught him well. He agreed. The tribute to Cat was expected to be a single 30-minute episode, but nearly everyone invited to participate did, so it filled three episodes to the brim.

Cat and I had a number of big plans for the future. We were about to begin a collaboration of sorts that, for Cat's part, would have defied the limits of generosity for most. I spent a fair amount of time in disbelief, pondering it, but it was nothing like the disbelief I still feel when attempting to contemplate her absence. As Sandra Grey said to me on that first unthinkable day, "Cat was too alive to be gone."

Cat taught me many things, including—not long ago—to give myself evenings and weekends to relax and recharge. I've been even more obedient since her passing, and it has improved my life more than any change in memory. I regularly "What would Cat do?" my way through tough situations. Some folks have Jesus, Buddha, or the Easter Bunny. I have a fat, Madonna-loving woman with a big laugh, the choicest manicures, and huge, ever-present sunglasses atop her head. Also the wisdom of a deity.

Cat is "with" me every day. But to keep her near in a more comforting, tangible way, I bought a coin-sized vial pendant to engrave and fill with dried, crushed petals from the bouquet she sent me for my birthday, shortly before her passing. I wear it on a long chain around my neck, and often rub it like a worry stone, the pad of my thumb buffing the frequent and final words she spoke to me from the other side of this world she so positively changed. The words now etched into the vial I use to carry a bit of her with me. The words I daily echo back to her, and mean with all my heart: "I love ya, you fat bitch."

FIGURE 24.2 Photo of Cat Pausé, courtesy Substantia Jones of The Adipositivity Project

FIGURE 24.3   Photo of Cat Pausé, courtesy Substantia Jones of The Adipositivity
Project

FIGURE 24.4   Photo of Cat Pausé, courtesy Substantia Jones of The Adipositivity Project

FIGURE 24.5 Photo of Cat Pausé, courtesy Substantia Jones of The Adipositivity Project

INDEX